THE HOUSE OF PITT

Chevening

THOMAS PITT, Governor of Fort St. George
Attributed to Vanderbank

THE
HOUSE OF PITT

A Family Chronicle

by

SIR TRESHAM LEVER, Bt.

LONDON
JOHN MURRAY, ALBEMARLE STREET, W.

First Edition . . 1947

Printed in Great Britain by
Wyman & Sons, Ltd., London, Fakenham and Reading.

CONTENTS

PAGE

ACKNOWLEDGMENTS ix

FOREWORD xi

BOOK I

RISE OF THE HOUSE OF PITT

CHAPTER

I. THE GOVERNOR OF FORT ST. GEORGE 3

II. IN THE REIGN OF QUEEN ANNE 29

III. THE FAMILY AFFAIRS OF THOMAS PITT 41

IV. AT THE COURT OF GEORGE II 61

V. "I KNOW THAT I CAN SAVE ENGLAND . . ." 80

BOOK II

REIGN OF THE HOUSE OF PITT

I. THE ACCESSION OF GEORGE III 119

II. GRENVILLE, PITT, AND AMERICA 151

III. IN THE REIGN OF GEORGE III (1) 166

IV. IN THE REIGN OF GEORGE III (2) 189

V. PITT AND FOX 214

VI. THE YOUNG PRIME MINISTER AND THE KING 234

CHAPTER   PAGE

VII.   THE PITTS, THE GRENVILLES, AND THE FRENCH REVOLUTION   .   256

VIII.   IN THE DAYS OF GENERAL BONAPARTE   280

BOOK III

DECLINE OF THE HOUSE OF PITT

I.   THE STANHOPES OF CHEVENING AND THE HOUSE OF PITT   .   303

II.   UNCLE AND NIECE   328

III.   THE PASSING OF THE PITTS   341

     L'ENVOI   369

     INDEX   371

LIST OF ILLUSTRATIONS.

THOMAS PITT, Governor of Fort St. George*   .   .   *Frontispiece*
   Attributed to Vanderbank

FACING PAGE

GOVERNOR PITT'S ACCOUNT OF THE PURCHASE OF THE GREAT DIAMOND †   14

HARRIET VILLIERS, Mrs. Robert Pitt † 26
   Kneller

ROBERT PITT, son of Governor Pitt † 26
   Kneller

LUCY PITT, Countess Stanhope, daughter of Governor Pitt* . . 48
   Artist unknown

ESSEX PITT, Mrs. Charles Cholmondeley of Vale Royal, daughter of
   Governor Pitt † 48
   Artist unknown

JANE INNES, Mrs. Thomas Pitt, wife of Governor Pitt* . . 54
   Attributed to G. Sharp

THOMAS PITT, Earl of Londonderry, son of Governor Pitt* . . 58
   Attributed to Vanderbank

AMELIA PITT, Mrs. William Spry, daughter of Thomas Pitt †. . 84
   Reynolds

CHRISTIAN PITT, Mrs. Thomas Saunders, daughter of Thomas Pitt †. 84
   Artist unknown

ELIZABETH PITT, daughter of Robert Pitt 96
   An old print
     British Museum. By permission of the Trustees

ANN PITT, daughter of Robert Pitt † 96
   An unfinished sketch

LADY HESTER GRENVILLE, Countess of Chatham* . . . 110
   Hudson

vii

FACING PAGE

THOMAS PITT, son of Robert Pitt† 138
    Artist unknown

PENELOPE PITT, Viscountess Ligonier, daughter of George Pitt of
    Strathfieldsaye 178
    Gainsborough
        Huntingdon Art Gallery, California. By permission of the Trustees

WILLIAM PITT, Earl of Chatham, son of Robert Pitt . . . 190
    From an engraving by Houston of a portrait by Hoare
        National Portrait Gallery. By permission of the Trustees

WILLIAM PITT, son of William Pitt, Earl of Chatham . . . 230
    Hoppner
        Cowdray Park. By permission of Viscount Cowdray

ANNE WILKINSON, Lady Camelford† 268
    Artist unknown

THOMAS PITT, Lord Camelford, son of Thomas Pitt† . . . 268
    Reynolds

ANNE PITT, Lady Grenville, daughter of Thomas Pitt, Lord Camelford† 320
    Hoppner

JOHN PITT, Earl of Chatham, son of William Pitt, Earl of Chatham* 346
    Romney

Chevening. By permission of Earl Stanhope, K.G.
†*Boconnoc. By permission of George Grenville Fortescue, Esq.*

ACKNOWLEDGMENTS

THE main body of Pitt Papers is in the Public Record Office, and I wish to express my sincere thanks to the Secretary of the Historical Manuscripts Commission and to the Deputy Keeper of the Public Record Office for the privilege accorded to me of examining these important MSS. in their wartime depositories: some of them were at Belvoir Castle, and the remainder at Market Harborough. There are also a considerable number of Pitt, Grenville, Stanhope and Lyttelton family papers at the British Museum, and I must thank Dr. Eric Millar, Keeper of MSS., and his staff for their kind assistance in my search through these interesting documents. In addition, I have examined the Pretyman Papers, formerly at Orwell Park, Suffolk, now in the University Library, Cambridge; and my gratitude is due to the Syndics of the University Library for the help afforded me and for leave, readily granted, to quote from these letters. I have also to thank the Trustees of the Huntingdon Library and Art Gallery, San Marino, California, for permission to reproduce the Gainsborough portrait of Penelope Pitt, Viscountess Ligonier, and to quote from the Stowe MSS. now in their custody, and Mrs. Julia L. Macleod of their Department of Manuscripts, who made special search through these multitudinous documents for papers of interest and importance in connection with the Pitt family. I am indeed grateful for her assistance.

Apart from these documents, I have been so fortunate as to have had permission to inspect a number of private collections. In this connection I must express my warm appreciation of the kindness of George Grenville Fortescue, Esqre. of Boconnoc, who placed at my disposal the whole of his unpublished Pitt material, of Earl Stanhope, K.G., for the use of his papers at Chevening, and of Viscount Cobham, who gave me free access to his three volumes of Lyttelton MSS. at Hagley. My thanks are also due to Lord Stanhope and Mr. Fortescue for kind permission to reproduce many of their family portraits. The Earl of Ilchester was so good as to send me copies of a number of letters formerly preserved at Holland House and now at Melbury; and the late Maud, Duchess of Wellington gave me all the information available about the Pitts as owners of Strathfieldsaye; to both of them my thanks are due.

I have been fortunate, too, in the aid I have received from professional historians: and I wish especially to thank Sir Charles Grant Robertson, the late Mr. D. A. Winstanley, Vice Master of Trinity College, Cambridge, and Professor Richard Pares, Professor of History in the University of Edinburgh, whose volume on the Reign of George III for the Oxford History of England is eagerly awaited; all three read my script and placed their great knowledge at my disposal. My gratitude is also due to Professor Basil Williams, who read my early chapters and answered with patience my many questions.

For advice on the illustrations generally, I have to thank Sir Henry Hake, Director of the National Portrait Gallery; and for permission to reproduce various pictures (apart from those already mentioned), I must express my appreciation to the Trustees of the National Portrait Gallery, the Trustees of the British Museum, and to Viscount Cowdray.

For aid in the general arrangement of the book and kindred matters I am much indebted to Mr. V. Cameron Turnbull; his help has been quite invaluable at all stages of my work. And last, but certainly not least, I tender my warmest thanks to Sir John Murray, who has taken a personal interest in this book which far surpasses anything that an author is entitled to expect from his publisher. Indeed, I am glad to have this opportunity of testifying that, but for his guidance, so generously offered, this history of the House of Pitt would be even more imperfect than it is. For his assistance I am heartily grateful.

T. L.

April, 1947.

FOREWORD

LORD MACAULAY, in his Essay on Horace Walpole's correspondence with Sir Horace Mann, complains that the great letter-writer is more concerned with the trivialities of life than with the leading events of the time. "The conformation of his mind was such," wrote Macaulay, "that whatever was little seemed to him great, and whatever was great seemed to him little. Serious business was a trifle to him, and trifles were his serious business. . . . In every thing in which Walpole busied himself, in the fine arts, in literature, in public affairs, he was drawn by some strange attraction from the great to the little and from the useful to the odd." It is because I realize that a like criticism could with some justice be levelled at this book that I would try to parry the blow before it falls.

The story opens in the reign of Queen Anne, it closes in the early days of Queen Victoria, a century and a half of human progress. Yet this is no history of England during those momentous years. The stupendous events of the time—the Wars of Marlborough; the Wars of Frederick; the Wars of Chatham, by which Canada was taken and the France of Louis XIV shaken and humbled; the War with America, which lost the Colonies to the English Crown; the French Revolution and the Wars of Napoleon, the first of modern Dictators; that beneficent movement that gave immortality to the names of Wilberforce and Granville Sharp, that noble crusade that had its birth in the unquiet seclusion of Epworth parsonage, that historic revolution that changed the face of Britain and settled for generations our future destinies, the sad record of Irish affairs, the turbulent history of modern India subsequent to the Governorship of Thomas Pitt—these happenings and many more receive scant notice within the pages of this book. I seek not to rival the many pens far abler than mine that have told the story of these events in a thousand volumes of stirring prose. My object has been at once more limited and less ambitious: I have sought no more than to tell the tale of a strange, eccentric, but brilliant family, whose members played a prominent part in the England of their day. The careers of some of them were great and glorious, of others wasted and barren, yet they were never dull, and the lives of most of them were bound up to a greater or lesser degree in the historic events of their time. Indeed, it is almost impossible to conceive of a Pitt being dull, for their progress was lighted by that magic flame that leads sometimes to imperishable glory,

sometimes to abysmal failure and even disgrace, but which, lead where it
will, banishes with its rays the black darkness of nonentity and the dismal
half-light of mediocrity.   What a queer lot they were—the quarrelsome
Governor with his great diamond and tiresome family; the illustrious
Chatham, gout-ridden and diseased; his sister Ann and her caustic wit;
Thomas, the brother of Chatham, poor deluded fool; the second William,
infant prodigy, battling against adversity; the first Camelford, repairing
the havoc wrought by his father's follies; the second Camelford, sailor,
duellist, brawler, maddest of them all; and Lady Hester, tall, stately, proud
and haughty, a little crazy too, for all her airs.   So they and many more
parade before us—ghosts called up from the eternal shades to play their
parts anew.   Yes, ghosts indeed.   But a part of England's history, too.
So let us watch them for awhile, smile at their antics, forgive their frailties,
and whisper a prayer of thanks that England is granted such men to guide
her on her way.   Churchill, Pitt, Pitt, Nelson, Wellesley, Churchill—
leaders and heroes every one!

BOOK I

Rise of the House of Pitt

CHAPTER I

The Governor of Fort St. George

FORT ST. GEORGE, Madras, 1702. His Excellency the Governor was sitting in his closet one afternoon towards the end of February or early in March, his friend, Mr. Benyon, writing at his side. The Governor was a short, thick-set man, broad-shouldered and of sturdy build. His mouth was small, his eyes were searching, his nose was coarse and wide with open nostrils, his chin firm as a rock; the whole face, hard and determined, wore an imperious look as that of one accustomed to command. But to-day the brow was knit, and the face bore a set and troubled look—as well it might—for there was much to cause anxiety to the inhabitants of the little fort over which Pitt had presided since his unanimous election by the Court of the East India Company on November 24th, 1697, as Governor of Fort St. George. For the Fort was under siege. A large force under the command of Daud Khan, general of the redoubtable Aurangzib, the aged Great Mogul, stood at its gates. The blockade had already lasted for several weeks, and the Governor was determined to hold out against the attackers, come what might. But the strain was great, and his solemn mood betokened the gravity of the hour.

As he sat, lost in meditation, his mind on the urgent problems of the day, a servant entered to announce that a certain Ramchund, with his companion Vincatee Chittee, was at the door and seeking an interview. On hearing these names, the Governor roused himself with alacrity, and as he did so a broad smile gradually spread across his face and lit up his features. The look of strain vanished in a flash and he hastily bade his servant admit the guests to his presence. . . .

The life of Thomas Pitt had been one long adventure. Member of a family of five surviving children of a country parson, Thomas was aged only nineteen when his father died in 1672. It was soon apparent to the ambitious youth that he must set forth into the world to make his fortune, and within a few years he is to be found in the eastern parts of India as an "interloper" or trader on the East India Company's ground and in defiance of their monopoly. He appears to have resided for some time at the small coast town of Balasore, south-west of Calcutta, where he met Richard

3

Edwards, the manager of the Company's factory in that town. Edwards soon introduced him to his friend, Matthias Vincent, who lived at Hooghly, situated on the river of that name and a few miles north of Calcutta, and acted as the Company's chief agent in Bengal. These two men, not being overburdened by scruples, had no qualms in associating with an "interloper" and their friendship for Thomas was soon further strengthened by his marriage to a niece of them both, for somewhere about 1679 he wed Jane, daughter of James Innes, the younger, of Reid Hall in Morayshire.[1] Exactly when young Thomas gave up interloping and took employment with the Company is uncertain, but he was assuredly in its service at about the time of his marriage, for it is recorded that at this period he made several journeys into Persia on their behalf as well as on his own. But sad to relate, he was frequenting bad company, and some obscure transactions in which he was involved with his friends led to his dismissal from the Company's service. He accordingly returned to England, but not before he had amassed a comfortable competence by methods that doubtless do not bear too close an inspection, and in London settled down with his wife to a life of ease and comfort.

This was in 1683, some ten years after the penniless parson's son first set sail for India in search of his fortune. Just thirty years of age, the enterprising Thomas emerges as a prosperous business man. He is already the father of one child, a son named Robert, and others—two more sons and two daughters—are to follow.

But Thomas Pitt was too ambitious to settle down to private life and obscurity in England. He had made money; he now determined to lay it out to his advantage. In 1688 he purchased from Lord Salisbury the manor of Stratford under the Castle, and was elected Member of Parliament for Old Sarum in the Convention Parliament and for new Sarum (Salisbury) in the parliament of 1690. The following year he became owner of the site of Old Sarum and of the votes attached to it. He also purchased estates in and around Blandford St. Mary, including the Manor House, which he re-built, and the Manor of Stratford, known as Mawarden Court, which he considerably enlarged. He was thus becoming a man of consequence; but he did not entirely give up his Asiatic interests, and he seems to have returned to India at least once before he went out in 1698. Accompanied by his eldest son, then about eighteen, he landed at Madras on July 6th, 1698, to take up his appointment as Governor of Fort St. George.

[1] The exact relationship of Jane Innes to Vincent and Edwards is not clear. Possibly she was a niece of their wives. Her grandmother was Margaret Stuart, Countess of Moray, whose father was an illegitimate son of James V of Scotland and therefore half-brother of Mary, Queen of Scots.

This was a critical period for the East India Company, for a new Company had recently been formed under a Charter of William III, and the agents of this new Company were despatched to the East clothed with the authority of British Consuls at almost the same time as Pitt went out to take up his Governorship. Of the three new Presidents, as they were termed, one whose residence was designated at Masulipatam, was a young relative of Thomas Pitt. "I received advice yesterday of my cousin John Pitt[1] coming out in the New Company's service as President of the Coast of Coromandel, and consul for the king," wrote Robert to his mother in England. "To all appearances, the old Company, in whose interest my father is, stands on a very bad footing, their servants in India being under the Consuls now come out and the sending of ambassadors to negotiate at Court being prejudicial to them." Then he concluded demurely, "I congratulate you on the birth of my young brother John."[2]

Young Pitt came out to India full of bounce and self-importance: and no sooner had he arrived than he commenced an acrimonious correspondence with his uncle. John's letter announcing his arrival is a model of pomposity:

"Sr: I did by some Early Shipps let you know that I had engag'd my Self in the Service of the Honble: English Company . . . lately Settled by Act of Parliament which determin'd yours in three years commencing last Michaelmas, and having gain'd the Coast cou'd not pass by without dropping an Anchor in Madrass Road, and wou'd salute you, had I not the Honour to bear his Majesties Commission which constitutes me his Minister or Consull for the English nation in Generall on the whole Coast of Cormandell including all your Settlements. If you think fit to pay the respect that is due to the Character with your fflagg lower'd the Compliment shall be returned you by

"Sr: Your affect. kinsman and servt.

"J. P."[3]

"I received yours the purport of which seems very odd as well as the Superscription," came the tart reply. "If you had read the Act of Parliament, and well consider'd it, you will find that it establishes my Masters in all their rights and priviledges in these parts till 1701, and afterwards 'tis

[1] John Pitt was probably a son of one of the brothers of George Pitt of Strathfieldsaye.

[2] Robert Pitt to Jane Pitt, Amoy, November 5th, 1699. The Court referred to is that of the Mogul, Aurangzib.

[3] John Pitt to Thomas Pitt, "From on board the De Grave, Capt. Wm. Young, Commander, in Porta Nova Road, July 26th, '99."

secur'd to them by their Subscription, therefore you can have noe power in any place of their Settlements, nor shall I own any till I am Soe order'd by those that intrust me.

"I am not unacquainted with what respect is due to the Kings Consull (whether you are one I know not) but you cannot (think) or ever have heard that an Ancient Fortification wearing the Kings Flagg, Shou'd lower it and Salute a reall Consull; but I take it to be your Obligation to have Saluted the Flagg ashore at your comeing to anchor which wee Shou'd have answer'd according to custome and good manners.

"What Liquors you have for me I desire you to send on Shore in these Boats. You must expect to find mee noe less zealous for my masters interest, than you are for yours and as you act the same will be return'd you by

> "Sr: your affection⁰ kinsman
> "and humble servant
> "THOS: PITT, GOVERNOUR."[1]

This answer does not seem unduly heated; but the young puppy to whom it was addressed scribbled hasty replies in which wrath is more conspicuous than prudence.

"I am sorry to find the zeal for your Masters has Transported you beyond Sence and Good Manners," he writes. "I shall Impute it in part to the heat of the Country which has altered your Temper.

"The Young Consull as you term him gives you this advice to mind the main Chance and not forfeit Old Saram &ca: and expose your Self to the World to boot; who I doe assure you will much censure and blaim this rashness of yours, and let me tell you your Masters will neither Thank you and bear you out in't. I came later from England than your advices.

> "J.P."

"I shall send your letters from Metchlepatam and doe not question A just Accompt from you of my private Affair. You'l know in the End I am not to be taught my duty by you.

> "J.P."

"July 28th '99."

His next onslaught is undated. "I'le take such measures to make you Sencible that my Commission reaches over all your Settlements and you

---

[1] Thomas Pitt to John Pitt, Fort St. George, July 28th, 1699.

your Selfe Shall be forc't to own and publish it in all your Forts and Settlements and beg pardon for the affront offer'd to the Charecter of his Majesties Consull.

"To Tho: Pitt Esqr.   In Madrass.

"J.P."

So John Pitt went on to Masulipatam further up the Madras coast, where he was mortified to find that the old Company's representatives, probably prompted by Governor Pitt, took not the slightest notice of him.

"Ye 8th ye King and flag was hoisted and his commis^n to ye Consull read in public to all ye English on shore," runs a contemporary account, "Mr. Lovell & ye rest belonging to ye old Factory was sent ye day before to come & hear ye commiss^n read, but they came not. 'Tis true they sent a letter to ye consull by ye Dubash ye night before, but he refused to receive it, then they sent it by an English young man, but ye Consull thought fitt not to receive it from him neither, & told him y^t he would hear no excuse, but did expect they should comply with his orders."[1]

And sad to relate, there was not very much that poor John Pitt could do about it, for bluster as he might, he had nothing with which to enforce his will. He could, of course, issue his high-sounding summons "To Mr. Tho: Lovell &C. English in the Service of the Governour and Company of Merchants of London Trading in the East Indies, in their Factory or elsewhere in Metchlepatam"; he could, of course, in the King's name, grandiloquently will and require them "to repair to our Factory to-morrow morning between 9 and 10 being the 8th Instant August, Upon hoisting the Flagg when I intend to open and read my Commission"; he could, of course, threaten them "fail not to appear as you'l answer the contrary at your Perill"; he could even sign himself "J. P. Consull"[2]; he could certainly do all these things, but when Mr. Lovell and his associates saw fit to ignore all this arrogant bravado, Mr. John Pitt must have been indeed puzzled to know what to do next.

Meanwhile, his uncle at Madras was laughing at his impotence; and on August 23rd, 1699, he issued a Proclamation to all the forts and factories within his Presidency denouncing John Pitt as an impostor and forbidding the servants of the old Company to have anything to do with him. But young John was perhaps beginning to feel rather foolish, for he seems to

[1] Extract from the Diary of William Tillard, a servant and later President of the New East India Company.

[2] John Pitt's Manifesto to the Servants of the old Company at Masulipatam, August 7th, 1699.

have written the Governor a more conciliatory letter,[1] to which his uncle replied in surprisingly mild terms. "'Tis your own ill nature and uneven temper makes you Censure your relations—from me you have mett with noe disappointments," he wrote. Then he reproved the young man for disrespect to the King's flag and continued: "If you pass by here you must behave your Selfe very Civilly, noe Drums, fflaggs, nor trumpets within our bounds, for here shall be but one Governeur while I am here. Your Advice is very good, and I returne it you, mind your trade which is your Masters business, and when the Moors have bang'd you and stript you of what you have, upon your Submission and begging pardon for what you have done, I may Chance to protect you here. I can't but laugh at your promising us protection; when you have neither forces power nor Interest in the Country. When ours are assign'd you, you may talk at that rate. . . ."[2]

While this wordy war was being waged by the two relatives, the Consul was becoming ensnared in difficulties in other quarters. In April 1692 John Pitt and a certain Trenchfield had been given the task of carrying a present of 15,000 rupees to Gingee for the Mogul's general, Zulficar Khan, in return for which and for aid given in the war he had successfully waged against the king of Golconda, the general had obtained a firman from the Grand Vizier, Assid Khan, conferring certain privileges. This treaty Pitt and Trenchfield brought back with them.[3] On the strength of this, John Pitt seems to have posed in England as an authority on Eastern questions, with the result that when it was decided to send out Sir William Norris, Member of Parliament for Liverpool, as Ambassador from the King to the Great Mogul, with the object of soliciting Phirmaunds or privileges for the English traders, he, whose knowledge of Indian affairs was negligible, was consulted on the many problems that were likely to present themselves.

Thus consulted, John Pitt advised the Ambassador to start his embassy at Masulipatam with the result that on September 23rd, 1699, his Excellency arrived off that town in one of his Majesty's ships and accompanied by three other men-of-war. No counsel could have been worse than to advise an Ambassador to the Mogul's Court to come to the little insignificant station at Masulipatam on the east coast, for, as John Pitt should have known perfectly well, the octogenarian Mogul, Aurangzib, was in fact at this time encamped somewhere in the Mahratta country on the western

[1] This has not been preserved.

[2] Thomas Pitt to John Pitt, November 12th, 1699.

[3] Talboys Wheeler, *Madras in the Olden Time*, Vol. I.

coast of India. But in blissful ignorance of this, the self-important Ambassador announced his arrival in grandiose terms:

"Sir Wm. Norris, to the Gentlemen of the English Company's Factory at Matchlepatam ffrom on board his Majesties Shipp *Harwick* rideing att anchor in the Roads before Matchlipatan on the Coast of Cormandell the 23rd of September 1699.

"Honrd. Gentlemen,

"I thought it Necessary to take the first Opportunity to Signify to you my Arrival on the Coast, which was (with the squadron under the Command of Comadore Warren) on the 20th Instant about Six in the Evening, And on Monday next I Intend to dissimbarque.

"This comes by a shipp in the Service of the Old Company, wherefor I think itt not Expedient to say any thing further than that I am

"Honrd. Gentlemen,

"Your humble Servant,

"Wm: NORRIS."

"All possible Provision is makeing (by the Governor in Cheife of this Province under the Great Mogull) for my Reception, with great grandure and all Imaginable demonstrations of ffreindshipp. A Supply of Wine and Strong Beer will bee Necessary by the first Opportunity."

"Shall get all things ready for your Lordship's reception on Monday and will advise you to-morrow what our of the day will be best to Land," came the somewhat dispiriting reply. "If your Excellency pleases, in my opinion 'twill be best to have only a Cold treat and the Severall tables ready spread cover'd, upon your Arrivall, for 'twill be impossible to hitt the time so exactly to have it hott and in Order besides 'twill be expected, it shou'd be done with a great deal of more Ceremony than what circumstances will admitt, for your Excellency cannot but be sensible wee must be in a little hurry, not being Yet well Settled, and every body with me unacquainted with India."[1] Whether the Ambassador enjoyed his "cold treat" and whether the "wine and strong beer" were forthcoming history does not relate! What history does relate is that the self-important Ambassador was detained at the out-of-the-way town on the east coast of India waiting for the Great Mogul, and that only after some three and a-half months' delay the misguided Consul at last summoned sufficient courage to write to the General whom he had once met seven years earlier.[2]

[1] John Pitt to Norris, September 23rd, 1699.

[2] John Pitt to "the Victorious and Noble Navob Zulpher Cawne, Metchlepatam the 10th Jany. 1699." This date should clearly be 1700 or in the old style 1699-1700.

The letter, written with sufficient bombast to impress the Ambassador with the Consul's intimacy with Zulficar Khan, drew forth no reply. The Ambassador was unknown to the General, and he would remember John Pitt, if he remembered him at all, as a minor servant of the East India Company who had once been admitted to his presence with a gift from the Governor of Fort St. George. So months passed. There comes a time, however, when the patience of the mildest is exhausted, and Sir William at length determined to sail to Surat and from that port to commence his march to the camp of the Great Mogul. But this was not before he had found time to write an indignant letter to the Court of Directors of the New Company to tell them what he thought of their precious Consul and all his works.[1] All this left Governor Pitt quite unmoved. "I will not trouble you with news——," he wrote to his friend, Sir Henry Johnson, "only tell you y^t ffort S$^{t.}$ George is in y^e same place I found it, notwithstanding the bouncing of Ambassad^{rs} & Consulls, the former not being able to doe any thing on this Cost [sic] is gone to Surat. They give out I am a dead man in the eye of the Law, & they say that one of the King's ffrigats is to fetch me home and that there will be Mandamuses and the Lord knows what, but lett them say w^t they will, I am sure they can prove nothing."[2]

We need not follow Sir William on his further travels. Suffice it to record that when at last he did arrive at the Court of the aged Aurangzib, it was only to find that the emissaries of the old Company had preceded him. Protracted negotiations ensued, but they led nowhere. "Your Ambassador is at the Camp eating rice and Curry at the King's charge," wrote Governor Pitt, "and notwithstanding the vast expense he has been at wee doe not hear he has effected any thing, nor will they I believe part with him till they have suck'd him dry." And of nephew John he writes humorously in the same letter: "My Kinsman and I are at as great a distance as ever, he at Metchlepatam, and I at ffort St. George, but whether it be Mellancholly or Madness occasions it, Duke Trincolo Swares Sometimes that he will Send for the Governor of ffort St. George in Irons to him, and was much of the same humour when he came into this roade, as you say to publish his powers. Did he ever write you that he dar'd do such a thing here, or that any body regarded his person or his power?"[3] At length, when it was clear that nothing would eventuate from his mission, Sir

---

[1] Norris to Court of Directors of the English Company, dated "ffrom on board the *Summers* in Metchlepatam Road," August 19th, 1700.

[2] Thomas Pitt to Johnson, "Octob^r 14th 1700."

[3] Thomas Pitt to Raworth, October 16th, 1701.

William retired in high dudgeon and sailed for home on the *Scipio*; but on the way he suffered an attack of dysentery and on October 10th, 1702, he died.

Within a few days of the Ambassador's departure the evil effects of the mission were seen in a Proclamation issued by the Mogul, interdicting all trade with the English and other Europeans and ordering that their persons should be taken into custody.[1] As a result of the King's decree, his general, Daud Khan, appeared on January 29th, 1702, with considerable forces at the little town of St. Thomé, only a few miles from Fort St. George.

When earlier in the month information of the approach of Daud had been brought to the fort, the Governor, knowing Daud's intense love for strong drink, had thought it wise to send out to the approaching general "forty bottles of brandy distilled here with all manner of spices."[2] Some parleying ensued, but in vain, and on or about February 6th the siege of Fort St. George began. It lasted for almost exactly three months, and was finally raised on May 5th when the Governor purchased the retirement of the enemy forces for the modest sum of 25,000 rupees. But between those dates there was much to cause anxiety to all the inhabitants of the fort. That was why Governor Pitt seemed *distrait* on the afternoon when we first met him, why his brow was knit and his thoughts elsewhere, till his servant aroused him from his lethargy to announce the arrival of Ramchund and his companion, Vincatee Chittee, and he hurriedly gave orders that they should be admitted to his presence.

To the north and westward of Madras lies the district and city of Hyderabad, and some five miles west of the capital of the Nizam's dominions is to be found the ruined fortress of Golconda, once the capital of a great and powerful kingdom of the Deccan, but subdued in 1687 by Aurangzib, the Great Mogul. This ancient stronghold was in the time of Governor Pitt the central market for the great group of diamond mines then being worked in the neighbourhood of Hyderabad. The proximity of these mines to Madras had for long tempted the residents in Fort St. George to speculate in diamonds, and Pitt had for some time been indulging in the fascinating pastime of sending diamonds to England.[3] During the Autumn of 1701—whilst Sir William Norris was still at the Mogul's camp and some four months before the appearance of Daud Khan at the gates of Fort St. George—a rumour came to Pitt's ears that a diamond of exceptional

[1] Hosbulhocum from the King with Assid Khan's seal, dated November 16th, 1701, in the 45th year of the King's reign.

[2] Consultation Book of Fort St. George, Wednesday, January 28th, 1702.

[3] British Museum, Addl. MSS. Nos. 22, 854-56.

size and quality had recently been brought from Golconda and was being offered for sale in and around Madras. Within a few weeks, the stone itself was brought for his inspection by a native diamond merchant called Ramchund. The Governor was not only able to make a thorough examination, but was fortunate enough to procure a model of the stone, and this he forwarded to his friend, Sir Stephen Evance,[1] the Court Jeweller and banker, together with a letter asking for advice.

He gave a full description of the stone: "itt weighs Mang.303[2]: and car$^{tts.}$426. It is of an excellent christaline water without any fowles, onely which will come out in cutting, they lying on the surface of the Stone. . . . Since I saw itt I have bin perusing of Tavernier, where there is noe Stone Soe large as this will bee when cutt. . . ."[2] In reply Evance bade his friend be cautious. "Wee are now gott in a Warr, the French King has his hands and heart full soe he can't buy such a Stone, There is no Prince in Europe can buy itt, soe would advise You not to meddle in itt, for the Interest Yearly would come to a great sum of Money to be dead, as for the Diamonds received per *Dutchess* can't sell them for 8s. a Pagoda."[3]

But the Governor had already yielded to temptation. The truth is that the wily Ramchund knew full well that Pitt could not resist a bargain and he early determined to do all he could to persuade him to buy the stone. With oriental cunning he commenced by asking a grossly extravagant price and thoroughly whetted the Governor's appetite by frequently leaving the temptation in his charge for some days and then withdrawing it. But so far the price had not been reduced from 200,000 pagodas, and as Pitt was declining to pay more than 30,000 pagodas, the prospects of a deal did not seem fair. And so the matter was left until sometime in February 1702, when Ramchund renewed the negotiations, in company with his friend, Vincatee Chittee. At last the time had come for a modification in the price, and at the end of the next interview this had been reduced first to 100,000 pagodas and then to an unspecified sum slightly below that figure. "When we agreed," as Pitt wrote some years later, "upon a day to meete and make a finall end thereof one way or other."

The great day came and Pitt and Ramchund met in the Company's

[1] The name might have been Evans, but Thomas Pitt always spelt it thus.

[2] Thomas Pitt to Evance, "Fort St. George, Novr. 6th, 1701." The Mangelin is a small weight varying in standard from approximately 1 to 1¾ carat. Jean Baptiste Tavernier (1605-1689) was a great traveller and the highest authority of his day on precious stones. The reference is, of course, to one of his books in which he gives advice on how to detect flaws in diamonds.

[3] Evance to Thomas Pitt, London, August 1st, 1702.

Consultation Room to see if they could come to terms; "I brought him down to 55,000 pagodoes, and advanced to 45,000, resolving to give noe more, and he likewise resolved not to abate, soe delivered him up the stone, and wee tooke a friendly leave of one another." This seemed final, but, sure enough, about an hour later the two natives returned, and it was to announce their unexpected call that the servant interrupted his Excellency's reverie at our first sight of him. No wonder a look of pleasure came over the Governor's face; it was clear that the price was falling fast: the stone was as good as his! And so it proved. At first Ramchund named 50,000 pagodas, then feigned to leave the room, and finally turned to say that 49,000 was his final figure. "But I still adhered to what I had before offered him, when presently he came to 48,000, and made a solemn vow that he would not part with it a pagodoe under; when I went againe into the closett with Mr. Benyon, and told him what had passed, saying that if it was worth 47,500, it was worth 48,000, so closed with him for that sum, when hee delivered mee the stone, for which I paid him very honourably, as by my books appears." So the great diamond was purchased for less than a quarter of the sum originally asked.[1]

But with the purchase of the gem, Governor Pitt's troubles had only begun; his next problem was how to get it back home in secrecy and safety. This task the Governor determined to entrust to his son, Robert, now about twenty-two years old.

It was not that the fond father had any illusions as to Robert's fitness for the task, for he must have looked with grave misgivings on the weak, feeble face, the shifty, furtive, deep-set eyes of his first-born; but several things conspired to force him to rely on his son as messenger. In the first place, Robert had never liked the East and had his reasons for being anxious to return home. Most of his time seems to have been spent in travels in China. "We live here very sociably together," he wrote from Canton. "Instead of bohea and damned strong sherry, and country beer, we drink every night good claret; and by midnight, after the shake of the elbow and

[1] The description of the negotiations is taken from Thomas Pitt's own account written at Bergen under date July 29th, 1710, and endorsed: "In case of the death of mee, Thomas Pitt, I direct that this paper, sealed as it is, bee delivered to my sone Robert Pitt." The paper was written to falsify accounts circulated by his enemies suggesting that he used dishonest means to acquire the great stone; for example, Alexander Pope maligned him in the oft quoted lines from *The Man of Ross.*

"Asleep and naked as an Indian lay,
An honest factor stole a gem away,
He pledg'd it to a knight, the knight had wit,
So kept the diamond, and the rogue was bit."

The last few words in the original MS. ran ". . . and was rich as Pitt."

several hearty curses, some people, by degrees, abate the commission on the gross."[1] To his mother he also wrote from Canton: "On my return to Madras I intend going home by the first ship that sails thence for England,"[2] and two months later from Fort St. George, "I arrived here on the 17th instant, and continue in my resolution of returning home. I find my father wavering in the matter, but unless his positive commands detain me, I design for England next September."[3] Later in the same year he returned to Canton, whence he wrote to his mother: "I hope to arrive at Fort St. George ten days before the *Bedford* sails, on which I design for England."[4] It was fortunate for Robert that his father had misgivings as to the *Bedford's* seaworthiness, for she was lost with all hands—and incidentally with a fine but smaller diamond belonging to Thomas Pitt. But the young man was bent on sailing for home for a purpose that soon became apparent, and his father, seeing his determination, was unwilling to say him nay. And besides, there was another reason that prompted the Governor to let his son return and take the diamond with him.

When Thomas Pitt sailed for India in 1698, he left his wife in entire charge of his affairs, with instructions to follow the advice of two friends, Peter Godfrey and Samuel Ongley, both members of the Court of the Old Company; and he left her in possession of ample funds and a pleasant country house, Mawarden Court, at Stratford, together with a residence at Blandford St. Mary. For a time, all went well. The Governor would send home valuable consignments, not only of diamonds and other stones, but also of merchandise of all sorts, which had to be sold in London, and the money laid out for the benefit of his family or remitted to him in India. It was not unnatural, therefore, for Pitt to express considerable anxiety as to the fate of these consignments, and to feel the most intense annoyance when he was fobbed off with vague and unsatisfactory intimations in place of positive facts. Thus, in February 1701, Ongley had written that Mrs. Pitt was pleading that ". . . she has occation for all the money in my hands to pay for some land that she has bought, of which I suppose she will give you an accompt. I observe you order me to pay what Madame Pitts shall require of me, which order I must obey she having the same from you."[5] Pitt was furious and he thus unburdened himself to his brother-in-law, Thomas Curgenven:[6] "My wife has writt mee little or nothing to

[1] Robert Pitt to Harrison, Canton, October 14th, 1701.
[2] Robert Pitt to Jane Pitt, Canton, December 12th, 1700.
[3] Robert Pitt to Jane Pitt, Fort St. George, February 20th, 1701.
[4] Robert Pitt to Jane Pitt, Canton, December 20th, 1701.
[5] Ongley to Thomas Pitt, "London the 26: ffeb: 1701 (-2)."
[6] Curgenven, the Rector of Folke, had married the Governor's sister, Dorothy.

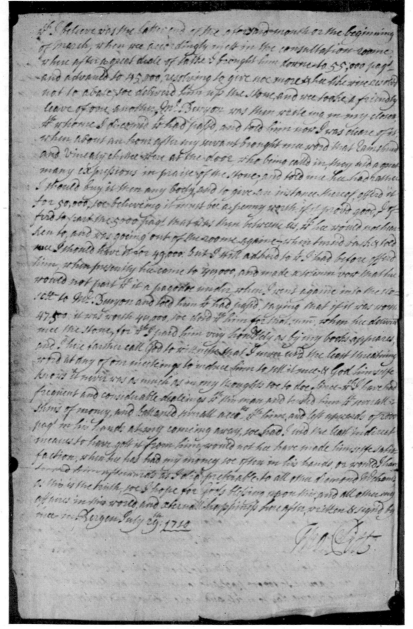

GOVERNOR PITT'S ACCOUNT OF THE PURCHASE OF THE GREAT DIAMOND
DATED FROM BERGEN, JULY 29TH, 1710. (*The last sheet.*)

the purpose this year, nor has sent me nothing, tho' I positively order'd her. She writes me God knows what that she is about purchases, but not a word of what some has cost or others will cost. I have noe manner of accompt of what I left her, what She has received or paid since, what I have hence sent her or what it Sold for, but all railings against one or other, which has very much expos'd my busyness and done me a great deal of prejudice. Soe that I find great inconvenience by trusting a woman with busyness which I will avoid for the future."[1] So he determined to send Robert home with both the diamond and a document revoking his mother's powers and appointing him and Sir Stephen Evance as trustees to act in her place. Thus it came about that Robert Pitt embarked for home on the *Loyal Cooke*, with the stone—if tradition is to be believed—hidden in a hollow made in the heel of his boot. He sailed from Fort St. George on October 9th, 1702, and reached England in May of the following year.

No sooner was Robert out of his father's sight than he was bombarded with letters of caution and advice about what was always termed his "great concern." He quitted Fort St. George with a memorandum of instructions as part of his luggage.[2] This was followed by further messages, all written in a more or less worried strain and all concerned with his great diamond. "The true value I must never expect;" he wrote, "but I hope you will never part with it for much less. I gave you an account of how to estimate the value, which I hope you are master of." There is more about the diamond and the great responsibilities devolving on young shoulders; then he ends significantly: "Avoid all vices, and an inconvenient or disreputable marriage."[3]

That was in October. In the following April, Thomas Pitt wrote once more urging his son to send full details and again in July acknowledging what appears to be the first letter he had received from Robert since his departure: "I enjoined you at parting not to be sparing of your advices, which you have hitherto neglected, and I believe you had hardly written to me from the Cape but for the accompanying bill, which I hope you took up for the ship's expenses and not for your own, for no one went better provided than yourself, in a condition to spare rather than want. . . ."[4]

Two months later the Governor wrote his son to announce the death

[1] Thomas Pitt to "the Revd. Mr. Thos. Curgenven at Folke near Sherbourne, Dorset," October 22nd, 1701.

[2] Thomas Pitt to Robert Pitt. Endorsed, "Memorandums to my son Robert Pitt on his going to England." It is dated from Fort St. George on the day of Robert's departure, October 9th, 1702.

[3] Thomas Pitt to Robert Pitt, Fort St. George, October 15th, 1702.

[4] Thomas Pitt to Robert Pitt, Fort St. George, July 23rd, 1703.

of the foolish Consul Pitt,[1] ". . . upon which I wrote a compliment to his lady who answered it and some months after wrote to me about interring her husband here, which I did not refuse her but would pay no respects to the corpse." Then he added regretfully: "When he came out of England his will was in favour of your brother John; but since he came into India he has made a new one and left him out, and every relation he had, except his uncle Nick, from whom he had expectations."[2]

But there was still no news from Robert, and in November Thomas writes him again: "I hope you have, long since, safely arrived in England and deliver'd that which, if itt answers my expectations, has not its fellow. I would wish, though, I abated something of its true value, that the Crown would buy it, for the like will never be had againe in these parts. . . . I strictly enjoin you to be dutifull to your mother, and loving to your brothers and sisters. . . ."[3]

As we have already seen, Robert had in fact long since arrived in England. How could he be so thoughtless as to leave his father for so long in anxious ignorance of his fate? At last all was explained. Robert Pitt was in love; and within a few weeks of reaching London he was married to Harriet Villiers, daughter of Lady Grandison and of the noble family of which the two notorious Dukes of Buckingham were members. Robert thus announced his marriage to his father: "You always advised me against a disreputable marriage which I have avoided by marrying a lady of family and character, with the approval of my mother and of Uncle Curgenven. . . . I hope I shall not be abandoned by you at a time when I have no other support but yourself, since my alliance with the greatest families in England is as much to your credit, as my wife will be a comfort to you when you know her. My present happiness is altogether due to you, as it was the universal report of your good and generous character that induced Lady Grandison to give me her daughter. Her age is 21, her portrait and letter, herewith, speak for themselves. . . ." and he concluded—"I hope to obtain some genteel employment by the intercession of her relations."[4] This

---

[1] John Pitt had died at Deverampant on May 8th, 1703. Extracts from Diary of William Tillard.

[2] Thomas Pitt to Robert Pitt, Fort St. George, September 17th, 1703. More than a year later, Robert replied to his father: "My cousin, John Pitt, died little lamented either by his relations or employers. It was reported here that you denied him Christian burial until I showed the copy of your letter to his widow." Robert Pitt to Thomas Pitt. London, December 18th, 1704.

[3] Thomas Pitt to Robert Pitt, Fort St. George, November 8th, 1703.

[4] Robert Pitt to Thomas Pitt, London, December 30th, 1703.

hope was never fulfilled; nor did she bring a great fortune with her. She appears to have had about £2,000, enabling the young couple to start life with a capital of between £8,000 and £10,000, no bad position for those days. As for Harriet, with her tall, slim body, her long, shapely neck, and her soft, appealing face, everybody spoke well of her: "a very virtuous fine young lady, with a good fortune,"[1] as one friend wrote to the Governor, and "as beautiful as sensible, and as well-behaved as most I have seen in my life,"[2] in the words of another. "I must declare I do not know a more accomplished person than Mrs. Pitt," wrote Sir Gilbert Dolben to Thomas, "it is a great dispute among those who have the pleasure of conversing with her, whether her beauty, understanding, or good humour be most captivating; and I am much pleased to hear her husband frequently express a just sense of her merit and his own happiness."[3]

But the Governor refused to be comforted. For one thing, his son had deceived him.[4] "In your letter of the 27th of May, you say there is a match on foot between you and the lady mentioned. I believe you play the same game with me as with your mother, who writes me you were married before she saw your wife; and I believe you were so before you wrote to me, for several correspondents tell me that was the first thing you did, which has justly brought you under the character of a giddy inconsiderate young fellow. I guess the cause of your writing so slender an account of my affairs, and take no notice of brother or sister, friend or relation; nor do you mention anything in regard to the delivery of many letters I sent to you. . . . As to your marriage, what I chiefly dislike is its suddenness; and much wonder you desire a present enlargement of your fortune, which, with your wife's cannot be much less than £10,000; a very good fortune for a young man qualified for business. I hope the great interest you value yourself on, will procure you some considerable employ."[5]

But to return to the Governor's "great concern," which must now be cut into a brilliant. Thomas Pitt had been reading Tavernier, and he had reckoned that, according to that authority, his diamond when cut into a

---

[1] Styleman to Thomas Pitt, London, November 18th, 1703.

[2] White to Thomas Pitt, London, January 20th, 1703-4.

[3] Dolben to Thomas Pitt, London, January 4th, 1705 (-6).

[4] Robert arrived in England in May, 1703, and he and Harriet were married within a few weeks. He advised his father in his letter of December 30th, 1703, when he had been married some seven months.

[5] Thomas Pitt to Robert Pitt, Fort St. George, September 12th, 1704.

single stone should weigh about 300 carats and be worth some £800,000,[1] that is to say nearly as much as the Mogul diamond, the largest stone in the world in Tavernier's day, weighing, as it did, 279$\frac{9}{16}$ carats.[2] As a matter of fact, this was an altogether exaggerated view because the Mogul weighed as much as 793 carats in its rough state, and Pitt's no more than 426 carats. But the Governor was buoyed up with hope and was anxiously awaiting news of the stone's cutting. "Mr. Cope had the cutting of it," reported Robert. "Our present design is a single stone, and we hope to make it a brilliant. It proves the first water, but will be diminished almost one half in cutting. We have so managed it that what is cut off is in great pieces, and will be sold for a good sum of money. Mr. Cope says that when finished it will weigh about 280 carats, and will be the wonder of the world."[3] This was encouraging enough, but the Governor's chagrin may well be imagined when he is next informed that his great jewel will in fact weigh no more than one-half of Cope's original estimate. "My son, by your direction, wrote to me in January 1703, when you had the stone in your hands about eight months and, as I suppose, begun to work it, that it would make a clean stone, a brilliant of 280 carats, and the pieces sawed off worth a great sum," he wrote to Cope. "Now you tell me it will be but 140 carats, and the pieces worth little that are sawed off. Certainly Mr. Cope's judgment cannot fairly vary so much, there being a window in the Crown of the stone when (it) went hence, and the body very clear, when the skilfull here could discover only two small flaws at one end. And then I cannot but make one remark more on the paper; after the nine pieces sawed off, the stone is still to lose 102$\frac{1}{2}$ carats in working, before finished. None can believe but that it was my interest to have preserved the magnitude of the stone, although there had been a flaw or so in it; and, as you told my son, 280 would make it the wonder of the world. I am sure it will be so, your paring it to 140. I will be speedily with you and discover more fully about the matter."[4]

[1] Thomas Pitt to Evance, Alvarez da Foncesca and Robert Pitt jointly, Fort St. George, January 28th, 1702-3. According to Tavernier a good quality flawless diamond weighing 1 carat is worth approximately £11 5s. 0d. To ascertain the value of a larger stone, the number of carats of its weight should be squared and then multiplied by the value of a 1-carat diamond. Thus according to this method of calculating, a 12-carat diamond of the highest quality is worth 12 x 12 x £11 5s. 0d.=£1,620. Tavernier, *Travels in India*, vol. 2.

[2] According to Tavernier's reckoning, the Mogul diamond was worth £879,245.

[3] Robert Pitt to Thomas Pitt, London, December 30th, 1703. The statement that it will be "diminished almost one half in cutting" seems strange seeing that the Mogul diamond was thereby reduced from 793 carats to 279$\frac{9}{16}$ carats.

[4] Thomas Pitt to Cope, Fort St. George, October 12th, 1705.

The poor man's anxiety must have been unbearable, for the same day he wrote off to his son in a hurry that did nothing to improve either his grammar or his spelling: "The disappointment in that grand concerne has not a little disquieted me, and you nor Sir Stephen, nor any one of you never as much as hinted what, in all probability, it would fetch, which you know, could not but have been some satisfaction to mee. . . . I charge you that you never permit the selling of it under £1,500 a carat, and that all my business be managed with the greatest secresye and quiete immagenable, and without ostentation." Then he adds somewhat unkindly—"But I thinke it is too late to forbid that, since you have sett up to live at the rate I heare you doe, which has not created me a little envye, and makes mee often remember Osborne, that the children are certaine trouble but uncertaine comforts."[1]

But before he received this testy outburst, Robert had already written a letter calculated to pacify an anxious parent: "Your grand concern is now almost finished," he assured his father. "It is a most glorious sight, but the outer coat so foul, and the flaws went so deep in it, that it will not come net above 140 carats, which still being not to be paralleled, is as inestimable as if it were much more. The reason why the pieces" (sawn off), "although well-spread, yielded no more was that they were very full of flaws; Mr. Alvarez and Mr. Cope both think they have been sold for their full value."[2] Moreover, Alvarez da Foncesca appears to have written Pitt a full account of the whole matter, and he replied cordially ". . . I assure you I think your favours to me in that matter are as inestimable as the thing it selfe," he wrote, "and I shall be greedy of an opportunity to acknowledge it otherwise than by words, for with the account you give I'me intirely satisfyed, tho very much chagrin'd last year when I was writ, that the magnitude would not be above halfe as much as was formerly writ, without giveing any reason for it."[3] A year later he wrote Foncesca hoping the diamond might be bought by "the Crown of England, for the honour of me and my posterity; and if wee have been successful this last Campaigne as before, I doubt not there will be money enough to buy it, and the parliament have a heart great and gratefull enough to present it to her Majesty."[4]

At length, in January 1707, Robert wrote his lengthy account of why the great stone lost so much weight in cutting, a letter that he would have

[1] Thomas Pitt to Robert Pitt, Fort St. George, October 12th, 1705.
[2] Robert Pitt to Thomas Pitt, London, January 3rd, 1705 (–6).
[3] Thomas Pitt to Alvarez da Foncesca, September 13th, 1706.
[4] Thomas Pitt to Alvarez da Foncesca, September 12th, 1707.

done well to have written at least a year before. He explained that this was entirely due to unexpected flaws and assured his father that the central portion of the stone was quite perfect; it was only the outer part that had been cut off where the imperfections had been found. To his father's lament that they had cut off more than was necessary, Robert explained that the three persons concerned—Evance, Alvarez and he—always visited Cope together, and that it was their joint opinion that "it was better to make it a pure stone of a less weight, than to keep it greater and have it foul; for the reason that its being at once the largest stone in the world, and without flaw, makes it more valuable." He quieted his father's suspicions that he had been cheated, "for there was never a piece sawed off that I did not myself put on the place whence it was taken, and see if it exactly fitted. Mr. Alvarez was the chief manager in the sale of the pieces, and he protested that he would not have given so much for them, and that, had they been his own, he would have sold them for the same money." Finally, he promises his father it is safely put away under lock and key and that he has never let a word drop as to its existence. "I have been asked about it by a hundred people," he writes, "and all the answer I ever made was that I wished it were true, or that they could make their words good."[1] These statements were fully substantiated by a joint letter subsequently despatched by Evance, Robert and John Dolben who had recently returned from India, and to this at last Thomas expressed himself entirely satisfied.[2] Finally he directed: "For some particular reasons with which I shall acquaint you when wee meete, I desire you, upon receipt of this to deliver to my kinsman, George Pitt, my large diamond cutt into a brillion by Mr. Cope, weighing about one hundred and thirty-six carratts."[3] So the stone was accordingly removed to Strathfieldsaye, where it remained until its owner's return to England in the autumn of 1710.[4]

Whilst this war of words was being waged, Robert Pitt was soon in trouble in other ways. It will be remembered that he returned to England charged by his father with the duty of taking over from his mother the management of the family affairs and administering them jointly with Sir Stephen Evance. Robert was then about twenty-four years old, and not

[1] Robert Pitt to Thomas Pitt, London, January 10th, 1706-7.

[2] Thomas Pitt to Evance, Dolben and Robert Pitt, Fort St. George, September 16th, 1707.

[3] Thomas Pitt to Evance, Dolben and Robert Pitt, "Near Bergen in Norway, May 30th, 1710."

[4] Strangely enough, nothing is known at Strathfieldsaye of the great diamond having ever been lodged there, but it appears likely that George Pitt did in fact keep it in his own house at this time.

unnaturally his mother did not take kindly to her supercession by her youthful son and another trustee with whom she was little acquainted. It is hardly surprising to find, therefore, that before long Robert and his mother were not agreeing. On December 30th, 1703, Robert had mentioned vaguely to his father that his affairs had been mismanaged; in January he reported a violent quarrel with his mother with regard to the control of some property near Salisbury which Jane claimed as hers by settlement.[1] At this stage, however, the Governor was still on affectionate terms with his wife and had recently written Robert: "My love to your mother, to whome I charge you all to be very Dutyfull;"[2] and again two months later: "I strictly injoyn you to be Dutifull to your Mother and loving to your Brothers and Sisters. . . . Give my Love to your Mother, my blessing to your Selfe, Brothers and Sisters, and service to all friends. . . ."[3] Indeed, hitherto Thomas had been receiving excellent accounts of his family who appear to have passed their time partly at Stratford and partly at Blandford. His cousin, John Pitt, often called "Cornet John Pitt" had written to him of them: "In my way ye last Sumer to my Quarters I cal'd at Stratford & stay'd fower dayes wth Mrs. Pitt & pretty family who were all in health and learne their bookes bravely. . . ."[4] Another cousin, Robert Pitt, a doctor, had also written the Governor a satisfactory account of his family: "As the news of your Recovery was very wellcome to me and all your Friends, I can acquaint you that my Cosen and Miss Essex are both in perfect Health";[5] whilst from the doctor's brother, Thomas, the Governor had heard that "Your Lady was a few dayes agoe at my house and lookes as well as ever I saw her."[6] "I saw my Cousin & your two Daughters very lately," wrote the same correspondent a year later, "who & your other children here were very well."[7] "Last year I was at the Bath," wrote Sir

---

[1] Robert Pitt to Thomas Pitt, London, January 20th, 1703 (-4).

[2] Thomas Pitt to Robert Pitt, September 17th, 1703.

[3] Thomas Pitt to Robert Pitt, November 8th, 1703.

[4] Captain John Pitt "To the Honble. Thos Pitt Esqre., Governor of Fort St. George, India. Gravend the 8th. Jan. 1701-2." Though the exact identity of Cornet Pitt is not certain, he was probably that John who was 4th son of the first George Pitt of Strathfieldsaye. He was aide-de-camp to the Duke of Marlborough and he it was who was commissioned to bring home the despatches of the victory of Blenheim.

[5] Dr. Robert Pitt to Thomas Pitt, January 21st, 1701 (-2). Dr. Pitt (1653-1713), was an eminent physician.

[6] Thomas Pitt to Thomas Pitt, January 27th, 1701. This first Thomas subsequently became a Master in Chancery.

[7] Thomas Pitt to Thomas Pitt, "February 7e 8th, 1702."

Thomas Littleton, Treasurer of the Navy, "where my wife's happiness was to become acquainted wth yr. good Lady & very much Obliged to her for her great kindness and Civility . . . particularly my good wishs attend a dainty boy of yrs. wch she had wth her at ye Bath."[1]

But Robert had not been long home before the relations between him and his mother rapidly deteriorated, and his sisters seem to have taken their mother's part. Essex, the elder, actually complained to her father of Robert's temper: "You cannot but know the reason why your sisters are not with you, as I have a letter from Essex who resents your ill-treatment of her, and so do I, who know your temper too well. Your brothers and sisters have no dependence on you, nor ever shall; and as my children behave themselves, one better than another I shall consider them, and no otherwise."[2] But Robert was also a mischief maker; and three months later, he writes to tell his father—"My sisters are at Bath with my mother, and we seldom meet except in the country during Summer. I always invite them to pass the winter in London with my wife, in order that they may have the benefit of masters and of the best society, but my civility is thrown away, they being, for some unknown reason, set against me." And then he adds: "I hope that the good accounts you have received of my marriage have induced you to approve of it, and that you will send your blessing to your little grand-daughter, Harriet, born in May last, of whom I have presumed to name you godfather. My dependence on your love and generosity has made me endeavour to put myself on a footing in the world becoming your son; but without your support I must soon sink under the pressure of my own narrow fortune."[3]

Robert must have known the bad impression this news would make on his father. The Governor had left his wife in possession of two country homes, and now she must leave them both to take a house at fashionable Bath where soon the scandal-mongers were busy. "I have heard from others, the truth of which I cannot question," wrote Thomas, "that that scoundrell rascally villain has been too intimate in my family, to the prejudice of my honour and their reputation for I make noe distinction between women that are reputed ill, and such as are actually soe; wherefore I have discarded and renounced your mother for ever, and will never see her more, if I can avoid it."[4] And again some two years later: "Why could

[1] Littleton to Thomas Pitt, October 1st, 1701. Littleton had been Speaker of the House of Commons from 1698 till 1700, and was Treasurer of the Navy from 1701 till 1710, when he died.

[2] Thomas Pitt to Robert Pitt, Fort St. George, September 12th, 1704.

[3] Robert Pitt to Thomas Pitt, December 8th, 1704.

[4] Thomas Pitt to Robert Pitt, Fort St. George, September 30th, 1706.

you not write like Mr. Shipman? He hinted to me that your sisters were with you and that your mother had been guilty of some imprudence at the Bath . . . let it be what it will, in my esteem she's noe longer my wife, nor will I see her more if I can help it . . ."[1] Seeing that these outbursts were the result of mere gossiping rumours, we are tempted to question the Governor's sanity. Perhaps misfortune was in part responsible, for William, the youngest of his boys, had recently died of small-pox. "What hellish planet is it," he asks Robert, "that influences you all and causes such unaccountable distraction that it has published your shame to the world; which has so affected me that I cannot resolve what to doe. I wish you nor none of your family be at the bottome of it. . . . Have all of you shook hands with shame, that you regard not any of the tyes of Christianity, humanity, consanguinity, duty, good morality, or anything that makes you differ from the beasts, but must run from one end of the kingdome to the other, aspersing one another and aiming at the ruine and distruction of each other?" Then he raves at the wretched Robert for having turned his mother and sisters out of his house. "But I see," he goes on, "your hand is against every one of them, and every one against you, & your brother William to his dying minute. How do you think this has chagrined mee, & what anxious as well as desperate thoughts has it brought into my mind, & dampt my desire of ever seeing you more, or any of you all, for I can promise myselfe noe comfort of you." But he belabours them all, for in the same letter he writes, "I no less resint what they did to your child at Stratford," though history does not relate what that enormity may have been.[2]

Eight days later, he writes in ever greater frenzy ". . . of the hellish confusion that is in my family, and by what I can collect from all my letters, the vileness of your actions on all sides are not to be paralleled in history. Did ever mother, brother, and sisters study one another's ruine and destruction more than my unfortunate and cursed family have done? and I wish you have not had the greatest share in it, for I cannot believe you innocent. This has so distracted my thoughts, staggered my resolutions, broken my measures, that I know not what to resolve upon, nor in what part of the world to seeke for repose. What I have fateagued for after this manner, and lived soe many years in exile from my country and friends . . . but to make my children easy in their circumstances and mee happy in their company; and haveing by God's blessing acquired such a competency as I never expected or could hope for, so as that I shall have been able to establish a

[1] Thomas Pitt to Robert Pitt, Fort St. George, November 24th, 1708.

[2] Thomas Pitt to Robert Pitt, Fort St. George, September 22nd, 1706.

family as considerable as any of the name except our kinsman G. P.,[1] and now to have all blasted by an infamous wife and children. It is such a shock as man never mett with, and whether I shall overcome it or sink under it, God knows. Is this the way to invite mee home? When I am well assured you are all of you thoroughly reformed I may think of it; but as matters stood at the writing of your letters, I think your company hell itselfe." Then he reverts to the turning of his mother and sisters out of doors, as he puts it. "You say your house has two rooms of a flour, and a closett, and, as I suppose, four or five storeys high. It was very hard you could not spare them one storey. I would have done it to your wife and children had they been twice as many. . . . Then, it is said, in all companies you expose your brothers and sisters, who ought to conceale their faults and support their character! It is ill to do any such thing to either, more especially your sisters, whose reputation ought to be as dear to you as your life; and I had rather you would cutt their throats and mine too, than that you should doe any *such* thing, or have as much as a thought to their prejudice. What makes you quarrel with them? Is it that you would have me thinke that you are the Saint of the family? Noe, I know you too well and parted with you when you were at man's estate, but left them all poor innocent children. . . . I have various thoughts of all your actions, and how barbarously and inhumane like you treat each other. Will dyed with complaints in his mouth against you. It is much that no one should be of your party; or it may be the designe is that I shall discard them all, and soe I might be the better able to contribute to the supporting of your extravagancies."[2] Yet this letter, terrible as it appears, seems to have done some good, for it evoked a joint reply from the whole family expressing regret for the past and a firm promise to live in harmony for the future.[3]

But of his eldest son's extravagance the Governor was also constantly complaining. Soon after his marriage, Robert had set up an establishment in the fashionable quarter of Golden Square. "Your son, my opposite neighbour, lives very handsomely," wrote John Wyndham to the Governor, "and in esteem with all good men, and also very happily with a good lady."[4] But the last thing Thomas wanted was his first-born to live very handsomely. "My letters from several friends are full of your extravagancies and in what vaine-glorious manner you went down to the election

[1] George Pitt of Strathfieldsaye, to whom Thomas Pitt always looked up as the head of the Pitts.

[2] Thomas Pitt to Robert Pitt, Fort St. George, September 30th, 1706.

[3] Pitt family to Thomas Pitt, London, February 10th, 1707-8.

[4] Wyndham to Thomas Pitt, London, January 27th, 1705 (-6).

at Old Sarum, and what charge you put me to in house-keeping while there. What is it that you mean by this? I find you have exhausted your own fortune and your wife's too; and are you now broaching mine? Have a care what you doe, for I assure you if I find a just cause, I will cutt off you and all your family from ever haveing to doe with any thing of mine. . . . I wish gameing bee not rife in your family, or otherwise you could never have spent soe considerable an estate in soe short a time. Whenever I am certain that any of my children game I will, by all that is good, disinherit them."[1]

Robert had been elected Member of Parliament for Old Sarum, and his election expenses were a great shock to his father. "When I hear in what manner you went down to Old Sarum against the election," wrote the irate parent, "sent down a man cook sometime before, coach and six, five or six liveries, open house for three or four months, and put me to about £500 charge. What was the need for this? It never cost me above £10 which was for a dinner the day of election."[2] Indeed, Robert was forced to give up his London house and retire to Enfield, where, as he wrote, he had taken a house and garden with 50 acres of land for £60 a year at a place called Forty Hill, "twelve miles from the Capital."[3] He begged his father for help—"our concord will be a comfort to you when you return, and then I shall hope to be no longer the abandoned child of your family, the only one who has had no provision of head made for him, his unfortunate wife, and three little children, although in the most need of all. I have been maligned to you as extravagant, without any grounds. My wife's fortune is untouched, and of my own I have spent £4,000 in nearly five years of married life. If my marriage so disobliged you at first, I am sure I have been sufficiently punished for it by daily anxieties of mind which almost drove me to despair."[4]

To this appeal Thomas Pitt did not lend a deaf ear. "I was over-joyed," wrote a delighted mother, "that your father was at last pleased to do a little for you as well as for your brothers and sisters, and dont in the least question but that he will increes yearly in his genourosaty to you all,"[5] which at least shows that the unfortunate quarrels with his mother had been for a time composed. But the father also wrote his son a characteristic letter in reply to his appeal: "Before you had wrote that long doleful

[1] Thomas Pitt to Robert Pitt, Fort St. George, September 22nd, 1706.
[2] Thomas Pitt to Robert Pitt, Fort St. George, September 30th, 1706.
[3] Robert Pitt to Thomas Pitt, London, January 10th, 1706-7.
[4] Robert Pitt to Thomas Pitt, London, January 8th, 1707 (-8).
[5] Jane Pitt to Robert Pitt, Stratford-near-Sarum, August 1st, 1708.

paragraph you should have better considered the necessity that induced me thereto. Did you not see how your mother had deserted my habitation and was wondering with my family which it was high time for me to provide for." Could there be a greater distortion of the facts? "In my will, which I have ordered to remain in Mr. Haworth's hands," the Governor continued, "there is a good provision made for you, your wife and children, who shall never be abandoned by me if they deserve otherwise, and you have no reason to grudge what I have done for your brothers and sisters, nor will I be tyed up by the direction of one child to what I shall do for the others. . . . Can you be so voyd of sense as not to see what I have been doing ever since I was soe fortunate as to purchase that Great Concern, which has been to use my utmost endeavour to acquire such a competency as to be able to provide for my family without being put under a necessity to dispose of that affair at an under rate, or it would have been of as little advantage to me as if I had partners therein; which, I thank God, I have effected if no extraordinary misfortune happens; soe, as soon as I come home, and get my estate remitted, I will make you and your family easy, to which you should think of contributing, not as yet hearing you have turned one penny in trade since you left me. Always spending and nothing comeing in will soon waste a better estate than I have got, and what I want a good purchase for is chiefly to settle you."[1]

But the result of these constant family quarrels was that in the end the father felt compelled to remove Robert from the trust and to place the younger children under the care of his brother-in-law, Thomas Curgenven, and his kinsman, George Pitt of Strathfieldsaye. The former, unfortunately, having become blind, was unable to act, but George Pitt, in Robert's words, "has shown himself friendly and zealous for the good of your family above expectation."[2] It was no easy task that the head of the family had assumed, but he seems to have been a moderate man of good sense and to have determined to do his best for all parties. "On the receipt of a letter from your father, at his landing in Norway, full of resentments towards you," he wrote to Essex and Lucy Pitt on one occasion, "I did, by the first opportunity, doe you the best service I could to him by letter. . . . I have since had another from him of a milder strain, which gives me hopes it may be in the power of your friends to pacifie your father, whose present displeasure seems to be founded on your disobeying his orders, which you cannot but remember I sufficiently cautioned you against. I have now nothing but to repeat . . . that you will both continue with your brother

[1] Thomas Pitt to Robert Pitt, Fort St. George, February 5th, 1708-9.

[2] Robert Pitt to Thomas Pitt, London, January 3rd, 1707 (-8).

ROBERT PITT, son of Governor Pitt

Kneller

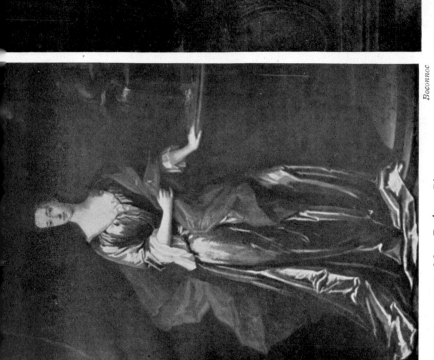

Bocomoc

HARRIET VILLIERS, Mrs. Robert Pitt

Kneller

till you receive other commands from your father. And . . . I pray keep a good correspondence with your brother, for the harmony your father will find amongst you will contribute more to the healing the unhappy differences that have bin in your family, than all the endeavours of your friends together."[1] He persuaded the Governor's two daughters to live with their brother and his wife at Enfield for a while, but they do not seem to have stayed for more than a few months. "My sisters continued to reside with my wife till last month," wrote Robert, "when contrary to the directions of their guardian they went to live with my mother, who has a house upon the Upper Terrace of St. James' Street. They say that your letters give them liberty to choose where they will live: and there has been no quarrel or disagreement between us. My mother has given up to them the £200 a year, which you allowed her, having sufficient of her own to maintain herself and them." He closed this letter with some significant words—"My wife intended to have written to you this day, but early in the morning was suddenly prevented by the birth of another son. We have now two boys and two girls."[2] This new child was christened in the parish church of St. James's, Piccadilly, where the entry in the register ran: "1708 December 13th. William of Robert Pitts Esqr. and Henrietta, born November 15th. baptised." Of this child much will be heard before our tale is done.

Whilst the Pitts were quarrelling in England, events in Madras were fast moving towards a climax. The acrimonious Governor was becoming increasingly difficult to work with. He was constantly being involved in bitter quarrels with members of his council, against whom he was wont to utter the most extravagant threats. In consequence it was not long before he had created for himself a number of enemies, anxious only for an opportunity to dislodge him. The mishandling by Pitt of a native outbreak in Madras proved their chance, and as the result of some obscure and uninteresting machinations the directors of the United East India Company[3] determined in September 1709 to recall the Governor.

Thankful to be released from his arduous duties, Thomas Pitt sailed for home during that autumn, and travelling by way of the Cape of Good Hope and Bergen in Norway, he at last reached England late in the following year. His fame, however, preceded him for whilst in Amsterdam, John Drummond, the famous Scottish merchant-banker, who had been long

[1] George Pitt to Essex and Lucy Pitt, "Stratfielsea, October 5th, 1710."

[2] Robert Pitt to Thomas Pitt, London, November 15th, 1708.

[3] In April 1702, the old and new companies had united on terms very favourable to the former. These terms were not a little due to the skill and vigour with which Governor Pitt had maintained his Company's interest.

settled there, wrote home eagerly to his friend, Robert Harley, who had just returned to office: "Governor Pitt from the East Indies is safe arrived here, and being recommended by Sir Steven Evans and several others to me, I think I have made him yours and have drunk your health with him. He will have a powerful purse, in England, and be a thorn in the side of some great men now at the head of the bank and East India Company if they should thwart you. Therefore if you can get him chosen in Cornwall pray do, for he will be more useful to you than ever Dolven was to your predecessor, and I hope you will make a better use of him. He will be here yet ten or fourteen days if not three weeks, and then for England."[1]

In this country Pitt's qualities were soon recognized and it was not long after his return before he was very generally known as the great President.

[1] Drummond to Harley, Amsterdam, September (12)—23 N.S. 1710.

CHAPTER II

In the Reign of Queen Anne

WHEN Thomas Pitt landed in England in the autumn of 1710, Queen Anne had reigned for rather more than eight years, and during the whole of that period the country had been at war. The War of the Spanish Succession is, of course, famous for the four great victories of the English hero. Whilst Marlborough's famous battles were being waged and won, however, an important but lesser-known campaign was being fought in Spain itself. The commander of the English and Dutch troops was a strange, quarrelsome, fussy little man of great energy, known to history as Lord Peterborough. Accompanying him was a tall, dark, handsome man with all the energy and none of the fussiness of his superior, James Stanhope by name, then aged about thirty-two and soon destined to succeed his superior as commander-in-chief of the British forces in Spain. He had an early success in the attack on Port Mahon, after which he returned to England in time to take part in the trial of Dr. Sacheverell.

This windy ecclesiastic was not endowed with much sense, but he was the proud possessor of an imposing presence and a loud voice which he was delighted to use on all possible occasions. He had preached many sermons of an inflammatory nature on the doctrine of non-resistance, and in 1709 he preached such a sermon to the embarrassed Lord Mayor and Aldermen of the City of London assembled in St. Paul's Cathedral. He also availed himself of this grand opportunity to assail the Ministers of the Crown and especially Marlborough's friend, Lord Godolphin, the Treasurer,[1] whom with rare invective he attacked under the name of "Volpone."[2] Instead of following the wise course of ignoring the empty-headed divine, Ministers, stung by his taunts, were foolish enough to stage a full-dress impeachment in Westminster Hall; and General Stanhope, just back from the battlefield and eager to join in the fray, took a prominent part in these proceedings. The charge against Sacheverell was that he had maintained that the means that had been found necessary to bring about the "glorious" Revolution of 1688 were "odious and unjustifiable," and all the managers of the

---

[1] They were also connected by the marriage of Godolphin's son Francis to Lady Henrietta Churchill, the Marlboroughs' eldest daughter.

[2] The title character of Ben Jonson's famous comedy, *Volpone, or the Fox*.

impeachment spoke to this article. General Stanhope expounded the theory of Locke that civil Government is based on a compact which itself implies the right of resistance by an aggrieved party. He spoke with sufficient force and energy to show that he was a power in the political world as he was already recognized to be in the military.

Meanwhile, there was rioting in the streets, the mob madly in favour of the parson, whom they regarded as the victim of ministerial malevolence; in consequence, troops were called out to quell the enthusiasm of the people and the Queen was assailed by excited citizens shouting "we hope your Majesty is for a High Church and Dr. Sacheverell." In this atmosphere, the decision of the peers was awaited with much anxiety, and when it was known that sixty-nine were for conviction and fifty-two against and that the sentence was no more severe than a suspension from preaching for three years, it was recognized that this was as good as a Government defeat, which was bound still further to weaken the Ministry and already indicated that the Whigs had lost the confidence of the country.

So thought the Queen; and encouraged by her favourite, Abigail Hill, now Mrs. Masham, and two new advisers, Harley and Shrewsbury, she determined to rid herself of the Ministers. On April 6th, 1710, the last terrible scene took place between Queen Anne and the Duchess of Marlborough, and they were never to meet again; on June 14th, Marlborough's son-in-law, Sunderland, was removed from office; on August 8th, Godolphin himself was peremptorily dismissed. The Queen declined to see the Treasurer and sent him no word of thanks for all his services. With brutal abruptness eight long years of loyal service were suddenly terminated, and in a few weeks Godolphin was followed into retirement by Orford, Somers and the other Whigs. Marlborough consented to retain his command, but the Whig Ministry was at an end, and the wealthy, muddle-headed, bibulous Harley found himself at the head of affairs. The new minister immediately dissolved parliament, and as a result of the General Election that ensued, the Tories were placed in possession of a considerable majority.

Meanwhile, the war dragged on. In the Peninsula, the Allied Army in Catalonia under General Stanhope and the Austrian Marshal Starhemberg, was slightly larger than the enemy, and the English general at any rate was eager for battle. But just as Stanhope was fiery and impulsive, so Starhemberg was slow and cautious. The Englishman urged an invasion of Aragon and battle with the enemy, and though the Austrian was opposed to the project, he was overruled by the impetuosity of his colleague. The resulting battle was fought at Almanara and proved a brilliant justification of Stanhope's plans. The Spaniards under Villadarias, were utterly routed, and to the joy of all England, the gallant Stanhope fought in hand-to-hand combat with Amezaga, the Commander of the Spanish Cavalry, and struck him to the ground.[1] As a result of this defeat, Villadarias was replaced by the Marquis de Bay, but as no confidence was felt in any Spanish general, Louis hastened to send one of his best marshals, the Duke of Vendôme. But before he could arrive, Stanhope had won a second and even greater success. The Spaniards, having crossed the river Ebro, had retreated along its southern bank to Saragossa. Once again the English general was for action, and the Austrian for caution, and once again the former's counsel prevailed. Battle was joined amongst the olive groves and vineyards to the south of the town and quickly resulted in an overwhelming victory for the allies. Saragossa was taken, and the remnants of the enemy fled south in confusion.

But at this point fortune veered. A few days after the battle, a council of war was held in the newly captured town to decide future policy. The turbulent Stanhope was anxious to march on Madrid forthwith; the cautious Starhemberg urged the closing of the Pyrenees passes before the undertaking of any further adventures. Hitherto Stanhope had been consistently right and Starhemberg as consistently wrong; accordingly the English commander's forward policy was preferred. On hearing this news at a supper party at Robert Harley's, Stanhope's former chief, Peterborough, blurted out to Swift that they could be sure of Stanhope losing all Spain before Christmas, and "that he would venture his head upon it,"[2] a prophecy that was amply fulfilled.

The march on the capital was soon accomplished. But no sooner had the town fallen than Vendôme crossed the Pyrenees at the head of about eight thousand French troops, and this force, added to what he could raise from Spaniards eager to repel the foreign invader, rapidly put at his disposal an army considerably larger than their enemies. It was soon clear that Madrid could not be held in the face of hostile troops in considerably greater numbers, and about the middle of November the great evacuation began. The retreat was organized in three parallel columns starting from Chinchon, a small town south-east of Madrid. Stanhope was at the head of the left-hand column, and it was agreed that he should retire northwards by way of Brihuega. On December 6th, rather more than three weeks after leaving Madrid, he reached this destination, where he halted for several days to rest his troops and to obtain the necessary stores: and there he was suddenly surprised by the enemy. Believing Vendôme to be on the far side of Madrid, Stanhope had not thought it essential even to send

[1] A medal commemorating the event is still preserved at Chevening.

[2] Swift, *Journal to Stella*, Vol. II.

out scouts to keep watch over the country surrounding the town. Suddenly the enemy appeared over the hill, and the English commander hastily sent his aide-de-camp to warn Starhemberg that his troops were surrounded and, to make matters worse, were short of ammunition. But it took the envoy five hours to make his way through the enemy's lines to the Austrian Marshal's camp at Cifuentes. The next afternoon Starhemberg set forth to aid the beleaguered force, but he moved slowly, and by nightfall had not arrived. Less than a thousand rounds of ammunition were left to the defenders, and their state was hopeless; so late that night the English general surrendered with some 4,000 British troops.[1] Thus ended in tragedy what had hitherto been a brilliant military career. It was some eighteen months before Stanhope, exchanged for the Duke of Escalona, was released from confinement and enabled to return to England. But though he was yet to render his country service both in politics and diplomacy, his military days were done.

Though the General Election held in the Autumn of 1710 was a resounding defeat for the party he supported, it was favourable to the fortunes of Thomas Pitt, who was returned for the safe seat of Old Sarum. The ex-Governor was a staunch Whig, and he suspected all Tories of Jacobite sympathies. It was this that had so distressed him about his eldest son when he had heard of Robert's Tory leanings, and had prompted him to write thus angrily from India: "I have been often thinking what box you have gott into in the House of Commons. I am afraid you are one of those children that are awakened with the rattle that is commonly nameing the Church of England, for which noe man have a greater veneration than myselfe; but I know it is often named within those walls to bring over a party, the consequence of which has been generally dangerous to the State."[2] And again even more explicitly two years later—"It is said you are taken up with factious caballs," he complained, "and are contriving amongst you to put a French kickshaw upon the throne againe, for no true English heart as the present Queen has (and pursues no other interest than that of her own nation) can please your party. If I find or hear of any child of mine that herd with any to oppose her present Majesty's interest, I will renounce him for ever."[3]

Thomas Pitt did not return to England unnoticed by those whose notice counted, for the fame of his great diamond had preceded him and was

[1] The original document, giving the terms of the capitulation signed by the Duke of Vendôme, is among General Stanhope's papers preserved at Chevening.

[2] Thomas Pitt to Robert Pitt, Fort St. George, February 6th, 1706-7.

[3] Thomas Pitt to Robert Pitt, Fort St. George, November 24th, 1708.

soon the talk of the town. "My dearist and best of children," wrote Lady Wentworth to her son Lord Raby, in Berlin, "for all the great scairsety of money, yett hear will be a gloryous show one the Queen's birth day, wonderful rich cloaths are preparing for it; thear was one that see Mr. Pit's great dyomont that I writ you word of and they say its as big as a great eg; I would have the sity of London bye it and mak a present of it to put in the Queen's Crown. . . ."[1]

Soon after his return Pitt took a large house in Pall Mall, which henceforth was to be his London home. There he kept an excellent cellar and a handsome establishment: he lavishly entertained many political friends, and also doubtless for his two daughters, whose futures had long caused him some anxiety. "My daughters are my greatest concern," he had written to his friend, Colonel Wyndham, a few years before, "and heartily wish they were well disposed of, which I have left entirely to my Cozen George Pitt. I have appointed the sum (£6,000 each) for their fortunes, which should not be unwilling to augment, if they were matched into such an honourable family of (sic) yours or those you mention."[2] Of Essex Pitt, the elder, we know little. Her face hard and rather stupid, her hair long and ill-kept, she lacked beauty, save for her grave blue eyes and a certain grace that was the attribute of youth. Moreover, she was reputed to be a peevish, spoilt young lady with many of the usual Pitt characteristics and a mind of her own. "We go to Mr. Bartmansemmer's very ofone, and are much in his favor," she wrote to her sister-in-law. "I was in hopes of gitting of him at one time, but, the other day, I was stroke dead all at once, for he told me he never desired to marry."[3] From her few extant letters we gather that Essex Pitt was even worse educated than most young women of her day. "I writ this in bed for I have such a pain in my head, and coff, that I cannot keep my head from the pellow. . . . I believe I shall never be well again, for my coff grows worst and worst every day."[4] "The house that is taken for my Lady Grendison . . . is in Jarman Street, amost opeset to Lady Barrymore's . . . I would have gone and seen it but have had no coatch to go anywhere. Master Tommy is very well. I think the town agrees with him, for he have a fine collor and groose fat. He is now visiting at my Lord Pembroke's."[5]

[1] Lady Wentworth to Raby, December 15th, 1710.

[2] Thomas Pitt to Wyndham, January 19th, 1708-9.

[3] Essex Pitt to Harriet Pitt, London, October 6th, 1712.

[4] Essex Pitt to Harriet Pitt, London, May 4th, 1711.

[5] Essex Pitt to Harriet Pitt, London, October 30th, 1711. "Master Tommy" is Robert Pitt's eldest son.

Very different was her younger sister, the Governor's favourite child. Lucy Pitt was a lovely girl with a straight nose, a beautiful well-formed mouth and narrow deep-set eyes that gave her a soft gentle appearance that was certainly indicative of her nature. Her marriage, which took place the year before her sister's, must have given old Thomas Pitt the greatest pleasure, for of all the men who visited him at his house in Pall Mall it may safely be surmised that none was more welcome than his prospective son-in-law, General Stanhope, just back from his captivity in Spain. In spite of the final catastrophe, James Stanhope was something of a national hero, for had he not won two notable victories and slain his man in single combat? Moreover, he was a staunch Whig, a notable and rising politician whom all respected and of whom the Governor could justly be proud. He visited the Pitt family almost immediately after his release, and it must have been plain for all to see that the master of the house was not the chief attraction that brought him to Pall Mall. In truth, the gay, middle-aged, war-worn warrior had no eyes but for sweet gentle Lucy Pitt, eighteen years his junior, and within six months he had won her as his bride. On February 24th, 1713, they were wed, and there then commenced for both of them eight years of happy married life, only terminated by Stanhope's premature death in 1721.

The governor's relations with his firstborn seem to have improved somewhat upon the father's return to England, due in part at least to the charms of Robert's wife. "The deportment of your daughter Pitt," he wrote to Lady Grandison soon after his return, "hitherto exceeds the character that either yor Ladyship or other ffriends have given her, which together wth the pritty children gives me entire satisfaction." But of his son he cannot speak so well. "I wish I could say soe of the Husband and the ffather," he continues in the same letter, "who I thought should be charm'd into a dilligent care of 'em and not to have spent all that has come to his hands. I wish I could have been soe happy as to have met you here, to have had yor advice in rectifying what I find amiss, and prevent the like for the future, for that I expected to have found in his hand a very considerable cost, but instead thereof not one penney, but rather in debt, w^h has soe irritated me, that was it not for his wife and children I would discard him for ever, this I impart to your Ladyship esteeming it the same as in my own breast, he being as nearly related to you as his wife is to me."[1] Not unnaturally, Lady Grandison was delighted at Harriet's success. "I am pleased to hear my dear daughter was so well received by Governor Pitt," wrote the proud mother, "it gives mee hopes I shall have the satisfaction to find you in his house when we meet. This I must impart to your

[1] Thomas Pitt to Lady Grandison, London, November 15th, 1710.

good management, for I am sensible of the difficultys you have to strugel with, while there are partys in your family, and I cannot but think it is a fault in your father to allow of it, as I shall tell him, you may assure yourself. . . . The General is much pleased to know you are in the Governor's house."[1]

But if Lady Grandison was happy at her Harriet's success, she was determined to do what she could to restore her erring son-in-law to the good graces of his father; and the subtle meed of flattery was the physic of her choice. "It gives mee all ye satisfaction I can desier as to yr kindness design'd my daughter and her children wch I do not doubt, but she will make it her care to desarve," she wrote to the Governor a few months later, "what faults has been in my son Pitt's managem[t] I impute to his being at so great a distance from you, for I thought it a great misfortune to want ye direction of a descrete parent when he was first to live in ye world, their are follys in youth yt will soon be over and then will be pardoned and forgot by a kind father, it pleas'd mee exstremely when I found my son was not to be drawn in to play, for that will ruin ye best fortune: ye considerable prospect he has, made many have designs on him when he was first marre'd. . . ."[2] The Governor does not seem to have been proof against such blandishments; and his attitude to Robert noticeably changed: he allowed him and his wife the sole use of Mawarden Court, his house at Stratford-under-the-Castle, as also his house at Blandford St. Mary, and the young couple's financial position was further eased by the passing over to Robert of the rents of Stratford. With Lady Grandison he remained on the friendliest terms, and the following year wrote to congratulate her on the birth of a grandchild to them both. "I was unwilling to omitt this opportunity by my friend Colonel Ottery of giving your Ladyship my humble service and to wish you joy of yo grand daughter who was born just time enough to have a small share in the lottery tis a brave bouncing girl and hope they bee fortunate there in."[3] Of this "brave bouncing girl," christened Elizabeth, more will ere long be told.

While these events were happening in the Pitt family, Marlborough was waging war on the Continent with his accustomed skill, and the Ministers were conducting secret negotiations with the French to see how

---

[1] Lady Grandison to Harriet Pitt, Bath, April 4th. "The General" is, of course, General Stewart, Lady Grandison's second husband. By "your father," she means Harriet's father-in-law.

[2] Lady Grandison to Thomas Pitt, Dromana, August 9th, 1711.

[3] Thomas Pitt to Lady Grandison, Pall Mall, November 21st, 1712.

best to bring the conflict to a speedy conclusion. In a few weeks the triumphant general was at the gates of Bouchain. When that fortress fell, the road to Paris lay open before him. Marlborough, anxious to take advantage of this position, sought the necessary supplies to enable him to push on towards the Capital. But the Ministers were determined on peace, and all he received was "a bamboozling letter from Lord Oxford."[1] The siege of Bouchain saw the end of what was perhaps the most brilliant of all Marlborough's exploits; it was certainly the end of his military career.

At home, the Tory Government was, or pretended to be, convinced that the war had been from the very beginning a gigantic mistake entered upon to enhance the personal interests of Godolphin and Marlborough; that England had not gained and was not likely to gain from it anything beyond empty military glory; that the interests of her allies had been preferred to her own; and that the sooner this country could be extricated from her foreign entanglements, the better it would be. Fortified with these sentiments, Ministers had but one thought, how best to obtain the most favourable terms possible from the French king. Their first expedient was ignominiously to remove from the command of the ever-victorious army the ever-victorious general, to replace him with an untried soldier of small experience, and after his departure from England to send him secret orders "that you avoid engaging in any siege, or hazarding a battle till you have further orders from her Majesty."[2] Furthermore, he was commanded "to disguise the receipt of this order" as it might have an ill effect if it became generally known! This was the predicament in which the Government placed their new general, the Duke of Ormonde,[3] upon his arrival in France. To Louis and his countrymen, our policy seemed to be nothing short of madness and they proceeded to take advantage of the occasion by putting forward a spate of demands, by withdrawing offers they had previously made, and by protracting the negotiations by every variety of artifice and deceit. At length, in March 1713, peace was signed at Utrecht on terms that were little better than those which had been rejected by the Whigs at Gertruydenberg a few years previously. Nevertheless, a day of thanksgiving was appointed, and the Queen and both Houses of Parliament went in solemn procession to give thanks to God for the peace of which nine men out of ten disapproved. A week or so later, Parliament was dissolved and at the ensuing General Election Governor Pitt and his sons Robert and Thomas were all returned.

[1] Harley had been created Earl of Oxford and Mortimer three months previously.
[2] Bolingbroke to Ormonde, May 10th (O.S.), 1712.
[3] The second duke, grandson of the splendid and abler first duke.

No sooner had the new parliament met than rumours began to circulate that the Queen was plotting with her Ministers to secure the throne for her Stuart relatives. No shred of evidence exists to support this charge; indeed, all that we know on the subject points in the opposite direction. While, however, it is certain that Anne had no desire to aid her Roman Catholic brother to regain his Crown, it is equally sure that she had little love for the House of Hanover, and a rooted objection to any prince of that House setting foot on the soil of England so long as she was queen. Judge then of her horror, when the agent, Schutz, urged on by the English Hanoverian leaders of all parties who were anxious to secure the succession by having a member of that family resident in England, went on April 12th, 1714, to the Chancellor Harcourt and demanded without warning a writ for the young Electorial Prince to be summoned to the House of Lords by his English title of Duke of Cambridge. There was no doubt that, as a Peer of the Realm, he was entitled to be summoned to take his seat, and Harcourt could only reply that he would consult the Queen. A meeting of the Cabinet Council was hastily called, and it sat that night in Anne's presence till the small hours of the morning. Finally, the writ was handed to Schutz accompanied by an intimation that he was not expected to present himself at Court; and angry letters were sent by the Queen to the Electoral Prince and to the aged Dowager Electress Sophia, who was at the bottom of the whole intrigue, that it would be highly undesirable for the Duke of Cambridge to avail himself of this opportunity to come to England. What would have happened next if the sprightly old lady had lived, it is difficult to surmise; but fortunately for all concerned, Sophia died within a few weeks—much to her annoyance, no doubt, for, though aged eighty-five, she had set her heart on outliving and succeeding the English Queen—and the new Elector, George, taking a more reasonable view of the matter, forbade his son to come to England, recalled the offending Schutz, and sent over a more experienced agent, Bothmar, to take his place.

So Anne had won the race, and ailing as she was, had outlived the old war-horse of Hanover who had for so long been waiting to occupy her place. But now, with the mists of death gathering upon her brow, the poor Queen was terribly alone. Her husband, "poor asthmatic 'est-il possible?' who always looked as if it were dinner time"[1] was dead; not one of her children had survived; her greatest friend, Sarah of Marlborough, had become a hated enemy and an exile from her native land; and Godolphin's quiet sagacity was no longer there to help in her perplexities. To

---

[1] Feiling, *A History of the Tory Party, 1640–1714.*

whom could she turn? To my Lady Masham,[1] the sly intriguing Abigail? To her Grace of Somerset, the "proud" duke's red-haired Duchess "Carrots," daughter of the last Percy of Northumberland and her Majesty's Mistress of the Robes? To her Ministers—the ageing drink-sodden Oxford or his debonair, pushful, intriguing rival, Harry St. John, Viscount Bolingbroke? These were not the stuff of which friends are made. There was none to help her, and the poor sickly invalid must struggle on alone until release should come.

The summer months sped slowly past, and all the time the enemies of Oxford strove mightily to bring him down. The insinuating Bolingbroke, anxious as ever for his own advancement, moved heaven and earth to effect his rival's overthrow, and the Tory party, split as it was from top to bottom on the question of the succession to the throne, united only on one desire— the removal of Lord Oxford from his post. At last the Queen gave way, and at a meeting of the Privy Council, held at Kensington Palace on July 27th, she announced in her own simple language the reasons that had brought her to dismiss her Treasurer from his office. These, according to Oxford's Secretary were manifold—"that the Lord Treasurer neglected all business, that he was very seldom to be understood; that when he did explain himself she could not depend on the truth of what he said; that he never came to her at the time she appointed; that he often came drunk; lastly, to crown all, that he behaved himself towards her with bad manners, indecency and disrespect."[2]

The scene at this last Council was tragic indeed. There sat the Queen, drooping with pain and exhaustion, whilst the rivals denounced each other across the table with every form of vituperation. Regardless of the presence of their sovereign, forgetful of the presence of a lady, these two men accused each other of every variety of vice—peculation, disloyalty, drunkenness—with unseemly passion and relentless rage. At last the ugly play was ended, and Anne, sick in mind and body, retired exhausted to her room. Two days later, on July 29th, she had an apoplectic fit. The release that the poor woman had so long desired could not now be long delayed.

Meantime, Lord Bolingbroke, taking it for granted that he would be summoned to replace the fallen Oxford, gave a dinner at his house in Golden Square to some of the leaders of the opposition in an effort to bring them to terms with the Tories. The rising Walpole was unfortunately away from London; but Stanhope, Pulteney, Craggs, and other prominent Whigs attended. The host "waxed eloquent on his devotion to the House of

---

[1] Abigail's husband had been created a peer in the New Year's Honours, 1712.

[2] Lewis to Swift, July 28th, 1714.

Hanover. His guests sat, grim, polite, incredulous."[1] The Whig terms were simple. They wanted, said Stanhope, assurance that the armed forces were in hands loyal to the House of Hanover; they required Marlborough to be in command of the army and Oxford of the navy; they did not seek office for themselves, but these conditions they must see fulfilled. Bolingbroke could not agree, and the party broke up with these words from the frank, manly soldier who had been spokesman for the Whigs—"Harry! you have only two ways of escaping the gallows. The first is to join the honest party of the Whigs, the other to give yourself up entirely to the French king and seek his help for the Pretender. If you do not choose the first cause we can only imagine you have decided for the second."[2] Bolingbroke equivocated and would not commit himself. So General Stanhope, determined to take no chances, assumed a leading part in organizing precautionary measures throughout the country. In this he was enthusiastically seconded by his father-in-law. To Thomas Pitt, the mere thought of a Stuart succession was anathema, and there were assuredly no lengths to which the old Governor would not go to help in preventing the success of any attempts that might be made to place the Pretender on the throne. So measures were pushed ahead to meet any emergency, for it was clear that the crisis, so long expected, was close at hand.

Two days after the dinner-party in Golden Square, Anne suffered a serious relapse. At noon of that day, July 30th, the Privy Council met at Kensington Palace. The Dukes of Somerset and Argyle hurried to the Palace where they arrived before the commencement of the Council, and exercising their rights as Privy Councillors went in to the meeting. They forthwith demanded that the office of Lord Treasurer should be filled instantly, for they feared that if the Queen died with that office vacant, Lord Oxford might take advantage of the confusion to return to his former post. This was quickly agreed to, and it was the unanimous view that the Whig Duke of Shrewsbury must have the White Staff. To Bolingbroke, who of course had counted on the office for himself, anything seemed preferable to the possibility of his rival returning, and accordingly he took a leading part in the proposal of Shrewsbury to the Council. A deputation was quickly formed, and on ascertaining from the seven doctors in attendance that Anne could be addressed, headed by Bolingbroke they went to the Queen's chamber.

There lay the poor helpless invalid in the great bed, a tormented gout-racked body with still a flicker of life within. None can tell how much she

[1] Trevelyan, *England under Queen Anne,* Vol. III.

[2] Williams, *Stanhope.*

knew of what was passing, though some say that the Queen mumbled to Shrewsbury that he was to use the staff for the good of his country: all that is certain is that her hand, guided by the Lord Chancellor, gave the Treasurer's staff into the Duke's custody. Thus the melancholy scene was ended. The delegation retired from the sick-room, and the Privy Council set to work to secure the safety of the Kingdom and to prepare for the peaceful Proclamation by the Heralds of the undisputed succession of King George. All that day they sat and far into the night; and all the next day also was not found too long for the transaction of the necessary business of the affairs of state. Late that evening the exhausted men retired for a little sleep, and the Council stood adjourned until eight o'clock the following day, Sunday August 1st. But even that early hour was too late. At six o'clock in the warm August morning the doctors called the Clerks of the Council from their beds to inform them that their patient could not live another two hours. The weary Councillors were hastily summoned, and Shrewsbury and a few of them reached the Palace in a very short time; but it was only to be told that the long expected had happened at last—at half-past seven o'clock the guttering candle had flickered and gone out.

CHAPTER III

The Family Affairs of Thomas Pitt

NOT long after the arrival of King George the list of appointments to ministerial posts was announced and it must have rejoiced the old Governor's heart that his favourite son-in-law, Stanhope, was nominated a Secretary of State. Indeed, he had only recently acquired a second son-in-law, for it was but a few days before the Queen's death that at St. James's Church, Piccadilly, Essex had married Charles Cholmondeley of Vale Royal in Cheshire.[1] But not only was Stanhope in high favour with the new dynasty, but the Governor himself was received by King George soon after his first arrival in England. "I was this day above an hour with the King and Prince," reported Pitt, "certainly their aspect promises prosperity to the Country. I showed them the Great diamond, which they admired and seemed desireous of it, but I believe, hope the nation will give it."[2] A typical Hanoverian sentiment!

On October 20th the new Sovereign was crowned. The next day Stanhope left the country on a mission to the Hague and Vienna, and it was only in January of the following year that he returned. He was just in time for the General Election and no doubt rejoiced with his father-in-law at the Whig triumph at the polls. Not only the old Governor, but all three of his sons were elected Members of Parliament at this time. The father and his firstborn, now elected for Thirsk and Old Sarum respectively, had both been members for some years; but with the two other sons the position was different. Thomas Pitt had first been elected to Parliament only in 1714 when he became Member for Wilton, and at this election he was re-elected for the same constituency. His younger brother, John Pitt, on the other hand, became an M.P. in 1715 for the first time, being elected for Hindon in the same county of Wiltshire. Both these sons had recently married—Thomas to Lady Frances Ridgeway, daughter of Robert, Earl of Londonderry, and John to Mary Belasyse, daughter of Thomas, Viscount Fauconberg. So the father might be thought to have much to

---

[1] Charles and Essex Cholmondeley were the grandparents of the first Lord Delamere.

[2] Thomas Pitt to Robert Pitt, Pall Mall, October 2nd, 1714.

rejoice him; all his children were married, his favourite child, Lucy, to one of the leading men of the day, and all three sons were with him in the House of Commons. But in spite of these apparent blessings there was, as we shall see, much to sadden the old man's declining years.

No sooner had the Houses met than it became plain that the Whigs were determined on revenge, for the King's speech contained some ominous words about the Pretender. Governor Pitt was a member of the Committee formed to draft the reply which assured King George that "It shall be our business to trace out those measures, whereon he bases his Hopes, and to bring the authors of them to Condign Punishment." Meanwhile, amidst these distractions and busy as he must have been, James Stanhope yet found occasion to do his brother-in-law a service. "I assure you that when in discourse with your father, the office of Clerk of the Green Cloath to the Prince was mentioned, it was onely looked upon, as you truely guess it, as an introduction to such future advancement as, I am confident, you will very justly be thought to deserve when you shall be better known to the King and Prince. I cannot precisely answer what you desire to be informed of, no establishment being yet made; but what I have heard is, that the salairy will be £500, the attendance little or none, at least as long as the two families live under one roof. There can certainly be no occasion for a new election for the reason you mention. I believe the establishment will be fixed in about a fortnight; and it will be a very great satisfaction to me if any endeavours of mine for your service are acceptable to you."[1] Whilst Stanhope was thus writing to his brother-in-law, Thomas Pitt was paying a visit to his daughter, Essex, at Vale Royal, her new home in Cheshire. Here grave news reached him: rebellion had broken out, and the Pretender's standard had been raised in Scotland by Lord Mar. Thomas Pitt heard of the rebellion with alarm, and knowing Robert's Tory propensities his first anxiety was lest his son should be compromised. "I reached home last night after a pleasant journey from Vale Royal. On my way at Coventry news met me of the arrest of three peers and six members of the House of Commons: among the latter being your bosom friend the Esquire of Combe.[2] . . . I hear that letters from his friends have been found among his papers, and hope there are none that can compromise you. I have heard since I came to town that you are strooke in with all your old hellish acquaintance, and in all your discourses, are speaking in favour of that villainous traytor Ormond. The designs of these packs of villains that are now taken up was noe less than to cut off

---

[1] Stanhope to Robert Pitt, London, September 16th, 1715.

[2] Edward Harvey, who had formerly sat for Old Sarum with the Governor.

the whole Royal family and sett the Cursed Pretender on the throne, in which miserable tragedy I should have had my share. God still avert it! Greater discoverys are expected will be made every day; let whose will be concerned, I wish they may have their demerits."[1] But though Robert was able to reassure his father, Thomas, nevertheless, was only partially comforted, and he continued to reproach his son for the company he kept. "Since last post, I have had it reiterated to mee that in all company you are vindicating Ormond and Bull, the two vilest rebells that ever were in any nation, and that you still adhere to your cursed Tory principles, and keep those wretches company who hoped by this time to have murthered the whole Royal family; in which catastrophe your father was sure to fall. . . ."[2]

Thomas did not wait long in London. Early in October, he posted down to Stratford and Blandford with the object of raising a regiment of Dorset men at his own cost to fight for the Hanoverian cause; and his second son, Thomas, in command of a regiment of dragoons, took a prominent part in the defeat of the rebels at Preston in the following month. How this must have rejoiced the father's heart: how the old man wished his first-born was of like mettle!

We have seen how, amidst all the distractions of a busy public life, James Stanhope found time to oblige his brother-in-law by obtaining for him a sinecure appointment in the Prince of Wales's Household. One would have thought, in view of Robert's constant complaints of impecuniosity, that he would have been grateful to his sister's husband and anxious to take up the appointment as soon as possible. But in fact this was not so. In the first place, he kept postponing the journey from Wiltshire, so that his father wrote anxiously to Harriet, "I did hope by this to have seene your husband in towne, and his not being soe, occasions various speculations."[3] The reason for the delay seems to have been an absurd reluctance to meet his sister Lucy, and he wrote to his father suggesting that she might be prevailed upon to postpone her visit to Pall Mall until after he had been. "I received yours of the 5th. to which I shall only answere that my house and all I have is at my owne disposall, and shall be soe," came the furious reply. "I think you have already put a more than ordinary slight on the Prince's favour, and those that obtained it for you. I do not doubt but you will still adhere to the advice of your old Jacobite friends, who I hope

[1] Thomas Pitt to Robert Pitt, Pall Mall, September 27th, 1715.

[2] Thomas Pitt to Robert Pitt, Pall Mall, September 29th, 1715. "Bull," of course, means Bolingbroke.

[3] Thomas Pitt to Harriet Pitt, Pall Mall, January 28th, 1715-16.

to live to see confounded and all their adherents. You may stay in the country or come; it is all one to mee."[1]

At length Robert condescended to visit his father, but no sooner had he arrived than he seems to have gone out of his way to offend the old man and his sister by deliberately ignoring her baby, being displayed in the proud grandfather's arms. Indeed, so strained were the relations between father and son that General Stewart wrote seriously to Robert to warn him of the folly of his ways. The kindly George Pitt, too, did his best to compose the quarrel. "The only opportunity I have had of being alone with your father," he wrote, "was the other day when he and his present family did me the honour to dine with us. . . . By his discourse I find his present concern is your want of affection to your brothers and sisters. . . ."[2] As a result of these warnings Robert seems to have made some amends and thanks also to the peacemakers, Stewart, George Pitt and Lady Grandison, the General was soon able to report some progress. He had twice called on Robert's father but found him from home. But "He at last made mee a vissett, and after siting a good while, without takeing any notice or giving any opportunity of mentioning you, my wife came into the rome, and sone after he fell into a violent passion, declaring his resentment upon a letter you writ to him, to which wee boath seemed to be strangers and exprest concerne that you should do anything to give him so great disturbance. Hee then said hee would bring the letter to sho us, which hee has not yet don. Upon this, my wife sent for George Pitt and . . . desired hee would endeavour to sett this affaire in a true light with your father, which hee promised. . . . Two days ago the girles being at my house, your father came to make them and us a vissett. My wife being in the rome, wee expected, after the girls were gon out, he would have shone us your letter . . . but still he tooke no notice of anything. At last my wife asked if hee had writ to you or heard lately from you, to which hee answered, in some passion, that hee had received a long letter from you which hee threw by without reading which . . . gave us boath a good deale of concerne. . . ."[3]

It is difficult to get to the roots of this somewhat sordid family quarrel or to know where to lay most of the blame. George Pitt is inclined to take Robert's side—"I am heartily concerned for the trouble you are under," he writes, "and as I am sensible you do not deserve such treatment, I shall embrace all opportunities of serveing you in the best manner I can; but find

[1] Thomas Pitt to Robert Pitt, Pall Mall, February 7th, 1715-16.

[2] George Pitt to Robert Pitt, London, March 17th, 1715-16.

[3] Stewart to Robert Pitt, London, March 31st, 1716.

your father industriously avoiding all occasions of speaking of you. . . ."[1]
On the other hand there is no denying that Robert's manners were extremely
unfortunate; and though always complaining of a shortage of money, he
had shown no alacrity to take up the appointment which his brother-in-
law had procured for him in the Prince of Wales's Household. "I received
yours of the 15th," wrote the irate old man in reply to a letter from his
daughter-in-law, "and severall others before from you and your husband.
The latter were so stuffed with complaints and directions to mee that made
mee very uneasye, and have taken a resolution to answere none of his letters.
None of my children shall ever prescribe to me who I shall take into my
house, or who I shall keepe out, more especially him that has been the
bane of my family, of which hee has given great proof not only whilest I
was abroad, but since. Soe lett him rely on those that have hitherto
steered his judgment, for I will have nothing more to doe with him."[2]

It was about this time that Thomas Pitt accepted the Governorship of
Jamaica: "I, this day, kissed hands of the King, the Prince, and the Princess
on being appointed Governor of Jamaica . . . Lady Grandison has just been
here to wish me joy of the honour the King has done me."[3] He was due
to leave before the end of the summer, but as the months went by it became
evident that he was by no means ready to sail. Towards the end of August,
he announced an important arrival in the family—"Yesterday morning
your sister Cholmondeley was brought to bed of a daughter,"[4] and to
Harriet's letter of good wishes he replied tartly, "I thank you for your
congratulations of my daughter being safe, and wish there was a better
harmony in my family than at present is, or as far as I can see, like to bee;
and that some of late, had not given mee just cause to revive my resentments. I know not by whose advice you have acted, nor your husband
who never followed mine. I am buisy night and day to prepare for my
departure, being what I most long to see."[5]

We may well imagine that Lady Grandison, seeing how things were
between her daughter's husband and the old man, was also very ready to
speed the parting proconsul. Judge then of her dismay when the date of
sailing was constantly postponed. Despite the difficulties, Lady Grandison
and her husband did all in their power to dissuade their perverse son-in-law
from ruining all his chances by crass stupidity. "There seems an appearance

[1] George Pitt to Robert Pitt, London, April 12th, 1716.
[2] Thomas Pitt to Harriet Pitt, Pall Mall, April 17th, 1716.
[3] Thomas Pitt to Robert Pitt, Pall Mall, June 19th, 1716.
[4] Thomas Pitt to Robert Pitt, Pall Mall, August 25th, 1716.
[5] Thomas Pitt to Harriet Pitt, Pall Mall, September 2nd, 1716.

of all things going well," wrote the General, "and your going to London with Mrs. Pitt and the children will, I believe, improve the good intentions your father may have; especially at this time when, I judge, his final settlements are to be made. If you do not find Tom in London, I hope hee will bee sent for to take his leave of his grandfather, so that hee may see all the infantry together, which I think should please him very much. . . ."[1]

"The infantry" were, of course, the young Pitt family, and Stewart was shrewd enough to know that old Thomas had a very soft spot in his heart for all his grandchildren. They were an imposing throng—Harriet, aged twelve; Thomas, the eldest son, two years her junior; William, already the old man's favourite grandson, aged eight; and three girls, Catherine, Ann and Betty, between the ages of ten and two—and there is little doubt that Thomas's affection for the children would go far to mitigate his rancour against his son. But the months passed. Summer gave place to autumn, and the leaves began to fall; yet Thomas Pitt did not sail. In December he was still in England arguing with the Ministry on the Governor of Jamaica's powers, and then an event happened which caused him to put all thought of Jamaica out of his mind. Early in 1717 overtures were made to him on behalf of the French Government for the purchase of his great diamond.

After protracted negotiations arrangements were come to whereby the purchasers were to deposit £40,000 in London in part payment, and the stone was to be brought to Calais to be examined by the celebrated Laurent Rondet, jeweller to the French Court. If his verdict was unfavourable, £35,000 of the deposit money was to be refunded; in the event of the diamond meeting with Rondet's approval, however, the price to be paid by the Regent Duke of Orleans was 2,000,000 livres (£125,000). This sum was to be paid by instalments, and in the meantime the Governor was to be given as security four separate parcels of the French Crown Jewels. On the conclusion of this preliminary agreement and with the deposit money safely in a London bank, Thomas Pitt, accompanied by his son-in-law, Charles Cholmondeley, and two of his sons, Thomas, a Colonel of Dragoons, and John, a Captain in the Guards, set forth for Calais.

The journey was not entirely uneventful, for it seems that the party stopped at the Crown Inn at Canterbury, where the poor Governor suffered the fright of his life. During the evening old Pitt excused himself from buying wine from the house on the plea that he always brought his own with him, being unable to obtain what he required on the road, and he invited the landlord, one Lacy, to taste it and give his opinion of its quality. This Lacy did, politely wishing he could have treated his guest to as good. So delighted was Pitt at this reply that after several glasses he grew sufficiently

[1] Stewart to Robert Pitt, Bath, September 7th, 1716.

convivial to tell mine host that he had taken a great liking to him and wished he could be of service. To this invitation Lacy, having heard of the famous diamond, but not of course for a moment suspecting its present whereabouts, jokingly replied that his visitor owned a pebble which could do him the utmost service. No sooner had he spoken these words than the Governor, thinking his secret was out, flew into a passion, started shouting that he would be murdered, and abused the unhappy innkeeper in the grossest terms. His family and officers of Thomas's regiment did their best to pacify him, but nothing would satisfy the old man but to have an escort of officers and their servants as far as Dover, where he gave them a second meal; and two of them were actually persuaded to accompany him to France.

At Calais it became necessary to convince Rondet of the quality of the diamond, and family tradition has it that great difficulties were experienced until the Governor's shrewd second son thrust a bank note into the jeweller's hand and bade him go over to the window to see the stone in a better light. It was then pronounced to be entirely perfect. So the transaction was concluded, and though the whole balance of the purchase money was never paid, Pitt retained possession of the jewels which he held as security, and it may be safely surmised that these were adequate compensation![1]

So Governor Pitt returned well pleased with his trip and thankful to have seen the last of an acquisition that had given him nothing but trouble. Indeed, during his ownership of the diamond he must have often recalled the ancient story of it having at one time been stolen by a slave in the Parteal mines on the Kistna, who concealed it in a gash in the calf of his leg until he could escape to Madras, where he fell in with an English skipper who lured him aboard, cut his throat and sold the diamond to Ramchund for £1,000;[2] and there is to this day a local legend that the ghost of the murdered slave still walks Queen Anne's Gallery at Swallowfield, the Governor's Berkshire home.[3]

But be that as it may, it was not long before he began laying out his money and his first purchase was the beautiful Cornish estate of Boconnoc, between Lostwithiel and Liskeard. "When I can get matters settled about

---

[1] For the subsequent history of the Pitt diamond, see Streeter, *The Great Diamonds of the World*.

[2] According to some, the skipper squandered the proceeds in drink and subsequently, in a fit of *delirium tremens* and remorse, hanged himself. Streeter, *The Great Diamonds of the World*.

[3] It is said that Wilkie Collins, who was a frequent visitor to Swallowfield, founded his story of *The Moonstone* on some of the legends connected with the Pitt diamond.

the Cornish estate," he wrote Robert, "I think it would not be amiss if you went down with Crissick. . . ."[1] Lady Grandison, of course, soon heard of the purchase, and anticipating that the Governor intended this family estate to descend to his eldest son, wrote anxiously to her daughter: "This will be a very proper time for my son Pitt to visit the Governor in London, as he will find only Colonel Pitt in the house. Lady Frances, Mr. Cholmondeley and family have departed for Cheshire yesterday. It is very expedient that the Governor should be kept in the good humour of thinking of buying an estate, which I cannot believe but must be designed for the head of his family."[2] Indeed, Lady Grandison proved quite correct, for the estate was subsequently left by the Governor to his eldest son, but not before he had greatly enlarged and improved it. "I find a great deal of trouble in settling my Cornish affairs. . . . You must know what a condition Boconnoc is in."[3]

This was not the only purchase that Thomas Pitt made at about this time, for he bought up land in London, Berkshire, Hampshire, Wiltshire, Dorset, Devonshire and Cornwall. But of all his purchases, his favourite was ever to be Swallowfield in Berkshire, "where however," according to his great-grandson Lord Camelford, "he contrived to throw away as much money in a very ugly place with no property about it."[4] This was no more than the truth, for he certainly did lavish large sums on alterations and improvements to both the house and the grounds, not the least of which was the beautiful five-arch bridge over the Blackwater that flows through the park which bears to this day the initials of the builder, "T. P. 1722." "I went on Thursday to Swallowfield . . . ordered many alterations which will, I fear, put me to vast expense. I wish I had a better head than Abbiss there. The house has been made much cheerfuller by the cutting down of trees."[5]

Whilst Thomas Pitt was buying up estates, James and Lucy Stanhope were busy founding a family. The marriage of the middle-aged General and the tender, quiet daughter of the Governor had been a great success, and it was not long before Lucy had become the mother of a numerous family. Unfortunately Stanhope's public duties took him all too fre-

---

[1] Thomas Pitt to Robert Pitt, Pall Mall, June 29th, 1717.

[2] Lady Grandison to Harriet Pitt, London, July 9th, 1717.

[3] Thomas Pitt to Robert Pitt, Pall Mall, May 19th, 1720.

[4] For the 1st Lord Camelford see family tree. This and other quotations from him are taken from the MS. entitled *Family Characters and Anecdotes*, addressed to his son, and dated December, 1781. The original is preserved at Boconnoc.

[5] Thomas Pitt to Robert Pitt, Pall Mall, August 16th, 1718. Abbiss was Pitt's bailiff.

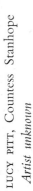

LUCY PITT, Countess Stanhope
Artist unknown

Chævening

ESSEX PITT, Mrs. Charles Cholmondeley of Vale Royal
Artist unknown

Boconnoc

Daughters of Governor Pitt

quently away, and within a few months of his marriage he had been obliged to go abroad on a diplomatic mission, which was protracted long beyond the time originally planned. This was the occasion for one of the few letters now extant from Lucy to her husband and it shows the tender love that she bore him. "My dear Mr. Stanhope's letter was very welcome to me, but I am sorry you are like to be absent so much longer I hoped you would, for I shall think every day on ye and count the minutes till I see you. . . . I have no satisfaction at anything while you are away. . . . I am my dearest love your most affec. Loveing wife L. Stanhope."[1]

Other letters written towards the end of their all too short married life show how undimmed was the love of this sweet girl for her soldier husband. "My Dearest," she wrote in the summer of 1719, "Yours wch I received y^r morning was very acceptable to me, for I was under a great deal of concern for fear you was not arived safe before ye very high wind we have had; ye children are I thank God very well: I am much as I use to be; my Father who dined wth me to-day is very much yours and wishes you all health and happiness; he is now I think in very good humer, my sister Londonderry was yesterday morning brought to bed of a daughter and they are both pretty well; I hope I will finde you in perfect health and am my Dearest most faithfully and affectionately yours, Lucy Stanhope."[2] The General's public work necessitated much of their private affairs devolving on his young wife, who proved herself extremely efficient and businesslike. In another letter written at this time, estate matters are happily blended with more intimate affairs. "My dearest, I am very glad to hear by yours you are in good health. Pray God continue it. I am not yet certain about my being breeding; but w^h I am will let ye know. I went y^{r}day sevenight to carry ye children to Chevening and have heard since they are very well, I thank God. W^n I was there Mr. Fort Mr. Stevenson and I were of opinion it would be much better to have ye offices selated ye tiles there being so bad and will be much handsomer; and ye extraordinary charge will not be above (as Mr. Fort says) a hundred and twenty or fourty pounds at most, so desire ye answer to it. I am to dine at my Father's who often asks after you and is in very good humer. Y^e children present thire respects to you in thire letters to me: I am my dear ye affect. and dutyfull wife, Lucy Stanhope."[3]

[1] Lucy Stanhope to Stanhope, August 18th, 1713.

[2] Lady Stanhope to Stanhope, "London, May ye 16, 1719." Soon after the death of his father-in-law, Lord Londonderry, in 1714, Thomas Pitt managed to have himself created Baron Londonderry, and in 1726 he was created Earl of Londonderry and Viscount Gallen-Ridgeway of Queen's County, both in the peerage of Ireland.

[3] Lady Stanhope to Stanhope, "London, June ye 2^d, 1719."

In the summer of 1717, Stanhope received his reward for services to the Crown, for he was raised to the peerage as Baron Stanhope of Elvaston in the County of Derby and Viscount Stanhope of Mahon, and in the following year he was raised to a higher dignity as Earl Stanhope. About this time James and Lucy Stanhope decided that they must have what all men most desire, a country home, and in June 1717 they purchased the beautiful estate of Chevening, near Sevenoaks, which is the family seat to this day; the purchase, as appears from the trust deed, being made in the names of General Carpenter, an old friend of Stanhope's, his cousin Charles Stanhope, and almost inevitably (it being Pitt property) the amiable and accommodating George Pitt of Strathfieldsaye.

Meanwhile, because of his disagreement with Stanhope on foreign policy, the King had seen fit to dismiss Lord Townshend and he was followed into retirement by his faithful friend and brother-in-law, Robert Walpole.[1] Other ministers also resigned and the government was accordingly reformed under Stanhope and Marlborough's son-in-law, Sunderland. The retiring ministers, bitterly resentful of George I's treatment of Townshend, soon found an ally in the King's jealous and resentful son, the Prince of Wales, who during his father's absence from the country, had contrived to attract his future subjects by a great show of affability and kindness; so that the comparative charm of the son after the frigidity of the father—a young, small, smiling, fussy German, who could just speak English though with a very guttural accent, accompanied by a charming and gifted wife, seeming altogether preferable to an old, small, plodding peevish German, with no knowledge of the English tongue, and accompanied by a train of horrific mistresses—showed to such advantage that the English began to look with increasing favour upon the heir to the throne. In consequence, when the King returned from his Electorate, he was highly incensed against his son and only too anxious for an opportunity to obtain his revenge.

Nor was it long before he saw his chance. To the disgust of the nation, a frivolous dispute at the christening of one of the prince's children was soon magnified into a gross public scandal, so that the King and his son—those two resentful little men, small in stature, thought and deed—were not on speaking terms. Only after a considerable interval, and thanks to the efforts of Stanhope and Walpole, was any sort of harmony restored to the royal family—a harmony which, though loudly heralded, was more apparent than real. Thomas Pitt, of course, was delighted. "This is to acquaint you of the great and good news of this day," he wrote to Robert, "which is a reconciliation between the King and Prince. The King sent

---

[1] Townshend's second wife was Walpole's sister, Dorothy.

for the Prince, who, after some time with him, came out, when drums, trumpetts, and collours displayed, the usual ceremonies to the Prince of Wales and Guards attended him home; and to-morrow it is expected that the Court of St. James's and that of Lesterfields unite in one, to the great joy of all that love old England."[1]

Thus, for Stanhope, in the summer of 1720 at the summit of his power and popularity, the future looked fair. Yet in a flash all was changed. The bubble of his popularity burst with that of the South Sea Company, and within a year he was no more.

Of the Ministers of the Crown, Stanhope was about the only one who was not implicated in the scandal of the South Sea Bubble. Yet, to judge from a somewhat obscure letter still extant from his brother-in-law, Lord Londonderry, he suffered some loss through the stupidity of his wife's relative. "This comes under my sister's cover and am under all the concern in the world that £20,000 of yr Lordship's money should be laid out in £4,400 South Sea Stock, wch is at the rate of about 455 pr. Ct., and immediately sold out again for £1,600 more for two mts, ending the 24th inst. to Messrs. Mitford & Merltins, bankers, then in as good credit as any in London, who have since broke and become bankrupt. So the Stock will be left on your Lordship's acct for your money when this was negociated stock sold at least 850 per Ct and at that time nobody would imagine but t'was an undeniable security. If Stock should rise up again to 350 per Ct your Lordship's and My Lady's account will be near in a ballance and you'l be no loossers which we hope and expect will on the meeting of parliament when some assistance and countenance may be give to cridit wch is now entirely at a stand. I must repeat to yr Lordship the very great confussion I am in on this account, but hope your Lordship will not condemn me by the consequence, by my good intentions and the improbability of what have since happen'd to cause this misfortune when I did it."[2] Though Lord Londonderry's spelling and grammar make his exact meaning obscure, it is clear enough that poor Lord Stanhope was a financial loser by the transaction! Yet, in spite of his innocence, he did not escape attack.

During the debate in the House of Lords, the young Duke of Wharton, perhaps the greatest rake and most abandoned libertine in all England, chose to deliver a violent and quite unjustifiable philippic against him, rather more

[1] Thomas Pitt to Robert Pitt, Pall Mall, April 23rd, 1720.

[2] Londonderry to Stanhope, London, October 12th, 1720. After the death of Lord Londonderry, his Executors were involved in litigation in respect of his purchase of South Sea Stock. The Statements of Claim can be seen in the British Museum, Add. MSS., 36, 152 ff., 203-206. There are also notes on the case in the Hardwicke Papers in the British Museum.

than hinting that Stanhope had fomented the quarrels between the King and his son. Roused to a white heat of passion, Lord Stanhope rose to repel the foul attack of this degenerate popinjay. But in the midst of his speech, he burst a blood-vessel in his head and had to be assisted home from the House of Lords. He was bled immediately and afterwards seemed somewhat recovered, so that Newcastle and Sunderland who came to take tea with him the following morning, reported him "pretty well." Soon after they left, however, he suffered a relapse, and died within a few minutes of this new attack.

The death of his son-in-law was a great blow to the Governor, who was chief mourner at Stanhope's funeral; and it was with a sad heart that he saw him buried at Chevening, the home he had loved but by pressure of work was so often prevented from visiting. No sooner was the ceremony over than Thomas Pitt had to set about looking after the Stanhope children, who had been left in his charge, and trying to comfort his daughter, whose pitiable condition was further saddened by the fact that she was pregnant. Some six months later, the Governor announced, "Your sister Stanhope was brought to bed Saturday the 19th of a brave lusty boy and a girl."[1] Poor sad Lucy. The shock of the sudden and unexpected loss of her much loved husband and the birth of these twins[2] seems to have been too much for her, and she gradually languished. "I returned from Cheevening Tuesday in the afternoon, where I left your sister Stanhope in an indifferent condition,"[3] wrote her father towards the close of the following year, and within a few months he had to report: "This is to advise you of the death of your sister Stanhope Sunday morning last, about eleven o'clock at Kensington, where she was hurried the Wednesday before by her physitians; and this day sennight she is intended to be interned at Cheevening. . . ."[4]

It would seem strange that Robert had taken so little interest in his sister's health that their father had to write not only to tell him of her death, but also to inform him of the course of her illness. Both Lucy and Essex had always shown him much kindness, and we have seen something of how Stanhope himself, amidst all the preoccupations of State affairs, had striven to be friendly. But all had been of no avail, and Robert was hardly on speaking terms with the members of his family, whilst his wife could do nothing better than try to obtain sinecure appointments at Court for her relations. Towards the end of 1722 Harriet wrote to Mrs. Howard,

---

[1] Thomas Pitt to Robert Pitt, Pall Mall, August 29th, 1721.

[2] She had had twins once before.

[3] Thomas Pitt to Robert Pitt, Pall Mall, November 8th, 1722.

[4] Thomas Pitt to Robert Pitt, Pall Mall, February 26th, 1722 (–3).

"whether the Lord of the Bedchamber to the Prince is appointed in my Lord Hertford's place. If not my brother Grandison would offer his services to his Royal Highness . . . if you think it proper (as he has been informed it is usual to make presents on such occasions), I will bring you a *thousand guineas* to dispose of to whoever is proper, but desire his name not to be used in vain; therefore I ventured to import this matter to you whose honour and secrecy I depend on."[1] No reply is extant to this presumptuous suggestion, but, judging from Harriet's next letter, it was certainly not favourable. "I aske y^r Pardon for ye freedom I have taken; & return you a thousand thanks for ye justice you did me in letting her Royal Hyness know my sincere wishes for her health & happyness," she wrote. "I believe my Brother could never intend a *bribe* to any of their Royal Hyness's family, but was informed a present was made usually on such occasions, which I should not have named to y^u but to be informed, as believing y^u must have heard more of such matters by liveing so long at Court I should oncly be glad to have their R.H's know my Brother's desier to serve them, whether it is accepted or not."[2]

The truth probably is that Robert was intensely jealous. The little worldly benefit he had derived from his union with the patrician Villiers family had caused him bitter disappointment. Then when other members of his family improved their positions the situation became intolerable. Lucy had married one of the leading men of the day and, as his wife, must have enjoyed many privileges which would otherwise have been beyond her station. Thomas, too, had advanced himself. He had married, it will be remembered, Lady Frances Ridgeway, Lord Londonderry's daughter; and though according to Lord Camelford, "a man of no character, and of parts that were calculated only for the knavery of business, in which he over-reached others, and at last himself," yet he had managed after the death of his father-in-law to be created Earl of Londonderry himself.[3]

Robert's other brother, John, "the Colonel" as he is often termed, could not emulate the example set him by Thomas and buy the honours of his father-in-law because Lord Fauconberg had a son to succeed him, but he became a great personal friend of the King and spent much of his time at Court. This was the more remarkable because he was a despicable person, "a sort of Comte de Grammont who," to quote Lord Camelford,

---

[1] Harriet Pitt to Mrs. Howard, November, 1722.

[2] Harriet Pitt to Mrs. Howard, November 1722.

[3] Both Thomas's sons, Thomas and Ridgeway, became in turn Earl of London-derry; the former died from a fall from his horse at the age of seventeen and the title became extinct on the death of the latter unmarried in 1765. The Pitt Earldom had, therefore, lasted only thirty-nine years (1726-1765).

"contrived to sacrifice his health, his honour, his fortunes, to a flow of libertinism which dashed the fairest prospect, and sank him for many years before his death in contempt and obscurity." Contemptible he certainly was, for he stooped to little stratagems and acts of fraud. For example, we hear of a complaint from one Sutton,[1] who had lent him £10 and could not get repaid. "When I met him at Swallowfield," wrote Sutton to Robert, "I was a little surprised to find that he took not the least notice to me of the debt, or made any offer for a time of payment. And after I mentioned it to him, all I could get was a note of his hand. To make amends for this, and the injury he did my horse by his riding post, he told me I should have his little Dartmoor gelding that was at Boconnock. This promise he renewed to me several times before divers witnesses, and yet, if we may judge of men's thoughts by their actions, I dare believe he did not design it at the time." Such mean acts only bring a man into contempt, for, as Sutton goes on to ask, "When gentlemen, persons of rank and distinction, can stoop to little vile actions, what can be more shocking than such an inconsistency of character and deportment?"[2]

We get one other glimpse of this charming officer and gentleman. On a certain day when the agent for the Boconnoc estate brings up the rents to his employer's London house, Colonel John stands in Pall Mall to see him in and out again; then he enters whilst the Secretary is counting the money over, sweeps the whole pile with his sword into his hat, and retires precipitately, chuckling meanwhile at the Secretary's dilemma at having to explain things away to his outraged employer. After that little experience, the Governor took good care of his keys when his youngest son was about. "The Colonel is at home again, so that we are all very happy if the keys were not carryed to the old gentleman's bed-side at 10 o'clock every night. . . ."[3] It was perhaps not altogether surprising that, when at last Thomas Pitt's Will came to be read, it was not found that his son, John, figured in it.

No wonder such a family was ever at sixes-and-sevens. Their mother had tried several years previously to compose their differences. "What you write about your son Willy I hope will be brought to pass," she wrote to her daughter-in-law, Harriet, "if you can prevale on your uncle Villers to have a little patience. When my Son Londonderry returns, I dare answer for him that he will indever to promote the affaire, who has allways promoted the interests of your children, and is very ready to do it again upon

[1] John Sutton was Governor Pitt's private secretary, so possibly this Sutton was his brother.
[2] Sutton to Robert Pitt, St. Stephen's Cornwall, September 16th, 1723.
[3] Hardy to Robert Pitt, Pall Mall, January 25th, 1725 (-6).

Chevening

ANE INNES, Mrs. Thomas Pitt, wife of Governor Pitt
Attributed to G. Sharp

all occasions, and indeed so are his sisters. I am certainly sorry that my son Pitt did not invite him to his house, for he intended to come if he had been invited, and no body could expect him without it, especially when he never did anything that in reason could cause his brother's anger, and is very ready to forget anything that his brother has said or done against him. But who can desire him that has received all injurys to make all the advances. But if my son Pitt wod be so wise as to follow the good example of his Master, the Prince and his followers, who was all so forward in being reconsiled to thare old friends that they never rested till they had kissed and imbraced them all, and the very next day made invitations to the Ministry." It may be doubted if the reconciliation between the King and his son went quite so far as that, but that of their "followers" certainly was more complete: and so, according to Mrs. Pitt, was it between the ladies. "Nay, the ladies too was so inclined to friendship that they did the same. My Lady Townshend and Mrs. Worpoole came to your sister Stanhope the next day to invite her; so that they which stands out now are petty singular, for the Prince and Princess has returned thanks to your brother Stanhope for the great services he has done to the nation and to them. So you see when eyes are opened and malitious storys sett in a true light, what vast allterations it makes in opinions, which I pray God give us all grace and humility to consider as we ought."[1] Brave sentiments. What a pity that they all fell on such deaf ears!

In all the circumstances, then, we may not be so very much surprised at the violent language of the old Governor. "My resentments against you all have been justly and honourably grounded," he wrote his luckless first-born, who was, as usual, asking for a loan, "and that you will find when my head is laid. Money I have none, for that all my bags are emptied, so have none to lend; but rather than I will want for anything I will sell all I have purchased. I need no people to incense me against you all; your actions have been too provoking and plaine, and the more I think on 'em the worse is my resentment."[2] And again a month later in the very letter he announced the death of Lucy Stanhope: "The misfortunes that all my sons has brought upon me, whereby you have wronged me of a great number of thousands, which has reduced me so low that I cannot lend you a much less sum that you desire; and all of you have brought me to these hard circumstances, which, I believe, will very speedily carry my grey hairs to my grave, and I care not how soon it is, for that I am surrounded with the plagues and troubles of this world."[3] But the pathetic old man was growing infirm.

[1] Jane Pitt to Harriet Pitt, Gravill Pitt, May 7th (1720).
[2] Thomas Pitt to Robert Pitt, Pall Mall, February 16th, 1722 (-3).
[3] Thomas Pitt to Robert Pitt, Pall Mall, February 26th, 1722 (-3).

"I . . . this morning was taken so very ill, with the loss of all my limbs, that I thought I should not have lived till this evening . . . and don't press me any further, for I cannot lend you the money and die in debt."[1] He recovered from this indisposition, however, and was soon almost his old bellicose self again; but life was very sad and a great disappointment to him. He was getting so tired, too, of his sons' constant plea for money: how he wished they were more like his son-in-law, the gallant Stanhope! But he had gone—and his beloved Lucy had gone too. How often it is that the best are called and only the scum remain!

But there was a brighter side to the picture, for the old man busied himself with the affairs of his grandchildren. He was guardian of the young Stanhopes, and doubtless these duties gave him pleasure. "I hope all my daughter Stanhope's children are at my house at Swallowfield this evening," he wrote Robert, "except Lady Lucy, who is with Lady Fane; and my Lord Stanhope we intend to put to Eaton after Whitsuntide, so that there is four children and their servants there, which I intend shall remain till they are fitting to go out to boarding schools."[2] Then there were Robert's children to see to, for the old man's resentments against their father did not in any wise affect his relations with them. "Tomorrow morning I sett out for Swallowfield," he wrote their father in the summer of 1721, "and shall call at Eaton to take your two boys with me, and some of their comrogues, and will sett them down there again on Monday."[3] But Robert's second son was their grandfather's special favourite. "I set out hence for Swallowfield Friday next; your son William goes with me."[4] And with rare prescience—"I observe you have sent for your son William from Eton. He is a hopefull lad, and doubt not but that he will answer yours and all his friends' expectation."[5] "I shall be glad to see Will here as he goes to Eaton . . ."[6] However, the parents and other children are not entirely neglected—"Monday last I left Will at Eton. If you and your wife, Heriot and Tom will come hither, you shall be very welcome and my coach shall meet you at Sutton."[7]

But Thomas Pitt had exceeded his allotted span. He was seventy-three

[1] Thomas Pitt to Robert Pitt, Pall Mall, March 12th, 1722 (-3).
[2] Thomas Pitt to Robert Pitt, Pall Mall, April 6th, 1723.
[3] Thomas Pitt to Robert Pitt, Pall Mall, August 10th, 1721.
[4] Thomas Pitt to Robert Pitt, Pall Mall, March 31st, 1724.
[5] Thomas Pitt to Robert Pitt, Pall Mall, May 12th, 1724.
[6] Thomas Pitt to Robert Pitt, Swallowfield, June 23rd, 1724.
[7] Thomas Pitt to Robert Pitt, Swallowfield, July 5th, 1724. The children mentioned were Robert's eldest daughter and son.

years of age and his long and active life was nearing its close. At last, late in April, 1726, the end came; after no more than two days' illness, the tired old man died at Swallowfield. He was buried at Blandford St. Mary, but no monument marks the spot where he lies. The curt entry in the register of his native parish, "Thomas Pitt Esqr. was buried May 21st 1726," is his sole memorial.

"I am under the dissatisfaction of being obliged to advise you of the death of my father, Thursday last att Swallowfield, after two day's illness," announced Robert to his first-born, then at Utrecht; "his distemper was a mixture of appoplexy and palsie."[1] He goes on to tell Thomas that virtually everything is left to him, and that he is "willing to forget your past slighting and disobedient conduct towards me, under the hopes of a thorough amendment for the future." He accordingly enclosed his son a letter of credit from Messrs. Benjamin and Henry Hoare "att the Golden Bottle in Fleet Street, the most eminent bankers in London" for £700 a year so as to enable him to pursue his travels, and admonishes that on no account is he to exceed the allowance, nor to draw more than £200 on any one bill. But it is not long before father and son are squabbling. It would appear as if Robert at first held extravagant views as to the degree of benefit he was to derive from the Governor's Estate, but on further investigation found that the prospects were far less favourable than he had anticipated. He accordingly sought to reduce Thomas's allowance by £200 a year, and when the young man complained that the original allowance, much less the reduced amount, was not sufficient to permit him to continue his travels, the father testily reproached him for having constantly sought his grandfather's protection and support against his father.

But Thomas was not the only victim of Robert's temper, for his younger son also came under the lash. "I recd yrs. of ye 25th. in which I find with ye utmost concern ye dissatisfaction you express at my expences," came William's reply from Oxford. "To pretend to justify or defend myself in this case could be, I fear, with reason thought impertinent; 'tis sufficient to convince me of the extravagance of my expences, that they have met with yr disapprobation, but might I have leave to instance an article or two perhaps you may not think 'em so wild and boundless, as with all imaginable uneasiness, I see you do at present. Washing 2-2-0 about 3-6 per wek. of which money half a dozen shirts at 4d each comes to 2s. per wk. shoes and stockings 1-19-0. Three pair of shoes at 5d each, two pairs of stocking one silk or worcestead, are all that make up this Article, but be it

[1] Robert Pitt to Thomas Pitt, Pall Mall, May 2nd, 1726.

as it will, since Sr. you judge my expence too great I must endeavour for ye future to lessen it and shall be contented with whatever you please to allow me. One considerable article is a servant, an expence which many are not at, and which I shall be glad to spare, if you shall think fitt in hopes to convince you I desire nothing superfluous; as I have reason to think you will not deny me what is necessary. As you have been pleas'd to give me leave, I shall draw upon you for 25£ as soon as I have occasion."[1]

The following January, William attempts to justify his expenditure to his testy parent. "After such delay, though not owing to any negligence on my Part, I am ashamed to send you ye following accompt without first making great apologies for not executing ye commands sooner.

Matriculation Fees.	0	16	6
Caution money.	10	0	0
Benefaction.	10	0	0
Utensils of ye Coll.	2	0	0
Common room.	2	0	0
Coll: Servts. Fees.	1	15	0
Paddesway Gown	8	5	0
Cap	0	7	0
Tea Table, China ware, bands etc.	6	5	0
Glasses	0	11	0
Thirds of Chamber & Furniture	41	7	8
Tea spoons	1	7	6
Summe totale	84	14	8
Ballance pd me by Mr. Stockwell	15	05	7

I have too much reason to fear you may think some of these articles too extravagant, as they really are, but all I have to say for it is humbly to beg you would not attribute it to my extravagance, but to ye custom of this Place: where we pay for most things too at a high rate."[2]

It was not long before Robert found himself involved in litigation of a most unpleasant nature with the executors of his father's Will, his brother Londonderry, his brother-in-law Cholmondeley, and a solicitor, William Chapple, who was also a connection by his marriage to Priscilla Pitt, the Governor's first cousin.[3] In November, 1726, Robert filed a Petition in

[1] William Pitt to Robert Pitt, "Trin. Coll: April ye 29th."
[2] William Pitt to Robert Pitt, "Trin. Coll: Janry. ye 20th, 1726."
[3] See family tree.

Chevening

THOMAS PITT, Earl of Londonderry, son of Governor Pitt
Attributed to Vanderbank

Chancery, alleging that his father had died possessed of personal property amounting to more than £100,000 and that his brother, Thomas, owed the estate upwards of £95,000. The Petition further averred that the heir and the Executors having sealed up the testator's papers immediately following his death under an agreement that the seals should remain unbroken till an inventory could be taken in the presence of them all, during his absence from London, in breach of this agreement, the Executor had broken the seals and carried off all the documents, money and jewels. In reply, Londonderry not only denied owing the Estate anything, but positively declared that he was owed by his father the sum of £10,000, and demanded payment forthwith. At the same time, John Pitt, the Governor's youngest son, was bringing an action against his Father's Executors, alleging that his brother Robert and the others had cheated him of his rightful benefits under the Will; and this sordid litigation continued long after Robert's death.[1]

There was also litigation between the brothers over the guardianship of the Stanhope children. James and Lucy Stanhope having left the latter's father guardian of their eldest son, the old Governor had delegated much of the detailed work involved to his second son, Thomas, who, so Robert asserted, had received sums from the Stanhope Estate for which he had rendered no accounts and now sought, by discarding all responsibility, to make his brother personally liable as the proper guardian of the infant. A second petition was accordingly filed in Chancery submitting that Lord Londonderry be ordered to account for the money he had received from the Stanhope Estate, so that the personal estate of Thomas Pitt should not be liable for claims on behalf of the young Lord Stanhope.

We do not know the results of these lawsuits, but clearly much of the Governor's money was dissipated by the time they had run their course. Indeed, Lord Londonderry sneeringly told his elder brother that he need not call himself residuary legatee because there would be no residue to inherit;[2] and though this was doubtless something of an exaggeration, it serves to explain why the descendants of the wealthy old Governor received so little benefit from all his accumulation. Be that as it may, worn out by these bitter family feuds, the wretched Robert survived his father by little more than a year, and his mother by less than six months;[3] he died in Paris on May 20th, 1727. He was a poor creature, mean, cantankerous, petty, unworthy of his notable father and the genius that was his son. Before going up to Oxford that son had been at "Eaton," whence he had written to

[1] British Museum, Add. MSS. 36178, ff. 11 and 256.

[2] Robert Pitt to Annesley, Swallowfield, November 27th, 1726.

[3] Jane Pitt died in January 1727.

his father a note still extant in his school-boy hand: "I write this to pay my duty to you and to lett you know that I am well; and it would be a very great satisfaction to me to hear how you do; I was in hopes of an answer to my last letter to have heard how you both did, and how I should direct my letters to you; for not knowing how to direct my letters has hindered me writing to you. My time has been pretty much taken up for this three weeks, in my trying for to gett into the fiveth form, and I am now removed in to it. Pray my duty to mama and service to my uncle and aunt Stuart if now att the bath."[1] His tutor had reported to Robert some years before his death:

"Yr younger Son has made a great Progress since his coming hitherto, indeed I never was concern'd with a young Gentleman of so good Abilities, and at the same time of so good a disposition, and there is no question to be made but he will answer all yr. Hopes.

"Yr. most Obedient and most humble Servant,

"WILL: BURCHETT."[2]

Prescient Mr. Burchett! The name of this younger son was William Pitt!

[1] William Pitt to Robert Pitt, "Eaton, Septemb^r. ye 29th."

[2] Burchett to Robert Pitt. Endorsed "Mr. Burchett's letter about my Son att Eton, Febry. 4th,, 1722."

CHAPTER IV

At the Court of George II

On a hot afternoon in June, 1727—a few weeks, that is to say, after the death of Robert Pitt—Sir Robert Walpole, the first Minister, hastened down to Richmond Lodge with momentous tidings. King George I had died on his way to Hanover and the Prince of Wales reigned in his stead. The new King, roused from his usual afternoon sleep, appeared, it is said, in a very testy mood and carrying his trousers over his arm. "Dat is von big lie," he exclaimed on hearing the news, and only the sight of Townshend's despatch convinced him of his father's death. Whereupon he hastily bade Walpole repair to Chiswick and take his instructions from Sir Spencer Compton, Speaker of the House of Commons, who was commanded to draw up the necessary declaration to the Privy Council.

King George II resembled in face, figure and temperament, the Duke of Plaza Toro as portrayed by the late Sir Henry Lytton. He was diminutive in build, nervous in habit, choleric in temper; and though he fancied himself as a domineering master in his own house, he was in fact entirely controlled by a large woman far abler than he. Personally courageous he certainly was. But this, and a lasting affection for his brilliant wife—to whom, Hanoverian-like he was never faithful—were his only virtues. His other traits were ignoble enough; he was fussy, testy, petty, vain, mean. Indeed, one of his most enjoyable recreations was to sit, purse in hand, and count his money: "Sir, I can bear it no longer!" once exclaimed Mary Bellenden, one of the bed-chamber women. "If you count your money once more I will leave the room!" and when he did not desist, she knocked the purse out of the prince's hands, so that the coins rolled all over the floor.[1] What a picture of the King of England is conjured up; a nursery rhyme come true! Nor were his other failings more regal. Many Sovereigns have been ill-tempered, but surely few so fractious as George II. He would storm at his wife, snub and insult her in public, rampage up and down the room like a madman, call his Ministers rogues and liars—and for what reason? Because some affair of State had gone awry? Because through

---

[1] Walpole, *Memoirs*, Vol. I. Mary Bellenden was a daughter of John, 2nd Lord Bellenden.

the bungling of a diplomat, some dire misfortune threatened to overwhelm the kingdom? Not at all; but for some trivial cause, such as that, in the words of his eldest daughter, "one of his pages has powdered his periwig ill, or a housemaid set a chair where it does not use to stand. . . ."[1]

Queen Caroline was of sounder mettle. Daughter of the Margrave of Brandenburg-Ansbach, and married to George, then the Electoral Prince of Hanover, when in her early twenties, she was perhaps one of the most brilliant women of her day. Yet she bore patiently with the petty pomposities, the puerile vanities of her strutting, stupid, choleric little popinjay of a husband: she guided his every step and instilled into his silly head every original thought that ever entered his empty brain; yet such was her self-effacement, such her tact, that he, finding her ideas in his mind, invariably believed them to be his own.

This was the King and this the Queen, whose hands Sir Robert Walpole respectfully kissed that June afternoon at their home at Richmond, before lumbering off to Chiswick in obedience to his Majesty's command to take his directions from Sir Spencer Compton.

Sir Robert Walpole came of a family that had been settled at Houghton for many generations, a race of jolly, easy-going, pink-cheeked Norfolk squires, devoted to all forms of outdoor sports and the pleasures of the table. "Come, Robert," his father had once said to him, "you shall drink twice, while I drink once; for I will not permit the son, in his sober senses, to be witness to the intoxication of the father"—and during the whole of his life all things rural usurped the first place in his heart and thoughts. Walpole's domestic life, needless to say, was no model, but he was no more lax than thousands of his contemporaries; indeed he was typical of the country squires of the time, loose-living, hard-drinking, and at the table liking "to talk bawdy" because, as he explained, in that all could join. As he gazes down at us to-day from the canvas of Van Loo,[2] we see him as he was—fat, smiling, comfortable, looking for all the world like a benevolent publican in fancy dress.

But Sir Robert Walpole was much more than a country squire playing at politics; he was the great financial genius who had reformed our revenue policy, the great Chancellor of the Exchequer who had revised and simplified the whole system of our taxation, the great peace Minister who had fostered our trade and invigorated our industry. He was the first Minister to recognize the true place of the House of Commons in the affairs of State

---

[1] Princess Royal to Hervey. Hervey, *Memoirs of the Reign of George II*, Vol. I.

[2] The Van Loo portrait of Sir Robert Walpole is in the National Portrait Gallery.

and to give and acknowledge to that assembly the supreme authority that it wields to this day. All the world knows the greeting that he gave to his old rival, Pulteney, when first meeting him in the House of Lords after they had received their Earldoms. "Here we are, my Lord, two as insignificant men as any in England,"[1] and we can almost hear his deep-throated chuckle as he rallied his old enemy with these familiar words. Before his day, the banter would have been meaningless; coming from him, it expressed a profound truth. The House of Commons was supreme: the House that was to re-echo the vibrant notes of the Pitts, of Burke, Canning, Peel, Disraeli, Gladstone—here was the centre of our national life, the seat of authority and the fount of justice.

When Walpole reached Chiswick, he lost not a minute in delivering the King's message to Sir Spencer Compton, who promptly avowed himself unable even to draw up the Declaration to the Privy Council without assistance, and begged Walpole to lend his aid. This Sir Robert very willingly did, and off went Compton to the King with his rival's draft Declaration in his pocket. But as Queen Caroline with her usual good sense was quick to realize, a situation so farcical could not last, and she took the earliest opportunity of insinuating into the mind of her spouse how greatly superior were the talents of the fallen Minister to those of his successful rival. The result was as might be expected: Sir Robert Walpole returned to power in a position even stronger than he had been before, until one day in April 1736, when a young soldier made a speech in the House of Commons that drew upon him the whole weight of the Minister's displeasure. "We must muzzle this terrible Cornet of Horse,"[2] thundered Walpole, and promptly dismissed him from the service. No treatment could have been more injudicious, for the dismissed Cornet chanced to be a young man of genius. But that was in the future; for the present the position of Sir Robert Walpole was unchallenged, his future secure, and all men were ready and anxious to do his bidding.

Whilst these events were passing in the great world, the Pitt family were growing up and both of Robert's sons, Thomas and William, went to Eton and Oxford. This was a sad period for the boys and for their sisters, for family deaths were plentiful. Lady Grandison, their grandmother, died in December 1725, and some six months later her husband, General Stewart, also died, but not before he had found a brief consolation in a second

---

[1] Walpole had been created Earl of Orford, and Pulteney Earl of Bath.

[2] Not of the Royal Horse Guards ("The Blues") as sometimes stated, but of Cobham's Horse, now the King's Dragoon Guards ("The K.D.Gs.").

marriage.[1] About the same time, too, the Pitts lost their other grandmother, the Governor's widow, who died in Paris, having renounced administration of Robert's estate. The result was that the unscrupulous Thomas, a foul-mouthed, foul-tempered man, soured by early disappointments, seized, in the words of his son, Lord Camelford, "whatever fell into his hands without account, either belonging to my grandfather or grandmother, keeping at arm's length every demand upon him, till somehow or other these litigations seem to have worn themselves out and slept by the acquiescence of all parties."

At first, indeed, fortune smiled on Thomas, for whilst he was at Oxford, he had chanced to see at the Opera one night the beautiful Christian Lyttelton, daughter of Sir Thomas Lyttelton of Hagley, and elder sister of one of William's Oxford friends, to whom the headstrong youth proposed the very next day. Surprisingly enough, he was accepted and a marriage resulted which, as we shall see, was to bring great unhappiness in its train. But young Lyttelton, William Pitt's friend, was delighted at the news: "I heartily congratulate you upon my sister's marriage and wish you may dispose of all your children as much to your satisfaction and their own," he wrote to his father. "Would to God Mr. P. had a fortune equal to his brother so that he might make a present of it to my pretty little M! but unhappily they have neither of them any portion but an uncommon share of merit which the world will not think them much the richer for."[2] There is no evidence that William Pitt ever contemplated marriage with Molly Lyttelton, but her young brother was clearly looking at the family through rose-tinted spectacles, for he himself had fallen for his friend's eldest sister, Harriot Pitt.

Meanwhile, William, who on leaving Eton had gone up to Oxford in January 1727, in the spring of 1728 went for a holiday to Utrecht, accompanied by his cousin, Lord Villiers[3] and a friend, Lord Buchan, whence he wrote to his mother playfully referring to his friend's passion for his eldest sister: "I am in pain for poor Lyttelton: I wish there was leagues of sea between him and ye Charms of Miss Harriot. If he dies I shall sue her for ye murder of my Friend."[4] He need not, however, have been unduly

---

[1] Lady Grandison appears to have been insane for some time before her death on December 26th, 1725. The General married a Mrs. Alstone about a month later, but died on June 4th, 1726.

[2] Lyttelton, *Miscellaneous Works*.

[3] On Lady Grandison's death, her son had been created Earl of Grandison, and Lord Villiers was his eldest son.

[4] William Pitt to Harriet Pitt, "Utrecht, April ye 8th, 1728."

anxious for "poor Lyttelton," whose transient affections were soon transferred to another sister, Ann; and before long he had more cause to sympathize with the wilting Harriot who, sad to relate, had become first secretly engaged and then privately married to Sir William Corbett's son against the express wishes of both families. "The pleasure you give me in the account of Kitty's recovery," wrote William to his sister Ann, "is disagreeably accompanied with that of poor Harriot's Relapse into an ill State of Health; which I too much fear will never be removed till her mind is made a little easy: I never think of her but with great uneasiness, my tenderness for her begins to turn to sorrow and affliction; I consider her in a great degree lost, and buried almost in an unsuccessfull Ingagement."[1] Harriot's conduct elicited no sympathy from Thomas, who seems to have played to perfection the role of outraged elder brother, to William's evident disapproval. "Poor Girl," he wrote, "what unnatural cruelty and Insolence she has to suffer from a Person that shou'd be her support and comfort in this distress: I have heard him say so many hard things upon this affair, that I think I do him no injustice to say he will be more inexorable than the Knight."[2] Poor Harriot's stamina was no proof against such treatment, and she soon pined away and died at an early age.

But this was only a trifling instance of Thomas Pitt's harshness, and the Lyttelton family's satisfaction at Christian's marriage was short-lived. "What you say of Tom Pitt amazes me," wrote George to his father. "I shall obey your advice in being cautious how I think any man my friend too soon, since he whose affection I was surest of has convinced me of my mistake. I confess I thought malice and illnature as great a stranger to him as to my poor Chris. I am glad you are so happy in your daughter, I love her dearly and resent any injury done to her much more than if it was done to me."[3]

Poor Chris: it was indeed. For some years, whilst their family consisted of daughters only, Thomas Pitt bore with his wife, though he left her for long periods at Boconnoc, their lonely Cornish home; when at last in 1737 was born the longed-for son who could one day cut the entail, the husband's feelings for his gentle mate seem to have turned to active aversion

[1] William Pitt to Ann Pitt, "Besancon, June the 5: 1733. N.S." Kitty was Catherine Pitt, the second of the Pitt girls. Little is known of her except that she married a well-to-do Irishman of good family, Robert Nedham or Needham, by whom she had several children.

[2] William Pitt to Ann Pitt, Newbury, November 17th, 1734. As a matter of strict fact, Sir William Corbett was a baronet, and Harriot Pitt's husband eventually succeeded his father in the title.

[3] George Lyttelton to Sir Thomas Lyttelton, March 11th, 1729.

so that he forced her to submit to what that son subsequently described as "every kind of insult . . . too painful to dwell upon." All this Christian endured for the sake of the children as long as they were at home; but when young Thomas was about seven his father suddenly and without warning put him to school at Marylebone, and at about the same time the two girls, Christian and Amelia, were sent to one at Chelsea. Only then did the mother rebel; the unhappy Mrs. Pitt, sad, lonely and deserted at dismal Boconnoc, at last left her cruel husband and took refuge with her father at Hagley. But Thomas was without mercy. She was summoned back to Cornwall only to hear her fate; he would allow her £100 a year to be doubled at the death of Sir Thomas on the condition that she should never see her children again. Thus she was crushed. Her few remaining years she spent in sadness at Hagley. "I hope she will live long to be a pleasure to her friends and a . . .[1] to her worthless husband,"wrote her brother, Richard, to his father in March 1750; but his hope was not to be realized, for the unhappy woman pined away and died in June of that year.

Ann Pitt, the third of the sisters and William's special favourite, was of very different mettle from her sister Harriot. With her strong, resolute, not unattractive face, she, in the words of Lord Camelford, "equal'd her Brother Lord Chatham in quickness of parts and exceeded him in Wit & in all those nameless graces and attentions by which conversation is enliven'd & indear'd"; and, according to the same authority her charms were sufficient to captivate Lord Lyttelton and to inspire some of his most elegant verse.

Born in 1712 and therefore some four years younger than this brother, she had at the early age of twenty become a maid of honour to Queen Caroline, and thus entered the intimate circle of beautiful and brilliant women who adorned the Court of George II. For sheer loveliness, Mary Bellenden, soon to marry Colonel John Campbell, many years later to become Duke of Argyll, and Molly Lepell,[2] who married the effeminate and malicious memoir-writer, Lord Hervey, stood high; for intellectual brilliance, the palm must go perhaps to Elizabeth Montagu, whose *conversazioni* at her Mayfair home were long the talk of the town; for charm of manner and amiability, poor deaf Henrietta Suffolk must be our choice: but supreme above them all stood the arch bewitcher of the age, the witty, enchanting, roguish Kitty, Duchess of Queensberry.

This was the circle that Ann Pitt joined when she became maid of honour to Queen Caroline; these were the witty, amusing, charming

---

[1] Blank in the original.

[2] Mary, daughter of Brigadier-General Nicholas Lepell.

people with whom Ann associated, and who, when absent, were wont to write her long and affectionate letters with much wit and banter. ". . . the Duchess desires you will, in the meanwhile, write everything that is quite improper to be written by the post, and which can be matter of curiosity," writes Kitty Queensberry's brother, Lord Cornbury. "I wish the Duchess would give me a reason to give you for her not writing herself," he adds, "for it is really very hard upon you to be forced to decipher my scroll." Then after much more of this light nonsense, the gay Kitty chips in: "The Viscount and I have quarrelled this half hour about which of us should write to you," she says, "it has ended, so it seems, that we have both, tho' neither; . . ."[1] "But if upon the whole you can discover that I think well of you, that I love you very much, and that I have a sincere value and esteem for you, I shall be satisfied"; writes charming Lady Suffolk, "and if you do not, you are the dullest ungrateful little beast that ever was or ever will be called a Maid of Honour."[2] From Bath she writes, "I have drank the waters a week, and in this time I have had a relapse into one of my violent head-akes, attended with low spirits and very bad nights. The fatigues of what is commonly called the *diversions* of this place would be insuportable to me; but I begun in a much retired life than is fashionable here. I have kept my resolution of never breakfasting abroad, and consequently have had little occasion for that same gown that gives Lord Pembroke so much uneasiness. . . ."[3]

When abroad, this amusing correspondent does not fail to give Ann a sprightly account of her travels. "I left Paris Munday was three weeks, and got to Aix La Chapelle the Sunday following. On the Tuesday, I began those waters as they are called, but in reality I drank eight half points of roten eggs very hot, and well salted, every morning; which set as light as a fether upon my stomach. I rise at five o'clock, breakfasted at eight, dined, at one, supt at half an hour after eight, and was in bed before ten."[4] On her return to England she follows this up with further details. "Supper was ordered, and I, like a good wife, went to see our chamber was clean aired, and in order," she wrote from Becklesworth. "I was contented with the appearance, but we were no sooner laid in the bed, but a warm dispute arrise which side of the bed smelt least; both was so powerfull we often wished for a pest smell. . . ." The next morning they continue the

---

[1] Cornbury and Duchess of Queensberry to Ann Pitt. Undated but about 1736–37.

[2] Lady Suffolk to Ann Pitt, London, June 24th (1735).

[3] Lady Suffolk to Ann Pitt, Bath, September 25th (1734).

[4] Lady Suffolk to Ann Pitt, "Spaw August 5th N.S." (1738).

journey. "In two hours we went five miles, where we mett our guide, and in half an hour after were overturned; no hurt. I had a small wound, but in a place where I hope it will be no eye sore. . . . We found miles and roads so very bad that we darst not bait, but performed our journey of twenty-two miles in about ten hours."[1]

No wonder that Ann's brother, William, then on the Continent, thought fit to write her a long letter of advice on how she should conduct herself in her new surroundings. It was during these years—1730 to 1735—that young William Pitt wrote those delightful letters to "his dearest Nanny" and "his dear little Jug," as he called Ann. Soon he is to become the great showman, the dramatic actor, the world statesman; but the metamorphosis has not yet been effected, so let us linger awhile in contemplation of the bright, gay, charming Cornet of Horse, that tall splendid figure of early manhood with the flashing eye and the great nose that ere long were to be the bane of his enemies, who with humour and understanding could rally his sister about the unwelcome attentions of a foolish clergyman: "Why shou'd I mention Ayscough's overthrow! That is a conquest perhaps of a nature not so brilliant as to touch your heart with much exultation; But let me tell you, a man of his wit in one's suite has no ill air: You may hear enough of eyes and flames and such gentle flows of tender nonense from every Fop that can remember, but I can assure you, Child, a man can think that declares his Passion by saying Tis not a sett of Features I admire, etc. Such a Lover is the Ridiculous Skew, who instead of whispering his soft Tale to the woods and lovely Rocks, proclaims to all the world he loves Miss Nanny. . . ."[2] or write amid a bear-fight in Lyttelton's rooms: "I am now lock'd in George's room; the girls Thundering at the door as if Heaven and Earth would come together. I am certainly the warmest Brother, or the coldest gallant in the Universe, to suffer the gentle Impertinences the sportly Sollicitations of two girls not quite despicable without emotion, and bestow my Time and Spirits upon a Sister: But in effect the thing's not so strange or unreasonable, for every Man may have girls worthy his attention, but few, sisters so conversible as my Dear Nanny. Tis impossible to say much amidst this rocking of the doors Chairs and tables: I fancy myself in a storm of the utmost danger and horror; and were I really in one, I would not cease to think of my dear Girl, till I lost my fears and Trepidations in the object of my tenderest care and sincerest zeal. Let the winds roar, and the big Torrent burst! I won't leave my Nanny

[1] Lady Suffolk to Ann Pitt, Drayton, October 18th (1738-40).

[2] William Pitt to Ann Pitt, Swallowfield, September 29th, 1730. In 1745, Ayscough married George Lyttelton's sister, Anne.

for any Lady of you all, but with the warmest assurance of unalterable affection. Adieu."[1]

With his favourite sister moving in these circles, we would expect to find young William joining the Court party on his return to England early in 1734. The Whigs, led by that wary old campaigner, Sir Robert Walpole, were supreme. His colleagues were nonentities like Harrington, Wilmington, Dorset and Grafton, the plodding Pelham and his brother, that curious mediocrity who enlivens history with his strange idiosyncrasies, Thomas Holles, Duke of Newcastle. The Duke was one of those peculiar people who are only happy when they are out of breath and with much more work on hand than they can possibly accomplish. He was constantly in this state, not because he really had so very much to do, but because he had so little method as always to be in a pother. He did not walk, he ran; he did not speak, he stammered and stuttered: he did not work, he fussed, fumed and fretted: "The Duke of Newcastle," said Lord Wilmington, "always loses half an hour in the morning, which he is running after the rest of the day without being able to overtake it," and in the witty words of Lord Hervey, he "made his entry with as much alacrity and noise as usual, mightily out of breath though mightily in words, and in his hand a bundle of papers as big as his head and with little more in them.[2] But William Pitt was a man of parts. He preferred, therefore, the comparative freedom of the Opposition which, he was not slow to see, numbered amongst its members practically all the best brains of the country: and at its head stood that queer, weak, unpleasant young man, Frederick, Prince of Wales.

Our chief contemporary source of information about the Prince is the famous memoirs of Lord Hervey; but Lord Hervey's pen was so dipped in gall that he was incapable of writing a good word about anybody. Moreover, so far as Frederick was concerned, Lord Hervey was not unprejudiced, for the Prince had had the effrontery to steal his mistress, Anne Vane, Lord Barnard's daughter and one of the Queen's ladies-in-waiting. When in June 1732 she gave birth to a child, who was given the ridiculous names of Cornwall Fitz Frederick after his reputed father, there was a most indecent rivalry for paternity between Frederick, Hervey and Lord Harrington, the Prince of Orange flippantly declaring that the infant was the "child of a triumvirate," for, sad to relate, Miss Vane was not in a position to adjudicate between the competitors. It is true that ere long Hervey recovered his mistress, and had the additional joy of assisting her to embarrass Frederick;

William Pitt to Ann Pitt, London, March 13th, 1731.

[2] Hervey. *Memoirs of the Reign of George II*, Vol. I.

but the Prince had done him an injury and for that there could be no for-giveness from the malevolent memoir-writer. Fortunately, perhaps, for all concerned, the disputed Miss Vane, who had long been subject to fits, departed this life shortly afterwards, as also did the poor innocent little Fitz Frederick; but Hervey and the Prince remained deadly enemies to the last. So we must not take too much notice of the former's views of Frederick; though with the best will in the world it is difficult to rescue him from Pulteney's verdict that he was a "timid, poor, mean, weak wretch."

This was the ostensible leader of the party formed in opposition to the government. But the chief brain of the Opposition was that strange mercurial figure, Henry St. John, Viscount Bolingbroke, whose exuberant nature and brilliant intellect, soured by twenty years of exile as punishment for his Jacobite activities, were now devoted to organizing and directing the opposition to the Walpole ministry. In this work he was assisted by Carteret, the great scholar, by Wyndham, the reformed Jacobite, and by Pulteney, whose speeches, we are told, "began like Demosthenes and ended with Billingsgate." Junior to these leaders were a brilliant galaxy of young men who sat at the feet of Bolingbroke and learnt their politics from the master—Murray, a rising barrister soon to be famous as Earl of Mansfield, Chesterfield, whose more solid parts were obscured by his incurable cynicism, Cornbury, the gifted brother of the Duchess of Queensberry; and last but by no means least, he who is best remembered by the honourable title of "brave Cobham."

Richard Temple, Viscount Cobham, lived in sumptuous splendour in his great palace of Stowe, near Buckingham. Here he kept open house and entertained in princely style the notables and wits of the day. Hating Walpole, who had had the effrontery to deprive him of his regiment owing to a political disagreement, Cobham had joined the malcontents in violent opposition to the Ministry, bringing with him his "cubs" or "the Boy Patriots" as they were called, his nephews George Lyttelton and the brothers Richard and George Grenville, and their great friend William Pitt.

In the summer of 1735, shortly after his election to Parliament, William paid his first visit to Stowe and it lasted over four months![1] Here he met those who were banded together in one overwhelming desire to end the supremacy of Sir Robert Walpole; here he imbibed his first lessons in public affairs; here, in the company of Cobham, Lyttelton and the Gren-

[1] At the General Election of 1734, Thomas Pitt had been returned for both Okehampton and Old Sarum, and as he elected to sit for the former his brother, William, and his brother-in-law, Nedham, sat for the latter. So on February 18th, 1735, William was returned for the borough of Old Sarum. Pitt went to Stowe early in July of that year and did not leave before the end of October.

villes, of Bolingbroke, Chesterfield, Carteret, Pulteney and Wyndham, the young member of Parliament was to prepare himself for his great destiny.

Nor had he long to wait for the opportunity to show his mettle. On April 27th, 1736, the Prince of Wales married the Princess Augusta of Saxe-Gotha.[1] No member of the Court party was allowed to make mention of this event in Parliament: it was left, therefore, to the Opposition leaders to play the absurd farce of moving a dutiful address to his Majesty conveying the congratulations of his faithful Commons; and Pulteney and Lyttelton moved and supported this address. They were followed by Pitt in a maiden speech, the effect of which was profound.

In the speech itself there was nothing remarkable; it consisted of a string of empty platitudes: but they were uttered in an obsequious tone of almost oriental humility which hid indirect but bitingly sarcastic references to the personal relations existing between the Prince and his father. In consequence of this speech, the all-powerful Walpole determined to make an example of the young Cornet. It was in these circumstances that Sir Robert, thundering out the famous words already quoted, dismissed Pitt from the service. Whereupon, the discharged soldier united himself more firmly to the Opposition by being made groom of the Bedchamber to the Prince of Wales.

Meanwhile, Frederick, urged on by the Patriots, intensified the feud with his father by his constant demands for more money, and finally by the crowning insult of removing his wife in the pains of labour from his father's roof. That mad coach-ride in the dead of night from Hampton Court to St. James's Palace has been described in a famous passage of Lord Hervey's Memoirs; and though the embittered writer is not entirely to be relied on, there is little that can palliate this rash act which endangered the life of both mother and child solely to satisfy the Prince's desire to slight his parents. Henceforth the breach was irreparable. The son, peremptorily ordered to leave St. James's Palace, retired to Norfolk House, St. James's Square, which thus became the birthplace of King George III, and from this vantage-point he became the hub of all the opposition to the King and his Ministers and the rallying centre for political intrigue throughout the country.

On November 20th, 1737, Queen Caroline died. Her last illness and death have been described by Hervey with a wealth of detail more suited to a gynaecologist's handbook than a volume of Court Memoirs.[2] Suffice it here to say that one result of her death was that Ann Pitt lost her place at

---

[1] Daughter of Frederick II, Duke of Saxe-Gotha (1719–1772).

[2] Hervey, *Memoirs of the Reign of George II*, Vol. III.

Court. For a time she joined her brother, and they set up house together in Pall Mall overlooking St. James's Square. At first all went well, but after a time Ann began to evince that restlessness that was to become more pronounced with age. In 1741 she went to France to visit friends recommended by Lady Suffolk and later to Argeville to stay with Lady Bolingbroke.[1] "Mrs. Pitt I found here who seems pretty well, because she is extremely happy with Lady Bolingbroke, who is equally so with her," wrote George Grenville to Lady Suffolk, "and indeed her situation here is too agreeable and convenient in every light for her to think of changing it by taking a long journey to a Town in any of the provinces; and as this was not part of her scheme before my arrival nor cou'd reasonably be so I must not think of seeing her except upon my return for England, when my Lord and Lady Bolingbroke have given me leave to take Argeville in my way."[2] Be that as it may, Ann's peregrinations did not apparently pass without comment. "I can not conceive what reasons the lady we talk'd of gives, or how she can imagine the Scheme in question is absolutely against my opinion," wrote William to Lady Suffolk. "She sent for me when I was in Town last week to ask me if what she heard of my sister's design was true. I said it was, that I thought it absolutely necessary for her health, and that you had procured her such recommendation in France as wou'd settle her there in the properest manner. It was astonishing she shou'd give herself the trouble to imagine any reasons for this scheme before she talk'd to me, and much more so afterwards . . ."[3] We do not know who the meddlesome gossip was, but certainly both to Lord Chesterfield and Lady Suffolk William expressed approval of these visits, though looking with no favour on their indefinite prolongation.[4] At length, during the autumn of 1742, Pitt vacated his house and moved to more modest bachelor quarters in Cork Street, Burlington Gardens.[5]

Meanwhile, the attack on the Ministry continued unabated and many a broadside had been fired with deadly effect by Pitt and his young patriots. Patriots? The very word brought a sneer from the Minister. "Patriots spring up like mushrooms!" he declared, "I could raise fifty of them within the four-and-twenty hours. I have raised many of them in one night. It

[1] Bolingbroke's second wife was a Frenchwoman, widow of the Marquis de Villette. She was a niece of Madame de Maintenon.

[2] George Grenville to Lady Suffolk, "Argeville, Sept. ye 1742 N.S."

[3] William Pitt to Lady Suffolk, "Stow July ye 30th, 1741."

[4] William Pitt to Chesterfield, August 6th, 1741: and William Pitt to Lady Suffolk, July 6th, 1742.

[5] William Pitt to Grenville, London, October 21st, 1742.

is but refusing to gratify an unreasonable or insolent demand, and up starts a patriot." But Walpole was soon to learn that the patriotism of Pitt and his friends was of more solid stuff. They attacked the Ministry for attempting to introduce a bill to give special powers to the magistrates in connection with pressing into the Navy; and when old Horace Walpole sought to intervene and reproved Pitt for his youth, the ex-Cornet turned on him with brilliant fury. "The atrocious crime of being a young man," he thundered, "which the hon. gentleman has with such spirit and decency charged upon me I shall neither attempt to palliate nor deny, but content myself with wishing that I may be one of those whose follies may cease with their youth, and not of that number who are ignorant in spite of experience. Whether youth can be imputed to any man as a reproach, I will not assume the province of determining . . . much more is he to be abhorred who, as he has advanced in age, has receded from virtue and becomes more wicked with less temptation; who prostitutes himself for money which he cannot enjoy, and spends the remains of his life in the ruin of his country." His assailant had also attacked him for playing a theatrical part, and to this Pitt replied with crushing effect: ". . . if any man shall, by charging me with theatrical behaviour, imply that I utter any sentiments but my own, I shall treat him as a calumniator and a villain . . . I shall, on such an occasion without scruple trample upon all those powers with which wealth and dignity entrench themselves; nor shall anything but age restrain my resentment, age which always brings one privilege, that of being insolent and supercilious without punishment."[1] From these telling blows the Ministry reeled. But it was his unsuccessful prosecution of the war that cost Walpole the elections of 1745, and after an obstinate struggle he was forced to resign.

Though the Opposition had gained the victory, Pitt and his young friends gained little from the change. The fallen statesman, created Earl of Orford, had meetings with Carteret and Pulteney, neither of whom had vindictive feelings towards him, and actually discussed with them the formation of the new Government. As a result of these deliberations, a Ministry was formed that had no desire to treat Walpole as Lord Oxford and Lord Bolingbroke had been treated on their resignations; so those who had shown the most hostility to the late Minister and had therefore contributed most to his fall—Chesterfield, Cobham, the Grenvilles, Lyttelton and Pitt—were excluded from office. Thus baffled in their hopes of advancement, these disappointed men cried aloud for vengeance on the fallen Minister. They accused him of corruption; they attacked his foreign policy; they begged the House of Commons to appoint a Committee of its members to sit in

[1] William Pitt, House of Commons, March 10th, 1741.

secret for the purpose of investigating the financial transactions operated by Lord Orford during his Ministry. But try as they would, Walpole had too many friends in both Houses to allow him to succumb to these wolves.

His successor, Lord Carteret, was of very different mould. He, unlike Walpole, was a scholar and a linguist; unlike him, too, he was without bitterness and never desired the undoing of a rival. He had a profound knowledge of foreign affairs, and being master of many languages, had a distinct advantage over his colleagues—an advantage which had been specially helpful to him during the reign of George I, who not unnaturally took more pleasure in discussing public affairs with Carteret in his native German tongue than with Sir Robert Walpole in dog-Latin. But there were other characteristics of Lord Carteret that were less attractive. He was proud, haughty, imperious, a shade too sure of himself and contemptuous of others to make loyal colleagues and lasting friends. "What is it to me," he once declared, "who is a Judge and who a Bishop? It is my business to make Kings and Emperors, and to maintain the balance of Europe!" Though a man of brilliant intellect and an orator of the first order, he wanted consistency and application, and his two daily bottles of Burgundy helped to make him that lolling, laughing, lazy being, whose spark of genius was snuffed out by the fumes of good red wine. This was the Minister who succeeded Walpole, and on the innocent head of Lord Carteret now descended most of the abuse that Pitt had for some time been pouring upon the perhaps less innocent head of his predecessor. With great violence and much eloquence, Pitt attacked the new Minister for the favour supposed to have been shown to the German dominions of the reigning House, and he dubbed Carteret "an execrable, a sole minister who had renounced the British nation." There was, of course, a familiar ring about this trumpeting, and the fairness of the attack may be judged by the fact that within a very few years Pitt was adopting much the same policy himself and was confessing that everything that he had learnt in public affairs he had learnt from Carteret.

On October 18th, 1744, died "those two old beldames," the dowager Duchess of Marlborough and Lady Granville.[1] Carteret, son of the latter, succeeded her in the peerage as Earl Granville; by the death of the former, the financial position of William Pitt was materially improved.

During most of that year Pitt had been suffering from gout, a complaint that was to prostrate him more frequently as time went by; and in May he had gone to Bath in an effort to get relief from the "cures." Whilst he was there, the flame of that very old firebrand, Sarah Marlborough, was

___

[1] Walpole to Mann, Arlington Street, October 19th, 1744.

at last extinguished, and when her Will was read it was found that she had left him £10,000 "upon account of his merit in the noble defence he had made for the support of the laws of England, and to prevent the ruin of his country."[1] In addition to this legacy, even more splendid prospects were held out to the young statesman by the terms of the Will. The Marlboroughs' only son, Charles, had died in 1703, and three years later a special Act of Parliament had been passed settling the family titles on his daughters. Thus on the duke's death in 1722, the dukedom passed to his eldest daughter, Lady Godolphin;[2] and on her demise without sons, to her late sister's son, Lord Sunderland.[3] Now Lord Sunderland had a younger brother, John Spencer, who was Sarah's favourite grandson. She accordingly left to him and after him to his infant son, John, all the residue of her unsettled estates with the express proviso that should the Spencer line fail, Lord Chesterfield should inherit her property at Wimbledon and Pitt her property in Buckinghamshire, Staffordshire and Northamptonshire, formerly the estates of Richard Hampden, Lord Fauconberg and Lord Crewe respectively; and she had also persuaded her grandson, John Spencer, to make a will leaving his Sunderland estates to Pitt should his own son die without issue. Within a few years John Spencer died, so that there only stood an infant between Pitt and this splendid inheritance; and though the infant survived and therefore Pitt never benefited, these provisoes swelled his importance in Whig circles. William's income, increased by the Duchess of Marlborough's legacy, was further augmented at about this time by an annuity of £300 a year from the Duke of Bedford, whose first wife had been John Spencer's sister,[4] so that he now found himself relieved from his straitened circumstances and placed in possession of an income of something approaching £1,000 a year.

Whilst Pitt's circumstances were thus improved, the position of Lord Granville had fast declined. Ministers were weary of his haughty arrogance; they could not abide his bibulous dictatorship: and at last the Pelham brothers—the dithery duke and the plodding Pelham—had forced the unwilling King to part with him. Whereupon they succeeded in forming

---

[1] In the same Codicil she left £20,000 to Chesterfield.

[2] Lady Henrietta Churchill (1681–1733), wife of Francis, 2nd Earl of Godolphin.

[3] Lady Anne Churchill, who had died in 1716, had married Charles, 3rd Earl of Sunderland, and it was their son, Charles Spencer, 5th Earl of Sunderland, who succeeded his aunt as 3rd Duke of Marlborough.

[4] The duke had married Lady Diana Spencer, daughter of the 3rd Earl of Sunderland. She died in 1735, and in 1737 the duke married Lady Gertrude Leveson-Gower, daughter of John, Earl Gower.

the Government that came to be known as the Broadbottom administration. In this, Chesterfield, Cobham, Lyttelton, George Grenville and other friends of Pitt were included; but not Pitt himself, for the King could never forgive some offensive, wanton and quite unwarranted reflections on his personal courage, which Pitt had had the temerity to make in a public speech in the autumn of 1743. The offender now saw his mistake, and he resolved to do all in his power to repair the damage. He resigned from the Prince of Wales's Household, and he gave the full force of his support to the Government in the House of Commons. The Pelhams, recognizing his talents and his powers, were anxious to obtain his services. But the difficulties were great, for George's memory was long; and it was only by positively humiliating their Sovereign that they were able to overcome him. Awaiting their opportunity, they acted suddenly and with skill. At the moment when the insurgent forces of the Young Pretender were marching on Derby, they resigned their places. In his extremity, George turned to Granville, but his efforts to form a Government were vain, and the Pelhams were returned to office with greatly renewed strength. Now the King was not able to refuse them any demand; he could only mutter that it was hard to be forced to accept as his Minister the Duke of Newcastle, who was not fit to act as Chamberlain to the most insignificant Court in Europe.[1] One concession only could he wring from his Ministers. If Pitt must join the Government, he should have no post that would require frequent audiences of his Sovereign. Accordingly, instead of becoming Secretary at War, a post he coveted, he was appointed Joint Vice-Treasurer of Ireland, and a few weeks later Paymaster of the Forces.

Thus commenced the eight most tranquil years of the whole of Pitt's tempestuous career.

While these events were shaping in England, another Pitt was presiding over the destinies of Fort St. George. It will be remembered that the foolish Consul Pitt, who to the disgust of his kinsman, old Governor Pitt, became President of the New Company at Masulipatam, died in 1703. He had been married, and had had a son, George Morton Pitt, born in 1693.[2] On her husband's death, Mrs. John Pitt was financially much embarrassed and as early as 1709 we find George signing a covenant as free merchant at Fort St. George and some six years later he sought the assistance of the Government in the recovery of his father's estate. In 1724, young Pitt was in England, when he received his commission to be second of Council

---

[1] Newcastle to Chesterfield, February 18th, 1746.

[2] See family tree.

at Madras, and he arrived on Boxing Day of that year to take up his new duties. In 1725 he became Deputy Governor of Fort St. David, and on May 14th, 1730, he succeeded James Macrae as Governor of Fort St. George.

The five years' residency of George Morton Pitt was not marked by any striking events. Indeed, in contrast with his predecessor, a canny Scot, Pitt seems to have been a gullible soul, for he had not long been installed in his new position before we read of him being imposed upon by a trick of quite remarkable crudity. Early in 1731, a certain Gruapa, a native entrusted with the sale of diamonds of exceptional value, came to the new Governor with the story of having in his possession a stone of extraordinary size and quality. No sooner had Pitt heard of this than he sought to emulate his great kinsman predecessor and to purchase this remarkable jewel. Having stimulated the curiosity of his victim, the wily Gruapa, after many excuses and procrastinations came to him in company with his two friends, Ponchola Kistna and Permaul, to say that he had brought the diamond with him but that he could not show it as the owner was not available at that time. He then handed over a large bulse sealed with three seals, which he stated to contain the diamond, and which could only be opened in the presence of the owner who would call on the Governor in a few days' time. In the meantime, would President Pitt kindly hand over 1,300 pagodas on account, as the owner was in immediate need of this sum? The money having been duly parted with, the three friends left the simple Governor with the bulse and his thoughts. The next morning the alarming intelligence was brought to Pitt that Gruapa had died suddenly in the night of no apparent symptoms; and when he was further informed that this same man had tried to sell a stone on very similar terms to the ex-President Macrae, who had declined to purchase it, his suspicions were at last aroused. It is hardly necessary to add that the bulse, on being opened, was found to contain only a large sandy stone of no value, and that President Pitt remained short of the 1,300 pagodas that he had so rashly advanced to the insinuating merchant. It may well be imagined that this hoaxing of the new Governor created no little mirth amongst the worthy inhabitants of Fort St. George.

Yet, in spite of his simplicity, when Governor Pitt sailed for home in January 1735, he had amassed an ample fortune. A few years after his return, he married the widow of a former governor of Fort St. George and in 1737 purchased Orleans House at Twickenham, but he did not long survive his marriage. Their daughter, Harriet, a noted beauty, made a great match, for she wed Lord Brownlow Bertie; but like so many Pitts she was a sickly girl and she died within a few years. Had she survived she would have become a duchess, for in 1779 Lord Brownlow, succeeding his nephew, became fifth Duke of Ancaster and Kesteven. On his death in February 1809, the dukedom became extinct.

The scene shifts. The tempestuous gales and mounting seas of public life are no more; and in their place is found the restful verdure of the English countryside. We are transported far from the city's din, from the clang of battle at the hustings and at Westminster, and from the torrid heat of the Indian summer, to a quiet country rectory in the heart of the West. There in his study sits the incumbent, tall and good-looking, whose placid mien seems to betoken that he is at peace with all the world. This scholarly cleric is the Reverend Christopher Pitt, Rector of Pimpern in the County of Dorset.

Christopher Pitt's forebears had been doctors; his grandfather, Dr. Robert Pitt, was first cousin to old Thomas Pitt, Governor of Fort St. George, and his father, Dr. Christopher, also practised the medical profession. But young Christopher, who was only twenty-four when his father died in 1723, had taken Holy Orders and in the previous year had been presented to the living of Pimpern by his relative, George Pitt of Strathfieldsaye.[1] At a comparatively early age he had shown an aptitude for poetry, and whilst still at Oxford, had written a panegyric on his connection, Lord Stanhope, who had died during his residence at the University,[2] and a complete translation of the works of Lucan.[3] In 1725 he published a verse translation of De Arte Poetica by Marcus Hieronymus Vida, Bishop of Alba, and in the following year he sent to Pope his rendering into English verse of the twenty-third book of the Odyssey, which the great man warmly praised. But it is his rendering into English verse of Virgil's Aeneid which he commenced in 1728 and completed ten years later, that rescues his name from oblivion and sets him among the poets. Whether his version is as great as that of Dryden or whether it be greater, critics may contest, but here is the verdict of Dr. Johnson, no mean judge: "If the two versions are compared," he writes, "perhaps the results would be that Dryden leads the reader forward by his general vigour and sprightliness, and Pitt often stops him to contemplate the excellence of a single couplet; that Dryden's faults are forgotten in the hurry of delight; and that Pitt's

[1] The second George Pitt of Strathfieldsaye (1662–1734), grandfather of the 4th George (1776–1803), created Baron Rivers.

[2] He matriculated from Wadham in April 1718 and in the following March was elected a scholar of New College where he stayed till 1732. Lord Stanhope died in 1721.

[3] This was never published in consequence of the appearance of Rowe's version in the same year.

beauties are neglected in the languor of a cold and listless perusal; that Pitt pleases the criticks, and Dryden the people; that Pitt is quoted, and Dryden read."[1] We may doubt whether to-day the one is quoted or the other read; but at least the humble songster of Pimpern is in company with the immortals.

But alas, the quiet poet did not long survive to enjoy the growing reputation that this great work brought him, for like so many of his family, he suffered from a severe form of gout that undermined his constitution and in the spring of 1748 his gentle spirit fled.[2] He left this world as unobtrusively as he had entered it, and now he is hardly known. Yet he has left a fragrant memory: may our epitaph be as happy as his. He was, writes Dr. Johnson, "reverenced for his virtue, and beloved for the softness of his temper, and the easiness of his manners. Before strangers he had something of the scholar's timidity or distrust; but when he became familiar, he was in a very high degree cheerful and intertaining. His general benevolence procured general respect; and he passed a life placid and honourable, neither too great for the kindness of the low, nor too low for the notice of the great."[3] And on his tombstone at Blandford, where he lies, are these words:

"He lived innocent, and died beloved."

[1] Johnson, *Lives of the English Poets,* Vol. III.   Article on Pitt.

[2] He died at Pimpern on April 15th, 1748.

[3] Johnson, *Lives of the English Poets,* Vol. III.   Article on Pitt.   The punctuation is Johnson's.

CHAPTER V

"*I know that I can save England . . ."*

A FEW years after Pitt assumed his new duties as Paymaster of the Forces the Prince of Wales died suddenly.[1] Since the General Election of 1747, when Frederick's party was almost wiped out, the Opposition had been reduced to a mere group. His party's electoral business had been mismanaged by the truculent Thomas Pitt, M.P. for Okehampton, who was Lord Warden of the Stannaries and Steward of the Duchy of Cornwall, and by Thomas's stupid brother-in-law, Dr. Ayscough,[2] Prince George's former tutor, who had once been the despised wooer of Ann Pitt. Bribery had been rampant—"As for Grampound I think we can carry it, but it must cost damnably dear. The villains have got ahead to that degree and rise in their demands so extravagantly, that I have been very near damning them, and kicking them to the devil at once. The dirty rascals dispise 20 guineas as much as a King's Sergeant does a half-guinea fee. If it had not been for the orders by your letter, spare neither pains nor money, I would not have gone on at such a rate . . ."[3] but it was all in vain. "With heaviness of heart I send this. . . . I spared no pains. The expense of that I do not begrudge, that was my own; but the money that was expended to so little purpose was not mine. . . . I did my utmost to have procured success,"[4] and again: "I shall be ashamed to look the Prince in the face after the hopes I had raised in him," wrote Thomas Pitt to his brother-in-law, "I am vexed to the soul. What can I say? That I have been betrayed by villains that I had reason to depend on."[5]

But in spite of Thomas's mortification, Ayscough had been encouraging —"You are too modest indeed when you talk of being ashamed to look your Royal master in the face. Why should you be ashamed of seeing him who would be very glad to see you? and who declares himself perfectly

[1] On March 21st, 1751.

[2] Mrs. Thomas Pitt and Mrs. Francis Ayscough were Christian and Anne, daughters of Sir Thomas Lyttelton of Hagley and his first wife, Christian, daughter of Sir Richard Temple of Stowe.

[3] Thomas Pitt to Ayscough, Boconnoc, June 13th, 1747.

[4] Thomas Pitt to Ayscough, "Mr. Gregor's, near Tregony, July 1st" (1747).

[5] Thomas Pitt to Ayscough, Trewarthennick, July 3rd, 1747.

well satisfied with your conduct. Thank God, we have a master who values his friends and servants, not according to their success, but to their zeal and sincerity in his service; and, as no one can have shown more of this than you have done in the late troubles and fatigues as you have undergone, so no one can be more in his favour and esteem,"[1]—and the Prince had been gracious: "Mr. Pitt. This is to return you my thanks for your zeal and trouble. You have shown the ennemy a better generallship than they can boast of; and though I could have wished to have carried Bligh, Drury, and Moreton, who so handsomely deposited their money, yet one at Grampound is more than I hoped for. Ayscough is to tell you my intentions upon another matter, which max's me very sore, for I never forgive treachery. My first rule is to reward and to punish; and with that maxim, much may be done. When you have settled matters in the West, I hope to see you at Clifden with your gunn, and you will allways find me, as you deserve of me, a constant friend."[2] He further showed his friendship by presenting Thomas Pitt with the portrait which Van Loo had painted of him a few years previously, which vast canvas still hangs in the gallery of Boconnoc.

And now he was dead, and unable to dispense those rewards—a peerage and the Vice-Treasurership of Ireland—that Thomas had been anxiously anticipating, for he had gravely impaired his estate in the Prince's service. It had all happened very suddenly; a neglected cold turned to pleurisy and an abscess on his breast ascribed to a blow received from a ball some years previously. "He died at a quarter after nine of Wednesday night," recorded Henry Fox. "His Majesty was surprised, and is infinitely affectionate towards the princess and the children, and has sent and wrote to her every day. The sons, the eldest at least, will come to St. James's; and his Majesty has the Duchy of Cornwall reverted to him. Poor Tom Pitt."[3]

"Poor Tom Pitt" it was, for his embarrassments had become desperate and his brother, the Paymaster, was requested to make it plain that he had nothing to expect from St. James's. Nearly two years before the Prince's death, Thomas had been forced to beg of Ayscough a loan of £4,000 of trust money arising from the sale of his grandfather's house, Swallowfield, and deposited in the doctor's hands.[4] Indeed, he was on the verge of ruin

---

[1] Ayscough to Thomas Pitt, July 7th, 1747.

[2] Frederick, Prince of Wales, to Thomas Pitt, Leicester House, July 7th, 1747.

[3] Fox to Hanbury Williams, "March 22nd–April 2nd., 1750–1."

[4] Thomas Pitt to Ayscough, London, May 5th, 1749. Thomas had sold Swallowfield in 1737 to a certain John Dodd for £20,770. As it was entailed, a special Act of Parliament had been necessary to enable him to do so.

and would probably have actually gone bankrupt but for the efforts of his brother-in-law and the generosity of the Prince of Wales, who seems to have given him the sum of £3,000 and certainly appointed him Warden of the Stannaries at a salary of £1,500 a year on various conditions, the chief of which was that the Prince should have the nomination of every Member of Parliament for the Pitt borough of Old Sarum.[1] Within a year, however, Pitt was applying to Ayscough for £5,000 from the trust fund, and Ayscough sets out a memorandum to show the financial position of the trust:

	£	s.	d.
July 6th. 1744—Remaining in Dr. Ayscough's hands of the trust money	8170	3	8
June 21st. 1749—Lent to Mr. Pitt out of this money	4000	0	0
Received from Mr. Pitt towards replacing it	1242	10	0
	£2757	10	0
	2757	10	0
If, therefore, Dr. Ayscough should advance £5000 further	5000	0	0
the whole advance to Mr. Pitt will amount to—	£7757	10	0

He then proceeds to show how insufficient is the security that Pitt has to offer, and suggests an alternative scheme which does not appear to have helped matters much.[2] And so things proceeded—constant bickering, repeated applications by the improvident Pitt to the trustee for assistance, and frequent grumblings that whatever is done is insufficient to rescue him from his embarrassments.

Since his wife's death Thomas Pitt had retired with his family to Boconnoc and there in dull seclusion the children were doomed to spend the next few years. The Lyttelton family tried to get in touch with the young

[1] A memorandum, unsigned and undated, but assumed to be about May or June, 1749, drawn up by Dr. Ayscough, is to be found amongst the Fortescue MSS. from Dropmore. This document sets out the terms under which the Prince was prepared to give Thomas Pitt the funds necessary to save him from ruin.

[2] Thomas Pitt to Ayscough in Lisle Street, Leicester Fields, London, June 19th, 1750.

Pitts, but this was not easy as the two families had long since been estranged. Some correspondence did pass, however, between Christian and Amelia Pitt and their uncle Charles Lyttelton, at that time Dean of Exeter and soon to become Bishop of Carlisle, and these letters, still extant, can be seen in the sisters' childish hands. Their mother had bequeathed them a small legacy. ". . . and I think there is no room to doubt but that my papa will apply it to our use," wrote Amelia to her uncle. "You did very right not to speak of the £100 you mention, for your speaking of it in your first letter was enough. Mr. Bennett has told me that my papa intends to pay it, but if he was not, I should be very sorry that, that, should occasion any difference between you, for I should be very glad to have all yr differences made up that we might have the pleasure of seeing you. . . . As for the watch, and rings, you may be sure he won't trouble his head about such trifles, and will never think of taking them out of your hands or mine. . . . I should be glad to know into whose hands my mother's papers fall into and whether there is any of my letters among them."[1] Nor were the girls forgotten by their Lyttelton grandfather, for some time later the other sister had occasion to write to the Dean. "We are quite ashamed after the trouble we have already given you to think of taking my grandfather's legacy out of such good hands as it is now in," wrote Christian. "But my papa has proposed to us to have it laid out in a suit of lace, a piece which will be of more use than any jewells. We beg Sir George will axcept of our duty and that we are in no hurry and desire he will take his own time for it. We should be much obliged to either of our aunts if they would be so good as to buy it for us to whom we beg you will present our duty."[2]

Apparently the worthy dean had his doubts as to his nieces' true preference for lace over jewellery, for a few weeks later they wrote him a joint letter. "I must beg leave to trouble you with this, to acquaint you that my sister and myself (with the consent of my father) would rather chuse to have this legacy my grandfather left us spent in lace than in earrings or any jewel whatever, for as we have no jewels to answer with a pair of earrings we think the money will go further and make more show in lace than in any single jewel, tho' no doubt you may have very handsome ones for the prise. Except I had a whole set of jewels, I would at any time chuse a handsome suit of lace than a pair of diamond earrings without any think else to wear with it. We should take it as a great favour if one of my Aunts would take

---

[1] Amelia Pitt to Lyttelton, "Feb. 22nd., 1750." This must be a mistake for 1751, as the mother died in June, 1750.

[2] Christian Pitt to Lyttelton, "Boconnock, Novber ye 12, 1752."

the trouble to buy it for us whenever it suits yours or their convenientcy."[1]
A further assurance comes from Amelia a few days later. "I have not told
my papa of your laying out of the money for I don't care to say more
than I need to him upon the subject," she writes, "and I believe he had
rather I should say as little as possible about it. I assure you it was our own
choice to have lace instead of earrings for we were saying one day that we
liked a handsome suit of lace rather than a midling set of jewels, upon which
my papa asked us if we should not like to (have) the money spent on lace
than in earrings, upon which we said yes. . . ." Apparently feelings between
the families was somewhat better, for she continues, "My papa will set
out very soon for London, if you would be so good as to perform your
obliging promise of going to visit him, we would be very glad, for, believe
me, there is nothing I wish so much as the uniting of our two families."[2]

The good-natured uncle was glad to comply with this request, but the
only thanks he got was an offensive letter from the petulant father. "Sir,"
he wrote, "I am sorry I had not the pleasure of seeing you yesterday, when
you took the trouble of calling here. With regard to my giving a receipt
as you desire, it is what, to deal frankly with you, I cannot comply with.
That trifling legacy to my daughters instead of making their mother's fortune
up, at least to them, equal to either of her sisters, is indeed beneath my
regard, and I do not think fit to concern myself about it one way or the
other. I must take notice that you are extremely mistaken in saying you
have substituted lace instead of jewels in compliance with my request, as
well as your nieces; for I am sure it should be very far from my thoughts to
make any request concerning a legacy which, in the light I see it, appears
so very despicable. I return you the boxes unopened for you to dispose
of them as you please, and you will execute that important trust of Executor,
especially in request to this legacy, in the most advisable and most agreeable
manner to yourself. I wish you a good journey and am, Sir, Your obed[t]
humble Serv[t] T. Pitt."[3] Not a nice letter; and so apparently thought Tom's
daughters, for soon afterwards Amelia wrote, "I cannot approve of my
Father's behaviour," and telling her uncle that she will be of age the following
month and willing then to give him "any discharge you think proper."[4]
This is soon followed up by the younger girl who proposes, "As my sister
is now of age, may not I choose her guardian for my share of the lace, and
by that means receive mine at the same time she does hers?"[5] Then

[1] Amelia and Christian Pitt to Lyttelton, "Boconnock, Jan[ry] ye 31st, 1753."
[2] Amelia Pitt to Lyttelton, "Feb[ry] ye 2d. 1753."
[3] Thomas Pitt to Lyttelton, "Bury Street, 27th, 1753."
[4] Amelia Pitt to Lyttelton, "May y[e] 26th, 1753."
[5] Christian Pitt to Lyttelton, "Boconnoc, ye 26. 1753" (June).

AMELIA PITT, Mrs. William Spry

Reynolds
Восток

CHRISTIAN PITT, Mrs. Thomas Saunders

Artist unknown
Восток

Daughters of Thomas Pitt

apparently the cautious Dr. Charles asks about methods of conveyance, for in August Christian writes him, "I do assure you it will come very safe by the carrier's horses from Exeter to Boconnock, and the quickest way from London to Exeter will be by Fry's flying Waggon. All our cloathes come to Boconnock by that means and even the stores when there is not enough to make it worth while to send it by sea come that way. . . ."[1]

So at last all is settled and the precious lace despatched to Cornwall. "I am excessively obliged to you for your indulgence towards me, in letting me have my grandfather's legacy before I was of age to give you a legal receipt for it," writes Christian, "but I give you my word, as soon as I am of age (if I am alive) I will give you a receipt in full for it"; and in an undated letter, Amelia joins her thanks for the lace which has arrived, "very safe," and begs her and her sister's "respectfull comp^{ts} to my Lady Lyttelton and thank her for the trouble she has taken in chusing the lace. It is excessively handsome, and if we had chose it ourselves it would not have been more to our liking."

Whilst this correspondence was passing between the dean and his nieces, his nephew, young Tom Pitt, was expressing a very proper spirit. "I assure you I am very glad to hear of Sr George's recovery," he wrote, "as I cannot but have the greatest concern for the safety of all my dear mother's relations; had it pleas'd God to have let me shew my affection to her dear person, how much greater would have been my satisfaction! But as she is gone to a place more worthy her goodness the only thing that remains is to shew my respect for her memory by my regard for the welfare of her family. But you indeed have laid me under double obligations by the tenderness you have shewn me, and of course my ingratitude would be double if I did not subscribe myself your most affectionate friend and nephew, Thomas Pitt."[2]

Young Tom was at Cambridge at this time, and it must have been during one of his visits to London that he first became acquainted with his Uncle William who at once interested himself in his nephew's prospects. And fortunate was he to have such a friend, for he had only been a few months at the University when there came the inevitable crisis in his father's affairs.[3] For some time there had been rumours of William's willingness to relieve his brother's position by the purchase of Boconnoc, and several years earlier that old reprobate, Richard Rigby, had reported them to his patron, the Duke of Bedford. "You are like to enjoy some more of the great Mr.

[1] Christian Pitt to Lyttelton, "Boconnock, August y^e 7, 1753."
[2] Thomas Pitt junior to Lyttelton, "Boconnoc, Nov$^{ber.}$ ye 9th, 1753."
[3] Thomas Pitt junior to Lyttelton, "Sunday, March y^e 25th., 1753."

Pitt's company, for I hear he is gone to Bath, to make a long stay there
for a violent disorder in his stomach. . . . He was going to Cornwall,
not I presume to figure in Waldegrave's parliament, if he had been
well; but more likely to purchase his brother's estate there."[1] But
whatever truth there may have been in the rumour, nothing came of the
negotiations, and by the following year the position of Thomas Pitt was
well-nigh desperate; his debts, long accumulated, had been increased by
the untimely death of his patron, and no longer could the clamouring
creditors be appeased. Faced with this dilemma, Pitt did what in those
days everybody did when in financial trouble, he applied to the Duke of
Newcastle. At first he wanted "a Government in America," but then he
changed his mind. "It was the particular circumstances attending my
situation which made me first think of applying for a Government in
America," he wrote, "not but could I have foreseen a probability of succeeding to an employment, consistent with the situation and rank I have
stood in at home, I should most certainly have made no application for
going into his Majesty's service in America. . . ." But he deserved something better than an exile abroad. "I hope I have in some degree acquitted
myself by securing the election of five members as appears by the memorandum left with your Grace. . . . I hope it is not vain arrogance in me to
say that there are very few private men who have it in their power to contribute so much to the support of an Administration as myself. . . ." So,
having met with "some disagreeable difficulties in settling my family affairs,"
he offers his services for an appointment at home. "Sir Thos. Robinson
having kissed hands for the place of Secretary of State, it would be an
eternal obligation . . ." and so forth, if he, Pitt, "could succeed to his employment in the wardrobe: for which I should think myself bound to make all
possible acknowledgments by zealous and faithful services."[2] So he
definitely refused an appointment in America, and some six months later,
when William was pressing this on his friend, Lyttelton, he stated cate-
gorically, "My Brother has declin'd going."[3]

Tom Pitt's application to Newcastle was not entirely in vain: he was not
offered Robinson's "employment in the wardrobe," but he was offered a
pension of eight hundred pounds a year to be granted during pleasure. This
he thought entirely inadequate, and he wrote promptly to Newcastle,
begging him to "endeavour to get this matter settled upon the footing I
had the honour to propose it, viz. a thousand pounds a year for a term of

[1] Rigby to Bedford, undated but about 1752.
[2] Thomas Pitt to Newcastle, "Bury Street, 24th. March, 1754."
[3] William Pitt to Lyttelton, "Bath, October 12th. 1754."

years, or for life, a matter very material to my affairs and of great consequence to me in my situation, but a very trifling consideration to the grantor."
And, he is careful to add ". . . as the obligation will be greater, so my attachment will be stronger, and that there is no return of gratitude, I shall not be
ready to make for such an act of generosity and benevolence . . ."[1]   A
month later, he receives his answer: he is given the choice of either a post
abroad or £1,000 a year on terms.   " . . . as the option now stands to be
made between the two," he writes to his benefactor, "I am greatly inclined
to that of the Government, and among many reasons I have for it, that, of
looking upon it, as being the only situation or post I can hope to be in for
doing my King and Country good service is my chief inducement.   But,
with concern am obliged to declare that, the situation and circumstances of
my affairs and family not permitting me to go thither so soon as the exigency
of affairs in that part of the world may require; I am therefore necessitated
to decline that service and obliged to accept of the thousand pounds a year
upon the terms his Majesty's goodness is pleased to grant it . . ."[2]

But, at the same time that he was pestering Newcastle, the wretched
Thomas turned to his brother for aid.   ". . . I must own to you that the situation of my affairs are so difficult and perplex'd and my circumstances so
extremely distressed," he wrote, "that my abode in London is rendered
very painfull to me and finding no absolute necessity for the carrying on
my affairs for my return to town, I could not prevail upon myself to relinquish the little ease my abode in the country gave me to throw myself
among my tormentors."   Then he goes into details of his distress.   "The
delays in settling the trust affairs and the disappointments I meet with in
the returns from my estates," are the cause of his embarrassments and
necessitate a retirement with his family to Cornwall.   "My children I
have taken from school, and my son I shall get instructed in his latin by
Mr. Leach, parson of Boconnock, till I can better afford to send him
abroad to school again.   My hounds I am oblig'd to part with and shall
let this house as soon as a tennant offers for it.   My sisters will be separated when I go into Cornwall.   Betty will be left at the Down House,
and Molly goes in to Cornwall.   I wish to God some way may be thought
of to provide for them, for I must repeat it, either of them living with me
is extremely disagreeable, and having so many uneasinesses in the world
it is too much to have my home, my retirement made uneasy to me.   For the
present I submit to it, trusting it will not continue long: at the same time
I must add that I shall at all times be ready to do everything reasonable,

[1] Thomas Pitt to Newcastle, "Boconnock, October 22nd. 1754."
[2] Thomas Pitt to Newcastle, "Boconnock, Nov^ber 7. 1754."

as far as my abilities go, to make their situation easy and comfortable to them. But God knows, my abilities at present are limited within very narrow bounds."[1]

Though no answer to this appeal seems to exist, it cannot have been favourable, for from another letter we gather that William had declined to see his brother. "Dr. Ayscough is now with me," wrote Thomas, "to whom I am indeed much obliged for the friendship he shows at this juncture, and the concern he takes in the unhappy situation of my affairs." Is there not some bitterness here at the contrast between Ayscough's sympathy and William's coldness? "It would have been a great consolation to me if you would have given me the meeting proposed," he continued, "to have heard what I have proposed, and to have given me your opinion and advice. Indeed, Brother, you need not apprehend any other uneasiness from our meeting than what the seeing distress would occasion. . . . I have given Dr. Ayscough in writing what I should have proposed to you by word of mouth if we had met and must refer you to his explanation if what I have wrote is not explicit enough; and I will still hope for your assistance as well as advice for the effecting the proposed scheme. I am ready and desirous of doing every thing that reason, justice, and honour require to the utmost of my power and abilities, but alas they are much circumscribed and restrained. It is most certain that the Scheme is the only means of attaining the end we are both so desirous of compassing, which is at all events to secure my sister Mary's fortune."[2]

But not only to his brother did the wretched Thomas appeal, for he turned too to his children, and with tears in his eyes begged advice from those he had so shamefully treated. Should they stay on at Boconnoc on a drastically reduced staff, or retire to some small country town where they would not be known, or should they live abroad until at the son's coming of age the entail would be cut? Wisely they chose the third alternative, and in March, 1755, they set forth. "I am just going on board ship for France," wrote Thomas to Newcastle, "I shall stay some little time at Rouen, untill I can determine upon the place for my fixt residence."[3] "Under these circumstances we took leave of poor Boconnoc, where I had passed the pleasing hours of childhood, and left it to neglect and to the mercy of creditors," wrote the son many years later. "Methinks I still hear the last cheer of the poor labourers assembled on the green before the house when the coach drove from the door."

[1] Thomas Pitt to William Pitt, undated.

[2] Thomas Pitt to William Pitt, Bury Street, August 8th, 1754.

[3] Thomas Pitt to Newcastle, "Dover, March 12th. 1755."

We can still picture the sorrowful cavalcade setting forth for London. Perhaps the half-crazed bankrupt paused awhile in the gallery of Boconnoc to gaze once more at the weak, vacant and typically Hanoverian features— the receding brow, the receding chin, the bulging eyes, the coarse nose—of him whose service had brought him to this pass; perhaps, as he looked up at the silly, childish face peering down at him from the vast canvas of Van Loo, a shaft of remorse may have stabbed him for the fate he had brought upon his innocent and unsuspecting family—the dissipation of a fine estate, the neglect of a beautiful property to the mercy of creditors, the dishonour poured upon a respected name. Then out by the front door comes the little party, into the full light of the wintery sun. One more fond look at the great house that for so long has been their home, and the sorrowing Pitts enter the coach that is to bear them to the Capital. As it rumbles over the stony drive and passes the little church beside the mansion, the poor villagers assembled on the green emit a feeble cheer— a sympathetic farewell from the simple Cornish folk to the unhappy family of the departing squire. And so the great coach rumbles on, through the lovely undulating deer park of Boconnoc which is now being swept by the keen pitiless winds of a winter's afternoon, past the great lake where the young Pitts must have boated and fished on many a sunny day, through the lodge gates with the keeper standing respectfully, his cap in his hand, into the cold, bleak world beyond . . . on, on to the Capital.

On arrival in London, young Tom was sent for by his uncles, William Pitt and Sir Richard Lyttelton,[1] who urged him not to accompany his father on his travels. Tom, recognizing the force of their arguments, agreed to stay; and William Pitt dictated the letter he was to write to his father stating his desires. "As the violence of my father's temper made it impossible to urge these arguments by word of mouth, and I knew him capable of any extremity to carry a point so important to him," recorded Tom in his subsequent account of these events, "it was concerted that I should elope from his lodgings in London and make the best of my way to Cambridge, and that the letter should be delivered to him some hours after my departure."

He hastened to chronicle his safe arrival to his uncle.

"I recv'd a letter from my father last night a copy of which with the answer I take the liberty to send you and will beg the favour of you to shew them to Sr. Richard. . . . I expect my father will come down immediately upon the receipt of my letter to Cambridge—I wish to God he may not think of it," he added apprehensively, "since it cannot be done without the oddest

---

[1] Lyttelton was made a Knight of the Bath in 1753.

appearance to the whole University."[1] The answer referred to does not seem to have been preserved, but this pathetic note may still be seen. "Indeed Son," it runs, "the consternation and anxiety which your not returning home to-day occasion'd and your letter brought me by Dr. Ayscough has thrown me into a great disorder and anguish to answer the particulars of your astonishing letter. I can only tell you that I expect you to dispose of your things and take up your caution money, quit Cambridge and return to me as soon as possible. If you want money more than is coming to you at the disposal of your Chambers and the Caution money you may draw a bill at three days sight upon me for it. I am too fataly for my own repose still Your affectionate tho' afflicted Father, T. Pitt."[2]

Further correspondence ensued between father and son during the coming months, when young Tom was peremptorily bid to leave the University without delay. "The answer to his letter came yesterday from my Father," he told his uncle, "when after the most heavy charges and violent abuses . . . he gives explicit orders to Courtail to surrender the Caution money, to dispose of my Chambers and to sell my books; and with the sum so raised he consents to discharge my bills (such expenses only as properly and immediately belong to the College) as far as the first day of this Vacation, and from that time allows me not a farthing."[3] Faced with this dilemma, the young undergraduate took refuge in Dr. Ayscough's house. There were many painful interviews with his father to be faced. "He almost broke my heart, but could not bend me from my purpose," he recorded. ". . . the conflict passed, he retired with my sisters into France, and I remained at my College in Clare at the joint expence of my two Uncles, my Father having, as I might well expect, cast me off and abandoned me to other friends. The violent emotions with which these scenes affected me left a sensible impression upon my health, and nervous disorders, which some time after increased upon me to a very alarming degree, owed their origin to anxiety of mind."[4] So young Tom stayed on at Cambridge, and his father, with Christian and Amelia, beat a hasty and very necessary retreat to the Continent, from which he did not return for three long years.

Whilst the elder brother was disgracefully escaping from his creditors, the younger, now Member of Parliament for the Duke of Newcastle's

---

[1] Thomas Pitt to William Pitt, Clare Hall, February 10th, 1755.

[2] Thomas Pitt senior to Thomas Pitt junior, undated.

[3] Thomas Pitt junior to William Pitt, Clare Hall, July 18th, 1755.

[4] The "nervous disorders" were epileptic fits from which Thomas suffered for some years, but he subsequently grew out of them.

pocket borough of Seaford, was striving to placate the malicious King; and realizing the necessity of retaining favour with his leaders, he acquiesced in those very measures of foreign policy which hitherto he had been foremost in condemning. But try as he might, he did not obtain that speedy advancement that he longed for and that he certainly thought his due. So the ambitious Pitt must needs continue patiently at his post, must see those with very inferior intellects promoted before him, must realize at last the dire consequences of slandering and insulting a King. Thus matters stood until early in 1754 the unexpected happened: the Prime Minister died suddenly. "Now I shall have no more peace!" was the oft-quoted comment of the old King. How true was this prediction events were soon to show.

We have seen how, when Mr. Pitt moved from his house in Pall Mall to his official residence at the Pay Office, his sister Ann preferred to stay on in France with the Bolingbrokes at their estate in Argeville. How long she remained abroad is uncertain, but she appears to have been in England for a while during the summer of 1744. "I imagine you have heard Lord and Lady Bullingbroke and Miss Pitt arrived in town from France on Wednesday night," wrote Lady Townshend to Lady Denbigh. "Lady Bullingbroke is at Mr. Chetwynd's house in Dover Street, and Miss Pitt is at Lady Suffolk's in Savill Row."[1] She was certainly here again in the summer of 1751, when she obtained the appointment of Keeper of the Privy Purse to Her Royal Highness and governess to the young Princess Augusta. During the intervening years, brother and sister can have seen or heard little of each other; but on Ann's return to take up her new appointment, William made a gallant effort at reconciliation. Two complaints, it appeared, she made of his conduct towards her; first that he tried unreasonably to control her activities, and secondly, that he had blabbed about the annuity of £200 that he had for some time been allowing her. He sets out these complaints in a long letter, owns to hasty temper at times, but absolutely denies one charge and offers an explanation of the other. "I was never so drunk with presumption," he writes, "as to expect *absolute* deference and *blind submission to my will*. A degree of deference to me and to my situation, I frankly own, I did not think too much for me to expect of you, with all the high opinion I really have of your parts." But this was wrong of him and he promises not to repeat the error. Then as to the complaints about the annuity, "I declare, upon my honour, I never gave the least foundation for those exaggerations which you say have been spread concerning it. I also declare solemnly, before God and man, that no consideration

[1] Townshend to Denbigh, June 22nd, 1744.

cou'd ever have extorted from my lips the least mention of the trifling assistance you accepted from me, but the cruel reports, industriously propagated, and circulating from various quarters round to me, of the state you was left to live in. As to the repayment of this wretched money, allow me, dear Sister, to entreat you to think no more of it. The bare thought of it may surely suffice for your own dignity and for my humiliation, without taxing your present income, merely to mortify me. . . . When I want and you abound, I promise you to afford you a better and abler triumph over me, by asking the assistance of your purse."[1]

The answer to this strangely pathetic appeal cannot have been too favourable, for William quickly followed it up with a second. ". . . I am ready to take shame before you, and all mankind, if you please, for having lost my temper, upon any provocation, so far as to use expressions, as foolish as they are angry : that you *had a bad head* will easily pass for the first : and a worse heart for the last. This you made me angry enough to say : but this I never was, nor I hope shall be, angry enough to think : and this, Sister, I am sure you know. As to the other word, which I am sorry I used because it offended you, I will again beg to appeal to your recollection, whether it was not apply'd to your forbidding *me ever to talk to you of everything that interested you* : and as to shaping your life in some degree to mine, which I believe were my very words, let me ask you, if you don't know that they were said in an answer to your telling me *that I had in several conversations directly explained to you that to satisfy me you must live with me as my slave."*[2]

At about this time Ann lost her appointment at Court and before long we find her retiring to the Continent once more. "My sister Ann is gone to winter in the South of France," wrote William to his cousin John.[3] Thus it was not until some months had passed that anything approaching the old intimacy between brother and sister was restored—"I am unable to express the load you have taken off my heart," wrote William early in 1753, "by your affectionate and generous answer to my last letter : . . . I will not give you the trouble to read any more : but must repeat, in the fulness of my heart, the warmest and tenderest acknowledgements of your goodness to, my dear Sister, your most affec. Brother, W. Pitt."[4] But even then things were never quite the same between them. William and Ann were perhaps too much alike in strength of character and obstinacy to be capable of living

[1] William Pitt to Ann Pitt, June 19th, 1751.

[2] William Pitt to Ann Pitt, Pay Office, June 20th, 1751.

[3] William Pitt to John Pitt, Bath, December 23rd, 1752.

[4] William Pitt to Ann Pitt, Pay Office, February 27th, 1753.

happily together: indeed, their whole relationship illustrates the truth of Horace Walpole's witty reply to the foreigner's inquiry if they were alike, that they resembled each other *"comme deux gouttes de feu."*[1]

But the disgrace of Thomas and the whims of Ann were not the only family trials that William had to bear at this time, for the escapades of Elizabeth, the "brave bouncing girl" of the old Governor's congratulatory letter upon her birth, must have caused him grave concern.

Elizabeth, who had, according to her nephew, "the face of an angel and a heart of all the furies," lived for some years with her elder brother at Down House, near Blandford, but when the crash came William provided her with a house, Grateley Lodge, where she openly lived with an eccentric peer, Lord Talbot. "Betty Pitt and her sister were at Ranelagh with Lord Talbot," wrote Charles Lyttelton to his father, "who I find has been her constant attendant at all publick places this winter. You may imagine this does not make her character much more shining than it was before."[2] Improvements to the lodge were soon undertaken with William's approval. "The alterations you projected here are in great measure executed, tho' not entirely and are what I am persuaded you will agree with me in thinking real improvements, and the walk round the fields extremely pleasureable which are at present fill'd with Dorsetshire sheep dress'd for sail with all the skill of the farmer. . . ." But, charming as Grateley may be, "yet I find as the winter comes on, the dais short, the weather bad, that I must be confined at home having intirely left off hunting." Therefore, "I should wish to remove to some town in the South of France just for the dead of winter and to return to Grateley Lodge the beginning of summer with a fresh supply of spirits which an intire change of scene never fails to afford. . . ." The place in France must not, of course, be too expensive, and "I sho'd think of living as retired at France as at Grateley, only that a new scene, a finer climat, and intire new objects and people about me I think of with infinite desire."[3] Apparently William asked for more details of her plans, for we find Elizabeth writing a few weeks later, "As a change of scene and of objects is singly the motive of my wishing to remove from Grateley just the melancholy dead of winter, what part of France I reside in is quite indifferent to me, where I can live cheapest and be most conveniently recommended is in my opinion most eligible: what

[1] Walpole to Hertford, Strawberry Hill, Easter Sunday, April 7th, 1765.

[2] Charles Lyttelton to Sir Thomas Lyttelton, Brook Street, April 29th, 1745.

[3] "Villiers Pitt" to William Pitt, "Grateley Lodge, Sept. ye 11th" (1751). One of Elizabeth's strangest eccentricities was to change her name from time to time, "Clara Villiers Pitt," "Villiers Clara Pitt," and "Elizabeth Villiers Pitt" being some of her choices.

you say in favour of the Banks of the Loire is sufficient to determine my choice. I think you seem mostly to recommend Blois. I should wish to avoid a town fill'd with English for many reasons." She proposes to set out in about a month's time, and to embark at Southampton. But "a footman that is honest and speaks French I should think necessary and where to find one is difficult. As I have never been abroad I am at a loss how to set about it and sho'd be glad to receive directions from my dear indulgent brother."[1] The dear indulgent brother received these suggestions favourably. So Elizabeth had further suggestions to make. ". . . My friend at Southampton informs me that the most commodious manner of my going to Bologne will be to apply to a Lord of the Admiralty to go on board the Fortune Sloop now stationed at the back of the Isle of White. She often runs over to the coast of France and that it is a favour often asked and never refused to any one of fashion and that in generall none but very small vessels go from Southampton. I have sent to Spit Head to enquire when the next sails for the South of France."[2] We do not know how William received this proposal, but he suggested an early meeting with his sister, who "will with great pleasure obey your summons for Monday at the Devises."[3] The meeting of brother and sister duly took place, and a few days later Elizabeth writes to announce a change of plan. "I find the expense of hiring a vessel from Southampton so considerable that it is necessary to save it in my journey by land, and have therefore determined for Nantes instead of Boulogne, the charge of the vessel being the same to either port and whichever I go to I must take a vessel on purpose. I have calculated the expense of going to Dover and find that it will not only be more inconvenient but likewise more expensive than the method I propose. I, therefore, my dear Brother, beg you will be so good as to obtain me a letter of recommendation to someone at Nantes. I shall set out the moment I receive it, my vessel and all things being ready for the embarkation."[4] The long-suffering William hastened to comply, and soon his fussy sister sailed. "The date of my letter informs you my great undertaking is begun," she wrote from Southampton on November 7th, "I hope to embark this evening on board a vessel of a hundred ton, eight hands on board, and very tolerable accommodations . . . if I am lucky I am told I may land at Nantes in four dais. . . . I have been here disagreeably enough these two dais but not unprofitably for having nothing to amuse me. I set about

[1] "Villiers Pitt" to William Pitt, "Grateley Lodge, Oct. yᵉ 1st 1751."
[2] "Villiers Pitt" to William Pitt, "Grateley Lodge, Oct. ye 10th. 1751."
[3] "Villiers Pitt" to William Pitt, "Grateley Lodge, Oct. ye 17th. 1751."
[4] "Villiers Pitt," to William Pitt, Andover, Oct. ye 24th. 1751."

the exchange of money and have bought thirty louis for twenty shillings, a price current in France for twenty two. . . ."[1] So the great journey began, being undertaken on an allowance of £200 a year from her brother—half granted so long as she behaved herself and half without conditions—and it was not long before she contrived to obtain a fresh notoriety that must have been most unwelcome for her family and friends.

The next we hear of the traveller is at Tours in the summer of the following year. Apparently William had written suggesting it was about time she returned: "that you desire it is the strongest reason possible for me to wish it," she wrote in June 1752. Then she sheds quite a new light on the whole matter. "It has been delayed," she states, "by my not having been able to prevail with my Lord Talbot to leave the neighbourhood of Grateley and by my firm resolution not to return to England till his Lordship has acquiesced to my request, which now being done I hope soon to revisit the long forsaken Lodge. And my reason for postponing my journey is to avoid the observations my returning immediately into the country upon Lord Talbot's leaving it might occasion. To put an end to the censures of the world equally prejudiciall to Lord Talbot and myself I have determined that we shall for the future live at a distance from each other, tho' as far as it depends on me upon the same footing of regard and friendship that ever subsisted between us. In case fortune ever sets him at liberty he has given his honour to offer me his hand, which is all in his power . . . Upon this head Lord Talbot has amply explained himself to my eldest Brother." At last William is given a glimpse of the truth, for the letter continues: "I flatter myself you will excuse the liberty I have taken in explaining my situation to you and of acquainting you that the effectual execution of this scheme was the first and great motive of my journey and long residence in France. I hinted something of this kind in a former letter, but timidity singly prevented my explaining myself thoroughly: and it now gives me infinite pain and uneasiness to entertain you upon the subject I am sensible must be so disagreeable to you: and was the reason I did not beforehand consult you."[2] So much for the dreary winter at Grateley!

But whilst touring in France Elizabeth had managed to compromise herself with a young French diplomat and writer, by name Louis Dutens. When Dutens had left for England, Elizabeth had given him a cordial introduction to her brother, the Paymaster, who had responded favourably.

[1] "Villiers Pitt" to William Pitt, "Southampton, Nov. ye 7th. 1751."

[2] "Villiers Pitt" to William Pitt, "Tours, June ye 11th. 1752." Lord Talbot's offer of marriage if he should gain his freedom came to nothing.

Pitt called on the diplomatist without delay and showed him every courtesy; soon they were on intimate terms and exchanging compositions. Then suddenly all was changed; the Frenchman called on Pitt and was not admitted. Elizabeth had discovered that Dutens had spoken lightly of his intimacy with her. "Immediately upon his leaving Tours," she wrote William, "a friend informed me that Mr. Dutens in a large company had given himself some very improper airs concerning me: and upon enquiring by four or five other people was acquainted yt he insinuated he was well with me, and yt if my family and fortunes answered his expectations when he came in to England he believed at my return I shou'd change my name: that in the mean time upon this footing I had given him letters of introduction to my family. . . . Upon this information I desired a gentleman to write to him from me, as I did not think it proper to trust a letter in his hands, to reproach him with his baseness and bid him return the letters of recommendation he had recd. from me intending the contents should be made publick at Tours. I find the whole family of the Dutens, except the uncle of Chatelneau, have endeavoured from vanity to propagate the story which has hurt me beyond what you can conceive, for in France a thing of this kind gaining credit sinks a woman to a degree of contempt." Such behaviour she will not forgive, and she therefore begs her brother "to order one of your footmen to give him the treatment he merits."[1] Pitt, it appears, took notice of his sister's complaints and thus the Pitt-Dutens intimacy came to an abrupt termination.

From France Elizabeth went to Italy. "I am glad you are aware of Miss Pitt," wrote Horace Walpole to Mann, "pray continue your awaredoms: I assure you before she set out to Italy she was qualified to go any Italian length of passion. Her very first slip was with her eldest brother, and it is not her fault that she has not made still blacker trips. Never mention this, and forget it as soon as she is gone from Florence."[2] But by this time, her good fame was completely compromised. "You certainly could not do otherwise than as you did with regard to the fair Miss Betty Pitt," wrote Lord Chesterfield to a friend. "There are some reputations *un peu hasardées* that one must suppose are sweet, but hers is really too strong, *et sent trop le relais* to be served up in good company. I have not seen her since her return, and probably shall not, as I frequent little company and as she is received by none. Her compliment to you was a very impertinent one, and I believe her brother will not thank her for naming him upon such an occasion."[3] In Italy Elizabeth suddenly became a Roman Catholic: "Miss

[1] "Villiers Pitt" to William Pitt, "Tours, June ye 11th. 1752."
[2] Walpole to Mann, January 28th, 1751.
[3] Chesterfield to Dayrolles, London, August 6th, 1753.

ELIZABETH PITT, *an old print*

British Museum

ANN PITT, *an unfinished sketch**

Boconnoc

Daughters of Robert Pitt.

* *On the back of the original are these words:—"Ann Pitt, Maid of Honor to Queen Caroline, Privy Purse to the Princess Dowager of Wales. Sister to the Earl of Chatham, Equal to her Brother in fine Parts, Unrival'd in Wit, Humour & Agreeable Conversation. Given in 1765 to Elizabeth, wife to Agmondisham Vesey of Lucan."*

Pitt, whom we have had here about two months, last Friday made a public abjuration of the Protestant religion, and became a Roman Catholic," reported Sir Horace Mann, our envoy to Tuscany. "Such a conversion would have been more taken notice of at Rome than it has been here."[1] She had also quarrelled with all sorts of people, usually about nothing. "Nobody could ever guess the motive of her quarrel with Mr. Montgomery, who was not conscious of having offended her, but still offered to make whatever submissions she might dictate for his supposed offence," wrote Mann. "Instead of accepting of this she, by degrees, worked herself up to such a pitch of extravagance as made all reconciliation impracticable, though even then she never particularised any motive, nor was it till long after his departure that she invented that of his having told her she was handsome." She also made herself foolish by pursuing first a Leghorn merchant, who was fortunate enough to escape from her toils, and then an Italian, young enough to be her son. "His family has been much alarmed, though he has assured them, without reason; that he knows her character too well by having avoided the danger she would have exposed him to, by fighting on her account." In Florence she went through a second ceremony of abjuring her religion, and the very next day sought an interview with Count Richecourt, the Emperor's Minister, to ask his protection because, as she said, her own country would disapprove of the action she had taken and would become her enemy. "I interrupted the Count," wrote Mann acidly, "by saying that I was very sure her nation would be as indifferent about the religion she professed as she was herself."[2]

In a few years she was back in England, where she interested herself in the promotion of a scheme for the building of magazines for the storage of corn to relieve the necessities of the poor. But she was soon also actively engaged in disputing about her financial affairs with the unfortunate Dr. Ayscough and with Thomas Cholmondeley of Vale Royal, son of Charles and Essex Cholmondeley, who was careful to take Counsel's opinion and to write William Pitt about his sister's attitude,[3] and violently accusing her brother of having cheated her out of £100 a year. "The famous Miss Elizabeth Villiers Pitt is in England," announced Horace Walpole, "the only public place in which she has been seen is the Popish Chapel; her only exploit endeavours to wreak her malice on her brother, William, whose kindness to her has been excessive. She applies to all his enemies, and, as Mr. Fox told me, has even gone so far as to send a bundle of his

[1] Mann to Bubb Doddington, Florence, March 15th, 1754.
[2] Mann to Bubb Doddington, Florence, June 7th, 1754.
[3] Cholmondeley to William Pitt, Vale Royal, April 13th, and May 23rd, 1761.

letters to the author of *The Test*, to prove that Mr. Pitt has cheated her, as she calls it, of a hundred a year, and which only proves that he once allowed her two, and after all her wickedness still allows her one. How she must be vexed that she has no way of setting the gout more against him."[1] A few years later she wrote Pitt to announce her engagement, but felt obliged to send the letter to another relative, probably Thomas Cholmondeley[2] begging "yt you will peruse and forward ye inclosed to Mr. Pitt as for some years pass'd we have no correspondence, but what ever cause of complaint I may think I have against his behaviour towards me, I sho'd be very sorry to deviate from the proper respect and civility due to his situation and ye near relation between us: forgive I beg ye liberty I take with ye upon this occasion." "Brother," she wrote to William, not "Dear Brother," as formerly, "Brother, from ye motive of respect and civility I think due to you from ye consideration of near relationship, your rank and personal character, I take ye liberty of acquainting ye I have accepted ye proposals of John Hannam Esq., of ye Middle Temple, and shall very soon change my condition: so I flatter myself yt a moment's reflection on ye involved and unhappy situation, from wch ye generous affection of this gentleman extricates me will render this change agreeable to you." Then with a note of defiance: "Give me leave upon this occasion, to inform you of some few particulars relative to Mr. Hannam, as he will soon become your brother by marriage: he is of Sr. William Hannam's family in Dorsetshire, a lawyer by profession of unexceptional character, remarkable for his ability, some years younger than myself and possessed of a fortune superior to my own. Ye annuity I injoy from you and ye liberty left me by my grandfather are vested in Trustees of my own nomination for my sole use and benefit and any additional settlement I positively decline: let my future conduct towards this gentleman alone entitle me to any further effects of his generosity: as it is, I being a considerable additional expense and a very small fortune to support it. Mr. Hannam has been three years acquainted with me, a judge of my conduct, morals, and manners,"—poor misguided Mr. Hannam!—"and as he can have no possible inducement in my situation to ask my hand but ye most disinterested affection I have reason to flatter myself with ye hopes of a great share of felicity, under ye protection of a man of his superior understanding and merit."[3] So we take leave of her. How Mr. Hannam

[1] Walpole to Mann, Arlington Street, January 17th, 1757.

[2] I am, however, informed by Lord Delamere that he has no Pitt correspondence at Vale Royal.

[3] "Villiers Pitt," to William Pitt, "Weybridge, May ye 11th. 1761."

fared we do not know, but on February 14th, 1770, the restless Elizabeth died, no doubt to the intense relief of most of those who had crossed her path.

It must not be thought, however, that all William's family relationships at this time were equally difficult, for at least one was particularly happy. We have seen how, when Thomas found himself in financial difficulties, William, jointly with the Lytteltons, assumed the responsibility of educating his brother's son. In 1751 the uncle started to write that famous series of letters to the future Lord Camelford, then aged fourteen, which were designed to guide him both in his studies and his general conduct through life. For reading he recommends the whole of Virgil's *Aeneid*, Pope's *Homer* and Dryden's *Fables*—"I am not sure if they are called Tales instead of Fables"—also Horace's epistles and Terence's plays.[1] But especially Homer and Virgil are recommended—"I hope you taste and love these authors particularly. You cannot read them too much: they are not only the two greatest poets, but they contain the finest lessons for your age to imbibe: lessons of honour, corage, disinterestedness, love of truth, command of temper, gentleness of behaviour, humanity, and in one word, virtue in its true significance. Go on, my dear nephew, and drink as deep as you can of these divine springs: the pleasure of the draught is equal at least to the prodigious advantages of it to the heart and morals."[2] When the young man was at Cambridge, his uncle warns him against an undue love of pleasure and bids him "qualify yourself for the part in society to which your birth and estate call you. You are to be a gentleman of such learning and qualifications as may distinguish you in the service of your country hereafter; not a pedant, who reads only to be called learned, instead of considering learning as an instrument only for action."[3] During the first quarter of 1754 which was probably the beginning of his nephew's residence at the University, the uncle wrote regularly to guide young Thomas on his way—application to studies, suitable friendships, religion, deportment before one's superiors, politeness or, as he prefers to call it, "benevolence in trifles" or the preference of others to ourselves in little daily, hourly occurrences in the commerce of life, are among the subjects discussed[4]— and throughout the whole of the correspondence there is breathed a tender affection of the uncle for the nephew that is rarely to be found. Here there is nothing of the haughty statesman whose very frown put his rivals

---

[1] William Pitt to Thomas Pitt, September, 1751.

[2] William Pitt to Thomas Pitt, Bath, October 12th, 1751.

[3] William Pitt to Thomas Pitt, Bath, January 12th, 1754.

[4] William Pitt to Thomas Pitt, Bath, January 29th, 1754.

to confusion: here is but the fond uncle guiding and advising the child of a luckless brother on whom fortune has placed a heavy hand.

Whilst uncle and nephew were corresponding affectionately, William Pitt was becoming more and more intimate with his cousin, John Pitt, one day to be known as the great Commoner of the West. George Pitt the second of Strathfieldsaye had married twice: by his first wife he was the father of George Pitt the third of Strathfieldsaye, and by his second he had two sons, John and William. This second wife, a great heiress, brought two magnificent estates, Encombe and Kingston, into her husband's family, for she was the daughter of Audley Grey, last of the Greys of Kingston, and a descendant of Lady Jane Grey's father, the Duke of Suffolk. When Laura Pitt died, she left all her wealth to her sons, and William, who never married, bequeathed his entire share to his brother; so John Pitt, usually known as John Pitt of Encombe from his princely property in Dorset, was a man of immense fortune and considerable political influence in his own county. He represented the local constituency in parliament for many years and between 1744 and 1757 held office in four successive ministries; and though these offices were only minor—he was a Lord of Trade in the Broadbottom, Pelham and Newcastle governments and a Lord of the Admiralty in his great cousin's first administration—he had much of the ability which distinguished without the eccentricity which marred the junior branch of the vast Pitt family.

Much of John Pitt's time was spent at Encombe, a few miles from Corfe Castle, a beautiful place overlooking the sea, and to this paradise William Pitt was a frequent visitor. The cousins, too, were often together at Bath, where William went to take the waters. "Adieu the hills (or halls) and rocks of Encomb, for this summer at least," he wrote sadly in August 1750. "I am a good deal out of order and shall set out tomorrow for Bath. . . . Come to me, my dear Pitt, if you can, and believe me you will do a real pleasure, and infinite good, to your ever affectionate, W. Pitt."[1] There are many letters like this; thus two years later we find him writing a bantering letter to his cousin. "In disobedience to my dear Pitt's prescription of sea-water, whey, etc., I have taken the liberty to get well, or very near it, by Bath Waters, Raleigh's Cordial etc. I should not have presumed so far, if I had not found myself supported by Doctor Moisir himself, which I trust will alleviate my offence in the eye of our learned brother of Encombe. . . ."[2] Then early in 1753 John Pitt marries, and William writes, regretfully: "Unfortunately disabled from attending your happiness in

[1] William Pitt to John Pitt, Stowe, August 11th, 1750.
[2] William Pitt to John Pitt, Bath, October 4th, 1752.

person, may I be allowed a line to you of the most sincere and affectionate felicitations? I will keep my word; it shall be but a line; for I love you too well, to take off your eyes from Mrs. Pitt for more than an instant, to read assurances of friendship, which, after all, you can never fully read but in the heart of your ever affectionate, W. Pitt."[1] Obviously Mr. William Pitt was a rather clumsy gallant, but he had an intense affection for his cousin of Encombe, a regard he maintained to the end of his life.

One other glimpse we get of the John Pitts in after days. "I enquired of Mrs. Howe about Mr. & Mrs. John Pitt, who I know are sometimes in your neighbourhood," wrote Lady Sarah Bunbury, "& I find that tho' she likes them vastly as being undoubtedly very worthy & agreeable people, it is a little Mrs. Pitts way to be uncertain, & Mrs. Howe in a little meek way said, 'I dare say she don't mean it but its a little distressing, for sometimes she is very fond of us, & sometimes takes no notice of us a whole winter.' Upon this Louisa said it had happened to her too to be treated the same, & had made her fear they did not like her, but afterwards she found it was her way, & upon Dean Marley's desiring her to go to Mrs. Pitts & assuring Louisa that it was not meant, she went and found her very civil and pleasing. . . ."[2] All of which goes to show that John Pitt of Encombe and his wife thought themselves powers in the land!

But to return to his greater relative. We have observed Mr. William Pitt going to Bath for the relief of the gout. Here he became a frequent visitor; indeed, for a time he owned 7 The Circus, and his tall figure and handsome face preceded, as it were, by the great nose, must have been a familiar sight in the streets and rooms of the Kingdom of Beau Nash. He was a frequent visitor, too, to near-by Prior Park, where he was hospitably entertained by that strange and lovable character, Ralph Allen.

At this genial host's friendly board there assembled all that was gayest and best in the fashionable world of Bath. Here frequently came that not very successful writer, Henry Fielding, who immortalized his host and benefactor[3] as Squire Allworthy in *Tom Jones*, and his sister Sarah, author of *David Simple*, who lived her rather drab life at Yew Cottage across the way; here, too, came another novelist of note, Samuel Richardson, a highly-strung little man, ever thirsty for praise. But a brighter light than either of these writers spent months together as a guest at Prior Park,

[1] William Pitt to John Pitt. The letter is headed "Sunday morning," but is not dated.

[2] Lady Sarah Bunbury to Lady Susan O'Brian, Castletown, July 6th, 1775.

[3] After his death in 1754, his four children were faithfully cared for by his brother John and by Ralph Allen.

for Alexander Pope actually completed the fourth book of the *Dunciad* under the Allens' kindly roof. Other guests were Garrick, ever a friend of Pitt's, his great rival, Quin, Thomas Gainsborough and his fellow-artist, William Hoare, who painted the only known portrait of Ralph Allen, and his familiar likeness of William Pitt.[1]

Not unnaturally the local member of parliament was frequently at Prior Park, the gardens of which must have been a constant source of joy to him whose hobby throughout life was the planning and laying out of grounds. He was often, too, with his old friends the Lytteltons at Hagley in Worcestershire, where he was consulted on the rebuilding of the house and the laying out of the park. Not far away was the Leasowe, the more humble home of William Shenstone, who had become a victim of the craze for pretentious landscape gardens and spent much time, thought and money in beautifying his property in the modern vogue. When at Hagley Pitt would frequently ride over to visit the poet and to offer his advice on possible improvements.

At his own house, too, South Lodge, in Enfield Chase, the Paymaster could exercise his skill. "I consider S. Lodge as an accession to the Common Stock and Republick of Sportsmen, which from its situation will bring peculiar advantages along with it and that the woodcocks and snipes of Enfield may be visited at seasons of the year when those of Hampshire will not be so accessible. . . ."[2] But he soon tired of the place and was glad to dispose of it in 1753. It was at about this time that Pitt paid his first visit to a house called Hayes Place, near Bromley in Kent, of which Mrs Montagu had a lease. He seems to have taken a violent fancy to the property, for at the termination of his friend's tenancy in 1756 he purchased it, and moved in that summer.

Another house that William Pitt was fond of visiting was Radway Grange near Edgehill in Warwickshire, where the owner, Sanderson Miller had a craze for designing his friends' houses for them. It was here that Pitt went in 1748 when the party consisted of George Lyttelton and Fielding who had just completed his masterpiece, *Tom Jones*, and the great writer read his story from manuscript to Miller and his guests sitting under the shade of the trees in the garden over their walnuts and port. How they must have enjoyed the rendering and especially the portrayal of their friend from Prior Park! In 1754 Pitt planted three trees at Radway to commemorate the occasion and later an urn was placed under them by another Pitt. In October 1908, when the urn required repair, it was found to

[1] Hoare's portrait of Chatham is now in the National Portrait Gallery.
[2] Legge to William Pitt, July 10th, 1748.

contain a sealed bottle in which was a sheet of paper recording the ceremony.[1]

To Radway, also came the Grenvilles with their cousins the Wests,[2] and perhaps it was here that Molly West first cast her loving eyes on their attractive friend, William Pitt. Pitt was ever intimate with this family—and once when he had to go to Tunbridge Wells for the cure, he and the Wests took a joint lease of Stone House on Mount Ephraim. Their near neighbour was Mrs. Montagu, the famous but rather dull blue-stocking, and many were their parties formed for going to the Assembly Rooms or for picnics into the country. During some of the time, Pitt was very ill. "While he continues under this oppression," wrote Dr. West, "I am afraid it will be impossible for me to leave him, as he fancies me of the greatest use to him as a friend and a comforter." Those were doubtless also the sentiments of the adoring Molly, who watched and waited anxiously and tenderly for his recovery. Pitt, of course, recovered, but the romance did not prosper, and Molly eventually became the wife of a young sea-captain, one day to become a famous Admiral and known to the world as Viscount Bridport. "I told you in my last that Miss West was to be married to Captain Hood," wrote Lord Lyttelton to Mrs. Montagu, "yesterday I had the pleasure to give her away to him at Hagley Church, after which we made a party to Mr. Shenstone's Arcadian farm in very fine weather. The pastoral scene seemed to suit the occasion, and the bride owned to him that the cascades and rills never murmured so sweetly before. . . . We dined and supped with Admiral Smith, who, though tortured still with the gravel, lost all sense of his pain in the joy of his friends. He is the best man in the world to be at a wedding where the bride is not *afraid*, but his mirth is rather too boisterous for a very timid young virgin. All that he said I can't tell you, though you are no virgin, but one thing I will for the sake of the answer. . . ."[3] In this case the blushing bride was certainly no timid young virgin, for though the gallant bridegroom was no more than thirty-one, Molly West was no less than fifty-four!

When the Wests were at Radway, so probably were the Grenvilles, for the cousins were good friends, and the West children, Gilbert, a minor poet, William, a future Admiral, and Molly, were frequent visitors to Stowe. So was Mr. Pitt. We have already caught a glimpse of him during

[1] Miller, *An Eighteenth Century Correspondence*.

[2] Mary, one of the daughters of Sir Richard Temple had married Dr. West, Prebendary of Winchester.

[3] Lyttelton to Mrs. Montagu, August 22nd, 1757. Admiral Smith was an illegitimate son of Sir Thomas Lyttelton, and therefore half-brother of the writer of the letter. George Lyttelton had been made a peer in 1756.

his first visit in the summer of 1735. But much had happened since then. Lord Cobham, the head of the family, had died in September 1749. He was succeeded in his titles by his sister, Hester, so Mrs. Grenville became Viscountess Cobham in her own right and her eldest son, Richard, was her heir. It is time we met this Richard, his brothers and his sister, Hester, for some of them are destined to play a prominent part in our story.

There were five Grenville brothers, Richard, George, James, Henry and Thomas, but three of them we can briefly dismiss. James was a bachelor. Henry, Sanderson Miller's special friend, is perhaps best known as the husband of the lovely Peggy Banks, the toast of the town.[1] Tom was a sailor of singular promise but lost his life in command of the *Defiance* in Anson's famous action. "He fought and died with the gallantry of Sir Philip Sidney," wrote his kinsman, George Lyttelton, and no one can improve that noble epitaph.[2] With the two remaining brothers, we are more intimately concerned.

Richard and George Grenville suffered from a common hallucination that must have surprised their contemporaries and has certainly astonished posterity—so far, that is to say, as posterity remembers them at all—that they were people of consequence in the public life of their country. No belief could have been more strange for none could have been more unfounded; yet they persisted in this view and nothing could divert their minds from the strange illusion. They had formed from early youth a friendly association with their young friend, Pitt, and that friendship and that union lasted into their more mature years. It no doubt suited both parties, for the Grenvilles were immensely rich and Pitt was a great genius, and the coalition of wealth and genius is ever a potent force. It is safe to say, then, that Richard and George were quick to see the advantages of the association, and in a very short time Pitt was treated almost as a member of the family. We have seen that as far back as 1735 he paid his first visit to princely Stowe, and staying there several months. Innumerable more visits were to follow, as the Grenvilles and their kinsmen, the Lytteltons, and to a lesser degree the Wests, formed the famous "Cobham Cousinhood." In the Grenville meshes, then, Pitt was soon entwined: by his own passions, as we shall see, he was soon to become more securely held, so that no power on earth could rescue him.

But the most astonishing aspect of the whole affair is this: Pitt probably —for love is blind—and the brothers certainly—for conceit is blinder—did not realize how great a preponderance of advantage accrued to the Grenvilles

[1] Margaret Banks, sister of John Hodgkinson Banks.

[2] Lyttelton to Thomson, May 21st, 1749.

in the association—how far greater was the gain of mediocrity linked to genius than that of genius linked to wealth and station. Thus, in 1766, when Pitt was at the very zenith of his fame, Richard publicly declared his absolute equality with him who was beyond doubt or cavil the first states-man in Europe; and when this political Tom Thumb was offered the First Lordship of the Treasury, with the nomination of the Chancellorship of the Exchequer and the Board of Treasury, he rejected the offer with lofty scorn. What a superb gesture! Nothing was good enough for the great Richard and his mighty clan; for—and this also is remarkable—they were not concerned solely with their own advancement but with the glorification of the all-important Grenville family of which Richard was the conceited head. To this mean object, they directed the whole force of their energies and achieved success worthy of a loftier cause.

Lord Cobham, the Grenvilles' uncle, died on September 13th, 1749, and as we have already noted, was succeeded in the Viscountcy by his sister, Mrs. Grenville of Wotton, their mother. But a Viscountcy for the head of this great family was thought to be quite inadequate, and the brothers were soon corresponding on the project of making an application to the Duke of Newcastle for an earldom to be conferred on Lady Cobham with remainder, of course, to Richard Grenville-Temple,[1] her eldest son.[2] On September 28th, only fifteen days after Cobham's death, Richard duly made the application. Even that hardened campaigner amongst political jobbers, the Duke of Newcastle, was shocked. "The only thing I shall submit to you, and that I shall leave entirely to your own determination, relates singly to the point of time"—it does not seem to have worried anyone that no services whatever had been rendered for which the great honour might be a just reward!—"whether it might not be as well to defer it 'till winter or some time after the meeting of Parliament, as to propose it just now, so soon after Lord Cobham's death and before you have had an opportunity of appearing at Court."[3] But delay was the last thing the

[1] Immediately upon Cobham's death, Richard Grenville had assumed his late uncle's name of Temple in addition to his own.

[2] Dr. Von Ruville states that the brothers acted on Pitt's advice, but I know of no evidence to support his contention. Von Ruville, *William Pitt, Earl of Chatham*, Vol. I. On the contrary, there is amongst the Stowe MSS., now in the Huntingdon Library, California, a long and interesting "last letter" addressed by Lady Temple to her eldest son, and dated June 25th, 1750, rather more than two years before her death. This remarkable document, commencing: "When this comes to your hands, I shall be no more——" breathes throughout that spirit of intense family pride that was so pronounced in her sons, and would seem to suggest that the Mother herself was very likely at the back of this unseemly application.

[3] Newcastle to Grenville-Temple, Claremont, September 30th, 1749.

Grenvilles wanted; and Richard made this abundantly clear in the reply he sent the wavering duke the very next day.[1] Newcastle saw plainly that there was no arguing: the thing must be done, and done it was. "October 15th at Leicester House," records Bubb Doddington, "The Grenvilles presented for the title of Temple."[2] So Lady Cobham became Countess Temple, and Richard Viscount Cobham until his mother's death on October 7th, 1752, gave him the Earldom, and as Earl Temple he is known to history.

There was yet another member of the Grenville family, and she has not yet appeared in these pages. The Grenville brothers, we are told, "all loved their sister Hetty in their several ways, Lord Temple with his coarse joviality, George in the priggish airs of protection, Jimmy jocose but with the most enduring faithfulness, while Henry, the youngest, seems at this time to have been very dear to her."[3] Of this Hetty, now the Lady Hester Grenville, more will ere long be told.

But we must leave the Grenvilles awhile, and return to Mr. Pitt, who is paying one of his periodic visits to Bath. His sister, Ann, is in France, but he must needs write to her. Their Aunt Essex has just died, but that is relegated to a postscript. A bigger player on the stage of life than Aunt Essex has just left it, for the Prime Minister is no more, and Pitt, crippled in the West, is unable to travel to London at the time of crisis. "Dear Sister,—I write to you under the greatest affliction, on all considerations Private and Public. Mr. Pelham died Wednesday morning, of a Feaver and St. Anthony's fire. This Loss is, in my notion of things, irreparable to the publick. I am still suffering much Pain with Gout in both feet, and utterly unable to be carry'd to London. I may hope to be the better for it hereafter, but I am at present rather worn down than relieved by it: I am extremely concern'd at the last accounts of your health. I hope you have Spring begun at Nevers, which I pray God may relieve you." Then comes the family news: "My sister Nedham has been ill of a Feaver here, but is well again. I have just received an account of Mrs. Cholmondeley's Death."[4] Poor helpless invalid. Yet wonderful to relate, he was to be a joyful bridegroom ere the year was out.

Before Pelham had been dead more than a few days it was determined that the Duke of Newcastle should be placed at the head of the Treasury; but what all men were asking was who was to be the leading Minister in the House of Commons. The three persons most eligible were undoubtedly

---

[1] Grenville-Temple to Newcastle, Stowe, October 1st, 1749.

[2] Melcombe, *Diary*, October 15th, 1749.

[3] Williams, *William Pitt, Earl of Chatham*, Vol. I.

[4] William Pitt to Ann Pitt, Bath, March 9th, 1754.

William Murray, Henry Fox and William Pitt. Murray, the Attorney-General, was by common consent the greatest lawyer of the day; but his aims were set upon his profession and he wholly lacked the vaulting ambition needed for political advancement. Pitt was ill at Bath; but had he been in London there would still have been the difficulty of overcoming the King's objection to the man who had so insolently baited him. There remained Fox; would he accept the leadership of the House of Commons in the new administration of the Duke of Newcastle?

To Newcastle, in search of a head for the House of Commons, Fox had much to recommend him. He was a debater of unrivalled skill, he was on excellent terms with the King and the Duke of Cumberland, and his indigence made him likely to be a pliant tool in the duke's hands. So approach was made to him. He was offered the post of Secretary of State with leadership of the House of Commons on the terms that the disposal of the secret service money—that is to say, in plain English, the bribing of Members of the House of Commons—should be in the hands of the First Lord of the Treasury, who would inform Fox exactly as to how this fund was being employed. Fox accepted these terms. But the next morning, when he met Newcastle face to face, he found that the duke had changed his mind, and was now anxious to secure Fox's assistance without yielding to him even that share of power that his previous offer implied. Fox retired angry and baffled, and wrote declining the proffered post but promising his continued services in his former position of Secretary at War. Whereupon Newcastle with evident relief handed the Seals of Secretary of State to a dreary and little known diplomat, Sir Thomas Robinson.[1]

To the invalid confined at Bath, this was agony. He was the victim of every emotion—first hope that, in spite of his illness, he might be summoned and consulted: then, at least partial resignation, for Fox, whom he regarded as more or less his equal, had been chosen, and this was a mortification that was not too hard to bear; and lastly, blank despair, coupled with the white heat of fury, for not only had he been passed over but he had been supplanted by a pompous nonentity. The news of this insufferable humiliation reached him by letter from Lyttelton late in the evening of March 23rd. He hardly slept that night, and early the next morning he wrote Newcastle that famous and terrible indictment that was in effect a declaration of war.[2]

[1] Afterwards Lord Grantham.

[2] William Pitt to Newcastle, March 24th, 1754. Curiously enough, this letter was not included in either the *Chatham Correspondence* or the *Grenville Papers*. It was first disclosed in an article on Chatham in the *Quarterly Review* No. CXXXI, where extracts from it are given from the Hardwicke MSS. The original is among the Newcastle Papers in the British Museum. Add. MSS. 32734, f. 322.

He sent it open to Lyttelton, so that he and the Grenvilles could read it before it was sealed and delivered. He also wrote to George Grenville and to Temple, hoping his letter would meet with "fraternal approbation," and then he added—for all this effort had over-taxed his strength—"I am so tired I cannot hold my head down to write any longer. A fine Secretary of State I should make."[1] A courageous pose, for he must by now have realized his great abilities!

Meanwhile, poor timid Newcastle was positively quaking with fear at Pitt's explosion, and both he and Hardwicke strove to pacify the irate invalid.[2] At first Pitt responded despairingly: "The weight of irremovable royal displeasure is a load too great to move under," he wrote to Hardwicke, "it must crush any man; it has sunk and broke me. I succumb; and wish for nothing but a decent and innocent retreat, wherein I may no longer, by continuing in the public stream of promotion, for ever stick fast aground, and afford to the world the ridiculous spectacle of being passed by every boat that navigates the same river.[3] But this mood quickly passed. He stayed on at Bath till the summer, but returned to London in June when he had an interview with Newcastle. The duke's shuffling and evasive replies made it evident that he had exerted but little effort to overcome the King's aversion, and Pitt fully grasped the baseness of the man who pretended to be his friend. So with the light of understanding dawning within, there swelled up such a torrent of passion that nothing on earth could stem, and he vowed that in the very next session of Parliament, he would show them what manner of man they had thought to humble and to silence with a few soft, empty words.

But even as he made his vow, he knew that never before had he felt so friendless, so utterly alone: all save the Grenvilles had failed him and none recognized his genius. He spent a sad summer that year at Radway, where his old friend strove to rally him. Thence he went to Astrop Wells to drink the inevitable waters. Later he planned to stay with Legge, the Chancellor of the Exchequer, at Holte in Hampshire, and after a visit to Bath he hoped to be able to get to his cousin's at Encombe.[4] Somehow these plans were upset, and by September we find him at Wotton where he was ever sure of a warm welcome. Here was the placid stillness of the English countryside; here the affectionate companionship of his best, his

[1] William Pitt to Grenville and to Temple, Bath, March 24th, 1754.

[2] Newcastle to William Pitt, Newcastle House, April 2nd, 1754, and Hardwicke to William Pitt, Powis House, April 2nd, 1754.

[3] William Pitt to Hardwicke, Bath, April 6th, 1754.

[4] William Pitt to John Pitt, Astrop Wells, September 10th, 1754.

truest friends; here was their sister with her sweet patient smile and soft, mellow voice. He had known her for many years, had seen her grow out of the school-room into womanhood, but had little noticed her. But now, when he was so tired, so bitterly disappointed, so desperately alone, there she was with her calm manner, breathing the very spirit of peace.

Lady Hester Grenville was thirty-three: yet she hardly seemed that age as she looked out upon the world with her fine noble face, full of self-confidence—or of pride, perchance, for how could she forget that she was a Grenville? She was tall, with a graceful carriage, and her head, surmounted by rich auburn hair, was set on a long, well-shaped neck. The general effect was of a great lady of unusual sweetness and charm. She was fond of country life, and had spent most of her days at Stowe and Wotton. She had many women friends, and one of her oldest and best was Elizabeth Wyndham,[1] who to the great joy of the family had married her brother, George. Nor had she lacked suitors. "You are either a little idle Bitch, or I am a sad unlucky Dog," wrote her brother Thomas, "for I have not seen a line from you this four months; I desire you will tell me in your next what it is that takes your time up so; if it is your Lovers, I excuse you but upon no other accounts."[2] Some two years later, her brother, Jemmy, had written playfully that he was "not a little glad there is a prospect of getting you off with Simon Truelove. He really deserves to have you, and it is impossible to look for a more advantageous proposal. My dear Meg, you grow old and it is time for you to think of a decent retirement from business. Tho' you have served me with great fidelity and attention, yet you will soon become incapable and burthensome. You are already so puny that you can scarce run after the young people enough to carry on their affairs. Besides with regard to my business you will be better able to manage it at present by marrying Simon than in any other manner. . . . Therefore let me hear by the very next post that the thing is concluded, otherwise never tell me again of the hardship of the times, nor expect me to supply your unnecessary demands."[3]

Then there is the charming Captain Geary: "I own I heard some expressions thrown upon your conduct at Tunbridge: I was told that you rode out at improper hours, that you breakfast'd before you drank the waters and drank the waters too late, and many other articles of complaint. Consider that we are in times of severity, and that if you misbehave you will

[1] Daughter of Sir William Wyndham and Lady Catherine Seymour, daughter of the sixth Duke of Somerset.

[2] Thomas Grenville to Hester Grenville, Villa Franca, August 29th, 1742.

[3] Thomas Grenville to Hester Grenville, September 29th, 1744.

be treated without mercy. My information came from good hands, from a *charming spirited honest young lady* who was at least as good a witness for me, and I am sure a less suspicious one than your *charming Spirited honest* Captain Geary. . . . I am told wonders of your horsemanship, but seriously ten miles an hour is rather too much for an invalid; pray remember that is an error, and confine your praises to your genteelness on horseback, and not your spirits, the former will never quit you and can do no harm, the latter may and will do you a great deal. . . ."[1] Then some two months later he is writing again about the charming Captain Geary, who "remembers his best respects to that fair, fair lady, my sister, and in her prevailing name asks a favour which I will grant him if possible. Is not this good in me? Se the advantage of having a brother in the Admiralty and make the best of it."[2] So George, in true Grenville style "obliges" Francis Geary in case he should marry his sister. Nothing came of this romance; but whilst the infatuation lasted, Francis Geary did not have things all his own way for he had a rival in Richard Berenger, Hester's first cousin,[3] who had a common bond with her in fondness for horsemanship. "If it was in my inclination as much as in my power to rain you with R. Ber: Dear Miss Grenville," wrote her future sister-in-law, Elizabeth Wyndham, "I would do it most infallibly in letting him know how cheaply you have used his most ecstatic expression of a little bit of felicity which I am persuaded he never confined to the narrow bounds of receiving a letter, nor could bear to have it mis-applied. But I have too much generosity to use undue arts and will, therefore content myself with endeavouring to rival you with him in horsemanship which I have already attempted and shall leave it to him to tell you what progress I have made."[4] But Berenger was no more successful than Geary, and in the years that follow we find him appointed "Gentleman of the Horse to His Majesty,"[5] asking his old love, now Lady Chatham, for some mark of her great husband's favour and notice,"[6] and soliciting subscriptions from the Pitt family to his book on horsemanship, shortly to be published. "It is very natural for me," he wrote to Hester, "and I hope not too presuming to sollicit the honour and advantage of being

---

[1] George Grenville to Hester Grenville, "Admty. Aug. ye 28th., 1746." Francis Geary, a captain in the Navy, subsequently became an Admiral.

[2] George Grenville to Hester Grenville, October 28th, 1746.

[3] Richard Berenger was the son of Moses Berenger who had married Penelope, daughter of Sir Richard Temple.

[4] Elizabeth Wyndham to Hester Grenville, June 17th, 1746.

[5] Berenger to William Pitt, November 27th, 1760.

[6] Berenger to Lady Chatham, The King's Mews, August 3rd, 1766.

Chevening

LADY HESTER GRENVILLE, Countess of Chatham

Hudson

permitted to enroll Lord Chatham's name with those of Lord Temple and the rest of the family. . . . As Ladies ride, and Ladies read, if your Ladyship should have the smallest inclination to give me your name likewise, it shall be recorded, and will make me proud and make me happy."[1]

But, to return to Hester Grenville, we find obscure references to various admirers from another of Hester's friends, Jane Hamilton, soon to be the bride of Lord Cathcart. In the summer of 1748, Jane tells Hester that Lord Pembroke greatly admires her;[2] and a year later writes after Elizabeth Wyndham's marriage to George Grenville, that she hears her friend is to follow Elizabeth's example "and make a happy man of one who has been long an admirer."[3] But within a few days she is writing again to apologize for her previous letter.[4] Later, there are references in Jane's letters to "the Cameleon Br. and the Chevalier Profond,"[5] but to whom the words refer we have no means of knowing. So we see that Hester Grenville had had many admirers. Yet she had never wed; and now she was thirty-three. Could it be that—consciously or unconsciously—she had loved Mr. Pitt all the while?

None, of course, can say; but one thing is certain, the great man had taken very little notice of her in times gone by. When he had first come to Stowe as a Cornet, she had been in the nursery; later she had seen him shine in the brilliant society that adorned her home. As she emerged to womanhood, he grew to middle-age, and the brilliant, romantic figure changed to the balanced statesman of genius with all his infirmities and all his worries. Now he was forty-six. Always he had been so proud, so sure of himself, so aloof—with an old-world courtesy towards women that was at once delightful and rather forbidding; but gradually circumstances had combined to bridge the gulf that divided them. The previous year when he had been sore stricken with his old enemy, Lady Hester had in a variety of ways shown her warm sympathy for his broken state, and he had evidently been deeply touched by her understanding. And now, though his health was better, his mental state was scarcely improved. Perhaps he had lost some of his self-confidence, perhaps his very dejection gave her the power over him she sought; perhaps . . . But who can tell? All we know is that one late September morning these two, as they walked by the lake in the grounds of Wotton, told each other of their love.

[1] Berenger to Lady Chatham, The King's Mews, May 24th, 1769.
[2] Jane Hamilton to Hester Grenville, May 15th, 1748.
[3] Jane Hamilton to Hester Grenville, July 20th, 1749.
[4] Jane Hamilton to Hester Grenville, August 1st, 1749.
[5] Jane Hamilton to Hester Grenville, June 18th and July 24th, 1750, and an undated letter of the same year. See also Tunstall, *William Pitt, Earl of Chatham.*

At this time of happiness, William's thoughts turned to Ann, and in spite of all that had passed, he hastened to give her the news. "I am now, Dear Sister, to impart to you what I have no longer a prospect of doing, with infinitely more pleasure, by word of mouth: it is to say that, your health excepted, I have nothing to wish for my happiness, Lady Hester Grenville has consented to give herself to me, and by giving me every thing my Heart can wish, she gives you a Sister. . . ."[1] Judging from the prim letter enclosed from "Your most faithful and Obed. Humble Servant, Her: Grenville," Ann may have felt that there was some exaggeration in her brother's remarks, but she nevertheless hastened to congratulate him on his engagement. To his old friend, George Lyttelton, Pitt wrote in a pleasantly humble tone not often to be come by in this proud man's correspondence. "You who know what it is tenderly and passionately to love the object of your perfect esteem and intire confidence," he wrote, "will best be able to estimate this happiness truly. I can add, if I may without vanity, that I have the Pride as well as the Joy to find every taste of my mind and more serious purpose of my Life correspond to those of Lady Hester Grenville. Would I cou'd add that my nature was as free from Defect and Weaknesses! . . . My obligations to Lady Hester are indeed infinite, for what, my dear Lyttelton, have I to lay at her feet in return for the invaluable present her goodness makes me, but a fortune very far from tempting and a health shatter'd and declin'd?"[2] Pitt must have taken special pleasure in writing to his cousin of Encombe because he had had to write to him earlier that year on the birth of his son—to be christened William Morton—"May the finest Boy (which I'll take your word for), and the most amiable woman (which I'll swear of my own knowledge)," he had written, "continue in perfect health, and every hour add to the happiness of a man who deserves and enjoys it."[3] Now he had to announce his own happiness: "I am the happiest man that lives," he wrote, "as well as the most honoured. . . ."[4] Jane Hamilton, now Lady Cathcart, was delighted: "I will burn my books if you are not happy together, but as you will remember I long ago gave you to him."[5] Legge hastened to rejoice with the loving couple, and humorously remarked to John Pitt— "I think the breed will be a good one, and can't fail to speak as soon as they are born. It is an acquisition to the corps of a married man; and heartily

[1] William Pitt to Ann Pitt, Bath, October 21st, 1754.

[2] William Pitt to Lyttelton, October 31st, 1754.

[3] William Pitt to John Pitt, Bath, May 18th, 1754.

[4] William Pitt to John Pitt, Bath, October 21st, 1754.

[5] Lady Cathcart to Lady Hester Grenville, November 4th, 1754.

THE MARRIAGE OF WILLIAM PITT

I wish them much happiness."[1] The Grenvilles, too, were delighted. Jemmy hastened to Wotton, and, as Hester told her lover, expressly thanked her for giving him as a brother the one man in all the world that he would choose to call by that name.[2] Henry regarded the marriage as an honour to the whole family.[3] And Lyttelton at Hagley, vainly awaiting a visit from his friend, was warm in his congratulations. "I shall never be entirely satisfied," he wrote, "until you visit us together, which I hope may be possible next summer, and then we will shake the old house to its foundations."[4] "As your friend I congratulate you," he wrote to Hester, "and as his I love you for the choice you have made."[5]

On Saturday, November 16th, William Pitt and Hester Grenville were married by Dr. Ayscough by special licence in her house in Argyle Street, and on the same day they left for the Wests' house at West Wickham, lent them for their short honeymoon. There they remained untroubled by the outside world for barely ten days. On November 25th Pitt returned to London. The great happiness that he had so suddenly and unexpectedly found had helped to restore his self-confidence. He was ready to face the world anew, to attack and slay the pigmies who had dared to pass him by, and to prepare himself for that great and glorious work that it was his destiny to fulfil.

When Pitt reached London, he wasted no time and was in his place in the House of Commons on the first day of the new session. Here he found a fellow-malcontent in Henry Fox, and the two disappointed ministers soon came to an unofficial understanding for launching a joint attack upon their leader. And their primary method of attacking Newcastle was to bait unmercifully the unfortunate man whom the duke had dragged from comparative obscurity into the full glare of public life.

Poor Sir Thomas Robinson was particularly vulnerable to attack of that kind. A large awkward man of many absurdities, the possessor of a very bass voice and an excessively portentous manner, he had been chiefly noteworthy when our Ambassador at Vienna for having written long and prosy despatches on innumerable subjects of but very moderate interest. He was wholly ignorant of the rules and customs of the House of Commons and was, therefore, about the very worst man who could have been chosen

---

[1] Legge to John Pitt, Downing Street, October 25th, 1754.
[2] Lady Hester Grenville to William Pitt, October 13th, 1754.
[3] Henry Grenville to Lady Hester Grenville, 1754.
[4] Lyttelton to William Pitt, October 26th, 1754.
[5] Lyttelton to Lady Hester Grenville, October 28th, 1754.

to face two such experienced campaigners as Pitt and Fox. "Sir Thomas Robinson lead us!" exclaimed Pitt contemptuously, "the Duke might as well send his jackboot to lead us!"—and so it proved. Newcastle, of course, would have been thankful to dismiss the two rebels from their offices, but courage failed him. Instead, he made efforts to win over Fox by the offer of a place in the Cabinet. For a time, he resisted the temptation; but his impecuniosity overcame his reluctance and in January 1755 he accepted the duke's offer.[1] Pitt, needless to say, was furious, but the wily Newcastle had had his first success: he had succeeded in dividing his enemies.

Whilst these squibs were being fired in the House of Commons, affairs abroad, both in America and in Europe, were lowering. On the threat of war in Europe, the King, on his annual visit to Hanover, was soon engaged in forming with the petty princes, a series of treaties to save the Electorate from the inevitable conflict. When this became known, there was a storm of indignation throughout England. In his perplexity Newcastle turned to Pitt. If only he could be prevailed upon to support the treaties, all might yet be well. He accordingly sent for the Minister, and held out splendid promises. His Majesty, who had hitherto practically refused to speak to Pitt, would now be civil and obliging; he should be given a Cabinet post and consulted on everything—there was nothing that should not be done if only he would support the Hessian subsidy. Pitt coolly declined place, but said that if the King felt so strong an inclination towards this particular treaty, he would on this one occasion deviate from his usual course and support it. "Well, and the Russian subsidy?" asked Newcastle eagerly. "No, no," said Pitt hastily, "not a series of subsidies." The duke could do nothing with his intractable colleague; and Hardwicke, called in to help, was no more successful. A responsible leader of the House of Commons had to be found; there was nothing for it, then, but to remove Sir Thomas from this position and to replace him by Henry Fox.

In November, 1755, the Houses of Parliament met, and one of the greatest debates in all its history ensued. "I remember that at Lyons I was taken to see the conflux of the Rhone and the Saone," declared Pitt, referring to the Newcastle-Fox coalition, "the one a gentle, feeble, languid stream, and though languid, of no depth—the other a boisterous and impetuous torrent; but different as they are, they meet at last," and with bitter irony "long may they continue united to the comfort of each other, and to the glory, honour and security of this nation." "He surpassed himself, and then I

---

[1] For full details of the negotiations see Ilchester, *Henry Fox, 1st Lord Holland*, Vol. I.

need not tell you that he surpassed Cicero and Demosthenes," was Horace Walpole's enthusiastic comment.[1] "Who is the Rhone?" asked Fox of Pitt after the debate. "Is that a fair question?" came the prompt reply. "Why," rejoined Fox good-humouredly, "as you have said so much that I did not wish to hear, you may tell me one thing that I do want to hear. Am I the Rhone, or Lord Granville?" "You are Granville," was Pitt's retort, for in truth they were one in their opposition to him. The effect of this oratory was that Pitt, Legge, and George Grenville were all dismissed from their places; whereupon Lord Temple with great generosity wrote his sister begging her to persuade her husband to accept a gift of £1,000 a year "till better times."[2]

Meanwhile, the war, which broke out in many parts of the world, went badly for England, but of all our disasters none was more humiliating than the loss of Minorca, and the failure of Admiral Byng to relieve Port Mahon. At this dire news, a storm of fury broke over England, and vengeance was demanded on the admiral, whose conduct was held to blame. The Duke of Newcastle began to tremble for his skin and to a deputation from the City of London which waited upon him, he blurted out with unfeeling venality—"Oh, indeed, he shall be tried immediately; he shall be hanged directly."

It was clear that affairs could not long continue thus, and that Pitt must be approached. But knowing his power he made an absolute stipulation that Newcastle should be entirely excluded from the new arrangements. At this, the ludicrous duke once more ran chattering from colleague to colleague in great distress begging for advice and listening to nobody. At length, when no one was found to face Pitt in the House of Commons, Newcastle had no alternative to tendering his resignation. So the way was made clear for Pitt at last; and after further negotiations, Lord Hartington, now through the recent death of his father, the fourth Duke of Devonshire, a conscientious and upright man, was with difficulty prevailed upon to form a Ministry with William Pitt Secretary of State. Thus he who ere long was to be known as the great Commoner with superb self-confidence set about his mighty task. "My Lord," he proudly trumpeted to Devonshire, "I *know* that I can save England, and that no one else can."[3] With that sublime boast the House of Pitt came into its own at last.

[1] Walpole to Bentley, November 16th, 1755.
[2] Temple to Lady Hester Pitt, November 20th, 1755. The whole correspondence between Temple and the Pitts is published in the *Grenville Papers*, Vol. I.
[3] Walpole, *Memoirs of the Reign of George II*, Vol. III.

BOOK II

Reign of the House of Pitt

CHAPTER I

The Accession of George III

"THE eyes of an afflicted, despairing nation were now lifted up to a private gentleman of a slender fortune, wanting the parade of birth or title, of no family allowance, but by his marriage with Lord Temple's sister, and even confined to a narrow circle of friends and acquaintances. Under these circumstances Pitt was considered as the only saviour of England." Thus wrote Glover[1] and he had good reason for his despondency. Things in America were looking grim; the French had seized Minorca, and Admiral Byng had failed to relieve the beleaguered garrison; and on the continent of Europe, a formidable confederacy of other powers was forming against the King of Prussia, who, in spite of the animosity of George II, was almost our only friend.

Amid these distractions, the new Ministry was formed. And it was not long before it became evident that it was unlikely to last for more than a very short time. Almost the first matter of consequence with which the Government had to deal was the trial of Admiral Byng, against whom the popular clamour was prodigious. The Court[2] found that whilst the Admiral was not guilty of cowardice, treachery or gross dereliction of duty, he was guilty of not having done his utmost to destroy the enemy fleet; they therefore recommended him to mercy. No sooner was the verdict known than efforts were made to save Byng, and in these Pitt and Temple played leading and honourable rôles. "The House of Commons, Sire," said Pitt to the King, "seems inclined to mercy." "Sir," was George's famous reply, "you have taught me to look for the sense of my subjects in other places than the House of Commons."[3] But all efforts were vain, and the Admiral was destined to suffer for his shortcomings on the quarter deck of the *Monarque* in the witty and familiar words of Voltaire, "*pour encourager les autres.*"[4]

[1] Glover, *The Memoirs of a Celebrated Literary Character.*

[2] The President was Admiral Smith, the Lytteltons' illegitimate brother, and one of its members was Francis Geary, Hester Grenville's one-time suitor.

[3] Walpole, *Memoirs of the Reign of George II*, Vol. II.

[4] Voltaire, *Candide*, Chap. XXIII.

The Ministry was clearly doomed. Pitt's advocacy of Byng's cause had lost him much popular support; moreover, he was positively loathed by the King, who was consulting Waldegrave as to how best he might be rid of his hated Ministers, and whether the timid Newcastle might somehow be tempted to return to office. Accordingly, early in April, Pitt was informed that his Sovereign had no further use for his services. The fall of Pitt was very ill received. The freedom of the City of London was voted to him; and soon nearly all the greater towns in the country were following this example. "For some weeks," wrote Walpole, "it rained gold boxes."[1]

Matters were further complicated by the motion for enquiry into the loss of Minorca, which had been tabled in the House of Commons. Newcastle and his colleagues only obtained an acquittal by a small margin; and if Pitt had seen fit to exert his powers against them, they might well have been impeached. But he was too wary to resort to such extremes. He was beginning to realize what the animosity of the Sovereign meant, and he was not anxious to add to his difficulties. George II was striving for a coalition of Newcastle and Fox; but the "Aspen Duke,"[2] far too old a campaigner to be tempted to join with one of the most unpopular men in England, was evolving a plan for forming a Government of his own with dependants and nonentities as his colleagues, and Sir George Lee and Sir Thomas Robinson were designed for high office in this imposing administration; but no sooner had he formed this resolve than he took fright, and he forthwith abandoned the whole project. Thus gradually, very gradually, the duke turned his enquiring eyes and stupid irresolute face towards the massive brow and hawk-like nose of the country's idol. True, he had promised the king never to have dealings with that hateful man; true, every instinct warned him against associating with that stormy petrel: better, far better retire to private life than play with such a firebrand. But the Duke of Newcastle was constitutionally incapable of retiring into private life; power was the food on which he flourished and the wine that rejoiced his heart; starve him of these, and he must wither and fade. Therefore, in spite of his plighted word, in spite of the dictates of his own reason, he gradually, very gradually, turned his gaze in the direction from which succour might possibly come. And so, at last, after all his efforts to find an alternative Government had failed, the fiery little king was forced to yield; and with much explosive abuse against all who had preferred to be, as he repeatedly put it, the footmen of the Duke of Newcastle to the friends

[1] Walpole, *Memoirs of the Reign of George II*, Vol. III.

[2] Walpole to Mann, Arlington Street, March 17th, 1737.

and counsellors of their sovereign, his Majesty submitted to the only practical solution of the imbroglio. The influence of the widowed Princess of Wales and her Leicester House clique was brought to bear on the haughty Pitt to abate a little of his arrogant demands, and out of the welter, confusion and discord there at last emerged a Government strong enough, resolute enough and determined enough to cope with the grave emergency of the hour.

It was time, indeed, for England to have a strong Government, for the outlook was not promising. Early in 1757 the Prussian army poured into Bohemia and attacked Prague. Daun, perhaps the foremost of the Austrian generals, was marching at the head of another army, to its assistance. On May 6th, the battle was joined, and in one of the bloodiest clashes of the whole war Frederick just managed to snatch a costly victory from the jaws of disaster. Of the remnants of the Austrian army, the greater part joined up with Daun, now hot on the heels of the victorious Prussians. About noon on June 18th, he came up with them. By dusk the Prussian army had lost some thirteen thousand of its bravest men. Nothing remained for Frederick but to raise the siege of Prague, to retreat in as good order as possible and by a devious route to extricate his army from Bohemia. The position of the King of Prussia seemed well-nigh desperate.

This was the position that faced Pitt on his accession to power. He was quick to see that everything had changed since those days when he had thundered against the despicable Electorate. Then he had deprecated continental entanglements: now, he perceived that Frederick, our only ally, was likely to sink under the weight of these attacks, and if he succumbed, France would be the more able to face us both in America and in the East. It was, therefore, imperative for us to lend him instant aid. So an expeditionary force of some 50,000 mixed troops was despatched under the Duke of Cumberland to defend Hanover against the French force advancing from Westphalia under the gallant d'Estrées, grandson of the great Louvois. Unfortunately, Cumberland's military talents were small; and on July 26th he was routed at the small village of Hastenbeck, near Hameln. In consequence, the whole of Hanover was overrun. No sooner had the victory been won than the French general was recalled through the intrigues of Madame de Pompadour, who gave his command to two of her favourites, the Duc de Richelieu, the victor of Minorca, and the Prince de Soubise. Richelieu was to attack Cumberland, Soubise, Frederick. Richelieu was quick to follow up d'Estrée's success; he forced the English to retire behind Stade, where he compelled the Duke to sign the ignominious Convention of Closterseven. The King was furious. "Here is my son who has ruined me and disgraced himself," was his greeting to Cumberland. But when the king complained to his Minister that he had given his son no orders to conclude such a convention, Pitt promptly replied, "But full powers, Sire, very full powers!"[1]

By this reverse Frederick's position was rendered still more desperate, and it was not until near the close of 1757 that the tide began to turn in his favour. Then on November 5th, his great victory at Rossbach over Marshal Soubise, followed in December by his defeat of the Austrians under Prince Charles of Lorraine at Leuthen near Breslau, turned the scale. The latter victory was overwhelming. Twenty-seven thousand Austrians that day fell in the awful carnage and Silesia was retaken by the all-conquering Prussians. The fame and popularity of the King of Prussia was prodigious so that it was easy for Pitt to obtain the assent of the House of Commons to the conclusion of a new convention with Prussia whereby we agreed to pay a subsidy to Frederick of £670,000, and to despatch an army to defend the king's western borders against the encroachment of France. This force was placed under the command of Prince Ferdinand of Brunswick, soon to prove himself one of the greatest soldiers of the age. So ended in triumph and glory the fateful year of 1757.

But the pendulum of fate was soon to swing back, and during the years 1758 and 1759 disaster dogged the King of Prussia. The only glimmer of light in the darkened sky was provided by the success of Prince Ferdinand of Brunswick in the west, where within a few weeks Zelle, Hanover and Hameln were all cleared, and by the glorious victory of Minden, though this was dimmed by the unseemly conduct of Lord George Sackville.

Early in 1759 further disasters faced the King of Prussia for Berlin was occupied by the enemy and the royal palace sacked; but later fortune veered, and successes were gained at Lignitz over Lauholn and at Torgau over Daun. Tidings of the former victory brought forth ebullitions of joy from the adoring Hester, who, dating her letter, "Tuesday, Glorious August 26, one o'clock," thus addresses her hero. "You was, my Life, a Prophet of this Victory, and expected it from the King of Prussia. Your sister had a second sight of it, for she was entertained all the night long with triumphs and trophies, which I told her displeased me greatly, and that I prayed Heaven we might not hear of something of quite a contrary sort. Thanks to Heaven, my forebodings proved false . . . I wait for the guns, and then Hayes bells shall speak for the King of Prussia, which I thought they never would again be employed in."[2] Even the Pitt children, we are told, had their part in the rejoicings; John, aged four, shouted "Hurrah!"

[1] Walpole, *Memoirs of the Reign of George II*, Vol. II. However, Pitt subsequently advised the King to repudiate the Convention.

[2] Lady Hester Pitt to William Pitt, August 26th, 1760

and little William, only fifteen months, scampered to his mother and kissed her for the welfare of the King of Prussia.

But in spite of the celebrations, it was soon apparent that Frederick was no nearer to a decision. In Germany and in all the surrounding countries that had experienced the devastation of battle, famine and distress stalked hand in hand, and with these horrors there came the inevitable revulsion amongst the people. Yet, in spite of the universal misery, in spite of the awful carnage, in spite of the accumulated misfortunes, the indomitable Frederick struggled on, grimly resolved to fight till the last man and the last beast should be destroyed or until he should lead his weary, blood-soaked troops to final and overwhelming victory.

While these tremendous events were soaking all Europe in blood, events scarcely less momentous were taking place in North America, where the English were making a gigantic effort to expel the French from Canadian soil. Here under Amherst's inspiring leadership, a great campaign was evolved for the simultaneous advance of three British armies. The first, starting from Virginia, was to capture Fort Duquesne and to advance on Montreal by way of the Great Lakes; the second, setting out from New York, was to take the Fort of Ticonderoga and Crown Point; the third was designed to attack Louisburg and advance down the Richelieu and St. Lawrence Rivers against Quebec. The troops under Amherst himself were completely successful, and Louisburg was speedily taken. News of this victory was joyfully received, and Pitt hastened to send a messenger on horseback to Hayes to apprise Hester. "My joy upon the news sent me by you, my Dearest Life, was inexpressible," she replied ecstatically, "so truly so that I have been obliged to take a whole hour to compose myself in, before I could find words to tell my Adored Man the infinite delight which I receive from this most glorious and happy event. Happy and glorious for my beloved England, happy and glorious for my most loved and admired Husband."[1] . . . And much more in the same vein. Ann Pitt, too, was overjoyed, and she celebrated the event in Bath. "I ordered a Bonfire," she wrote, "so placed as to be sure no bonfire ever was for the beauty, upon a rising ground before the Circus (where my Brother's House is), 10 hogsheads of strong beer round it, which drew all the company I cou'd desire, and enabled them to sing 'God Bless great George our King' with very good success, with the help of all the musick I cou'd get in the Circus. The whole town was illuminated, which, as it is the prettiest in the world, was the gayest thing I ever saw. I am in love with the place and have quite set my heart upon making it my home, especially since I have

---

[1] Lady Hester Pitt to William Pitt, August 18th, 1758.

seen a house made on purpose for me. . . ."[1] But Louisburg was not the
only success of this time, for Ticonderoga and Crown Point were also soon
taken. Unfortunately, however, General Abercromby, before Quebec,
suffered a severe repulse and was forced to beat a precipitate retreat. Thereafter, he remained in camp for the rest of the season until recalled by an
impatient minister in Downing Street. Meanwhile, others fared better:
Forts Frontenac and Oswego on Lake Ontario were captured by
Bradstreet, and gallant old Forbes seized Fort Duquesne and renamed it
Fort Pitt.[2]

The following summer, Admiral Boscawen at Lagos destroyed the
French fleet under de la Clue, which had put to sea from Toulon, and in
September Quebec was captured. This time our troops were commanded
by a general of thirty-two named James Wolfe, a man of a very different
type from Abercromby. Though odd in appearance and eccentric in
manner—"Mad is he?" said the king to one detractor, "then I wish he
would bite some of my other generals"—this red-headed, snub-nosed,
chinless young man was one of Pitt's *protégés*, and he had gone out to Canada
at the minister's earnest request, charged with the important task of capturing
Quebec. The glory of this enterprise is unquenchable; the battle lasted
but one hour at the end of which time the garrison had been overpowered
and the city taken.

Before the year was out, a great victory at sea removed all fear of a
French invasion. In November the Brest fleet under Conflans sallied
forth from harbour and was immediately pounced upon by the gallant
Hawke. In the ensuing fight, two of our ships went aground, but the
enemy flagship was burned, six others were destroyed, and many of the
rest of that splendid fleet of twenty-six ships were battered to splinters amid
the rocks and shoals of Quiberon Bay.[3]

But it was not only on the continent of Europe and in the Western
Hemisphere that Frenchmen and Englishmen faced each other in deadly
conflict, for in India, too, their opposing interests led to mutual rivalry.
We have seen how, largely owing to the force and ability of Governor Pitt,
the two East India Companies were in April 1702 united on terms very
favourable to the older Company, of which Pitt was so loyal and useful
a servant. Five years later, on March 3rd, 1707, old Aurangzib died at

[1] Ann Pitt to Lady Suffolk, August 26th (1758).

[2] Now the great city of Pittsburg.

[3] The greatness of Hawke's action consisted in his going into Quiberon Bay,
then held by many to be unsafe, in order to complete the destruction of Conflans'
ships.

the advanced age of eighty-nine after a reign of forty-six years, and at his death the power and glory of the Mogul Empire speedily waned. Chaos ensued. The north-west of India was invaded by the warlike Afghans, whilst central India fell a prey to the savage Mahratta princes who soon had in their power the feeble and degenerate successor of Aurangzib, still known by the proud but empty title of Great Mogul. Clearly the European traders in India, French and English alike, would soon be in peril, for they owed the security of their concessions to the protection of the Mogul, who now could protect them no longer. It was, therefore, not long before the merchants took sides in the conflict and allied themselves with one interest or the other, and a Frenchman of genius, Dupleix by name, Governor-General of all the French establishments, was soon scheming to drive the British out of India. Not unnaturally, the English civilians in India soon took fright, for the danger seemed extreme. Indeed, the whole province of the Carnatic, save Madras, fell into French hands and the prospect for the English along the Coromandel Coast looked gloomy in the extreme. At this moment the whole position was changed by the daring and skill of Robert Clive, an obscure English clerk in the service of the East India Company, who succeeded in convincing his employers that war with France was inevitable and that if Dupleix was not overcome the fate of Madras would be sealed. He further persuaded them to give him command of a small army with which he promptly seized Arcot, the capital town of the Carnatic, and defied all the efforts of the enemy to dislodge him. That was in 1751. By 1753, when Clive returned to England, he had driven the French out of the Carnatic and had brought about the disgrace of Dupleix and his recall to France.

Two years later, Clive returned to India with the rank of colonel to serve in the army of the East India Company. No sooner had he landed than he set about the subjugation and conquest of the great province of Bengal, then ruled by an unamiable youth, Surajah Dowlah by name, a drunken sadist with all the vices so often encountered in the harem-reared princes of the East. This monster and his depraved friends were consumed with a fanatical hatred of the British, and they only awaited an opportunity of venting their spleen on those they deemed their mortal foes. A pretext was easily found, and when the English merchants at Calcutta, in expectation of war with France, began to fortify their settlement without having obtained express permission from the Nabob, Surajah Dowlah immediately marched against Fort William, arrested the servants of the Company and their families there, and at a season when the fierce heat of Bengal is scarcely tolerable to the native, let alone to the European, thrust his one hundred and forty-six prisoners into a tiny guard-room, known by the fearful name of the Black Hole of Calcutta. From this dreadful ordeal only twenty-three survived. To avenge this barbarous, inhuman crime, Clive was sent from Madras with a small force. Fortunately, Surajah Dowlah, a coward surrounded by traitors, promptly fled, and his companions hastened to betray their ruler to the English. On June 23rd, 1756, with a force of no more than 3,000 men, Clive defeated some 50,000 at Plassey. Surajah Dowlah was captured shortly after the battle, and on his deposition Meer Jaffeir, one of the traitors who had betrayed him, was made Nabob in his place. The deposed ruler, brought before his triumphant successor, grovelled in the dust and jabbering in the paroxysms of his fear begged for mercy; but that divine quality which he had never shown to his victims was not to be granted him at this dread hour. Mouthing and bellowing in his agony of terror, the ruthless slayer was dragged forth from the presence of his betrayer to a secret chamber, and there remorselessly done to death by barbarous, unknown hands.

This was the posture of events abroad when in the autumn of 1760 George II suddenly died. On the morning of October 25th, he rose at his usual hour of six o'clock, "looked, I suppose, if all his money was in his purse,"[1] and drank his chocolate. Shortly afterwards, the attendants heard a heavy fall followed by a stifled groan, and rushing in found the king on the floor having cut his right temple against a bureau. He gave but one gasp and expired. Lady Yarmouth, hastily summoned, sent a servant hurrying for Princess Amelia, who was not, however, informed of the fatal event. The Princess, who was nearly blind and very deaf, fancying that the king spoke to her, leaned over him and put her face close to his in an effort to catch his words. Then for the first time did she perceive that she had lost her father for ever.

We left young Tom Pitt at Cambridge, where, since his father's departure for the Continent, he had been maintained by his uncles Lyttelton and Pitt. And to this favoured undergraduate there came one of the first letters written by his relative from his new home at Hayes. "Lady Hester was safely delivered this morning of a son. She and the child are as well as possible, and the father in the joy of his heart. It is no small addition to my happiness to know you will kindly share it with me. A father must form wishes for his child as soon as it comes into the world, and I will make mine—that he may live to make as good use of his life, as one that shall be nameless is

[1] Walpole to Montagu, "Arlington Street, October 26th, 1760. I tell a lie, I am at Mr. Chute's."

now doing at Cambridge. . . ."[1] More will be heard in due course of the
infant, christened John, whose entry into the world was thus heralded by a
proud and loving father.

Tom Pitt was a frequent visitor to his uncle and aunt during the vacations
from Cambridge, and another member of the family came to Hayes in
July 1757, for Ann Pitt returned from her long sojourn abroad. "Lady
Hester's Behaviour," she wrote to Lady Suffolk, "has been upon that occasion, and upon every other since her marriage, beyond what I can give you
any notion of, but by her own letters, which I have kept, and will show you,
and which have given me a most sincere esteem and friendship for her.
But I was so sunk, and my mind so overcome with all I have suffered, and
I do not believe anything in the world could have made it possible for me
to get out of this country but my brother's sending a friend to my assistance . . ." She was eager to come home, but she was ill and the journey
difficult. ". . . 7 days from Lyons to Sens where I came very much fatigued
and even with a little fever, which I did not want, and was too happy to
stop in Me de Villette's house . . ." where she was well looked after. She was
full of praises for the kindness of her brother ". . . who has always seem'd
to guess and understand all I felt of every kind, and has carried his delicacy
so far as never once to put me in mind of what I felt more strongly than
any other part of my misfortune, which was how very disagreeable and
embarrassing it must be to him to have me in France. You may believe
I will be out of it the first minute that is possible. . . ."[2]

She stayed with the Pitts for some months and then visited Clifton
and Bath in search of relief from the gout. "I think I am better in some
respects," she wrote to Lady Suffolk from Clifton, "but as nobody thinks a
long course of these waters wou'd be good for me I shall get to Tunbridge as soon as I can. I propose leaving this place next week but as I

---

[1] William Pitt to Thomas Pitt, Hayes, October 10th, 1756. He also wrote to
George Grenville the same day—"Lady Hester is as well as can be in her situation—
She had a sharp time, but not longer than two hours and a half. There was notice
enough to have Hunter and all comforts about us. . . . Mrs. Grenville, I am sure,
and perhaps you, will forgive my talking nursery: the young man meets with general
applause for stature and strength: Nurse Cresswell looks with satisfaction, and Nurse
Long with envy, upon such quality and quantity. He is, however, as they flatter
me, without appearance of heaviness, notwithstanding his size." William Pitt to
Grenville, Hayes, October 10th, 1756. Another child, christened Hester, had been
born to the Pitts at the Pay Office about September of the previous year. The
Dictionary of National Biography gives the date of Hester's birth as October 18th, but
this cannot be correct as Pitt makes mention of the child,—"the little woman" he
calls her—at an earlier date. William Pitt to Lady Hester Pitt, September 20th, 1755.

[2] Ann Pitt to Lady Suffolk, Sens, July 10th (1757).

have some complaints that are not convenient for a courtier, such as pains in my limbs and swellings in my legs, I shall try bathing a few days at the Bath, rather than Buxton, which my Brother advised me to since I have been here, as thinking what I believe to be true that my disorders come from a want of perspiration, but I hope Tunbridge will do me good, and if it does I shall be glad to try one winter with my friends in England before I go abroad again. . . ."[1] At Bath, where we find her two months later, she consulted Ralph Allen's friend, Dr. William Oliver, famous for the biscuit, who is "Very sure I am gouty and shou'd have the gout. . . ."[2] In due course she returned to London, apparently in a sudden and insane desire to marry the wealthy Lord Bath, then in his seventy-fifth year. "I hear my Lord Bath is here very lively, but I have not seen him, which I am very sorry for, because I want to offer myself to him. I am quite in earnest and have set my heart upon it; so I beg seriously you will carry it in your mind, and think if you could find any way to help me. . . . He can want nothing but a companion that wou'd like his company, and in my situation I shou'd not desire to make the bargain without that circumstance, and tho' all I have been saying puts me in mind of some advertisements I have seen in the news papers from gentlewomen in distress, I will not take that method, but I want to recollect whether you did not once tell me as I think you did many years ago that he once spoke so well of me that he got anger for it at home where I never was a favourite . . ."[3] Fortunately perhaps for both of them, Ann's wish was never fulfilled.

In the winter of 1758, William found a curious means of making use of his sister's services. The French, it appears, had captured a bundle of unsigned letters, which, as they requested an answer to Lady Yarmouth's lodgings in Kensington, they imagined to be from Lady Yarmouth herself. That virtuous lady in her distress appealed to Pitt for assistance, and he persuaded his sister to write to her friends at the Court of Versailles and explain the mistake.[4] So successful was the plan that William and Hester were especially requested to thank Ann on Lady Yarmouth's behalf.[5]

But if William and Hester Pitt could make use of Ann when it suited them, they were not always so pleased to see her in London. Thus when

[1] Ann Pitt to Lady Suffolk, "Clifton, June the 22nd." (1758).

[2] Ann Pitt to Lady Suffolk, "Bath, August 19th." (1758).

[3] Ann Pitt to Lady Suffolk, Friday, November 10th (1758).

[4] William Pitt to Ann Pitt, "St. James's Square, Nov. 7th, 1758."

[5] William Pitt to Ann Pitt, "Saturday morning," and Lady Hester Pitt to Ann Pitt, "St. James's Square, Friday, Nov. 14th."

at about this time[1] the restless woman, depressed and in poor health, came
from the west of England to the Capital in the hope of a pleasant reception
from her brother and his wife, she was chagrined to receive an angry letter
from Hester explaining that the great Mr. Pitt was too busy to write himself.
"He is very sorry to find that you are ill," she wrote, "and wishes me to
tell you that you have mistaken him in thinking he meant to express any
Desire of His as to your going, or staying, which he always meant to leave
to your own Decision, but only to offer you his opinion, and never proposes to take upon Him to give you any further advice with regard to the
place of your Residence which you have all right independent of anything
with respect to Him to determine as you please for yourself. I am extremely
concerned to hear your disorder is increas'd so much as to have made your
return to Kensington necessary, as I fear your situation There must be very
uncomfortable and disagreeable, without servants, or any of those con-
veniences which are so particularly of consequence when any body is ill.
I hope most sincerely to have the pleasure of hearing you are better, and
able to prosecute whatever may be thought best for your Health."[2] Empty
words ! Would not an offer of help have been kinder ? So apparently
thought Ann, who seems to have written her brother to reprove him for
such unfeeling conduct towards her. The letter is not preserved, but it
drew a defensive reply. "I desire to assure you that all Idea of *quarrel* or
unkindness, (words I am grieved to find you cou'd employ) was never
further from my mind than during your stay in this neighbourhood," he
wrote. "On the contrary, my Dear Sister, nothing but kindness and
regard to your good on the whole has made me judge it necessary that we
shou'd not meet during the continueance you think fit to give to an excursion so unexpected and so hurtfull to you. I beg my dear Sister not to
mistake my wishes to see Her set down for a time, quiet and contented
within her own resources of Patience and fortitude (merely as being best
and only fit thing for Herself) so very widely as to suppose that my situation
as a Publick Person is any way concern'd in her residing in one place or
another. All I meant is that, *for your own sake*, you should abstain from all
desultory jaunts, such as the present, the hearing of you, all at once, at
Sion, next at Kensington, then every day going, and now not yet gone,

---

[1] As the three letters quoted below are not dated with the year, it is impossible
to fix the exact time of Ann's unfortunate visit to London. As, however, Lady
Hester's letters are addressed from St. James's Square, they must have been written
later than Lady Day 1759, when the Pitts took a lease of the house there, now
known as Chatham House, and as she signs herself H. Pitt, they must have been
written before October 1761, when she was created Baroness Chatham.

[2] Lady Hester Pitt to Ann Pitt, "St. James's Square, Monday, January 29th."

certainly carries an appearance disadvantageous to you in this view; I have refused myself the pleasure of seeing you; as considering your journey and hovering about London as too imprudent and restless, or as too mysterious, for me not to discourage such conduct by remaining unmixt with it. This is the only cause of my not seeing you, nor can I give you a more real proof of my affectionate regard for your welfare than by thus refusing myself a great pleasure and, I fear, giving you a Pain. I offer you no advice as to the choice of your residence. I am persuaded you want none. You have a right and are well able to judge for yourself in this point, but if you will not fix some where you are undone."[1]

Ann was clearly hurt, but she wrote a dignified reply: "Dear Brother, I am going to set out to return to Bath, but as the letter I receiv'd from you yesterday leaves me in great anxiety and perplexity of mind, I can not set out without assuring you, as I do with the most exact truth, that there was no mistery in my journey here, nor no purpose but the relief I proposed to my mind. If I had known before I left the Bath that you disapproved of my leaving that place at this time, or of my coming to Town, I wou'd not have done as I have done, and wou'd not even have come near it, tho' the advice given me at Oxford with regard to my health, made me desire to make use of the interval in which I was order'd not to try the waters again, to have the pleasure and satisfaction of seeing you and some of my friends, and as I hoped that satisfaction from you in the first place, I will not dissemble that I am very much disappointed and mortified in not having seen you, but as the hurry of important business you are in, and the relief necessary to make you go through it, made it possible for me not to interpret your not seeing me as a mark of unkindness, I never used the word but to guard against other people rising it, upon a circumstance which I thought they had nothing to do with.

"When I writ you word from the Bath that I had thoughts of coming to Town for Christmas, I desired nothing so much as to do what was most proper according to my situation, and consequently to have your advice, which I told you very sincerely I wish'd to be guided by preferably to every other consideration, you best know how I am to attain the end I have steadily desired for years, as you know I writ you word from France (before my spirits were as much disordered as they have been since) that I desired nothing so much as a safe and honourable retreat, that wou'd leave me the enjoyment of my Friends, without which help and support I find by a pain-full experience that it is impossible for me to support myself."[2]

[1] William Pitt to Ann Pitt, undated.
[2] Ann Pitt to William Pitt. As this letter in the original MS. is undated and unsigned, it may have been a copy kept by Ann for future reference.

There does not seem to be much of the old gay Ann of those happy far-off Court days in this melancholy letter. But Ann Pitt was genuinely ill. "I set out yesterday because I understood you desired it," she wrote to William, "but as I was not well enough to travel, I was so ill at the first stage, that the apothecary who saw me thought as I did myself that it wou'd be impossible for me to get safe to the Bath if I persued my journey, therefore I came back here and hope you will approve of my taking the rest and quiet that is indeed very necessary."[1] We do not know William's reaction to this, but it is good to hear of her a few years later back at her house in Kensington Gravel Pits, then of course the heart of the country, and entertaining the fashionable world at what Horace Walpole called Pitsburg.[2] "They ask me a thousand questions about Pitsburg; I tell them it is a vile *guinguette*, that has nothing but verdure, and prospect, and a parcel of wild trees that have never been cut into any shape, and as awkward as if they had been transplanted out of Paradise; that you fancy you are making something of the house, but that you have been too long out of France not to have lost all taste; that you will not have so much as an antechamber full of cooks, chafing dishes, and footmen in dirty nightcaps."

"We had last Monday the prettiest ball that ever was seen at Mrs. Anne Pitt's, in the compass of a silver penny," he wrote to his friend, Lord Hertford. "There were one hundred and four persons, of which fifty-five supped. The supper-room was disposed with tables and benches back to back, in the manner of an ale-house. The idea sounds ill; but the fairies had so improved upon it, had so be-garlanded, so sweetened, and so desserted it, that it looked like a vision. I told her she could not have fed and stowed so much company by a miracle, and that, when we were gone, she would take up twelve buckets full of people. The Duchess of Bedford asked me before Madame de Guerchy, if I would not give them a ball at Strawberry. Not for the universe. . . ."[3] And later the same year—"I am just come from a little impromptu ball at Mrs. Ann Pitt's. . . . It was entertaining to see the Duchess of Bedford and Lady Bute with their respective forces, drawn up on either side of the room. . . ."[4] Indeed, Ann must have been good company; she enjoyed entertaining, was musical, sang a little, was an enthusiastic patron of performers on French horns, and on at least one occasion brought a troupe to a party of Horace

[1] Ann Pitt to William Pitt, "Kensington, Sunday night."

[2] Walpole to Ann Pitt, Paris, October 8th, 1765.

[3] Walpole to Hertford, Arlington Street, February 24th, 1764. Walpole often spelt the Christian name Anne, but it was usually spelt without the final "e."

[4] Walpole to Hertford, Arlington Street, December 3rd, 1764.

Walpole's to entertain his guests. When well, and not being bullied by her brother, she had a bright and lively manner, and was intensely popular with the lord of Strawberry Hill and his gay friends. "My resolutions of growing old and staid are admirable," wrote Horace Walpole jokingly to Lord Hervey, "I wake with a sober plan and intend to pass the day with my friends—then comes the Duke of Richmond and hurries me down to Whitehall to dinner—then the Duchess of Grafton sends for me to loo in Upper Grosvenor Street—before I can get thither, I am begged to step to Kensington, to give Mrs. Anne Pitt my opinion about a bow-window—after the loo, I am to march back to Whitehall to supper—and after that am to walk with Miss Pelham on the terrace till two in the morning, because it's moonlight and her chair is not come."[1] Great fun! But Ann entertained staider company than gossiping Walpole. "Yesterday morning the Duchess insisted on my going with her to see Mrs. Anne Pitt's little improvements," wrote Mrs. Delany, "as out of a very ugly old house, and a flat piece of ground, with a little dirty pond in the middle of it, she had made an uncommon pretty place; she says she has 'hurt her understanding' in contriving to make it so. . . ."[2]

But to return to Tom Pitt. If he was a frequent guest at his uncle's table and a favoured recipient of his uncle's advice, he was already in these early days beginning to display his Pitt-like inability to remain for long on friendly terms with his family. For some time, as we have seen, William had contributed to the cost of his nephew's education, but gradually as he found his own expenses rising he had pleaded poverty as an excuse for contributing less to his maintenance. Tom did not suffer in the slightest, for his Lyttelton uncle cheerfully assumed those responsibilities that Pitt could no longer support, but young Pitt chose to make this a grievance, and he subsequently wrote in scathing terms of the parsimony of the one uncle in contrast to the generosity of the other. Thus, when a few years later Pitt had again to announce a birth in his family, he did so to his brother-in-law, Grenville,[3] only and ignored his nephew. The name of this son, like the name of his father, was William Pitt.

When in London, Tom was in the habit of staying with his Lyttelton uncle, and it was in the course of one of these visits in 1759 that he received a note telling him that an old friend would be glad to see him at a certain tavern in Bond Street. Thither he repaired with all haste to encounter to his great astonishment his father home from his travels.

[1] Walpole to Hervey, June 11th, 1765.
[2] Mrs. Delany to Mrs. Dewes, Whitehall, August 25th, 1768. The duchess was presumably Mrs. Delany's intimate friend, the Duchess of Portland.
[3] William Pitt to Grenville, Hayes, May 28th, 1759.

For three years Thomas Pitt senior and his daughters had remained abroad. "A letter from those good girls, my sisters, has just come to my hands, and I doubt not you will partake of my joy and satisfaction to hear they are in good health; the letter is dated from Rouen, but they are going to Paris," wrote Tom to his Uncle. "They give a charming account of Normandy, and seem at present in the best of spirits that could be hoped for; indeed, the people are civil and every body is good humoured."[1] At Utrecht they fell in with young Lord Shelburne, then nineteen, who was so much charmed by Pitt's company that he spent the whole night talking with him. Pitt, it appears, abounded in anecdotes of the Prince of Wales and his circle, was full of his own grievances, and branded his brother with every form of abuse. Had he not assisted that thankless brother with money, when they had been boys together? Had he not been instrumental in obtaining for him the Cornetcy of Horse? Sir Robert Walpole had offered him, Thomas, any terms not to bring his brother and his brother-in-law Lyttelton, into parliament; had he not preferred his family's interests to his own and thereby laid the foundations of William's future greatness? And how had his ungrateful brother repaid him for all these sacrifices? "Sorry am I to say," wrote Camelford from information doubtless supplied by his aggrieved parent, "that dividing soon after in their political systems in which my Father was shipwreck'd at the time that his Brother rose to the top of everything, there was not a moment through the course of their lives when these obligations seem to have been remember'd, tho the situation of my Father when his Brother was first Minister was so reduced as to solicit in vain the appointment to the Swiss Cantons as an object of his ambition." But it was not only an appointment to the Swiss Cantons that Thomas Pitt had been seeking, for though abroad, he had not let the Duke of Newcastle forget him. A certain Mr. Potter, the Member for Oakhampton, had died, and Pitt wishes "to succeed him in his employment and in his vacant seat in Parliament" in place of his pension of £1,000 a year. "I flatter myself my pretension will not appear altogether trivial or despicable, or my application unreasonable." Then he adds mendaciously: "I am upon my return to England, an agreement being made between me and my son, by which my affairs will soon be accommodated."[2] But the duke has already recommended Admiral Rodney for the seat in parliament, and he also cannot oblige Pitt

---

[1] Thomas Pitt to William Pitt, Cambridge, March 29th, 1755. William replied: "I rejoice extremely to hear that your father and the girls are not unentertained in their travels." William Pitt to Thomas Pitt, Pay Office, April 9th, 1755.

[2] Thomas Pitt to Newcastle, "Utrecht, 28th June 1759."

in respect of the Irish Employment vacant by Potter's death, which, he is careful to explain, "is one of the most beneficial ones in the King's Disposal, and as Mr. Potter's Death had been long expected, I have been under Engagement for it for some Time, and have on that account refused many applications, which have been made to me for it."[1] Pitt, of course, was deeply mortified. "I have stood in an other light . . . and now to find myself so sunk is mortifying indeed. It raises very unhappy reflections, because I cannot account for this change from any other cause than the disorder in my private affairs, brought upon me meerly by my misfortunes. . . ."[2] Later in the same year he borrowed £1,000 from his agent, Robert Andrews, on the understanding that he, Pitt, would cause Lord Pulteney to be re-elected for the pocket borough of Old Sarum, and on other conditions;[3] but history does not relate whether they were ever fulfilled!

But if Tom was astonished to see his father back in England, he was also alarmed, for he was in considerable risk of being arrested for debt. His son, therefore, could hardly have welcomed the news that his father had walked openly from Westminster Bridge, and that as he thought he was in bad health he had resolved to come home with the object of coming to arrangements with him and his creditors whereby he might be enabled to take up his residence in England once more. He made his son promise to keep his return a dead secret, even from Lyttelton, and it was not until he had extracted this promise that he would permit young Tom to go in quest of a safe place for him to hide in.

Tom Pitt was just twenty-one, and as a result of his father's return there now fell to his lot the unenviable task of unravelling the tangled skein of his parent's affairs, his sisters' dowries, acrimonious discussions with his aunt, Mary Pitt,[4] who demanded money which she maintained was owed her by her recalcitrant brother, and endless interviews with the great William, who definitely and firmly declined "coming into the proposal

---

[1] Newcastle to Thomas Pitt, "Newcastle House, July 6th. 1759."

[2] Thomas Pitt to Newcastle, "Hague, July 10th. 1759."

[3] "An Agreement made this fifth day of December 1759 between Thomas Pitt the Elder of Boconnoc in the County of Cornwall Esquire of the one part and Robert Andrews of the Parish of St. George Hanover Square of the other part. . . ."

[4] Mary Pitt (1725-1782), the youngest of the family. She never married and little is known of her. She is thus described by Lord Camelford: "She had neither the beauty of two of her sisters, nor the wit and talents of her sister Ann, nor the diabolical dispositions of her sister Betty. She must always, I believe, do right to the best of her judgement, but that judgement was liable to be warped by prejudice and by a peculiar twist in her understanding which made it very dangerous to have transactions with her."

you mention with regard to my name appearing among the Creditors who are to sign the Letter of Licence in question." And even if he could conquer his natural repugnance to the plan, ". . . not the smallest advantage to the unhappy man in question can possibly result from it. If the *hostile* creditors are disposed for their own sakes to sign a letter of Licence, your Father is safe, and if they are not so disposed, my signature wou'd draw none after it. May every facility attend you, my Dear Nephew, in the good work of filial Duty! and I desire here to repeat to you in the most earnest manner my strongest Instances, that you will put the consideration of me and mine entirely out of the question."[1]

Some idea of the state of things between the brothers may be gathered from Tom's account of the transactions. First, William demanded repayment of the £500, together with interest, which had been advanced for a seat in parliament at Old Sarum; then he claimed satisfaction for the interest he had in a house in Pall Mall which many years before had been sold to Lord Temple. The first of these claims Thomas Pitt admitted; the second he indignantly denied. "My father with amazement denied any such promise—call'd upon him to produce proof of it in writing or by word of mouth; or any witness that for 30 years since the transaction the claim had been made upon him. He gave the lie direct to the fact. . . . What," asks the despairing Tom, "what could a son answer to a Father under such circumstances? My Father protested he would not yield—my Uncle persisted in the demand—I enforced it with entreaties—my Father lost all temper—reproach'd me in the bitterest terms, broke off all further treaty and forbade me his House. My poor sisters by this means thrown off at once from all their hopes betook themselves to supplicate their Uncle in the most moving stile to consider the situation of them and the family and for their sakes to desist from his pretensions—he haughtily replied that he had given his determination thro his Attorney which he should abide by." Was ever a young man in such a quandary?

But at last the task was fulfilled, at last what he deemed his duty was done: "I bound myself to pay my father's debts," he wrote, "gave £5,000 a piece to my sisters, settled the claim of Mrs. Mary, calculated principal and interest with Mr. W. Pitt; in short I left not one person or claim unsatisfied." When all these negotiations were completed, Thomas Pitt and his two daughters went to live at Abbot's Anne, a small estate of his in Hampshire, and young Tom, doubtless feeling that he deserved a holiday, set off for a tour on the Continent.[2] "Young Mr. Pitt, nephew of *the* Pitt,

[1] William Pitt to Thomas Pitt, Hayes, June 16th, 1759.
[2] *Observations on a Tour to Portugal and Spain, 1760*, by John, Earl of Strathmore and Thomas Pitt, Esq. Brit. Mus. Cole's MSS. Vol. XLIV.

is setting out for Lisbon with Lord Kinnoul," wrote Horace Walpole, "and will proceed through Granada to Italy, with his friend Lord Strathmore. . . . Mr. Pitt is not only the most ingenius young man, but the most amiable one; he has already acted in the most noble style—I don't mean that he took a quarter of Quebec, or invaded a bit of France, or has spoken in the House of Commons better than Demosthenes nephew; but he has an odious father, and has insisted on glorious cuttings of entails on himself, that his father's debts may be paid and his sisters proved for."[1] Accompanying the two friends was another young man, Philip Francis by name, one day to acquire a sinister fame. "Lord Strathmore and Mr. Pitt are most amiable young men," he assured his father, "so that I cannot travel in better company."[2] But his next letter gave ominous news. "Young Mr. Pitt is troubled with fits," he wrote. "He had one last night so terrible that he cannot be moved."[3] As he became older, poor Tom Pitt grew out of the affliction, but it was to darken the whole of his early life.

We soon have news of the travellers in Lisbon, whence Tom wrote a spritely letter to his uncle, the dean. "The Country could be beautiful if it had Trees or Grass," he wrote, "but Olive yards, Vineyards and orange gardens which are better in description than reality supply the place of the one and patches of barley which with straw is the only fodder for their mules and horses, serves instead of natural Verdure. The Climate however is so fine that it embellishes every scene and gives every thing a peculiar cheerfulness. The weather is they say uncommonly hot for the season, the Spring is so far advanced that we have Ranunculus, Hyacinths and Jessamine, and even Roses in the Gardens, not to mention peas and strawberries which are extremely good . . . One thing you would miss exceedingly which is butter, for as they have no grass, they can have no milk and all their butter comes from Holland or Ireland. . . ." Most of the town has been destroyed by a recent earthquake. "They have still frequent shocks, one not six weeks ago but they do no mischief." Then follow some comic remarks on the Spanish. "The people are more wretched than can be imagined, poverty seems to preside universaly among all ranks of people and makes their pride appear more ridiculous. If two muleteers or Carters meet in the street they never fail to take off their hats gravely to each other and salute each other with the title of Signor, as if they were the first Nobility of the country. Murthers are here so

[1] Walpole to Mann, Strawberry Hill, February 3rd, 1760. Lord Kinnoul was British Ambassador to Portugal.

[2] Philip Francis to Dr. Philip Francis, Portsmouth, February 14th, 1760.

[3] Philip Francis to Dr. Philip Francis, Portsmouth, February 21st, 1760.

common that there is little notice taken of them, and if you see them happen
under your Window you have nothing to do but retire. Blows are look'd
upon as the height of infamy and if anyone chooses here to play the Buck
and thresh his footman or a man who affronts him in the street he may
depend upon being stab'd for it on the first opportunity so that he has
nothing to do but to be beforehand with him. Yet there is no servant in
your house the meanest creature who would kill a calf tho' he has no scruple
about sheep, poultry, etc., but you must send for a profest. Butcher for
that purpose they being already infamous and marrying into each other's
familys. In short their manners and customs are so strange that I shall not
be sorry to leave them which I shall do as soon as Lent is over."[1] Three
months later, the travellers are in Madrid. "I arrived at Madrid the 3rd
of this month after a very tedious and uncomfortable journey thro' the
worst of Spain," wrote Thomas to his uncle William, "and have endeavoured to entertain myself here ever since as well as I am able in expectation of the great festivals upon the King's Entry which is still put off
for some days. . . . Since we have been in Madrid Lord Bristol presented
me to the Royal Family, the King was very gracious and hoped we should
find more amusement at Naples than he feared we should in Spain. . . .
We propose staying here still some time till the King's Entry and the
Festivals are over, after which we intend making a Tour into the South of
Spain . . . and thro the south of France to Turin, having obtained a Passport
from Versailles, by means of the French Ambassador at Lisbon."[2] Early
in the following year, we find the travellers in Genoa. "A fortnight ago
I had two sheets from Mr. Pitt, dated Genoa, Dec. 23," wrote a friend to
Thomas Gray, the poet. "He spends the winter with Sir Richard Lyttelton,
and hopes to pass the end of the carnival at Milan with Lord Strathmore,
who has been ill at Turin, but is now quite recovered."[3]

It was not long before Thomas Pitt senior was suffering further misfortunes. Needless to say, he did not fulfil his promise to make his son an
allowance, and young Tom was forced to file a bill in Chancery against him,
though he later regretted having done so, believing that his father really
was not in a position to pay. And then on top of that trouble, his two
daughters left him. Christian, the younger, had become engaged to a
certain Thomas Saunders, who until recently had been Governor of Madras
and had just returned to England with a considerable fortune. At first
Thomas Pitt encouraged the match, but later he put all manner of difficulties

[1] Thomas Pitt to Lyttelton, "Lisbon, 24th, 1760 March."
[2] Thomas Pitt to William Pitt, Madrid, June 30th, 1760.
[3] Brown to Gray, London, February 9th, 1761.

in the way of the lovers so that they determined to marry in secret. The inevitable quarrel ensued, as the result of which they left the house taking Amelia with them. "Let me congratulate you on the marriage of Miss Kitty Pitt," wrote Mrs. Montagu to Dean Lyttelton, "she is a rich and happy bride. Governor Saunders has charmed Lord Lyttelton by his good sense and behaviour. Miss Emily is with her sister and I hope they will live very happily. It must be a great felicity to these young Ladies to live under the dominion of a reasonable and worthy man, after having suffered all that pride, passion and tyranny could inflict; and I hope our friend at Lisbon will feel himself relieved of many cares. He could not but feel himself solicitous for young Ladies in their situation."[1]

The desertion of his daughters drove Thomas Pitt distracted. At first the half-demented man had thoughts of returning to Switzerland, then of staying on at Abbot's Anne, then of retiring to Cornwall; but his restless, crazy spirit for long would not let him come to any decision. Then his creditors became pressing once more, and there was only one way of escaping their attentions: he must enter the House of Commons and as an M.P. elude their importunities. "As to his own burroughs he now tells me his affairs are such that they cannot be finally ended under eight or nine months," wrote his agent to Newcastle, "and till they are ended, he shall be liable to arrests and vexatious actions from his creditors, and therefore he proposed to choose Mr. Coke at Okehampton, and one other at Old Sarum, that shall be named, and to fill the other seat at O. S. himself, under an engagement to relinquish it at the time his affairs are settled, which he thinks will be before the House meets next winter, and therefore intends to make no use of his election, but to secure himself from his creditors. . . ."[2] And then a few days later: "He bids me assure your Grace with the utmost truth and sincerity, that he has fairly and honestly no other motive to desire being chosen at O. S. than what I have mentioned . . . and that he will religiously keep his engagement to vacate his seat again, when his perplexities are ended, to whoever he shall be directed to fill it with."[3]

So at the General Election of 1761 Thomas Pitt was duly elected Member of Parliament for the pocket borough of Old Sarum, and was thus enabled to laugh at his creditors from the safe portals of the House of Commons. And the creditors must have been pressing, indeed, for there had been some hitch in the promised pension, and recently Newcastle had required a letter from Pitt with regard to it. To this, Pitt replied: ". . . I readily comply (although I must own that such a requisition implies some suspicion to my

[1] Mrs. Montagu to Lyttelton, March 1760.
[2] Andrews to Newcastle, February 28th, 1761.
[3] Andrews to Newcastle, March 2nd, 1761.

THOMAS PITT, son of Robert Pitt

Artist unknown

prejudice) . . ."[1] But that, of course, was all nonsense, and at last Pitt
realized that he had been deceived by the slippery duke, as so many of his
contemporaries had been duped before him. Thomas was furious. ". . .
this agreement was concluded several months ago, and in consequence of it,
on my part, every point is perform'd . . . that has yet fallen into my power
to perform, but the only article in my favor remains still unperform'd.
What has been the pretences (for pretences I am very sorry now to find they
were) for what I then looked upon to be only delays in the performance on
your Grace's side?" The first excuse was that he had "incurr'd the displeasure of Lord Bute by some engagements I had made concerning the
Burrough of Bossiney . . ." and he well remembers the duke "pressing me
to submit to his Lordship's desire and give up my agreement at that place . . ."
Then another excuse was found ". . . the hurry of the Elections, which
postpon'd my affairs; and then the hurry of affairs in Germany was made a
reason for deferring the putting the last hand to it; and last of all . . . I am
told that for the finishing my affair . . . there wanted only my writing a
letter to your Grace . . . setting out various facts" yet having done all that
had been required of him, the duke informs him that ". . . the annuity for
my life will not be granted without some stronger assurance that O.S. shall
be at the K . . . g's disposal for my life also.   My Lord Duke," he adds
furiously, "Is that just? Is that honest? It is super-adding a condition
after the agreement was made . . .   I do positively assert that this very same
point was mention'd early in the beginning of the negotiation and I did
absolutely reject it, and farther I do affirm that, had it been insisted on, the
negotiation would have been stopt short. . . .   For God's sake! my Lord
Duke, if this which is now requir'd is the *sine qua non* of the executing the
only article of the agreement in my favor, how comes it that it has been kept
in reserve till now? Why was it not declar'd at the first? . . ."[2]   In
January 1706, his grandfather, the old Governor, had written to his son,
Robert, Thomas Pitt's father, in these terms: "If you are in Parliament, show
yourself on all occasions a good Englishman, and a faithful servant to your
country. If you aspire to fame in the House, you must make yourself
master of its precedents and orders. Avoid faction, and never enter the
House pre-possessed, but attend diligently to the debate, and vote according
to your conscience and not for any sinister end whatever. I had rather see
any child of mine want than to have him get his bread by voting in the
House of Commons."[3]   How far the old man's grandson had fallen from
these standards!

[1] Thomas Pitt to Newcastle, "Chettel Down, near Blandford, May 30th. 1761."
[2] Thomas Pitt to Newcastle, "Chettel Down, near Blandford, June 29th. 1761."
[3] Thomas Pitt to Robert Pitt, Fort St. George, January 16th, 1705-6.

Delighted, no doubt, at his ingenuity, Thomas suddenly determined to take unto himself a second wife, and he secretly married the daughter of a certain General Murray. After the wedding the bride and bridegroom went to the Dower House at Boconnoc, which had been specially prepared for their reception; but no sooner had they arrived in Cornwall than he fell ill, and a fortnight later had a stroke and died. "Is Sir Richard Lyttelton with you, and Mr. Pitt?" asked Horace Walpole of Mann. "The latter's father was just married again; but to make his son some amends for giving away a jointure of £600 a year, is just dead—very happily for his family."[1] His son was in Italy with Sir Richard Lyttelton. "It was at St. Cassiano that the same post brought me a letter from the poor man to notify his marriage and one from my uncle to inform me of his death." "I am sorry to write to you on a melancholy occasion, and to impart to you the loss of one so near to you. Your Father was seised with an apoplexy ye 10th. and, notwithstanding all proper assistance, expired ye next day, at Chettle Down. This event was notify'd to me by Mr. Murray, father of Mrs. Pitt, now a Relict, and I conceive jointured on your Estate. I hope this will find you in perfect health."[2] On receipt of these tidings, Tom hurried back to England, there to be greeted by further news that caused him infinitely more sorrow: his sister, Christian, had died after the birth of a child. Mrs. Montagu was signally mistaken in her estimate of Saunders. "I am not surprised at what you say of Governor Saunders' absurdity and brutal disposition," wrote Sir Richard Lyttelton in a letter of condolence to his nephew. "He must have been a brute indeed to have behaved ill to poor Kitty, who certainly had sweetness of temper and complacency enough to have reclaimed and softened the most obdurate nature. But since she was so unfortunately circumstanced, it was on the whole better for her (tho' poor creature, she deserved a better lot) and better for you, who would have often been made unhappy by her sufferings and could never have had any pleasure or comfort in her society, that God should have taken her out of a situation that threatened so much misery."[3]

Back in England, Tom Pitt determined to settle down. At first he lodged for a while in Sir Richard Lyttelton's house, but later he took a small residence at Twickenham, thus becoming a neighbour of Horace Walpole. "Mr. T. Pitt has taken a small house at Twickenham within a stone's throw of me. This will add to the comfort of my Strawberry-tide. He draws Gothic with taste, and is already engaged on the ornaments of

---

[1] Walpole to Mann, Strawberry Hill, July 3rd, 1761.

[2] William Pitt to Thomas Pitt, St. James's Square, July 21st, 1761.

[3] Lyttelton to Thomas Pitt, June 1761.

my cabinet and gallery."[1] It was not long before young Pitt found a name for his house which should remind him of his travels. "I am very happy, as I told you, in my new neighbour, Mr. Pitt; he calls his small house Palazzo Pitti; which does not look as if he had forgotten you, and sounds pleasantly in my ears."[2] Later, the wanderer paid a visit to Boconnoc, and a dismal scene of desolation met his eyes. The furniture had been auctioned. Nothing remained but the books, which were heirlooms, and a few boxes of old China saved from the clutches of the creditors. The gardens were overgrown, the walks could no longer be distinguished, and the woods had been practically destroyed. Great groves of ancient oaks had been cut down within sight of the windows, and the very lawns had been broken up and left in ridge and furrow. At first poor Tom was discouraged at the awful scene of ruin that met his eyes, but gradually he recovered; and then he determined to restore the home he loved to some degree of order. He fitted up beds in the attics, chairs and tables in the old dining-room and the library, and so he contrived to make it possible to pass a few summer months there in tolerable comfort. Similarly, without doors he slowly recovered the gardens from the shambles they had become and managed to restore the beautiful park to something of its former glory. This was a labour of love, indeed, and young Tom worked with a will to make his home habitable once more.

A few years later, Amelia Pitt married a certain Dr. William Spry, a lawyer, but she was no more fortunate in her choice than her sister had been. Spry was later appointed a Judge of the Admiralty Court in Barbadoes, from which position he was subsequently advanced to the post of Governor. And in Barbadoes at length he died, having first, in the words of Tom Pitt, "buried his poor wife, who had experienced from him such treatment as determined me not to wear mourning for his death."

Thus of the family of Thomas Pitt, young Tom alone survived.

When apprised of his succession, George was out riding near Kew in the company of Lord Bute. He immediately proceeded to Carlton House, the residence of his mother, there to receive the Privy Council.

King George III had just completed his twenty-second year, and seldom has a new reign opened with brighter prospects. For nearly fifty years England had been ruled by a foreign Sovereign; for nearly fifty years the occupant of the throne had been a contemptible creature of loose morals and irascible temper; for nearly fifty years the most favoured companions

[1] Walpole to Mann, Arlington Street, April 13th, 1762.
[2] Walpole to Mann, Arlington Street, April 30th, 1762.

of the monarch had been, not the great leaders of Church and State, but a troupe of upstart and unattractive mistresses. Now at last, in the autumn of 1760, there mounted the throne a tall young man with a frank, engaging countenance, proud of his English blood—to his first king's speech he added in his own hand the memorable words: "Born and educated in this country, I glory in the name of Britain; and the peculiar happiness of my life will ever consist in promoting the welfare and warm attachment to me I consider as the greatest and most permanent security of my throne"[1]—and against whose private life there could not be a whisper of reproach. Yet few men really knew their new Sovereign, for he had been brought up in the strictest seclusion and, save for his brothers and sisters, had never been allowed to enjoy the society of young people.

The prince's education had been sadly mismanaged and neglected. His knowledge of history, the foundations of the Constitution, and the functions of monarchy was imperfect; his appreciation of literature and the arts was entirely lacking. "Was there ever such stuff as a great part of Shakespeare?" he exclaimed to Fanny Burney on one occasion, and then with more caution, he added, "Only one must not say so."[2] His manner of speaking was hurried, halting and repetitive. He would exclaim "What! What!" and "Hey! Hey!" unceasingly. This made him seem to strangers trivial and shallow. But beneath this trifling exterior there were to be found qualities at once more durable and more substantial. He was sincerely religious though in a rather prudish way; he was a dutiful son; he was an honest man striving to do what he conceived to be his duty. "Though none of my ministers stand by me," he once exclaimed to Lord Chatham, "I will not truckle."[3] In other words, he was intensely obstinate: to give way was to him always to truckle. Coupled with this trait, there were others still more unpleasing; he was arrogant, secretive and prejudiced, uncharitable in his judgments, of uncertain temper, sullen, priggish; and above all, he was imbued with a grossly inflated idea of the legitimate powers of the monarchy.

It was not long before the opinionated new monarch began making mistakes. The first was made two days after his succession, when his Groom of the Stole, Lord Bute, was sworn of the Privy Council; from which

[1] The passage is usually quoted as "I glory in the name of Briton," but the manuscript containing George III's speech from the Throne, now in the British Museum, makes it quite clear that the King wrote "Britain" and not "Briton."—Brit. Mus. Add. MS. 32684, f. 121.

[2] Frances Burney, Madame D'Arblay, *Diary*, December 19th, 1785.

[3] On May 30th, 1767.

the wily courtiers were not long in perceiving where the new and brightest star in the royal firmament was to be found.[1]

The favourite was just forty-six when we first meet him riding with the new king near Kew. His early years had been passed in obscurity in the island of Bute, where he had contrived to pass his time in agricultural and botanical pursuits and to live on very moderate means in quiet contentment with his excellent wife, only daughter of that notorious miser, Edward Wortley Montagu and the remarkable Lady Mary. The Butes came to England after the revolution of 1745 and resided at Caen Wood near London. Two years later a chance encounter brought Bute in touch with Frederick, Prince of Wales, who was captivated by the charms and graces of this personable nobleman; so that in 1750, he was made a Lord of the Bedchamber to the Prince of Wales. But Frederick had no exaggerated notions of his friend's abilities. "Bute is a fine, showy man," he would say, "and would make an excellent Ambassador at any court where there was no business."[2] A fine, showy man he certainly was with a handsome face, engaging carriage, and a shapely leg—attributes to grace and adorn a court. Moreover, he had a certain taste in literature and a certain knowledge of science that no doubt stood him in good stead in the society that thronged to Leicester House. But his experience of public affairs was entirely lacking, and it may be safely assumed that so long as the Prince lived his abilities were rated at their just value. It was only after Frederick's death that the favourite became a power in the land; and then, when the public watched this accomplished political Malvolio receiving the highest trust and confidence from the widowed princess, they were not slow to draw their own conclusions.

The inevitable result of all this was that Bute became intensely unpopular. In the first place, he was a Scotsman with the ill-starred name of Stuart; then he was a royal favourite, and men mumbled under their breath the hated name of Buckingham; but worse still, he was proud, reserved, haughty, and like so many upstarts, to inferiors morose and scornful. In his manner of speaking, he was slow and ponderous—"Minute Guns," once exclaimed Charles Townshend, as the words fell from him one by one—and in his method of negotiation he was tortuous and intriguing. So as people saw this pompous, inexperienced, showy man strutting about the person of the

[1] But people really in the know were well aware of Bute's importance long before 1760. As Professor Richard Pares has kindly pointed out to me, both Pitt and Newcastle had negotiated with him in the Seven Years War as a man likely to be of consequence in the new reign; and Waldegrave knew all about him.

[2] Waldegrave, *Memoirs*.

new Sovereign, many a brow was knit and many a lip was curled; and men began asking, in the words of a witty jest, what fuel the king would burn in his chamber—Scotch coal, Newcastle coal, or pit-coal.[1]

In his first declaration to the Privy Council, George spoke of "this bloody and expensive war," words which, though subsequently emended on Pitt's demand to "expensive but just and necessary war," showed the way the wind was blowing. On March 21st following, Parliament was dissolved, and five days later it was announced that Bute himself was appointed a Secretary of State. In the General Election which followed, young Tom Pitt, who since his parent's death held the controlling interest in the parliamentary representation of Old Sarum and a large share in that of Okehampton in Devonshire, was duly elected Member of Parliament for the former, thus showing how little he considered himself bound by his father's promise to the Duke of Newcastle to vacate the seat to his nominee so soon as he had escaped from his creditors. Indeed, he had decided views on his parent's conduct. "I am obliged to you for the trouble you have taken in explaining to me the circumstances of my Father's agreement with respect to O.S.," he wrote to Andrews, "but cannot imagine why you think it can affect me in any degree whatever. I cannot conceive that his Ma^{ty} or any of the Administration will think me bound by any promise or agreement made personally by my Father without my knowledge or concurrence from which I co^d draw no manner of advantage, but which was on the contrary so evidently to my prejudice, and if they had thought differently I sho'^{d} probably have heard from some of the Ministry on this subject. I have been often grieved at the scandalous traffick he made of his Parliamentary interest, but cou'd they (the Ministers) suppose me bound in other respects, they wou'd certainly alter their opinion when they come to know that my father was under a previous engagement to myself to elect me at O.S. when I consented to the raiseing so large a sum for the payment of his debts, and this agreement ought certainly to have taken place of every other consideration."[2]

William Pitt was not unwilling to treat with the enemy but in his own way, and at his own time. Meanwhile, events moved in England's favour. In 1759, the small West Indian island of Dominica was seized, and in September of that year, after Amherst's capture of Montreal, all Canada was surrendered by the French. In the same year, Belleisle was captured and the expulsion of the French from India became a certainty. These successes, together with Pitt's well-matured plans for the capture of St. Lucia, Grenada and Martinique, gave him further advantages over the enemy. Accordingly,

---

[1] Walpole to Mann, Arlington Street, December 5th, 1760.
[2] Thomas Pitt to Andrews, August 21st, 1761.

when negotiations opened in 1761, the English Minister felt satisfied that his bargaining counters were such as would enable him to extract the most favourable terms from his adversary.

Of the suggestions advanced by the French Minister, Choiseul, Pitt rejected the proposals to limit the Canadian boundary at Niagara and was not prepared to submit to the return of Ile Royale to the French. Indeed, he would have made further difficulties with regard to the Newfoundland fishing rights but for the opposition in his Cabinet,[1] when the negotiations were brought to an abrupt stop by the sudden intransigence of the French agent, who was at this very time coming to terms with the Marquis Grimaldi, Spanish Ambassador in Paris for an alliance between their two countries. When an understanding with Spain appeared secure, Choiseul, on July 13th, suddenly withdrew many of his concessions and at the same time had the audacity to demand that England should satisfy various Spanish grievances. Pitt was not the man to stand for such temerarious demands, and in his haughtiest tone he informed the French that we were not accustomed to discuss an ally's grievance with an enemy.[2] On September 18th the Cabinet met to consider Pitt's proposal to recall Lord Bristol[3] our Ambassador to Madrid, and to strike instantly with an overwhelming force against the Spanish fleet. But he addressed what he afterwards termed a "trembling Council." The whole Cabinet, with the exception of Lord Temple, opposed any immediate declaration and sought rather to temporize. When it was clear that they had no following in the Cabinet, the two ministers drew up a paper, which they addressed to the king, in which they urged their reasons for advocating the immediate recall of the British Ambassador.[4]

At the meeting held at St. James's on October 2nd Pitt met his Cabinet for the last time. It was indeed a solemn occasion for it was generally expected that the great Minister would resign. There was a full attendance —old Granville, Lord President, how different from the fiery Carteret of

[1] It would seem as if Pitt's difficulties with his Cabinet were brought about as much by his dictatorial and offensive manner as by disagreement with his proposals. On one occasion he thumped the table and shouted at Ministers to such an extent that the three Dukes of Bedford, Devonshire and Newcastle who dined together afterwards at Newcastle House, disgustedly determined to attend no more Cabinet meetings so long as he was Minister. The King managed with difficulty to move two from this resolve, but Bedford remained adamant.

[2] William Pitt to de Bussy, July 24th, 1761.

[3] The eldest son of Lord Hervey, the memoir writer, and his wife, the beautiful and fascinating Molly Lepell.

[4] The famous "Advice in Writing" is printed in the Grenville Papers, Vol. I. It differs only verbally from the copy in the Newcastle Papers, Brit. Mus. Add. MSS., 32928, ff. 225-6.

long ago; truculent Temple, the Privy Seal; proud Devonshire, timid Newcastle; shrewd Mansfield; Hardwicke, back from mourning his wife;[1] Anson, a great seaman but weak in council; Ligonier, commander-in-chief but now of great age and long past his prime; and Mr. Secretary Pitt. Only Bedford, who had sworn he would never attend a Cabinet at which Pitt was present and was keeping his word, Halifax and Henley, the Lord Chancellor, were absent. The proceedings were opened by Pitt, who briefly stated the reason for their meeting and that he adhered to his opinion in writing of September 18th. He was followed by the Lord President, and all the Ministers present gave their views. But not one of them uttered a word in support of Pitt. Only Temple was at his side, and he was too angry to speak: mumbling a few ill-chosen phrases to the effect that he adhered strongly to the opinion he had already given the king, he snatched up his papers and flounced from the chamber.

At last Mr. Secretary Pitt rose—not to plead with his colleagues, for the proud man knelt to no one save the sovereign himself—but to justify once more his position and to take his leave. No new argument had been put forward, no new advice offered the king to make him change his views. The very honour of England was at stake. "Spain's conduct in putting forward her grievances under the shield of England's enemy, with whom we were at war, is the highest indignity that ever was offered to the Crown of England, and it will fix an eternal stain upon that crown if no answer is returned to Spain's avowal of her action. Moreover, prudence bids us strike before the enemy is prepared: You are *now* at war with the House of Bourbon," he declared, "but, for open war with Spain, you are prepared and she is not." And he concluded with these haughty words, "Without having ever asked any one single employment in my life, I was called by my Sovereign and by the voice of the people to assist the State when others had abdicated the service of it. That being so no one can be surprised that I will go on no longer since my advice is not taken. Being responsible I *will* direct, and will be responsible for nothing that I do not direct." Thus ended the memorable meeting and with a few words of thanks for the courtesy shown to him by the Council, Pitt left the Board.[2] Three days later he had an audience of the king, when he formally resigned the Seals.[3]

[1] Lady Hardwicke had died on September 19th.

[2] For very full information on the Cabinet Meetings held between August and October 1761, which led up to Pitt's resignation, see the *Newcastle Papers* (Brit. Mus. Add. MSS. 35870, ff. 297, 301, 303, 310). See also Grant Robertson, *England under the Hanoverians*, Appendix V, Williams, *William Pitt, Earl of Chatham*, Vol. II, and Williams, *Carteret and Newcastle*.

[3] At the same time that Pitt and Temple resigned, their kinsman, James Grenville resigned the subordinate office of Cofferer. Grenville to Bute, October, 12th, 1761.

To his surprise and joy the monarch was gracious. "I confess, Sire," he declared, "I had but too much reason to expect your Majesty's displeasure. I did not come prepared for this exceeding goodness. Pardon me, Sire, it overpowers, it oppresses me." Whereupon the proud unbending servant burst into tears.

Unfortunately for his popularity, Pitt accepted a peerage for his wife and a pension of £3,000 a year for himself, Lady Hester, and their eldest son; and, perhaps through the rather petty malice of the young king and his favourite, the resignation and the rewards were published in the same Gazette.[1] For a time all the world was in arms. The Great Commoner was mere common clay after all. The new Lady Chatham became Lady Cheat'em. Every variety of insult was hurled at the unhappy pair to such an extent that Pitt felt constrained to defend himself to his friend Warburton. "The cause then of my resigning the Seals," he wrote, "was a difference of opinion with regard to measures to be taken against Spain, of the highest importance to the Honour of the Crown and to the most essential national Interests. Lord Temple and I submitted to the King, in writing and sign'd by us, our most humble sentiments, which being over-ruled by the united opinion of *all* the rest of His Majesty's servants, I resign'd the Seals on Monday the 5th of this month, in order not to remain responsible for measures which I was no longer allow'd to guide. Most gracious publick marks of the King's approbation of my services follow'd my resignation; they are unmerited and *unsollicited*, and I shall ever be proud of having receiv'd them from the best of Sovereigns."[2] Nothing could be clearer than that! Yet the abuse continued, and unfortunately in this Ann Pitt joined. On her return from abroad she had asked her brother to use his influence to obtain her a pension, but he had declined. He had wished her well, ". . . but having never been a Sollicitor of favour upon any occasion, how can I become so now without contradicting the whole tenour of my Life?"[3] Later she had succeeded in obtaining a pension for herself and in announcing this good news to her brother she had been careful to explain ". . . that it is entirely to my Lord Bute that I owe the obtaining such a favour, as I cou'd never have presumed to ask if I had not been encouraged by his benevolence and generosity, which I must feel so long as I have life to feel the comfort and happiness which I owe to the King, singly through his intercession."[4]

[1] October 10th, 1761.

[2] William Pitt to Bishop of Gloucester, "St James's Square, Octre ye 15th, 1761."

[3] William Pitt to Ann Pitt, November 24th, 1760.

[4] Ann Pitt to William Pitt, "Tuesday 5 o'clock" (December 30th, 1760).

William replied the same day in a priggish letter that does him no credit. Congratulating Ann on her pension, he wrote, "On your account I rejoice at an addition of income so agreeable to your turn of life, whatever repugnancy I find, at the same time, to see my name placed on the Pensions of Ireland. Unmixt as I am in this whole transaction, I will not doubt that you will take care to have it thoroughly understood. Long may you live in health to enjoy the comforts and happiness which you tell me you owe to the King, singly through the Intercession of Lord Bute, and to feel the pleasing sentiments of such an obligation."[1] To this cold, unfeeling missive, poor Ann returned a mild answer. She thanked her brother and his wife for their good wishes, "but as I have the mortification of finding that for some reasons which I can not judge of, you feel a repugnancy to the mark of favour I have had the honour to receive and desire,— it may be thoroughly understood that you had no share in the transaction. ... I will take care to explain the truth, by which it will appear that you are no way concern'd in it, and that it has no sort of relation to your situation as Minister, since my request was first made to the Princess many years ago, as Her Royal Highnesses servant.... And through the Provision I have been so happy to obtain from His Majestys Bounty is of the utmost importance to me, and answers every wish I cou'd form with regard to my income, yet when I was allow'd to say how much wou'd make me easy, I fixed it to a sum, which I flatter myself will not be thought exorbitant, or appear as if I had wanted to avail myself of the weight of your credit, or the merit of your services to obtain it. As to your objection to your name being upon the Irish Pension, I do not believe that any mistake can be made from mine being there. And as to my self, I very sincerely think it an honour that is very flattering to me, to have received so precious a mark of the Royal favour, and to have my name upon the same List not only with some of the highest and of the most deserving persons in England, but even with some of the greatest and most glorious names in Europe. If I have tired you with a longer letter than I intended, I have been led into it by the sincere desire I have that an advantage so very essential to the ease and comfort of the remainder of a Life, which has not hitherto been very happy, shou'd not be a cause of uneasiness to you."[2] So when her sister-in-law wrote pompously to announce ". . . that his Majesty has been graciously pleas'd to confer the Dignity of Peerage on your Brother's Family by creating me Baroness of Chatham with Limitation to our sons. The King

[1] William Pitt to Ann Pitt, "Tuesday Decr. 30th, 1760."

[2] Ann Pitt to William Pitt, undated and unsigned, so it may be assumed this was a copy of Anne's letter, which she kept for reference.

has been further pleas'd to make a grant of Three Thousand pounds a year to Mr. Pitt for his own Life, Mine, and our Eldest Son's, in consideration of Mr. Pitt's Services. We do not doubt of the share you will take in these gracious marks of his Majesties Royal approbation and goodness—"[1] it is hardly surprising if Ann was anxious to take her revenge and was only with difficulty dissuaded by her friends from sending her brother a copy of his previous letters. Nevertheless she told everybody what she had a mind to do, so that it became the common talk of the Town.

It was not long, however, before the popular fancy veered, and Pitt became the national hero once more; so when on November 9th he attended the Lord Mayor's banquet, at which the King was present, the young Sovereign was hardly noticed, and Bute was attacked by the mob; but the fallen Minister received a great ovation. It was an unfortunate occurrence, for Pitt had no desire to show disrespect to the King; he had only agreed to attend the banquet at the earnest solicitation of Temple and had consented against his better judgment. He long regretted this error of judgment.[2]

Within three months the wisdom of Pitt's advice to the Council became apparent. Spain at last showed her hand; and on June 2nd, 1763, war was declared by England. Hostilities were speedily successful, which is scarcely surprising seeing that Pitt had laid all the plans and Martinique, St. Vincent, St. Lucia, Grenada, together with Havana in the West Indies and Manila in the Philippines, were captured by our forces. It was in the midst of these successes that Bute suddenly decided on a frivolous pretext to withdraw the subsidy that we had hitherto been paying to the King of Prussia. Fortunately for Frederick at this moment his old enemy, the Tsaritsa Elizabeth, died; and she was succeeded by her nephew, the half-witted Duke of Holstein, as Tsar Peter III. Unlike his aunt, this crazy youth entertained an enthusiastic veneration for Frederick which evinced itself in his kissing his portrait and calling him master. His reign was short, but even in the space of a few months he contrived to lend invaluable aid to the hard-pressed King of Prussia; his end, however, cold-blooded and horrible, came with relentless speed. At the bidding of a mistress, niece to the Chancellor, Count Woronzow, Tsar Peter had dared to slight his consort. Stung by the insult, the redoubtable Catherine put herself at the head of a conspiracy against the feather-brained ruler. The Guards mutinied; the nation rejoiced;

[1] Lady Hester Pitt to Ann Pitt, "Sunday morning."

[2] The letter of invitation—Beckford to William Pitt, Soho Square, November 6th, 1761—was endorsed by Lady Chatham "Mr. Beckford, 1761, to press my lord to appear with Lord Temple, to which he yielded for his friend's sake, but, as he always declared, both then and after, against his better judgment." The attack on Bute is described by Pitt's solicitor—Nuthall to Chatham, Friday, November 12th, 1761.

and the Senate hastened to proclaim her Sovereign as Catherine the Second.[1] Her husband, unconscious of those happenings, was taken at Oraniebaum, where he was living quietly with his mistress in a villa on the seashore, and was removed to safe lodgment near the capital. There a week later the unhappy man was strangled by a gigantic ape-like man, Alexis Orloff by name, known as "The Scarred" to distinguish him from his brother, who was Catherine's favourite. Thus miserably perished Frederick's most recent ally, perhaps the most hapless ruler that Russia had ever known.

By the spring of 1762 Bute was supreme, and it only remained for him to compass the retirement of the poor old Duke of Newcastle, who amid many groans and lamentations, retired to Claremont, refusing all rewards for his forty years' service to the Crown. By the winter all the preliminaries of peace were settled, and Bedford was sent on an embassy to Paris to sign the Articles with Choiseul and Grimaldi. The terms were less favourable than anything Pitt would have agreed to, and proved very unpopular. Indeed, it has long been thought that it was only by lavish bribery of members, for which the services of that past master, Henry Fox, were enlisted, that the safe passage of the peace preliminaries through the House of Commons was secured; and a familiar passage from Walpole supports this view.[2] It has now been established, however, that this accusation against Fox is a gross exaggeration.[3] Some bribery there may have been, but to the national war-weariness rather than to intense bribery must the result be attributed—a result which was achieved in face of the opposition of Pitt, who, though disabled by a violent attack of gout, spoke for three hours and twenty-five minutes against the measure, to the huge delight of the crowd who all that time waited without to cheer their crippled hero as he was borne in triumph from the House of Commons to his home.

In the eyes of the Court these events—the retirement of Pitt, the ascendency of Bute, the conclusion of the war, the Treaty of Paris—constituted a major victory. "Now my son *is* King of England," was the triumphant boast of a foolish mother. Posterity does not echo that cry.

---

[1] One day to be known as The Great, and also "the Semiramis of the North."

[2] Walpole, *Memoirs of the Reign of George III*, Vol. I.

[3] Namier, *The Structure of Politics at the Accession of George III*, Vol. I.

CHAPTER II

Grenville, Pitt, and America

BY the union of Bute and Fox two of the most hated men in England had been called to the highest posts in the State. The former was loathed as a Court favourite. The latter, detested by the mob for his rapacity, was abhorred by the Princess of Wales and her clique because of his supposed support of the King's wooing of Lady Sarah Lennox. Nor did Fox improve matters by the energetic and malevolent measures he planned for the complete overthrow of the great Whig party that had been in power without intermission since the House of Hanover came to the Throne. When the indignation of the populace was at its height, it was suddenly announced that Lord Bute had resigned—probably because he lost his nerve, found himself unequal to his post, and realized that his unpopularity rendered him more of a liability than an asset to George III. With the retirement of Bute came the resignation of Fox, who was elevated to the Upper House with the title of Holland, the same which his wife had borne since the previous year.

On the political exit of Bute, George Grenville, who to the indignation of his brother and his brother-in-law, had not resigned with them in 1761, kissed hands as First Lord of the Treasury and Chancellor of the Exchequer. The two Secretaries of State were Halifax and Egremont, the latter closely connected to Grenville by marriage,[1] and the three Ministers came to be known as the "triumvirate." Another relative of Grenville came into the Ministry, for young Tom Pitt was given his first experience of office, being appointed by his uncle one of the Lords of the Admiralty—not much to the King's enthusiasm, it would seem: "as my D. Friend thinks it is right to humour Grenville with young Pitt I will not refuse it. . . ."[2]—and thus still further widened the breach between himself and his Uncle William, who had been so good to him.

Grenville was a lawyer, and there was little in the law and custom of Parliament that he did not know. But the head of an administration demands other qualities and of those he was singularly deficient. Though a

[1] Lord Egremont was son of Sir William Wyndham and his first wife, Lady Catherine Seymour, daughter of the 6th Duke of Somerset. Their daughter was the wife of George Grenville.

[2] George III to Bute, "18 m. pt. 3." (April 12th, 1763.)

man of undoubted ability, he was grave, dry, slow, deliberate and pertinacious; he had an unfortunate propensity for invariably looking on the darkest side of things; he was parochial in his outlook, methodical, obstinate, parsimonious, a lover of detail, always ready to take the narrow as opposed to the broader view. His opinions were sound rather than brilliant, his speeches correct and sensible, but at the same time cold, abstract, dull. In short he was a bore, perhaps one of the greatest bores in history. With the King his manner was hectoring and prosy; he was like a schoolmaster lecturing a pupil. "When he has wearied me for two hours," George complained to Bute, "he looks at his watch to see if he may not tire one for an hour more."[1] For sheer stupid obstinacy the King was, in Grenville, to find his match.

The King's Speech at the end of the session referred complacently to the conclusion of peace on conditions "so honourable to my Crown and so beneficial to my people." As the terms of the peace treaty were by many considered grossly inadequate, these provocative words rang out like a challenge; and so they seemed to John Wilkes, Member of Parliament for Ailesbury. This debauched and depraved man, the associate of that dissolute cleric-poet who had the effrontery to bear the honoured name of Churchill and other of his kidney, had founded a paper called the *North Briton*, in which he alternately execrated and ridiculed the Scottish Prime Minister whom he hailed as the fount and origin of all our troubles. But it was not always at Bute that these two cast their poisoned barbs for any who aroused their ire or excited their ridicule were sure to find themselves defamed or mocked by the scurrilous *North Briton*; and in the forty-fifth, and what proved to be the last number, issued on April 23rd 1763, appeared a bitter onslaught on the King's Speech and on the references therein to the unpopular peace treaty. A wise statesman would probably have treated the vapid attack with the contempt it deserved, but the foolish Grenville ordered a General Warrant to be issued against "the authors, printers and publishers," whoever they might be, of the offending paper.[2] Under this warrant Wilkes was immediately seized in his own house and in due course he was lodged in the Tower.

It was not long before the prisoner applied for a writ of habeas corpus and when he appeared before Lord Chief Justice Pratt, he pleaded privilege as a Member of Parliament. However unsavoury a being Wilkes might be, it was evident that, whether general warrants were legal or not—and the Court did not pronounce on that point—the plea was good and he was

---

[1] Walpole, *Memoirs of the Reign of George III,* Vol. II.

[2] A General Warrant is, of course, a warrant that does not specify by name the person or persons against whom it is issued.

entitled to his discharge. Wilkes was accordingly released from custody whilst the king could only show his chagrin by depriving him of his commission in the Buckinghamshire Militia. Thus ended the first act of the drama of John Wilkes.

On August 20th Lord Egremont died suddenly. Faced with this unexpected event, George III had no alternative to summoning him whom but five months earlier the favourite had vowed never more to approach. Thus it came about that one hot August afternoon William Beckford, Lord Mayor of London[1] and Pitt's intimate friend, posted down to Hayes with an anxious message from Bute; and a few days later an interview took place between Pitt and Bute at the former's house in Jermyn Street. The proud Commoner spoke freely, but he absolutely declined to ask an audience of the king. "But suppose his Majesty should order you?" asked Bute. "The king's command would make it my duty," was the prompt reply, "and I should certainly obey it." The royal command soon came; and at noon on Saturday, August 27th, Pitt duly presented himself before his Sovereign.

During the progress of the audience, which lasted three hours, George Grenville arrived at the palace, and seeing in the court the familiar chair with its great boot specially constructed for its owner's gouty leg, knew that his brother-in-law was closeted with the king. Whilst in fact George had apprised Grenville of his intention to see Pitt, the sight of the invalid chair could not have been pleasing to the Prime Minister.[2] He was on the worst possible terms with his brother-in-law since he had been ridiculed in the House of Commons during a recent debate on a proposal to tax cider. When many objections had been raised to the suggested tax, Grenville had in his peevish tiresome voice asked members where else they would have taxes laid. "Let them tell me where . . . I repeat, Sir, let them tell me where!" And then from Pitt, who sat opposite, there came in almost this same querulous tone a line from a popular song of the time—"Gentle Shepherd, tell me where?" The House dissolved into guffaws of laughter and Gentle Shepherd became Grenville's nickname for many a day.

A very full account of Pitt's audience has been left by Lord Hardwicke who was informed by Pitt of all that passed,[3] and though no definite

[1] He was the father of William Beckford (1760-1844), the eccentric author of *The History of the Caliph Vathek*.

[2] Walpole's statement is not correct—"It was on the 28th. of August that Mr. Grenville, arriving at Buckingham House, was struck with the apparition of Mr. Pitt's chair and servants in the Court. This was the first notice he or the public received of a phenomenon so little expected, at least by the latter." Walpole, *Memoirs of the Reign of George III*, Vol. I. George Grenville's own Diary under date "Friday 26th" shows the contrary.

[3] Hardwicke to Royston, September 4th, 1763.

conclusion was come to at this meeting and the king requested his presence again on Monday, Pitt felt sanguine of a favourable issue. But during the week-end, a secret meeting took place between the king and Grenville. As a result of this, when Pitt presented himself at the palace on Monday, he found the king in a very different mood.[1] After some courteous preliminaries, George informed Pitt that he had carefully considered all that had been said at the previous audience; then with much repetition and circumlocution in short staccato sentences punctuated by many "what, whats" the wily monarch talked airily of the necessity of what he called supporting his honour. Passing lightly from that embarrassing theme, he went on to propose Lord Northumberland as head of the Treasury; and when Pitt demurred, the king named Lord Halifax as an alternative choice; then, to the minister's suggestion that perhaps the Paymastership was better suited to his abilities, "But Mr. Pitt," rejoined the king, "I had designed that for poor George Grenville—he is your near relation, and you once loved him!" Somebody said that when Pitt bowed to majesty, you could see the great nose between the long legs. He gave the king just such a bow on this occasion: it was the only response vouchsafed to the king's unwelcome proposal!

Hitherto it would seem as if George had done most of the talking. Now it was Pitt's turn, and he commenced to enumerate the Ministers he desired to appoint. The mere mention of them was too much for George's patience. "Well, Mr. Pitt, I see (or I fear) this will not do," he declared. "My honour is concerned, and I must support it." So the remarkable audience ended, and Pitt left his obstinate sovereign to support his honour as best he could. The king was thus forced into the humiliating position of having to request Grenville to remain his Prime Minister and of listening to a lengthy and most uncourtly discourse from that pedagogic statesman on the iniquities of the secret baleful influence behind the throne.

When the new Session of the House opened in the winter, the second act of the Wilkes drama began. In the Lords, the reprobate Sandwich rose to complain of a scandalous, obscene and impious libel written by Wilkes, called an "Essay on Woman," which was a parody of Pope's famous "Essay on Man." The sight of the debauched Sandwich turning on his former friend was outrageous enough, and at Covent Garden theatre, where *The Beggar's Opera* was being played, Macheath's words "That Jemmy

---

[1] According to Grenville's Diary of these events, the King told him on Sunday, August 28th, that he would not accept Pitt's terms. If, therefore, Grenville is reporting correctly, nothing that Pitt said the following day was responsible for the King's changed attitude.

Twitcher should peach I own surprises me" were greeted with a shout of delight from the entire audience. From that time forward the nickname of Jemmy Twitcher was constantly applied to Sandwich to his dying day.

Meanwhile, whilst being equally assailed in the Lower House, Wilkes was involved in a duel that all but cost him his life. As soon as he could move, he beat a hasty retreat to the Continent, and after long and heated debates was in his absence expelled from the House of Commons. These untoward events gradually led to the popular belief that Wilkes was a persecuted man, and "Wilkes and Liberty for ever" became the popular cry.

The House of Commons soon showed its malice. First it ordered No. 45 of the *North Briton* to be burnt by the common hangman; then it sought to declare that "Privilege of Parliament" does not extend to the case of writing and publishing seditious libels." But this partiality was vehemently opposed by Pitt, not for any tenderness towards the *North Briton* or its author—for both he had nothing but contempt—but because he was against the surrender of privilege. "I condemn the whole series of *North Britons*; they are illiberal, unmanly, detestable," he declared. "The author of these Essays does not deserve to be ranked among the human species; he is the blasphemer of his God, and the libeller of his king. I have no connection with him; none with any such writer. I neither associate nor communicate with any such man. . . ."[1]

It was at about this time that a remarkable piece of good fortune came Pitt's way. A wealthy West-country baronet, Sir William Pynsent by name, had been a member of the House of Commons in the time of Queen Anne, but had resigned in disgust at the peace of Utrecht and had lived ever since in retirement on his estate of Burton Pynsent near Langport in Somerset. There in moody seclusion the eccentric recluse remained for half a century, when the Peace of Paris stirred in his heart a wave of admiration for the statesman who had preferred to resign to compromising the honour of England; and he determined to leave to that man, though a complete stranger, the whole of his property.[2] Thus at Pynsent's death on January 12th, 1765, Pitt unexpectedly found himself in possession of a splendid estate with an income of about £3,000 a year.[3] The property lies in the valley of

---

[1] *Parl. Hist.,* Vol. XX.

[2] Lady Chatham in a letter preserved at Chevening states positively that her husband and Pynsent had never met. Dr. von Ruville tries to prove the contrary, but he is not convincing. Von Ruville, *William Pitt, Earl of Chatham,* Vol. III.

[3] The validity of the Will was disputed and it was not for some six years that the case was finally settled in Pitt's favour, but he nevertheless entered into possession forthwith. See *Brown's Cases in Parliament,* Vol. VI, *Tothill v. Pitt.*

the Parrett, a small river flowing into the Bristol Channel from the south, on the side of a ridge of hills forming the northern boundary of the parish of Curry-Rivel. High placed on the very top of this ridge stood the mansion, a large irregular building which had been erected at different periods and composed of various materials. The front faced squarely to the north with distant views over the flat country between the Mendip and the Quantock hills, the channel and the Welsh mountains. The south front overlooked a fine park, well wooded and studded with elm, oak and other trees of great antiquity. The rooms within were large and well proportioned, the gardens surrounding the house were well kept and delightfully laid out with rare and choice plants. Yet, in spite of the evident charm of the place, no sooner had the Pitts settled in their new inheritance than they commenced costly additions and alterations to the property. "Capability" Brown, the famous landscape gardener was employed; architects and builders were entrusted with the task of enlarging the mansion—a new library for Pitt, a "bird room" for Lady Chatham. Nor was the bounteous benefactor forgotten, for to the north-west of the house and at no great distance a lofty column, known as the Burton Steeple, was erected to the memory of Sir William Pynsent. Pitt's brother-in-law, Temple, assisted with the improvements. "I shall with the greatest pleasure facilitate as far as in me lyes, the favourite object of enlarging round Burton Pynsent, at the expence of Hayes, and I wish your estates in Somersetshire may not only rival the great Peter but extend as wide as the sight from the top of the monumental column on the black Promontory, which, through determined purpose, not blind chance, I shall most certainly see next Summer, as well as the rising towers and I hope flourishing plantations, which your active mind has plan'd and expeditious right hand already executed, so far breaking in upon Mr. Brown's department by adorning the country, which you were not permitted to save."[1] So the work went briskly ahead, and it was not long before the Pitts decided on disposing of Hayes, so as to facilitate their plans for their new property. A ready purchaser was found in Thomas Walpole,[2] nephew of Sir Robert, who took over the place in December, so happy and settled did William and Hester feel in their new home.[3]

At almost the same time that the death of Sir William Pynsent brought Pitt this splendid heritage, an Act of Parliament was passed that, though

[1] Temple to William Pitt, November 5th, 1765.

[2] Second son of Horatio, 1st Lord Walpole of Wolterton. He was a well-known merchant and banker, in partnership with his father-in-law, Sir Joshua Vanneck.

[3] When Burton Pynsent was subsequently sold by the second Lord Chatham to pay his gambling debts, the purchasers, some people called Pinney, pulled down a large portion of the mansion, and only that part built by Pitt still stands.

little noticed at the time, was to bring great and dire consequences in its train. In the days of Sir Robert Walpole, a plan had been laid before the Prime Minister for taxing America without the colonists' consent. But that sagacious old cynic would have none of it. "I have Old England set against me," he remarked to Chesterfield, "and do you think I will have New England likewise?"[1] But Grenville, less wise, cheerfully rushed in where Walpole had feared to tread. He had inherited a load of debt; moreover, an army of twenty thousand men was required to be maintained in the Colonies, so was it unreasonable that they should be asked to defray some of the expenditure? It was an evil hour for England when the ill-judged and ill-considered proposals were laid before Parliament.

Pitt was horror-struck, for he quickly foresaw the probable consequences of his brother-in-law's temerity; but he could do nothing, for his old enemy had him in thrall. Only from his sick-bed could he watch in feverish anxiety the almost careless and thoughtless passing of this dangerous measure.

So Grenville's Government continued, and it was not until the spring of 1765 that the king determined to make yet another attempt to rid himself of his hated ministers. At last in the hour of his dire need, George III despairingly summoned to his aid his uncle, the Duke of Cumberland, who despatched Lord Albemarle to Hayes to learn Pitt's terms. Though obviously very ill, the invalid was on this occasion clear and precise. He stipulated that England should make an alliance against the House of Bourbon, that those who had lost their employment through the expression of their opinion in Parliament should have their positions restored, that army and navy promotion should be granted solely on merit, that General Warrants should be declared by Parliament to be illegal, and that the cider tax should be repealed. On these conditions being reported to him, the young king, determined to evade the issue, instructed his uncle to see what could be achieved by personal persuasion. So on a hot Sunday morning in May, 1765, the Duke of Cumberland, very fat and rather "scant of breath"[2] went posting down to Hayes with an escort of the Guards.

What took place at this interview with Pitt and Temple, hastily summoned from Stowe, has been variously reported.[3] On one thing alone are all reports agreed. Nobody could understand a word of what the invalid was saying. On the visit of Albemarle, Pitt had been clear and concise;

[1] Coxe, *Life of Sir Robert Walpole*, Vol. I.

[2] "Our son is fat and scant of breath." *Hamlet*, Act v, Sc. ii.

[3] Cumberland's version appears in Albemarle, *Memoirs of the Marquis of Rockingham*, Vol. I, and Pitt's in *Grafton, Autobiography*. (Ed. Sir William Anson.)

now he enveloped his meaning in a cloud of verbiage. He was haughty, vain, bombastic, loquacious, oracular: in short, he was at his worst, his most detestable mood. It was clear that nothing could be done with him. "Yesterday the Hero of Culloden went down in person to the Conqueror of America at Hayes and though tendering almost carte blanche-blanchissime for the Constitution, and little short of it for the whole red book of places —brought back nothing but a blank refusal. Words cannot paint the confusion into which everything is thrown."[1] Meanwhile, Grenville was taking advantage of the strength of his position to make himself even more odious to his sovereign, whom he insisted on lecturing in his most pedagogic manner. At last George III could bear it no longer and determined to see what he himself could do with Pitt. At an audience on Wednesday, June 19th, and at another three days later, the king and Pitt came to a complete understanding. The harassed sovereign was by now prepared to agree to almost any terms that would release him from the bonds of the hated Grenville, and he therefore made no difficulty over Pitt's requirements. All seemed settled, and then suddenly and without warning the ship foundered on a rock hidden beneath the surface of the water.

For the leadership of the House of Lords Pitt regarded his brother-in-law as indispensable. On Monday, June 24th, therefore, Temple was summoned to Hayes and offered the position of First Lord of the Treasury and Leadership of the House of Lords. To Pitt's astonishment and dismay, his relative resolutely and uncompromisingly declined the offer. His dear brother was in too weak a state of health and too much would fall on his shoulders; his dear brother was too tender-hearted towards the followers of the Scottish favourite; all manner of excuses were offered, all manner of explanations were given why he, Temple, could not accept. And then, after hours of argument, some slight corner of the truth was exposed to view. There were certain "tender and delicate reasons which must always remain a secret" why he could not possibly join the Administration. During the previous months, the estranged brothers, Temple and Grenville, had become reconciled, and when the former had resumed once again his intimate terms with his brother-in-law he no doubt longed for the return of those happy far-off days of the brotherhood. A Ministry of the brothers, with George, William and himself on terms of absolute equality was what the proud, vain Temple dreamed of. This that he was being offered was something very different. It is almost incredible that a man of Temple's moderate abilities could possibly fancy himself as the equal of a genius like William Pitt, but so it was. To his sister he wrote in indignation of

[1] Walpole to Hertford, "Arlington Street, Monday evening, May 20th, 1765."

"... being stuck into a ministry as a great cipher at the head of the Treasury, surrounded with other ciphers, all named by Mr. Pitt. ... My brother, James, is no stranger to my thoughts upon this matter, even after cool reflection on my pillow, and I told the king and my Lord Chancellor to this effect, amongst a variety of other things, that though I was most willing to sacrifice my brother's pretensions, as he was himself, to Mr. Pitt's indisposition towards him, for the sake of public and general union, yet as that in my opinion was not in the plan, I would not *go in like a child, to come out like a fool.*"[1] And so this vain, stupid man refused; and Pitt, chagrined at his failure, retired to Burton Pynsent in high dudgeon. "All is now over as to me," he wrote to Lady Stanhope, "and by a fatality I did not expect, I mean Lord Temple's refusing to take his share with me in the undertaking. We set out to-morrow morning for Somersetshire, where I propose, if I find the place tolerable, to pass not a little of the rest of my days."[2] And on taking leave of Temple, he mournfully quoted the lines of Virgil:

> "*Extinxti te meque, soror, populumque, patresque*
> *Sidonios, urbemque tuam.*"[3]

The iron had entered into his soul.

Thus deprived of the services of Pitt, the king was forced to look for deliverance from Grenville to other quarters, and he found his salvation by taking in the Whig opposition under its nominal leader, the Marquess of Rockingham.[4] Lord Rockingham accepted the Treasury, the gallant Conway became leader of the House of Commons, and the Duke of Grafton Secretary of State. A mere lute-string administration, fit for summer wear, was Charles Townshend's acid comment; and so it seemed. The new Premier himself was an honourable, well-meaning but inexperienced young man of great possessions. But he was blessed with one inestimable advantage, for he had as his private secretary a young Irishman, Edmund Burke by name, who though admittedly "too accustomed to dwell in the altitudes of the intellect to be really successful in the rude warfare of parliamentary

---

[1] Temple to Lady Chatham, Stowe, July 27th, 1766.

[2] William Pitt to Lady Stanhope, Hayes, July 20th, 1765.

[3] Virgil, *Aeneid*, Lib. IV., verse 682. Christopher Pitt's translation of the lines runs thus:

> "You, by this fatal stroke, and I, and all
> Your senate, people and your country fall."

[4] The true leader of the Administration, however, was, until his death, the Duke of Cumberland, though as a Prince of the Blood he could take no office in it.

life,"[1] was undoubtedly a genius of the first order. Conway, the friend and cousin of Horace Walpole,[2] was a brave soldier, but a weak and vacillating statesman. Grafton, even younger than Conway—he was but thirty-one—was chiefly known for his love of sport and for his unfortunate association with Nancy Parsons, immortalized by Gainsborough, and the most famous courtesan of her day.

From this weak Administration, Pitt stood haughtily aloof. Yet before long they were eagerly, almost humbly, seeking his aid. But all hopes, if there really were any, of persuading him were wrecked by the king: he had made so many attempts himself that he declared it was Pitt's turn to solicit him. So matters stood when Parliament met for a memorable session on January 14th, 1766.

The speech from the throne referred to the many hostile acts that had been committed in America since the imposition of the Stamp Act. The debate which ensued resolved itself into a duel between the pedantic, logical, pedestrian mind of the cool, talented Grenville and the burning, all-mastering enthusiasm of the mighty genius of Pitt. The Great Commoner did not long leave the House in doubt as to where he stood: he spoke early in the debate and with his usual power.[3]

"I stand up in this place, single and unconnected," he said; and turning to Grenville, he spat forth these contemptuous words: "As to the late Ministry, every capital measure they have taken is entirely wrong." Then it was Conway's turn—"To the present gentlemen, to those at least whom I have in my eye," and he looked straight at the gallant soldier, "I have no objection; I have not been made a sacrifice by any of them. Their characters are fair, and I am always glad when men of fair characters engage in his Majesty's service . . ." and he had advised them to engage. "But, notwithstanding—I love to be explicit—I cannot give them my confidence: pardon me, gentlemen, confidence is a plant of slow growth in an aged bosom; youth is the season of credulity." Then, casting a shaft at Newcastle whose "overruling influence" he deplored, the great orator poured forth such a mighty cascade of words as to overwhelm in the bubbling waters of his eloquence those who would oppose his will and doubt his sincerity.

"When the resolution was taken in the House to tax America, I was ill in bed. If I could have endured to have been carried in my bed, so great was the agitation of my mind for the consequences, I would have solicited some kind hand to have laid me down on this floor, to have borne my

[1] Winstanley, *Lord Chatham and the Whig Opposition.*
[2] His mother was a sister of Sir Robert Walpole's first wife.
[3] Bancroft's report of Pitt's speeches on this occasion is the fullest, but that of Sir Robert Head is the most usually consulted version.

testimony against it. It is now an Act that has passed. I would speak with decency of every Act of this House, but must beg indulgence to speak of it with freedom." The speaker then dilated on the supreme importance of their deliberations. ". . . America being neither really nor virtually represented in Westminster, cannot be held legally, or constitutionally, or reasonably subject to obedience to any money bill of this kingdom. . . . The Americans are the sons, not the bastards of England. As subjects they are entitled to the common right of representation, and cannot be bound to pay taxes without their consent. . . . In an American tax, what do we do? We, your Majesty's Commons of Great Britain, give and grant to your Majesty, what? Our own property? No, we give and grant to your Majesty the property of your Majesty's Commons in America. It is an absurdity in terms." Then the speaker turned to the question of representation. "I would fain know by whom an American is represented here? Is he represented by any Knight of the Shire?" he asked, "or will you tell him that he is represented by any representative of a borough? a borough which, perhaps, no man ever saw. That is what is called the rotten part of the Constitution. It cannot endure the century. . . . The idea of a virtual representation of America in this House is the most contemptible that ever entered into the head of men. It does not deserve a serious refutation. . . . I shall never own the justice of taxing America internally until she enjoys the right of representation. In every other point of legislation, the authority of Parliament is like the North Star, fixed for the reciprocal benefit of the parent country and her colonies. . . . The power of Parliament, like the circulation of the human heart, active, vigorous and perfect in the smallest fibre of the arterial system, may be known in the Colonies by the prohibition of their carrying a hat to market over the line of one province into another, or by breaking down a loom in the most distant corner of the British Empire in America, and if this power were denied, I would not permit them to manufacture a lock of wool or a horseshoe or a hobnail. In everything you may bind them except that of taking their money out of their pockets without their consent. Here I would draw the line:

"*sunt certi denique fines,*
Quos ultra citraque nequit consistere rectum.

"I know not what we may hope or fear from those now in place; but I have confidence in their good intentions. . . . I could not refrain from expressing the reflections I have made in my retirement, which I hope long to enjoy, beholding, as I do, ministries changed one after another, and passing away like shadows."

The great orator ceased. For a time the House was hushed in an awe-struck silence. At length Conway rose to declare himself and most of the Government in general agreement with Pitt's views. He was quickly followed by Grenville, who expatiated on the recent disturbances in America, and hotly denied the contention that the Colonists could not be taxed by the House of Commons. Parliament taxes the India Company and great towns such as Manchester that are not represented; also the palatinate of Chester and the bishopric of Wales were subject to taxation before they sent representatives. Protection and obedience are reciprocal. Great Britain protects America; America must yield obedience. Then he turned savagely upon his brother-in-law. "Ungrateful people of America!" he cried. "When I had the honour to serve the Crown, while you yourselves were loaded with an enormous debt of one hundred and forty millions, and paid a revenue of ten millions, you have given bounties on their lumber, their iron, their hemp and many other things. You have related, in their favour, the Act of Navigation, that palladium of British commerce. I offered to do everything in my power to advance the trade of America. I discouraged no trade but what was prohibited by Act of Parliament."

Stung by these taunts, Pitt rose instantly to reply. He lamented that liberty of speech in the House had been imputed a crime: "It is a liberty I mean to exercise." Then he poured forth a fresh torrent of his eloquence. "The gentleman tells us America is obstinate; America is almost in open rebellion," he cried; then in ringing tones he ejaculated the famous boast, "*I rejoice that America has resisted.* I come not here armed at all points with law cases and acts of Parliament," he continued, "with the Statute Book doubled down in dog's ears to defend the cause of liberty. . . . I draw my ideas of freedom from the vital powers of the British Constitution, not from the crude and fallacious notions too much relied upon, as if we were but in the morning of liberty. . . . The gentleman tells us of many who are taxed, and are not represented . . . many of these are represented in other capacities. . . . Not one of the Ministers, who have taken the lead of Government since the accession of King William, ever recommended a tax like this. None of them ever dreamed of robbing the colonies of their constitutional rights. That was reserved to mark the era of the late Administration. . . .

"The gentleman asks, when were the Colonies emancipated? I desire to know when they were made slaves. The profits to Great Britain from the trade of the colonies are two millions a year. That was the fund that carried you triumphantly through the last war . . . and shall a miserable financier come with a boast that he can filch a peppercorn into the Exchequer to the loss of millions to the nation? . . .

"A great deal has been said without doors of the strength of America.

It is a topic that ought to be cautiously meddled with. In a good cause, on a sound bottom, the force of this country can crush America to atoms. But on this ground, on the Stamp Act, when so many here will think it a crying injustice, I am one who will lift up my hands against it. In such a cause, your success will be hazardous. America, if she fall, would fall like a strong man. She would embrace the pillars of the State, and pull down the Constitution along with her.

"Is this your boasted peace?" he asked in stirring tones. "Not to sheath the sword in its scabbard, but to sheath it in the bowels of your countrymen? . . . The Americans have not acted in all things with prudence and temper. They have been driven to madness by injustice. Will you punish them for the madness you have occasioned? Rather let prudence and temper come first from this side. I will undertake for America that she will follow the example. There are two lines of Prior's, of a man's behaviour to his wife, so applicable to you and your colonies that I cannot help repeating them:

> "'Be to her faults a little blind,
> Be to her virtues very kind.'

"Upon the whole I beg leave to tell the House what is really my opinion. It is that the Stamp Act be repealed absolutely, totally and immediately; that the reason for the repeal should be assigned, because it was founded on an erroneous principle. At the same time, let the sovereign authority of this country over the colonies be asserted in as strong terms as can be devised, and be made to extend to every point of legislation whatsoever; that we may bind their trade, confine their manufacturers, and exercise every power whatsoever, except that of taking their money out of their pockets without their consent.

"Let us be content with the advantages which Providence has bestowed upon us. We have attained the highest glory and greatness; let us strive long to preserve them for our own happiness and that of posterity."

The effect of this remarkable outpouring was profound. Rockingham had no illusions as to the effect of Pitt's powers;[1] and Grafton, now satisfied that the Government could not continue without Pitt, hastened to call on the Great Commoner, and had a two-hour interview with him. Pitt on this occasion was unambiguous: "if he was called on to form a proper system, it must be with the two present Secretaries, and first Lord of the Treasury, they *co-operating, willing*, and *thoroughly confidential*: any honours or favours to be shewn to the Duke of Newcastle, but not to be of the

[1] Rockingham to George III, January 15th, 1766.

Cabinet, as his perplexing and irksome jealousies would cast a damp upon the vigour of every measure. . . ."[1]

As a result of this interview, Grafton had an audience of the King, who was at last prevailed upon to allow him and Rockingham to enquire of Pitt whether he would consent to come into the King's service, and whether, if Temple should decline, this would still mean that Pitt would decline also. To the first of these questions, according to Grafton, Pitt replied that he would wish to serve with the present Ministers "but there must be a *transposition* of offices:"[2] to the second question Pitt said that Temple's refusal of office would not affect his own action.[3] The demand for a change of offices, however, was distasteful to Rockingham and on the King's instructions he called at Pitt's house to terminate the negotiations at a personal interview.[4]

So the weak Rockingham government continued in power. After many doubts and much hesitation, it was at last decided to repeal the obnoxious Stamp Act, but to accompany the repeal with a Declaratory Act affirming in clear and unmistakable terms the right of Parliament to tax America. The Repeal passed, not without considerable difficulty, largely through the active assistance of Pitt.[5] Meanwhile though Lord Rockingham had looked with such disfavour on Pitt's demand for a change of offices, he was fully conscious of the almost insuperable difficulties of carrying on without him; and on February 26th he sent him a formal memorandum. "He wished to God Mr. Pitt would give some plan for arranging an Administration, putting himself at the head of it."[6] This was very different language, but Pitt still declined to listen. "The King's

[1] Grafton, *Autobiography*, ed. Sir William Anson.

[2] Grafton, *Autobiography*, ed. Sir William Anson.

[3] The King's memorandum of this interview among his papers at Windsor is endorsed: "Precis of the D. of Grafton's and Lord Rockingham's conversation with Mr. Pitt. Jan. 18th., 1766." There is another copy in the Bute MSS.

[4] The King's distrust of Pitt is evident. "I think Y sending a written answer to Mr. P. extrem'ly dangerous, and therefore am clearly of opinion yt. Y even seeing him alone is preferable. . . . I recommend it strongly to Y to avoid a long Conversation by saying Y business only permits Y to call for a few minutes; be extrem'ly civil but firm in what Y say. . . ." George III to Rockingham, Queen's House, January 21st, 1766. Rockingham to George III, "Grosvenor Square, Tuesday p.m. near 5 o'clock Jan ye 21st., 1766."

[5] Pitt, Camden and Shelburne opposed the Declaratory Act, but without success.

[6] Memorandum of a Conference with Lord Rockingham (read by Nuthall to Pitt), Wednesday, February 26th, 1766.

pleasure and gracious commands alone shall be a call to me," he declared; "I am deaf to every other thing. The sum of things is that I am fitter for a lonely hill in Somersetshire than for the affairs of State."[1] So things continued into the summer, when matters were suddenly brought to a head by the resignation of Grafton, now more than ever convinced that the Administration could not satisfactorily continue without Pitt. George now had no alternative to summoning the recluse from Somerset, and on July 7th he wrote bidding him to come with all speed to town.[2]

On receipt of the King's summons, Pitt immediately penned one of his usual effusions for such occasions and hastened to London.[3] On the route to the Capital, his old retainer, honest John Smith, met his master's coach four miles on the London side of Marlborough careering along at a great speed. "Lord a mercy!" exclaimed the worthy yeoman to Lady Chatham, "going at such a rate!"

Pitt reached London on July 11th, and lodged with Alexander and Molly Hood at their house in Harley Street. Unfortunately the rapidity of the journey had affected his health. "I write this hasty line to my dearest life from the house of the Hoods; where I am perfectly well lodged. The history which I am happy to think my love wishes to hear is this, that I got safe to town, not over well, having found the fatigue of the first day too much for me. The bile was roused, and a little quickness of the pulse made my own Esculapian skill necessary. I am, upon honour, much better to-day; have been at Richmond, and returned to a five o'clock chicken, which, had you been with me, would have been a happy banquet. . . . May Heaven keep my love and our dear children well, and may I hear soon that you are all delighted with Weymouth! I expect many sage reflections from William, upon the public papers. Many blessings and tender kisses to them all. My pen is stopt by company entering. Good Night."[4] At his audience at Richmond Pitt had been given *carte blanche* for forming a Government. As soon, therefore, as he had recovered from the effects of the journey, he set about with what speed and alacrity his health would permit, the forming of what in happy phrase Edmund Burke has called his "Mosaic Administration."[5] Of its melancholy course to its inglorious close, the sad story must now be told.

---

[1] William Pitt to Shelburne, February 24th, 1766.
[2] George III to William Pitt, Richmond Lodge, July 7th, 1766.
[3] William Pitt to George III, "July ye 8th., 1766."
[4] William Pitt to Lady Chatham, Harley Street, July 12th, 1766.
[5] Burke, House of Commons, April 19th, 1774.

CHAPTER III

In the Reign of George III (1)

In the *London Gazette* of July 30th, 1766, it was announced that William Pitt had been raised to the peerage. The news was very ill received. The common people felt that their hero had deserted them, and even in the great man's home circle the tidings were not universally welcomed. "My Lord Pitt is much better, Lady Hester quite well, and Mr. William very near it," reported the family tutor to Lady Chatham. "The last gentleman is not only contented in retaining his papa's name, but perfectly happy in it. Three months ago he told me, in a very serious conversation, he was very glad he was not the eldest son, but that he could serve his country in the House of Commons like his papa."[1] Two days later the faithful Wilson gave Lady Chatham an amusing account of how first news of the new honours was received in the family circle. "At nine in the morning," he wrote, "(earlier by two or three hours than the postman generally comes) a letter from Mrs. Betty to Lady Hester Pitt was brought in by the Coachman. She instantly broke the seal, but in opening the letter the superscription accidentally catched her eye, upon which she was in the greatest distress imaginable and ran directly to Mrs. Sparry to know what she shou'd do, supposing that it belong'd to your Ladyship. Mrs. Sparry (who had just rais'd her head and rubb'd her eyes to read the letter which she had received from your Ladyship, and who was consequently yet uninformed) naturally received the account as it was represented, only with somewhat less concern; said it was an accident, that it cou'd not be help'd, desir'd her to lay it down and said that she wou'd take care of it and inform your Ladyship how it all happen'd. By this time the maids, who had all receiv'd letters and read them with greater Dispatch, alarm'd the whole house, and congratulations were so thick from every quarter that it's not easy to say how any one behav'd, but on the whole I am fully persuaded that the congratulated were much more compos'd than the congratulators. Lady Hester was a perfect pattern to the most improv'd understanding, and

[1] Wilson to Lady Chatham, Weymouth, August 2nd, 1766. Lord Stanhope quotes young Pitt as saying: "I want to speak in the House of Commons like papa," but that appears to be incorrect. Stanhope, *Life of William Pitt*, Vol. I.

Lady Harriot was very little behind her, I assure you; his Lordship was somewhat more elevated but by no means more to any improper degree, and Mr. William was not less animated than any one on being complimented as the only surviving Mr. William Pitt. . . ."[1]

We left the new peer at the Hoods' house in Harley Street. Audiences with the King at Richmond and meetings with various colleagues over the week-end made him so ill that he left his friends' house for one at North End on Hampstead Heath, where the air was thought to be cooler and more bracing. "Mr. Pitt has a fever at Mr. Dineley's at Hampstead," recorded the arch-gossip, Horace Walpole to Lady Suffolk. "Lord Temple arrived on Monday, and has been with the fever two or three times, but whether he has caught any of it or not, remains an impenetrable mystery."[2] And to Lord Holland he recorded the same day: "Mr. Pitt is at Mr. Dineley's at Hampstead and has a fever. Lord Temple arrived on Monday, has seen the King, and been at least three times at Hampstead. Still there is nothing but rumours and guesses."[3] Temple certainly had an attack of that fever that blew him out like a bull-frog to feeling the equal of his brother-in-law, and when he saw that he was to be treated as a subordinate, however high-placed, he retired in high dudgeon to Stowe. "The intended basis of the new, virtuous and patriotic Administration," he wrote sarcastically, "is to be the Rump of the last, strengthened by the particular friends of Mr. Pitt, the whole consisting of all the most choice spirits who did in the last Session most eminently distinguish themselves in the Sacrifice by the rights and honour of the whole Legislature and Kingdom of Great Britain. At the head of this I might have stood a capital cypher, surrounded with cyphers of quite a different complexion, and the whole under the guidance of that great Luminary, the great Commoner, with the Privy Seal in his hand."[4] With the departure of Temple, Pitt's difficulties were largely overcome, but the weakness in the House of Commons was quickly apparent and Chatham was soon searching for new adherents. But men were weary of his haughty manners and insolent ways and they would have none of him. Parliament met on November 11th, 1766, and the tone and conduct of Lord Chatham on various occasions gave great offence. He was more imperious, more quarrelsome, more tyrannical than ever. Then in December the proud minister suddenly

[1] Wilson to Lady Chatham, Weymouth, August 4th, 1766.

[2] Walpole to Lady Suffolk, "Arlington St., Thursday morning" (July 17th, 1766). "Dineley" was Charles Dingley, who was to obtain a momentary notoriety for his opposition to Wilkes at the Middlesex Election of 1769.

[3] Walpole to Holland, "Arlington St., July 17th., noon." (1766.)

[4] Temple to Grenville, "Stowe, Friday 6 o'clock a.m. July 18th, 1766."

proclaimed himself suffering from the gout and announced that he must retire to Bath to drink the waters. Early in the new year it was given forth that the Prime Minister was better, and on January 11th he set out for London. Soon, however, a fresh bout compelled him to turn back whence he came. He remained prostrate at Bath until February 15th when he set forth once more. This time he reached Marlborough, where yet another attack forced him to retire to bed in the Castle Inn. This noble pile, originally built by Inigo Jones, had only recently become a hostelry,[1] and it was certainly not accustomed to the bustle and confusion that reigned within its doors during the fortnight's sojourn of the illustrious invalid. Practically the whole accommodation was taken up by the noble lord and his vast retinue of grooms, valets, pages and other attendants, and it was even said by the wags that the inn servants themselves were compelled during his residence to don the blue and silver livery of the Earl of Chatham.[2] There he remained until March 3rd, when at length he arrived in London. Then the thick mantle of imbecility descended upon his mind and henceforth all was darkness, silence and confusion.

Meanwhile, the gouty Chatham remained hidden from the public view. Immediately upon his return to London he had repaired to Charles Dingley's house in Hampstead and there in the surrounding country he could be seen from time to time. "I was with Lady George last night where I met with Cunningham, who told me he had seen Lord Chatham in his chariot, with a servant sitting by him," wrote Lady Temple to her husband; "he looked very grave and sadly. Whatever was become of Lady Chatham, this looks as if they would not let him go out by himself, for he certainly does not like the company of servants."[3] Gradually, however, even this ceased, and for more than a year Chatham became invisible. To all who begged for an interview, he lent a deaf ear: to the remonstrances of the King, he returned an answer, full of humility, but in the same sense. Almost all Chatham's letters at this time were written in his wife's hand and were to the same effect. With admirable patience and understanding, the young King persisted in his efforts to rally the invalid, and again and again he begged him, if only for a few moments, to see the Duke of Grafton. "Your duty and affection for my person, your own honour, call on you to make an effort," wrote the Sovereign, "five minutes' conversation with you would

---

[1] In 1843 the building was bought for the use of Marlborough College.

[2] Lord Macaulay states this as a fact. Macaulay, *William Pitt, Earl of Chatham*, 2nd Essay. It seems fairly well established, however, that this was only a popular joke, and that in fact all the servants in the Pitt family livery were really part of his retinue.

[3] Lady Temple to Temple, April 18th, 1767.

raise his spirits, for his heart is good; mine, I thank God, want no rousing;
my love to my country, as well as what I owe to my own character and to
my family, prompt me not to yield to faction. Be firm and you will find
me ample ready to take as active a part as the hour seems to require. Though
none of my ministers stand by me I cannot truckle."[1] And in the same
letter the King even offers to call on his great Minister at North End House.
This at last had its effect, and the invalid replied that he would see Grafton
the very next day.[2]

The sight that met the young Duke was indeed a shock. He had
expected to find his leader very ill, but he was hardly prepared for so awful
a transformation. The nerves of the invalid were so affected and the great
mind was so sunk into lethargy that the mere appearance of his colleague
caused him to quiver with pain and confusion very embarrassing to the
visitor. No wonder that the interview was painful in the extreme.[3] But
it was also fruitless; Chatham could hardly be got to grasp what Grafton
said, and he was unable to offer any suggestions save to beg him to remain
at his post. So Grafton retired discomfited and the solitude of the invalid
was undisturbed once more.

For days together he would sit in a small room on the top floor of
North End, leaning over a table, his head in his hands. Seldom could even
his wife gain admittance, and when on occasions she did, he scarcely noticed
her. No domestic was ever suffered to enter the room, and he signified his
wants by knocking on the floor with his stick. His meals were served
through a hatch in the wall, still to be seen; and only when the servants
had gone was this opened to take out and to replace the dishes.[4] At times
he was seized with other strange cravings. In the spring of 1767 he begged
the owner to agree to the addition of thirty-four bedrooms to the house
and to the acquisition of every property surrounding it which interfered
with the view. He had long since given up all thought of his own affairs,
and in the summer of 1769 these had been entrusted by a Power of Attorney
to his wife.[5] In September, the family moved to Burton Pynsent in the
hope that the mild breezes of Somerset might bring healing in their wings.
No sooner was the move made than the invalid determined that he must
buy back Hayes immediately: only the air of Bromley could restore him.

[1] George III to Chatham, "Richmond Lodge, May 30th, 1767. 34. m. past 2 p.m."

[2] Chatham to George III, North End, May 30th, 1767. (From an imperfect
draft in Lord Chatham's hand.)

[3] Grafton, *Autobiography*, ed. Sir William Anson.

[4] Whateley to Grenville, July 29th, 1767.

[5] Chatham to Nuthall, "North End, August 17. 1767."

At first Walpole refused to sell, but offered to lend the house. This, however, would not suffice, nothing short of ownership would effect a cure. At length Walpole yielded,[1] and the invalid hastened to send a letter of profuse thanks, though it appears he was made to pay heavily for his whim.[2] By Christmas, Hayes was ready, and the family set out from Somerset. They stayed on the way with the George Pitts at Wandsworth Hill,[3] and by the end of the year were once more installed in their old house.

The malady from which Chatham was suffering was, it seems, "maniodepressive insanity" aggravated by lifelong gout, and in later life probably complicated with Bright's disease and perhaps prostate trouble.[4] The effect of these disorders was so to derange his mind that he alternated between periods of intense mental depression and of attacks of nervous excitement bordering on insanity. Indeed, the genius of Chatham, with its gleam of savagery, was akin to insanity, and it was therefore of the first importance that he should have the best possible advice. Unfortunately, at this time he put himself into the hands of a new physician, Dr. Anthony Addington,[5] who, according to Walpole ". . . originally was a mad doctor. The truth, I believe, is that Addington, who is a kind of empiric, has forbidden his doing the least business, though he lies out of town, and everybody sees him pass in his coach along the street. His case I should think, is a symptomatic fever that ought to turn to gout; but Addington keeps him so low that the gout cannot make its effort. Lord Chatham's friends are much alarmed, and so they say is Addington himself; yet what is strange, he calls in no help."[6] The King urged the invalid to see his own physician,[7] but Chatham would hear nothing of it, and he replied that he placed his entire confidence in Dr. Addington.[8]

The wonder is that Chatham ever survived his treatment. Little

[1] Walpole to Chatham, London, October 30th, 1767.

[2] Chatham to Walpole, November 1st, 1767 (from a draft in Lady Chatham's hand). Walpole had paid Chatham £11,780 for Hayes, but when he bought it back Chatham had to pay Walpole £17,400 for the property. See Chatham MSS. Public Record Office, 51, 61. But Walpole had greatly improved the property. The purchase money was found by a sale of portions of the Pynsent Estate.

[3] Walpole to Mann, Arlington Street, December 25th, 1767.

[4] I am grateful for these details to Sir Charles Grant Robertson, who informs me that George III, curiously enough, suffered from the very same complaints.

[5] Father of Henry Addington, afterwards Viscount Sidmouth.

[6] Walpole to Mann, Strawberry Hill, April 5th, 1767.

[7] George III to Chatham, "Richmond Lodge, June 15th, 1767, 5m. past 8 a.m."

[8] Chatham to George III, "North End, June ye 15th., 1767 ½ past 12." The copy in the Chatham Correspondence is in Lady Chatham's hand.

meat, no alcohol and plenty of fresh air in a clear, dry climate would seem to have been the prescription he needed. Yet Addington almost completely reversed this regime; he advised him to eat plenty of meat, to drink port wine, hock and madeira, and not to take too much exercise. That Chatham survived is due in no small measure to the noble woman whom Coutts, the banker, called "the cleverest *man* of her time in politics and business." On her fell the burden of his affairs. She conducted his correspondence, educated and tended his children, guarded his finances, and lavished upon the half crazy invalid the most devoted care. Thus matters dragged on until the autumn of 1768 when Chatham, seizing upon a petty excuse to bring matters to a head, resigned his office of Lord Privy Seal. Grafton begged him to reconsider his decision;[1] the King added his entreaties, almost his commands. ". . . I think I have a right to insist on your remaining in my service," he wrote, "for I with pleasure look forward to the time of your recovery, when I may have your assistance in resisting the torrent of factions this country so much labours under."[2] But Chatham was not to be moved from his purpose. "My health is so broken," came the reply, "that I feel all chance of recovery will be entirely precluded by my continuing to hold the Privy Seal, totally disabled as I still am from assisting in your Majesty's Councils. . . ."[3] There was no more to be said, and on October 14th, 1768, Lord Chatham laid down his last office under the Crown.

When on July 7th, 1769, Chatham suddenly made his appearance at a levee, he was surprised and shocked to find many changes in public affairs and the name of the Duke of Grafton, still the nominal head of the Administration he had formed, had been dragged in the mud by an anonymous writer of peculiar vituperative brilliance known by the *nom-de-guerre* of "Junius," now generally identified as a clerk of the War Office, Sir Philip Francis. Further trouble had been found for the Ministry by the return to England of the arch-firebrand, Wilkes, followed by the unfortunate affair of the Middlesex Election. Of these proceedings Chatham could not approve, and on being summoned to the King's Closet, he determined to let his Sovereign know his views. George was gracious,[4] but whether he liked

---

[1] Chatham to Grafton, "Hayes, Wednesday, Octo. 12th., 1768." Grafton to Chatham, "Grosvenor Square, Octr. 12th., 1768." Both these letters were the next morning forwarded to the King under cover of one from Grafton to George III. "Grosr. Square, Ocr. 13th., 1768 5m. past 8 a.m."

[2] George III to Chatham, Queen's House, October 14th, 1768.

[3] Chatham to George III, "Hayes, October ye 14th., 1768."

[4] Chatham to Temple, July 7th, 1769.

his haughty subject's harangue is much to be doubted. Certain it is that news of this twenty minutes' audience was soon abroad. Was he sent for? queried Burke to Rockingham: "If he was not sent for, it was only humbly to lay a reprimand at the feet of his most gracious master, and to talk some insignificant, pompous creeping, explanatory, ambiguous matter, in the true Chathamic style. . . ."[1] Thus in uncertainty ended this remarkable audience: the two actors in the drama were never again destined to meet face to face.

Not long before Chatham's sudden appearance at Court, an event had occurred which was soon to prove of great consequence to the future politics of the period. Through the mediation of Lady Chatham and the good offices of young Tom Pit, who, it will be remembered, had politically allied himself to his uncle, George Grenville, a complete reconciliation had been effected between the great man and the Grenville brothers, an event that was trumpeted abroad by the pompous Temple in typically bombastic terms.[2] To cement this friendship, the noble Temple had paid a visit in form to Hayes, which the Chathams had promised in due course to return. At first this was prevented by the illness of William "whose state keeps us extremely anxious, though in some respects hopeful enough. The whoop-ing-coughers are, I thank God, almost well. William's precarious situation will, we fear, hardly allow Lady Chatham to be absent a day from him which cruelly comes between our ardent wishes towards Stowe. Work-men at the same time must drive us from Hayes, and our purpose is to move as soon as practicable to Chevening, the house of Lord Stanhope, eight miles distant from this place."[3]

To Chevening the Chatham family moved as soon as William had sufficiently recovered; so it was not until a week after his reception at Court that the return visit to Stowe could be paid. But though it had been delayed, it was to be in the grand manner. "Your goodness has en-couraged us to come in the true patriarchal way, and to bring you no less than three children, Hester, Harriet, and Pitt, who are almost in a fever of expectation till the happy day comes. Old and young count the hours with equal impatience till the pleasure of a letter from your lordship fixes our motions."[4] Lord Temple soon fixed their motions, and we have a lively picture of Chatham's idea of travelling in the true patriarchal style: "Lord Chatham passed by my door on Friday morning," wrote Burke, "in a

[1] Burke to Rockingham, Gregories, Sunday, July 9th, 1769.
[2] Political Register, November 25th, 1768.
[3] Chatham to Temple, Hayes, July 7th, 1769.
[4] Chatham to Temple, Hayes, July 10th, 1769.

jimwhiskee drawn by two horses, one before the other,—he drove himself. His train was two coaches-and-six, with twenty servants, male and female. He was proceeding with his whole family (Lady Chatham, two sons and two daughters) to Stowe. He lay at Beaconsfield, and was well and cheerful, and walked up and down stairs at the inn without help."[1]

It was not long before Lord Chatham, eager to voice his dissent from all that had been done, presented himself before his brother peers in the House of Lords, swathed in flannel and supported by crutches. Men might loathe Chatham, but they could not but respect him; for here he was once more—as ever the stricken invalid, but now bowed down with the infirmity of age—standing forth proud and unafraid before his fellows, and by drawing men's attention to the state of the nation discharging what he conceived to be his duty to his God, his country and his king. The state of our foreign affairs he pronounced most critical; the state of our American affairs he declared in poor shape, our unhappy policy having alienated the affections of the Colonists from the motherland and having driven them to excesses which he at once comprehended and deplored. At home the liberty of the subject had been invaded by the arbitrary and unjustifiable expulsion of Wilkes from the House of Commons following the farce of the Middlesex Election, for by a resolution of the lower House alone had a subject been unconstitutionally deprived of his rights and the electors of Middlesex of their free choice of a member.

On the Lord Chancellor these words had an almost magical effect, for to the astonishment and dismay of Ministers, Camden suddenly rose in his place to denounce his colleagues as traitors to the Constitution.[2] From this unexpected outburst from the Keeper of the King's Conscience, it was evident that a new Lord Chancellor must be sought; and Ministers were not slow in seeking an adjournment to give them time to find a successor. But this proved no easy task. The Seals were refused by Dunning; they were declined by Sir Eardley Wilmot. They were then offered to Charles Yorke, a younger son of the late Lord Chancellor Hardwicke. Yorke, a brilliant lawyer and ambitious man, at first accepted the offer; but he rapidly sank under the vehement reproaches of his family and friends, who dubbed him traitor to their cause, and in a few days he died, probably by his own hand. This gloomy tragedy sounded the knell of the Ministry, and on the morning of Monday, January 22nd, the Duke of Grafton resigned. A wise king would have sent forthwith for Chatham, Rockingham or Grenville. But George III was not wise and he would have no dealings

---

[1] Burke to Rockingham, Beaconsfield, July 30th, 1769.

[2] Camden, House of Lords, January 9th, 1770.

with those he regarded as his mortal enemies. All that was wanting was a man sufficiently brave and at the same time sufficiently docile to the royal pleasure to undertake what appeared to be a thankless and well-nigh impossible task. Accordingly, in the hour of his extreme need, the King turned to the fat, podgy, rather stupid face of his Chancellor of the Exchequer, the amiable North, and fervently implored his assistance.[1] The appeal was urgent and not to be denied. In an evil hour for his country, in an evil hour for his fame, the good-natured North took pity on his Sovereign and undertook to rescue him from his embarrassments.

It is some time since we followed the fortunes of Tom Pitt. It will be remembered that on the accession to power of George Grenville, young Tom had hitched his wagon to that star and had been given a subordinate appointment in his uncle's ministry. This, not unnaturally, had been anything but pleasing to his imperious Uncle William, and had resulted in something of a breach between them. This breach had been healed, at least in part, by the reconciliation between Chatham and the Grenville brothers, in the bringing about of which Tom Pitt had played an honourable rôle. In the autumn of 1770 the bonds between uncle and nephew had been drawn closer by the death of Sir Richard Lyttelton. "I am just going to London to visit my nephew, Mr. Pitt," wrote Chatham to Shelburne, "on the late melancholy event of Sir Richard Lyttelton's death."[2] But it was not until the following summer that Tom really came into the news when we hear this piece of fashionable intelligence. "Tom Pitt is going to marry a Miss Wilkinson, a great fortune, sister to Jack Smith's wife," wrote Walpole to his old friend, Lady Upper Ossory, adding as an afterthought, "I don't believe your Ladyship cares much about these Jacks and Toms."[3] But even if these aristocratic correspondents are not much interested in the fates of Jacks and Toms, the more plebeian reader may well be; for behind this marriage hides a tragic tale, some mention of which must now be made.

During the summer of 1758, a certain Mr. Pinckney Wilkinson, a rich merchant of Burnham, Norfolk, accompanied by his wife and his two daughters, journeyed to Bath. Mrs. Wilkinson, something of an invalid,

[1] George III to North, "Queen's House, Jan. 22nd., 1770. 13 min. pt. 7 a.m." and "Queen's House, Jan. 23rd., 1770, 40 min. pt. 10 a.m."

[2] Chatham to Shelburne, Hayes, Wednesday morning (October 4th, 1770). Tom Pitt erected to the memory of his uncle an obelisk still to be seen in the park of Boconnoc.

[3] Walpole to Lady Upper Ossory, Arlington Street, June 27th, 1771. Lady Upper Ossory had previously been the wife of the Duke of Grafton, the Prime Minister.

seldom left her room, and her husband mostly stayed with her. In the evenings, however, it was not unusual for the girls, Mary and Anne, to visit the public rooms, and there in due course they made the acquaintance of a certain Captain John Smith of His Majesty's Brigade of Guards, and a former aide-de-camp to Lord George Sackville. The partiality of the gallant Captain seems to have been directed more to the elder Miss Wilkinson, but his attentions were not such as to occasion remark from any member of her family. In any case, the Wilkinsons' stay at Bath was not protracted, and before the end of the summer they returned to their house in London. Then for two years they disappear from our view—until, in fact, the summer of 1760, when we meet them once again, this time drinking the health-giving waters of salubrious Tunbridge Wells. There a strange thing happened. The Wilkinsons had not been settled at this resort more than a few days before the two girls, apparently by accident, suddenly encountered their Bath friend of two years ago. This time Captain Smith renewed his attentions with somewhat more assiduity, and he was soon inviting himself to dinner with the family. Mr. Wilkinson, who does not seem to have made Smith's acquaintance hitherto, was somewhat surprised at these proceedings but was too courteous to make any comment; but when, shortly afterwards, the Captain by the same method invited himself to breakfast, Mr. Wilkinson began to take particular notice of his daughter's friend. Some two days later, during the temporary absence of Mr. Wilkinson in London, Captain Smith made a formal proposal of marriage to Miss Wilkinson, who promptly told her mother: which intelligence Mrs. Wilkinson did not delay to disclose to her husband immediately upon his return.

On being apprised of this most unwelcome news, the portly merchant took an extremely unfavourable view of the proceedings. He was a rich man; his daughters were heiresses; and it did not take him long to discover that Captain Smith was penniless. It took the wealthy father but little time to come to the conclusion that the Captain was an adventurer, and he did not hide his views either from his daughter or her suitor.[1] Furthermore, he gave his views more tangible shape by an alteration in his will, thereby bequeathing his whole fortune to his two daughters in equal shares provided they married with his consent, but should Mary marry Captain Smith,

[1] Sir N. W. Wraxall's views of Smith, however, were more favourable. "Captain Smith, Sir Sydney Smith's father, I very intimately knew, who was himself a man of distinguished personal courage, strictly conscientious and incapable of asserting any fact that he disbelieved. He never entertained an idea that Lord George was withheld by unbecoming personal motive from advancing at Minden." Wraxall, *Historical and Posthumous Memoirs*, Vol. I.

"such marriage promising nothing but ruin and beggary," he then bequeathed her only £10,000 "to be laid out in the public funds, in the names of trustees, and settled to her separate use and that of her children. . . ."[1] Now things having got to this pass, they continued very much as they usually do in such circumstances. Poor Mary Wilkinson was constantly in tears, constantly overwrought, so that before long her health suffered. Faced with this dilemma, Mr. Wilkinson did what most fathers do in like cases; whilst setting his mind resolutely against the marriage, he yet for the sake of his child's peace of mind gave her some slight food for hope that at some uncertain future date he might possibly be prevailed upon to look with less disfavour on the project. As to the Captain, the origin of all the trouble, by a threat of immediate departure from Tunbridge Wells, Wilkinson prevailed upon him to give a positive undertaking that he would at once leave that place and that he would not attempt either to see or to correspond with his daughter during the rest of their visit. Smith promptly gave the undertaking and left for Stoneland Lodge, a property in Sussex, about six miles away belonging to Lord George Sackville's father, the Duke of Dorset. And thus matters stood when on September 15th the Wilkinsons returned to London.

But they had not long been settled before a lady appeared who represented herself as a friend of Captain Smith's and entreated Miss Wilkinson to go to him immediately as he was seriously ill at Stoneland Lodge. Mr. Wilkinson expressed himself in emphatic language to his daughter, and swore a most solemn oath that if Mary should marry Smith, he would never see her again. But the love-lorn girl was beyond all human aid. Within a few days of the receipt of the message she left her father's house to join her lover; within a week they were married in the Duke of Dorset's parish church, the ceremony being performed by the husband of the lady who had come to London on the Captain's behalf. The outraged Wilkinson did the only thing that in the circumstances was left him to do; he destroyed the will he had made in July and on December 6th he signed a new will leaving her but £5 together with an annuity of £400 for her separate use. However, during the next few years he made several fresh testamentary arrangements the final upshot of which was that Mary was to receive the £10,000 secured to her and for her children after her death, as originally provided.[2]

And so the years passed, and very unhappy years they were for poor

[1] Extract from Will of Pinckney Wilkinson made at Tunbridge Wells, July 28th, 1760.

[2] Codicil to Will dated December 6th, 1760, dated June 8th, 1764; Wills dated September 25th, 1765, and August 3rd, 1768.

Mary Smith. Captain Smith, it seems, having acquired his wife without her money, soon demonstrated what manner of man he was. He constantly ill-treated and frequently assaulted her, with the result that she came almost to fear for her life, and there were nights that she had to spend wandering abroad to avoid the insults and the lashes of her impassioned husband. One thing and one thing alone prevented her from leaving him —the mother's intense love for her children. Thus matters stood when in 1771 Tom Pitt came awooing Anne Wilkinson. Of course, he heard the whole sad story from her, for Anne had ever done all in her power to lighten her sister's burden; of course he was anxious to play his part in helping her who was soon to be his sister-in-law; but apart from paying the Captain's debts, which amounted at this time to some £1,500, there was little that he could do to improve what was so obviously an impossible situation.

Hitherto the attitude of Mr. Wilkinson to these matters had been that of the outraged parent; his daughter had defied him and she must suffer the consequences. But Tom Pitt had not been long married to the younger Miss Wilkinson[1] before he was forced to state to his father-in-law in no uncertain terms that the question had long since ceased to be whether he would restore to favour an offending child and was now the far more serious one whether he could refuse protection to a child who went in fear for her life; and so serious a view of the situation did young Tom take that he actually went to the length of secreting his sister-in-law into his house so that her father could not by reason of his oath refuse to see her. The upshot of these desperate proceedings was that on March 21st, 1772, Mr. Wilkinson, accompanied by his two daughters, his son-in-law, Tom Pitt, and a solicitor by name Dagge, presented himself at the house of Lord Mansfield to swear the peace against John Smith.

The old judge, having listened intently to all that was said, requested the presence before him of the cause of the trouble. Accordingly, Captain Smith, accompanied by two friends of both parties, Lord Dartmouth and Lord Chief Baron Smythe, duly arrived at the house and was put in another room. Then the negotiations began, and message after message passed from one room to the other, the disinterested parties doing all they could to compose the differences of the Smiths and to satisfy the requirements of Mr. Wilkinson; and in these negotiations Tom Pitt played a lively and honourable part. At length, after many comings and goings, an agreement was arrived at, the terms of which were set out in two papers. In one, signed by Smith, it was agreed that he would separate from his wife, give

---

[1] They were married on July 28th, 1771.

up the care of his children to their grandfather "for their good," and that Mr. Wilkinson would pay him £200 a year so long as the separation should continue, as well as settle the future debts of his daughter: the other, signed by Wilkinson, merely stated that he would pay his son-in-law £200 a year during the separation and his daughter's future debts, making no mention of the children. These papers were exchanged between the parties. This seemingly satisfactory compromise having been reached, Lord Mansfield, ever a lover of peace, prevailed upon Mary Smith to write a kind letter to her husband in order to pacify the extreme agitation of his mind which, he said, was bordering on distraction, and without any mention of the unhappy past to revert only to new hope for the future. This letter having been penned, Tom Pitt had the extreme satisfaction of bringing the Smith children to their grandfather's house, where they were received as members of his family.

Thus concludes the first part of the grim little tale; the conclusion of the sordid tragedy must ere long be told.

During the last months of 1770 and the spring and summer of 1771— at about the time that Tom Pitt was wooing and winning Anne Wilkinson —there was frequently to be seen in the fashionable drawing-rooms of London a twenty-two-year-old Italian aristocrat of distinguished appearance and attractive manners. Tall and commanding in form, he had a face that showed at once unusual intelligence and power; his forehead was lofty, and around it fell in careless disarray the more unruly locks of his great head of flaming red hair. His name was Count Vittorio Alfieri. A member of one of the noble families of Piedmont, he had been born at Asti. He was also connected with several other families of an antiquity equal to the Alfieris, for his father, Antonio Alfieri, married late in life the young widow of the Marquis of Cacherano, already the mother of three children, and by her had two,[1] first a daughter and then a son. When that son, christened Vittorio, had barely passed his first birthday, his father died; his mother, who was still young and handsome, married for the third time, the Chevalier Hyacinth de Magliano, a distant relative of her second husband, and with him she lived for many years in placid harmony and contentment. Count Alfieri then, was noble, well connected, handsome. Moreover, he was known to be rich, passionate, eccentric, with a nice taste for literature and an intense love of horses. It may, therefore, be well imagined that these qualities assured him a warm welcome in the fashionable circles of the capital.

[1] A third child of the marriage, born posthumously, died in infancy.

NELOPE PITT, Viscountess Ligonier, daughter of George Pitt of
Gainsborough   Strathfieldsaye

George and you in the midst of improvements, and the intended disposition of your Gallery I thought very pleasing. . . ."[1] The previous year, Pitt had been appointed our Minister to Turin, and it is while he is at this post that we first hear that all is not well between George and Pen Pitt. Phelps, it seems, is the confidant of them both. "My long Letter to Mrs. Pitt which you heard with attention, and the Intreaty that she would disprove the Allegations contain'd in it . . . remain in force; and having not been answer'd, I know not how I can more effectually instruct your kind intentions, than by referring you to this Letter. Two other long Letters upon ye same subject she has since recᵈ . . . you cannot have a better guide (from me at least) in the good work you seem inclin'd to undertake, than these papers." But the mediator should consult both sides. "Should you not find in Her the same disposition to be open and frank, should she scruple shewing you these Letters, you may assure yourself yᵗ· her backwardness will proceed entirely from her Tenderness for my precious Character, and her unwillingness to shew with how much Injustice I accuse her. But since you are equally a friend of both, she has my ready consent to expose me to you by shewing you these Letters, as I am very thoroughly persuaded yᵗ· you know me to be sincere in all I have laid to her Charge, and yᵗ· I think no earthly Blessing could equal her convincing me of it's Injustice."[2] Whether the peace-maker Phelps was successful, we do not know; but there was no open breach, and some seven years later Pitt was appointed British Ambassador at Madrid, a post he held for less than a year.[3] George Pitt, who in the past had badgered Pitt for a diplomatic post and believed, quite wrongly, that he owed his Turin appointment to his cousin's graces, had more recently been urging his claims to be elevated to the Upper House,[4] declaring that he was determined not to return to his duty without

---

[1] Phelps to Penelope Pitt, "Lausanne, Oct. 12th." (1762.)

[2] George Pitt to Phelps, "Turin, Feb. 5th. 1763."

[3] February 1770 till January 1771.

[4] George Pitt to Conway, Half Moon Street, September 24th, 1765 and August 28th, 1765, and George Pitt to Rockingham, Half Moon Street, October 5th, 1765. The last of these letters was endorsed: "An interview in consequence of this note gave Mr. Pitt clearly to understand that he was to expect nothing but opposition from the Administration." The letter of September 25th to Conway bears this note in George Pitt's hand: "Gen. Conway's letter in answer to that of September 24th, to which this is a reply, cannot in justice be shewn without his permission." These four letters were subsequently sent by Pitt together with a covering letter to George III and they are now in the Royal Archives at Windsor. Sir John Fortescue is mistaken in supposing the covering letter from Pitt to the King, which is undated, was written in 1766, and in printing it under that date in the King's published papers, *The Correspondence of King George III from 1760 to December, 1783*. Ed. Fortescue, Vol. III.

some mark of royal favour.[1] "My pretensions to a Peerage are so many and of so strong a Nature," he had written with sublime self-confidence, "that upon My Word, My Lord, even an enemy could not oppose them."[2] But he had to wait another ten years before his wish was granted, for it was not until 1776 that he was at last ennobled as Baron Rivers.

But though there was no open breach between the George Pitts, it is to be feared that the marriage was not a happy one ; and Horace Walpole, ever a staunch friend and admirer of the wife, is frequently a caustic critic of the husband. "I am sorry you saw no more of Mrs. Pitt," he wrote to his friend, Sir Horace Mann. "She is the most amiable of beings and the most to be pitied ; her brutal, half-mad husband, with whom she is still not out of love, and who has heaped on her every possible cruelty and provoking outrage, will not suffer her to see, or ever to hear from any of her children."[3] Of these children, four in number,[4] the beautiful Penelope soon won the heart of Captain Ligonier. They were married in 1766 at the British Embassy in Paris, and soon returned to England to join in the gay life of the fashionable London of George III. In 1770, the old Field-Marshal died at the advanced age of eighty-nine, and though his English earldom died with him his Irish Viscountcy devolved by special remainder upon his nephew. So it was to the drawing-room of the popular Lord and Lady Ligonier that Count Vittorio Alfieri repaired with such alacrity during his second visit to England in 1771.

But not only in their house, but in their box at the Opera and elsewhere in public was the passionate young Italian constantly seen with the fair Penelope Ligonier and her lord, so that the censorious began to whisper and the sceptics to doubt. All went well for a while however, for so long as they remained in London, Alfieri could see the lady without any undue risks being run, but as summer approached the bombshell fell ; Lord Ligonier announced that he and his wife were about to spend the next few months at a country house that he had recently taken near London,[5] and that they would not be back in London until winter came. The prospect of

---

[1] George Pitt to Chatham, Half Moon Street, August 1st, 1766.   [2] George Pitt to Chatham, Half Moon Street, December 17th, 1766.

[3] Walpole to Mann, December 22nd, 1772.   [4] See family tree.

[5] "A country seat sixteen miles from London," Alfieri, *Memoirs* (English translation), Vol. I. There is, however, a local tradition that the events about to be recorded in fact took place at a house in Strathfieldsaye park and the late Maud, Duchess of Wellington, was good enough to show me the site near the head of the lake where the house once stood. The truth probably is that Penelope lived there after her divorce from Ligonier and before her second marriage, but there cannot of course be any certainty as to that. All that is known is that the first Duke of Wellington in taking possession of the Strathfieldsaye estate had the house demolished because he so strongly disapproved of Penelope and all her works!

separation from the object of his affections drove the ardent Italian almost
to frenzy; he could not bear to live without her; and in his passionate way
he vowed that death itself was preferable to a long separation. To his plea
the fair Penelope did not turn a deaf ear. Indeed, the lovers agreed that
they could not bear to be parted; and that, in spite of the obvious risks,
they must continue to meet whenever an opportunity could be found.
So it was arranged between them that on an occasion when Lord Ligonier
had to spend a night in London for the transaction of some business, his
wife should not languish in a lonely bed.

At last the happy night arrived. The unsuspecting husband duly went
to London, and Penelope left open the gate in the garden wall. Her lover,
having stabled his horse at a local inn, slipped through and spent the night
in his mistress's arms. At dawn he left, but not before it had been arranged
that the adventure should be repeated two nights hence, when Lord Ligonier
would be again absent from home. Alfieri was in the highest spirits, but
the two days that lay ahead of him stretched forth into eternity. His
passionate nature was so wrought up by impatient expectation that he was
almost in a frenzy. Part of the time he passed raving in his chamber,
part in galloping furiously over the countryside and leaping recklessly over
hedges and ditches to the imminent hazard of his neck. On the second
day of this torment, whilst riding out with his friend, Marquis Caraccioli,
he spied a huge gate and on the impulse of the moment set spur to his
steed and went straight for the formidable obstacle. The result was to be
expected; the horse failed to clear the gate, and it and its impetuous rider
came to the ground. In a few moments, Alfieri felt the most excruciating
pain; a doctor was summoned, and he pronounced his shoulder to be broken
and his collar-bone dislocated. The bones were promptly re-set, and the
patient was ordered to bed. This accident took place on Saturday; Sunday
evening was the time of his assignation. In spite of the surgeon's orders,
in spite of the agony of movement, Alfieri determined to keep the appointment, and at six o'clock the following evening he duly set forth in a post-
chaise—riding being now impossible—and suffering torment from the
jolting of the carriage, he in due course arrived at his destination.

This time the garden gate was shut—which was curious, for Penelope
had certainly left it open, according to arrangement. This suspicious
fact might have given Alfieri to pause, and had he troubled to look round,
he might have caught sight of a dark, shadowy form lurking in the under-
growth. But the passionate Italian was too exalted to take account of such
trifles; he had no thought for hidden watchers; he had but one thought, the
object of his affections: so, in spite of this hindrance, in spite of his injuries,
he scaled the wall and in a few moments was in the arms of his love. At

dawn he returned the way he had come; that afternoon he was back in London again.

On Tuesday evening, Alfieri visited the Opera and was accommodated in the Spanish Ambassador's box. During the course of the performance the door at the back was opened, and he heard his name pronounced in a peremptory tone. He left the box immediately and in the passage outside found himself face to face with the grim form of Lord Ligonier. The injured husband promptly enquired into the meaning of Sunday night's escapade and let it be seen that he would be grateful for an explanation of the other's conduct. At first, Alfieri denied everything; but when it became obvious that Ligonier knew every detail and finally told him that his wife had confessed, he realized that further denials would only be ridiculous. So talking they came to St. James's Park.

It was clear that the matter could be concluded in only one way and though no seconds were available it was not long before the two young men drew their swords. At this moment, Ligonier noticed for the first time that his companion's left arm was in a sling, and he politely enquired if this would not hinder him from defending himself. But Alfieri, though he knew he was no swordsman, would hear of no delay. The duel went as might be expected. Alfieri, whirling his sword round with much force but no effect, slashed away savagely and with great resolution; his opponent, coolly parried those reckless blows and in a few moments quietly passed his point through Alfieri's right arm, between the wrist and the elbow. The Italian felt nothing and went whirling on; but Ligonier, courteously pointing out that he was wounded, pronounced himself satisfied and sheathing his sword promptly walked off. Alfieri, seeing that his wound was but a scratch, tied his handkerchief round it with his teeth and returned to the Opera. But he was too restless now to sit and listen to the music as if nothing had happened, and in a few moments he left the theatre and made for the house of Penelope's sister-in-law, who had connived at the whole intrigue. There to his astonishment he found Penelope herself. It seemed that she, having heard that her husband had gone to London to fight her lover, after sending a messenger to warn him rushed up herself. The messenger had failed to find Alfieri, and as Lord Ligonier, in a very gloomy state had returned to his house in a cab, they had all surmised that he had killed his opponent. Great rejoicings, therefore, attended the latter's arrival practically untouched.

Alfieri was now in a state of almost frenzied excitement. He had come through the ordeal of the duel without ridicule, and the outraged Ligonier soon made it plain that he was suing his erring wife for a divorce. Before long, therefore, he could be united to his mistress. But, whereas the Count was in this joyous mood, the prospective bride, much to his astonishment and alarm, appeared anything but content; indeed, she seemed overwhelmed with grief. She constantly wept. She continuously complained in a querulous, hysterical voice that her lover's intentions were not honourable, that she loved him to distraction, that he would never wed her. To a man of the Southern temperament of the Italian, this behaviour was less than bearable. He stormed; he raved; he became distracted; he conjured her to explain herself; he swore by all the gods that he adored her, would never leave her, would wed no one else, and much more in the same key. At last by slow degrees he dragged the truth from his reluctant mistress. After a long and hesitating preamble, punctuated with many sighs and tears, she confessed that she was unworthy of him; that he could not, would not, ought not to marry her; that before she had loved him, she had loved another. . . . "Who, then," exclaimed the romantic Italian; who had been his predecessor? Then came the climax, and the awful truth struck him like a mortal blow on the temple—his predecessor had been no romantic figure, no great lover like himself, but—oh, horror of horrors!—none other than her husband's head-groom! To the aristocratic soul of poor Alfieri, this intelligence was shattering: the humiliation he felt at his rival's social status was almost worse than the rivalry itself. Then of a sudden he remembered the locked garden gate on the second night of his adventure. It was indeed the groom who had locked it, and standing in the shadows had seen Alfieri climb the wall; whereupon he had promptly taken his revenge by making a clean breast of everything to his master! A painful scene ensued between the lovers in which the outraged and horrified Count informed Penelope that he could never wed her, but that as her frank confession had to some degree mitigated her offence, he would consent to live with her, unknown and unnoticed, in some obscure corner of Europe or America, provided only she never attempted to pass for his wife. Having worked himself up to a state of emotional ecstasy by this false spirit of self-abnegation, he impetuously flung himself from the room, slamming the door behind him.

Returning home, he threw himself on his bed and attempted to sleep; but the tumult of his mind made this impossible, and at the first gleam of dawn he rose from his restless couch. Hardly knowing what he did, he idly took up the previous day's newspaper and with a glassy stare cast his eyes over the pages. At first he saw nothing, but as he stared on he suddenly observed his own name standing out in large letters amid the print. Springing up and focusing attention on the sheet, to his consternation and dismay he read a detailed and circumstantial account of his whole amour. To his heated and distorted brain, the words stood out like fiery darts.

In a flash he was undeceived; at last he saw all—at last he realized that Penelope's frank, spontaneous confession of the previous evening was nothing but the story the newspapers of the morning had published to the world. Transported with rage and humiliation, he rushed to his faithless mistress, heaped a thousand reproaches on her offending head, cursed her for her duplicity, bade her an eternal farewell, and swore solemnly that so long as he lived he would never set eyes on her again. But he had not been gone more than a few hours before he returned, flung himself into her arms, and whispered a thousand nothings into her receptive ear. Thereafter, he continued to visit her daily till, finding herself the talk and ridicule of the town, Penelope determined to leave England and to retire to a convent in France. Alfieri accompanied her to the coast and exercised every art to delay her departure; day after day he continued to linger with her, ashamed and furious at his weakness, but unable to burst the bonds that bound them together. At last at Rochester they parted: the Count returned to London, and she, accompanied by her patient, long-suffering sister-in-law, retired to France and from the eccentric life of her temperamental lover.

Of the future careers of the chief actors in this story, a few words will suffice. George Pitt pursued untiringly his efforts to obtain a peerage,[1] until at last in 1776 his efforts were rewarded.[2] Lord Ligonier, having obtained his divorce, soon sought consolation in a second marriage with the daughter of Lord Chancellor Northington; he subsequently became a general in the army and an earl; but he did not long survive these honours, for he died in 1782. Count Alfieri became a world-famous figure, one of his country's greatest poets and dramatists, and the accepted lover of Princess Louise of Stolberg, Countess of Albany, the discarded wife of Charles Edward, the Young Pretender. After the death of her sottish, dissolute husband, these two were never parted until death came to Alfieri on October 8th, 1803. In the great church of Santa Croce near the tombs of Michael Angelo and Machiavelli, he sleeps; and over his body arises his monument, the work of Canova—a richly adorned sarcophagus in

---

[1] George Pitt to North, December 25th, 1772. "Stratfieldsay," January 3rd, 1773, "Hertford Street, Tuesday Jan. 12th., 1773." "Hertford Street, Jan. 16th., 1773," and "Hertford Street, Jan. 28th., 1773."

[2] In 1776 Pitt was created Baron Rivers of Stratfieldsaye, and in 1802 Baron Rivers of Sudeley Castle. On the death unmarried of his only son in 1828, the barony of Rivers of Stratfieldsaye became extinct, but that of Sudeley Castle devolved on his grandson, Horace William, son of his daughter Louisa and Peter Beckford, her husband. As Louisa was Pitt's second daughter, I suppose the special remainder was so arranged because Penelope had no children.

white marble—placed there by the Countess as a tribute to his memory. When she died more than twenty years later, she was laid at his side.[1]

And Penelope? Only once does she emerge from the obscurity into which she passed as the vessel took her from the shores of Dover on that unhappy afternoon in 1771. Twenty years later, in the spring of 1791, Alfieri and the Countess of Albany were embarking from Dover after a few months' visit to this country. The poet went on board shortly before the Princess to see that everything was prepared for her. Just as he was stepping aboard the vessel, he happened to glance at a number of persons assembled on the shore, and as he did so the first object that met his eyes was the former Penelope Ligonier, still beautiful and hardly altered from what he remembered when they parted at Rochester twenty years back. For a moment, scarcely believing his eyes, he gazed uncertainly at her; but as he did so, she turned in his direction, and a kindly smile of recognition told him that he was not mistaken. He did not know—and his aristocratic soul would have revolted at the knowledge had he been aware of it—that some few years back Lady Ligonier had married an obscure individual of the name of Smith, a trooper in the Blues;[2] and as their eyes met that day, Alfieri found himself bewildered with a multitude of conflicting emotions. He longed to speak once more to his former love, but at the same time he feared to do so, feeling himself emotionally unequal to an interview. But no sooner had he reached Calais than he determined to communicate with her forthwith, and he accordingly wrote her a long letter, recalling their former friendship, expressing the remorse he felt at having been the cause of her degradation, and assuring her of his warm concern for her welfare.[3] The letter he sent to a banker in Dover for re-direction. A month later this remarkable answer reached him in Brussels:

"You cannot doubt but that I am sensible of the marks of your remembrance, and of the interest you so kindly take in my fate, or that I received them gratefully; the more so, as I cannot regard you as the author of my misfortune, although the sensibility and uprightness of your heart make you fear so. You are, on the contrary, the cause of my deliverance from a world in which I was never formed to exist, and which I have never regretted a single instant. I know not if in that I am wrong or if a blamable pride and firmness delude me; but I constantly foresaw what has happened to me and I thank Providence for having placed me in a more fortunate situation than I have merited. I enjoy perfect health, increased by liberty and

[1] She died on January 29th, 1824, at the age of seventy-two.

[2] The marriage took place at Northampton on May 4th, 1784.

[3] This letter has not been preserved.

tranquillity. I seek only the society of simple and honest people, who pretend neither to too much genius nor to too much knowledge, who blunder sometimes, and in default of whom I rest satisfied with my books, my drawings, my music, etc. But that which most assures to me a fund of happiness and real satisfaction, is the friendship and immutable affection of a brother whom I have always loved above all the world, and who possesses the best of hearts.

"It is in compliance with your wishes that I have given you such long details of my situation, and permit me, in my turn, to assure you of the real pleasure which the knowledge of the happiness you enjoy, and which I am persuaded you have always merited, causes me. I have often, during the last two years, heard you spoken of with pleasure in Paris and in London, where your writings—which I have not yet been able to see—are admired and esteemed. I understand that you are attached to the Princess with whom you are travelling, and judging from her charming appearance she seems well qualified to make you happy. It is said, too, that she also fears you; that I can well believe. Without desiring it, or perhaps without perceiving it, you have irresistibly that ascendancy over those who love you.

"I desire for you, from the bottom of my heart, the continuance of your prosperity and of the real pleasure of this world; and if by chance we should meet again, I shall always have the greatest satisfaction to learn that it is so from your lips. Adieu,

"PENELOPE."

"Dover, April 26th."

Adieu, Penelope. You never saw or heard from your poet-lover again. You slid back into obscurity for the long remainder of your mortal span, till at last your summons came, and a raddled, tired old woman, you were ferried by the aged boatman across the stream. Poor Penelope Pitt. Poor weary soul. Sleep on, Penelope, sleep on into Eternity.

CHAPTER IV

In the Reign of George III (2)

FREDERICK, LORD NORTH, eldest son of the first Earl of Guilford, was but thirty-seven years of age—six more than George III—when he became Premier in 1770. But though his life had been short it had been full, and as Chancellor of the Exchequer he had shown himself to be a financier of no mean abilities. Moreover, North was a well-read man of wide interests, an excellent linguist, and something of a scholar. It was not, therefore, to any untried inexperienced amateur that George III turned in the hour of his need.

But if the abilities of North were by no means negligible, his personal appearance was anything but attractive. His body was fat and ungainly so that he was slow, clumsy and awkward in his movements; his nose was turned up; his chin receded; his mouth seemed overfilled with a tongue too large for it; and owing to his grave short-sightedness his eyes were unpleasantly prominent. Yet in spite of these obvious drawbacks, there was much to recommend Lord North to the House of Commons, for in spite of his unlucky lack of grace, he was always an entertaining and, at times, a really powerful speaker, with a lively sense of the ridiculous and marked powers of ridicule of which he availed himself with consummate ability. Moreover, he completely lacked that vaulting ambition that so marred the lives of many public men of his day and his equable temperament was in happy contrast with that of many of his contemporaries. In the House of Commons this last quality was at times apt to prove disconcerting to the Opposition, for what could be more discomfiting to an impassioned opponent who, after levelling the fiery darts of his invective at the Minister's inoffensive head, found that his eloquence had merely lulled the intended victim into a restful and untroubled slumber? Yet at times appearances were apt to be deceptive, for it is on record that on one occasion an Opposition member, thinking that the Premier was fast asleep in his place on the Treasury Bench, exclaimed in a voice of thunder: "Even now the noble Lord is slumbering over the ruins of his country." Slowly, very slowly, the massive inert frame was seen to heave, and a sleepy voice was heard to issue from the depths of the recumbent Minister's ungainly form, "I wish to Heaven," it muttered, "I wish to Heaven that I was!"[1]

The new Government had only been in office for about a month when Chatham took occasion to thunder against "the invisible, irresponsible, and most pernicious counsels of a Favourite . . ." who, though abroad,[2] still yielded influence at home. "Who does not know the Mazarinade of France—the Mazarin absent was Mazarin still. . . . When I was earnestly called upon for the public service I came from Somersetshire with wings of zeal. I consented to preserve a peace which I abominated; a peace I would not make, but would preserve when made . . . I own I was credulous; I was duped; I was deceived; for the same secret invisible influence still prevailed, and I found that there was no original administration to be suffered in this country!" This rubbish was promptly dubbed by the Duke of Grafton "the effect of a distempered mind brooding over its own discontents." "I rise, my Lords, neither to deny, to re-retract, nor to explain away the words I have spoken," replied the impenitent Chatham. The king was always gracious, he declared, but ". . . all the obstacles and difficulties which attended my public measures were suggested, nourished and supported by that secret influence to which I have alluded. . . . A long train of these practices has at length unwittingly convinced me that there is something behind the throne greater than the throne itself."

Such unjustifiable language coming from Chatham was bad enough; but when the Lord Mayor of London, the vulgar, turbulent Beckford, and his Common Council took to aping the Minister and hinting to the King in thinly veiled words at a similar charge, things had become well-nigh intolerable. And to make matters worse, Chatham showed his satisfaction at their effrontery by writing to one of the Sheriffs a cordial letter of warm congratulation. Indeed, his unfavourable temper and in-sufferable arrogance were thoroughly discrediting the Opposition. Per-haps he was not entirely unconscious of his ineffectiveness, for after the Session of 1770-1771 he seldom appeared again in the House of Lords until the final scene; then he had divested himself of the ill-fitting cloak of party leader and had donned a far worthier garb—the mantle of elder statesman. Henceforth, only in this more becoming guise does he make his appear-ance in the House of Peers—a strange, lonely, decrepit, but noble figure, resolved to spend his ebbing strength in an attempt to lead an imperious monarch and a misguided nation from the crooked lanes of irretrievable folly along the straight, broad highway of prudence and of justice.

[1] Russell, *Memoirs of Charles James Fox*, Vol. I.

[2] Bute had gone abroad for the sake of his health during the winter of 1769.

WILLIAM PITT, Earl of Chatham, son of Robert Pitt
From an engraving by Houston of a portrait by Hoare

But before events in America were to call the great man from his retreat, most of his time was spent in Somerset. "I know not when I shall set my feet eastward. The Metropolis is no inviting scene. The Place where I am is as comfortable winter-quarters as Hayes; the climate softens, the plough affords some amusement; my garden will soon give more. . . ."[1] "I am many hours every day in the field," he reported to Dr. Addington, "and as I live like a farmer abroad, I return home and eat like one. . . . The boys all long for ale, seeing papa drink it; but we do not try such an experiment. Such is the force of example, that I find I must watch myself in all I do, for fear of misleadings: if your friend William saw me smoke, he would certainly call for a pipe."[2] He sought the help of Alec Hood and Nuthall, his solicitor, in improving his estate. Meanwhile, Hester takes over the dairy and soon excites the admiration of the neighbours. "She is a woman of business," comments Farmer Petty to Mr. Bowring. "What a fine woman to breed out of!" is Mr. Bowring's typical reply. "Such a family is not elsewhere to be seen!" they both declare in chorus.[3]

Amidst such surroundings the children grew up, and two letters from the youthful William in his bold, childish hand may still be read by the curious. "Dear Mama," he had written, "As I cannot rest satisfied without making the best apology in my power for what has passed, and not being able to have the pleasure of offering my excuses in person, I trust you will allow me by letter to express how truly I am sorry for having done improperly and sincerely I beg your pardon. I hope that you will have arrived safely in London, and that your cold will be better to-morrow. Believe me, Dear Mama, your most Dutifull and most affectionate son, William Pitt." Then follows a postscript: "James begs his duty to you and desires to express that he feels exceedingly sorry for what he has done and hopes you will have the goodness to pardon him."[4] One wonders what youthful escapade evoked this contrite epistle! The other letter describes a visit to Brighton. "I think the drives about Brighthelmston are very pretty. We see a great many sea gulls. On Friday evening between 6 and 7 o'clock a man came here and immediately went down to the beach and gave two guineas and a half between 2 sailors to row him to France, but he had not gone far before he was driven back by the winds, yet he went off again in the morning."[5] All the children, and especially William and Harriet,

[1] Chatham to Lyttelton, Burton Pynsent, February 16th, 1772.
[2] Chatham to Addington, Burton Pynsent, November 23rd, 1771.
[3] Chatham MSS. Public Record Office.
[4] William Pitt to Lady Chatham, Hayes, May 27th, 1772.
[5] William Pitt to Lady Chatham, "Brighthelmston, July 26th."

were delicate from birth. As infants they were tended by Mrs. Sparry, the nurse affectionately known as "Pam"; as boys and girls their well-being was supervised by Edward Wilson, the tutor; and very carefully they were tended as it would seem: "The Ladies and Gentlemen continue all perfectly well, and are greatly improv'd in their looks since their coming to Brighthelmston," wrote the tutor to their mother, "Master Pitt seems to verify the proverb *laugh and grow fat*, but his neck is just as it was; this morning he went into the water; my Lord was to have gone too, but Mrs. Sparry heard him cough twice in his sleep last night, so we thought it best to defer it two or three days longer."[1] The father, it seems, arranged the children's studies, and his curriculum had changed little since nephew Tom's days. The two girls, Hester and Harriet, had lessons with the boys and rewarded their parents' efforts by growing up into charming young women with broad and independent views.

But work though they must, it is satisfactory to know that the family were not above a childish effort to obtain a holiday from lessons, and in the Chatham papers there is preserved a mock Petition, probably in James's youthful hand, addressed to their Mother: "Lady Harriot Pitt and Mr. James Pitt present their best respects to Lady Chatham; they will take it as a great favour if her Ladyship will be so obliging as to excuse Lady Hester and Lord Pitt their lesson that they may have the pleasure of their company. Thursday evenings four o-clock, Hayes." Let us hope that they were successful! The writing and declaiming of plays was a favourite pastime amongst the Pitt children, and about this time was acted a five-act tragedy in blank verse written by William and entitled "Laurentius, King of Clarinium"[2] but whether it is the play referred to in the petition is impossible to say.

When the parents were parted they invariably exchanged particulars as to the children's health. "Dear boys look charmingly. . . . I found, on my arrival, all at Church, Mr. Wilson preaching. Beef of Old England ready—not at an Old England hour—at four o'clock, on account of evening service. . . . The sea continues kind to our race; Pitt and William striving who shall by good looks, carry the vogue among the ladies of our Vaux-hall."[3] "It is a delight to see William see nature in her free and wild compositions; and I tell myself, as we go, that the *general mother* is not ashamed of her child. The *particular loved* mother of our promising to be

[1] Wilson to Lady Chatham,"Brighthelmstone, August, Tuesday the 11th., 1767."

[2] The original manuscript of this play is preserved at Chevening.

[3] Chatham to Lady Chatham, "Lyme Regis, Sunday, 6 o'clock p.m., June 6th. 1773."

has sent the sweetest and most encouraging of letters to the young Vauban. His assiduous application to his profession did not allow him to accompany us. He was generously occupied in learning to defend the happy land we were enjoying. Indeed, my life, the promise of our dear children does me more good than the purest of pure air. . . . Pray tell dear little tar, that I am in his debt for acquiescing so prettily to the restriction about hunting, and that I am impatient to repay the loss by some safer and fitter pleasure. His letter is quite pretty."[1] A few days later, Hester reported to her husband an amusing mishap at Burton Pynsent: "Yesterday we had such a deluge," she wrote, "as not even Seaby himself ever *remembers in all his memory*.' A sea-spout having, in its travels, mistaken our drowned land for sea, poured down upon us with such violence that all was in alarm—the peachicks in danger of being drowned; Bradshaw afraid his bed would be carried away by the water that poured over it. Between the fear for his family and the misfortune threatening his apartment, his perplexity was delightful."[2] Apparently something of the storm was felt at Lyme Regis. "I am happy to hear that Burton is safe from the discharge of the *blundering* sea-spout," came the reply. "That being so, I must rejoice in the alarm past; as Bradshaw's fears are too comic to have been lost. Our thunder here was very *handy* (in the Somerset tongue) *near*, but no hurt to any. William was reading to me, and no more moved his eye out of his book, than Archimedes left his geometry when the town was stormed. Pitt looked round, but rather as an engineer, to consider if the breach was practicable. How happy that our respective corps continue well, and that they furnish such ample matter of interchanging the praises of their amiable behaviour and affectionate attentions!"[3]

In the autumn of 1773, William commenced residence at Pembroke Hall, Cambridge. He was accompanied by his tutor, Wilson, who remained with him for a time to watch his health, but his studies were under the care of the Rev. George Pretyman, who remained his lifelong friend and bequeathed to posterity a dull and artless biography of his former pupil.[4] But soon his health failed and the faithful Mrs. Sparry went to

---

[1] Chatham to Lady Chatham, "Lyme Regis, Tuesday, past five, June 8th., 1773." The young Vauban is, of course, a reference to Lord Pitt, who was destined for the army, and "dear little tar" to James Charles, who was intended for the navy.

[2] Lady Chatham to Chatham, Burton Pynsent, June 15th, 1773.

[3] Chatham to Lady Chatham, "Lyme Regis, Wednesday, one o'clock, June 16th., 1773."

[4] Pretyman, afterwards Bishop of Lincoln and of Winchester, subsequently took the name of Tomline on the bequest of a large estate. His life of Pitt he never lived to finish.

nurse him.[1] "I hope Pam will have infused Ideas of buttoning coats, and using particular caution if Cambridge weather resembles ours,"[2] wrote an anxious mother. When he returned home he was put under the care of Dr. Addington, who prescribed plenty of air, exercise and port wine. In the summer of 1774, he returned to Cambridge and resumed his interrupted studies. Meanwhile, his strength increased and his health improved.

Towards the end of the year, the elder of the Pitt sisters, Hester, married her second cousin, Mahon, Lord Stanhope's son, a tall, awkward, angular young man of advanced views. "I wish I could find words to express what I feel at this moment," wrote Lady Stanhope to Lady Chatham. "I often wish that I had had a daughter, and in her I think I shall have one as dear to me as if so by birth. My boy is so good that I hope he'll make your daughter as happy as I expect she will make him, or I shall be sadly disappointed in both. I do think that it will be the cleverest match that has been for a great while; the union of two good hearts and two good heads must surely turn out well. I can't tell you how I long to embrace *our girl*."[3]

Meanwhile it had been decided to send Pitt to Canada on the Governor's staff. "My son's ambition is to become a real officer," wrote Chatham. "He is aware how much is to be learned, read, seen and done, before he can tell himself he is an officer; and my satisfaction will be complete in seeing him placed where all those wants can be best supplied. He will be proud and happy in accompanying General Carleton to America. . . ."[4]

James Charles was early destined to be a sailor, and it was arranged that one of the Hood brothers, Samuel or Alexander, should take young Pitt with him. "When I hear you have hoisted your flag," wrote Chatham to Alex. Hood, then treasurer of Greenwich Hospital, "poor Lady Chatham and I will call a council of heavy hearts, about our loved little boy. As things come nearer I confess I tremble. Twelve years old is a very tender age for actions."[5] Not until 1776, however, did James go to sea, and then

[1] This was the origin of the story that Pitt had his nurse with him at the University. Moore, *Diary*, Vol. V.

[2] Lady Chatham to William Pitt, undated.

[3] Lady Stanhope to Lady Chatham, undated.

[4] Chatham to Carleton, October 15th, 1773. (From a rough draft in Lord Chatham's hand.)

[5] Chatham to Hood, January 1773. For correspondence generally between Chatham and Hood and between Lady Chatham and Hood on the boy's service, see *Bridport Papers*, Brit. Mus. Add. MSS. 35,192, and Chatham MSS., Public Record Office, 23.

he joined Alex's brother, Captain Samuel Hood, in the *Marlborough*. He was soon reporting a narrow escape. "I am excedingly sorry to inform you that the *Marlborough* has had a most terrible accident," he wrote to Alex Hood, "which is that about 6 o'clock yesterday morning, the fore magazine blew up, by which we lost killed and wounded 63 people amongst whom were a great many of our best men. It was owing to some embezelled powder which was concealed in the store room which (as they were clearing out the Gunners stores) ketched fire and communicated to the magazine, but however there was then only a few cartridges which had been drawn out of some of the guns before they went ashore but there was a good deal of the deck foreward and started the beams about the Bows. Thank God I have escaped quite unhurt," he added, "tho' I was standing upon the Gangway by the anchors seeing them load the Lighter (which was alongside) with Ballast."[1]

But whilst the Chathams were happy in their growing children, they found time to take an interest in less intimate family affairs. In the summer of 1766 Chatham's sister, Catherine Nedham, wrote of the death of Lord Grandison, their uncle, and that she is "in the Entail of his Estate after you and your Heirs and my nephew Pitt and his Heirs." Then she adds quaintly, "I suppose my mourning should be deeper and longer than is usual for an uncle; I beg you will be so good as to direct me what is proper." Then there follows news of her family. "My son George is detain'd by business in London. . . . Son William who is with me desires his respectful compliments to you, he goes to London in a few daus to keep his Commons as Term is begun."[2] Some two years later we find her writing to Hester Chatham again. "I am much concern'd that yr. son William has had a long disorder, but rejoice to hear he is got over it. He is a most charming, Sensible Boy, and indeed yr la[sP] is particularly happy in the praise deserv'd and given to all your children by every body that sees and knows them . . ."[3] Then there is welcome news from Charles and Essex Cholmondeley's son, Thomas, who had recently married. ". . . my wife was happily deliver'd of a Daughter at half an Hour past seven this evening," he wrote to Lady Chatham in the summer of 1766. "She and the child are as well as possible; which is a full Compensation to me for the want of a son . . . no person can have been or is better attended, than she is by Mrs. Blackwell, and your old Nurse Linney; for both we are obliged to your Ladyship's

[1] James Charles Pitt to Hood, "Portsmouth Harbour, Marlborough, July 6th 1776."

[2] Catherine Nedham to William Pitt, Howberry, June 1st, 1766.

[3] Catherine Nedham to Lady Chatham, Howberry, October 2nd, 1768.

recommendation."[1] His request is readily granted that Lady Chatham should stand godmother to the child "who will therefore be very happy in taking the Name of Hester from your Ladyship; and with your Ladyship's consent we think to desire the Favour of Mrs. Mary Pitt to represent your Ladyship at the Christening. . . ."[2] But the impatient Thomas the following year can announce the birth of the longed-for son. ". . . at half an Hour after five o'clock this morning my Wife brought into the World a Brother to your little god-daughter; who so far from suffering by the Birth of a Son will endear herself still more to her Parents by their being blest by one of each Sex: Both our Children, thank God, are in good Health; and the Mother after a short easy Labour (during which she was duly attended by the same Person whom your Ladyship recommended, is as well as possible."[3] Then there was news from Chatham's nephew, Tom, whose marriage with Anne Wilkinson was proving fruitful. "About half an hour after one this afternoon," he recorded in 1772, "Mrs. Pitt made me a present of a fine girl after about an hour of pretty serious business. Thank God both She and the child are well, and myself happier than I can describe."[4] A few years later, he too was the father of a son. "Mrs. T. Pitt is brought to bed of a son, and very well at Boconnoc," recorded Mrs. Delany in February 1775.[5] "The kind congratulations from Hayes upon the Birth of our little Cornishman affords us no small addition to our pleasure even at a time when the measure seems almost full," he wrote to his aunt. "The success you have had in the education of so many young people is, I assure you, a very solid comfort to me in the prospect that lies before me and will give me no small encouragement in the exercise of new duties that are devolved upon me."[6]

But even amid these family distractions all was not sunshine for the ageing Chatham. In 1773 he was seriously ill; in 1775 he suffered a second visitation of his former affliction, which lasted two full years; in 1777 he was smitten with a slight stroke, causing him to fall from his horse and to lie

---

[1] Cholmondeley to Lady Chatham, "Beckenham, 9th of July 1766, 9 o'clock in the Evening."

[2] Cholmondeley to Lady Chatham, Beckenham, July 19th, 1766.

[3] Cholmondeley to Lady Chatham, Beckenham, August 9th, 1767. The son, whose birth is here recorded, subsequently became the first Lord Delamere.

[4] Thomas Pitt to Lady Chatham, Hertford Street, September 10th, 1772.

[5] Mrs. Delany to Mrs. Port of Ilam, "St. J. P." (St. James's Place), "February 28th, 1775." The child was born on February 19th.

[6] Thomas Pitt to Lady Chatham, "Boconnock, March 3rd, 1775."

senseless for several minutes.[1] And on top of ill-health came financial
worries.   Always lavish in expenditure, he had recently squandered vast
sums on Burton Pynsent and still more of his capital on the re-purchase of
Hayes at an extravagant price.   His resignation of the Privy Seal had cost
him £3,000 a year, and though he had been granted a pension of a like sum
it was worth little more than £2,000 after the deduction of taxes and fees;[2]
moreover it was constantly in arrears.   Eventually Lord North proposed
to the King that the pension should be made up to an effective £3,000 a
year and that he should be permitted to substitute another of his son's lives
for his own.[3] But George III's reply was not encouraging.[4]

Gradually things became worse, and Hester, now in financial control,
tried vainly to re-sell Hayes to Thomas Walpole, or to let either Hayes or
Burton Pynsent.   One ray only was there amidst the gloom: she succeeded
in selling to Lord Clive Chatham's house in the Circus at Bath.   Outlying
portions of the Burton Pynsent estate were also disposed of to local farmers,
and some of the worst extravagances she managed to cut down.   But
creditors were pressing, and these shifts were no more than palliatives; so
the Chathams were forced to borrow from their friends.   A clerk in the
Privy Council Office, by name Jouvencel, who lived rent free in one of the
houses on the Hayes estate, made it his business to enquire into the annuity
arrears.   In 1773 they were two months in arrear: in 1776 four months.
Things were desperate.   Banker Coutts, anxious to do what he could,
wrote to the Secretary of the Treasurer who, to his intense disgust, had not

[1] This was long unknown, but was finally disclosed by two confidential letters
from Camden to Grafton, July 27th and October 29th, 1777.

[2] Statement of P. Jouvencel to Chatham:

Quarter's Annuity			£750	0	0
Subtract—	£	s.	d.		
Treasury Fees	2	11	0		
Fees at the Polls	4	16	6		
Fees at the Auditors	9	10	0		
Fees to Tellers	22	10	0		
Shilling Duty	37	10	0		
6d. Duty	18	15	0		
4s. Land tax	150	0	0	245	12	6
				£504	7	6

Chatham MSS.   Public Record Office 47.   See also Williams, *William Pitt, Earl of Chatham*, Vol. II.

[3] North to George III, Ross, August 8th, 1775.

[4] George III to North, Kew, August 9th, 1775.

even the courtesy to reply.[1] In the summer of 1777 Coutts reported that by Michaelmas the quarterly payments would be a year in arrear.[2] In the following January, however, payment was at last made up to Lady Day, 1777, leaving the sum of £1,500 still due. But the kindness of friends did not end there. Coutts advanced Chatham several thousand pounds; Jouvencel £500; and brother-in-law Temple came to the rescue with another £1,000.

Whilst things were in this sorry pass, poor Lady Chatham had a fresh burden to bear. Her beloved youngest son, James Charles, whilst stationed at Gibraltar had involved himself in financial difficulties. At all costs this must be kept from his ailing father, and in April 1777 the distracted mother turned for help to her nephew, Tom. "Our son James . . . by an imprudence, pardonable only at *Fifteen* has run into a most unfortunate excess of expence . . ." which was causing her the greatest distress. ". . . I don't know where I am, for it is of the utmost importance to my Lord's Recovery that he shou'd not be acquainted with this circumstance. Is it possible, my Dear Sir, that you cou'd lend me your Friendly Aid on this occasion. . . ." Would he lend her £1,000? "This will be more *by half* than the Demand, come to my knowledge, but it has distress'd me so thoroughly, that I shall not feel at ease without a reserve for fear of any accident, or at (thank God) my Lord being better, may think of a journey, or something that may make an immediate call, which it might be unfortunate not to be able to answer."[3] Apparently Tom's generosity was equal to his aunt's demands, for ten days later she writes to thank him: "The kindness of your Letter, in answer to mine, is such as makes me feel it impossible to find expression to thank you for it, in a manner that agrees with the sense I have of it. . . ."[4]

But of all the friends, Alex and Molly Hood were the most accommodating. They rented Hayes; they interviewed prospective purchasers and were most assiduous in singing the praises of the estate to them; and Hood advanced first a further £1,000 on the already much mortgaged Hayes, and later a further £6,000 secured on Burton Pynsent. Altogether Hood and his wife's family, the Wests, advanced over £10,000, yet Chatham's chief acknowledgment was to ask for more ! In May 1775, the good-natured Coutts himself placed a loan of £1,000 to Chatham's credit. In December, 1775, when Hood was given command of the *Robust*, he was advised by

[1] Coutts to Lady Chatham, October 15th, 1775. The original is endorsed in Lady Chatham's hand, "Answer'd Oct. 16th."

[2] Coutts to Lady Chatham, Strand, August 12th, 1777.

[3] Lady Chatham to Thomas Pitt, Hayes, April 8th, 1777.

[4] Lady Chatham to Thomas Pitt, Hayes, April 18th, 1777.

his own banker, Henry Hoare, that in consequence of the American crisis, all mortgages were being called in. In consequence, Thomas Coutts the following February sold £14,000 3 per cent Consols to yield £9,794, and himself advanced the balance to repay Hood his £10,000 together with the interest due upon it. On the very same day, Mrs. Frances West and the Admiral's son, Temple West, paid £3,000 to Chatham's account with Coutts. Thus were the Pitt finances kept from breaking-point.

It was against such a background of ill-health and financial stress that Chatham made his last appearances in public life. On his recovery from his illness he hastened to write to his nephew, of whose generosity he was entirely ignorant, to herald his return to health. Then he gives his views on the nation's troubles. "I tremble for news from America. Till the event (which in every alternative, must be ruin) is known, the Date of England's greatness seems protracted for a few days. Sad (?) demise of more Public Happiness and Prosperity than Providence has ever given to a Nation or infatuated Counsels have ever thrown away."[1]

Indeed, whilst Chatham had been farming and ailing in Somerset, our relations with the North American Colonies had taken a sinister and terrible shape. Lord North's efforts to placate the Colonists by the removal of all duties save only those on tea had been wholly unsuccessful; the iron had set into their souls; and on July 4th, 1776, the American Congress formally adopted the Declaration of Independence, which claimed that "the Colonies are, and of a right ought to be, free and independent states." It was the very Magna Carta of American hopes and aspirations: it was a clarion call to liberty and justice.

Meanwhile, as the war progressed fortune did not favour our arms, the crowning disaster being the surrender of General Burgoyne at Saratoga. The full impact of this defeat was quickly felt, for early in 1778 France, anxious to avenge past humiliations, exulted to stab us in the back by recognizing the independence of the Colonies and making a formal alliance with America. Never had our fortunes seemed lower, and in our time of need, all eyes turned towards the greatest living Englishman who was passing a lonely life—tormented by gout—in the distant county of Somerset. The venerable statesman had done such great and wonderful things for England, had been so proud of her; would he not now return, and by the very force of his genius, conduct her back along the path that leads at once to honour and to glory?

Meanwhile, the Chathams had been in some anxiety over the situation of their eldest son, Lord Pitt, now in Canada with Carleton, and it must

[1] Chatham to Thomas Pitt, Hayes, September 25th, 1777.

have been a great relief to them to hear from a certain Major Caldwell that in June 1775, he was safe and well.[1] To Caldwell Lady Chatham replied on her lord's behalf, explaining that they had left it to their son's discretion whether he should remain in arms against the Americans or return home. "I wished him to weigh the matter well; and should his conscience dictate to him to resign his profession, not to take any step without having first maturely considered the nature and delicacy of it. Should he find no opinions in his mind to make it distressing to him to continue in a profession which he loves and admires, I advised him not to think of making the sacrifice."[2] The Americans also, it appears, felt the position to be delicate. "If Lord Chatham's son should be in Canada, and in any way fall into your power," wrote their Commander-in-Chief, Washington, "you are enjoined to treat him with all possible deference and respect. You cannot err in paying too much honour to the son of so illustrious a character and so true a friend to America."[3] But the problem soon settled itself, for in September Carleton sent Lord Pitt home with despatches,[4] and from this mission he did not return. "Lord Pitt returned home," wrote a poor mother pathetically, "why may not my poor boy do so too?"[5] Lady Chatham wrote to Carleton to explain. "Feeling all this, Sir, as Lord Chatham does, you will tell yourself with what concern he communicates to you a step that, from his fixed opinion with regard to the continuance of this unhappy war with our fellow subjects of America, he has found it necessary to take. It is that of withdrawing his son from such a service. . . ."[6]

But not only by such an act of protest did he show his disapproval of the war. In May 1777, accompanied by William, he managed to crawl to the House of Lords, and in two speeches that lacked much of the fire but little of the boldness of former days, he begged the Ministry to bring hostilities to a close. "You cannot conquer the Americans," he cried. "You talk of your powerful forces to disperse their army, but"—and he raised his support as he spoke—"I might as well talk of driving them before me with this crutch." There was much more besides, but the House would have none of it, and Chatham's motion was rejected by a large majority.[7]

[1] Caldwell to Chatham, Quebec, June 2nd, 1775.
[2] Lady Chatham to Caldwell, Hayes, July 1775.
[3] Washington to Arnold, September 14th, 1775.
[4] Carleton to Lady Chatham, Montreal, September 21st, 1775.
[5] Mrs. Boscawen to Mrs. Delany, Glan Villa, December 13th, 1775.
[6] Lady Chatham to Carleton, February 14th, 1776.
[7] Chatham, House of Lords, May 30th, 1777.

"My father's first speech took up half an hour, and was full of all his usual force and vivacity," was William's comment to his mother. "I only regretted that he did not always raise his voice enough for all the House to hear everything he said. . . . He spoke a second time . . . in a flow of eloquence, and with a beauty of expression, animated and striking beyond conception."[1]

Chatham followed up this speech with four more, in all of which his hatred of the war and his loathing for France were skilfully blended. "My Lords, if I were an American as I am an Englishman, whilst a foreign troop was landed in my country I never would lay down my arms—never—never —never!" He would not grant independence, but by reconciliation alone could the war be won, for America herself was strongly biased against France to an understanding with the mother country. "Notwithstanding the temporary intrigues with France, we may still be assured of their ancient and confirmed partiality to us. America and France cannot be congenial; there is something decisive and confirmed in the honest American, that will not assimilate to the fatality and levity of Frenchmen." On Lord Suffolk who declared it justifiable "to use all the means that God and nature have put into our hands," including the Indians, Chatham turned with unrestrained ferocity. "I am astonished! Shocked! to hear such principles confessed . . . principles equally unconstitutional, inhuman and unchristian!..." He concluded with the usual reference to his age and infirmities. "My Lords, I am old and weak, and at present unable to say more; but my feelings and indignation were too strong to have said less. I could not have slept this night in my bed, nor reposed my head on my pillow, without giving vent to my eternal abhorrence of such preposterous and enormous principles."[2]

But though the eyes of all men turned to Chatham in our hour of need, he was now a dying man and quite unequal to the task assigned to him. One more public appearance only did he make, but that one is a part of history itself. On April 7th, the old man, though very weak, accompanied by his three sons and his son-in-law, came to the House of Lords and on the arm of William and Mahon and with Pitt and James Charles in attendance, the veteran statesman entered the Chamber. At his first appearance, every man rose, and the great assembly of peers, perhaps scenting that this was to be a notable day in England's history, reverently made an aisle for him as he tottered to his seat on the bench of earls. As the little procession passed,

---

[1] William Pitt to Lady Chatham, "Hotel, King's Street, Saturday morning, May 31st., 1777."

[2] Chatham, House of Lords, November 20th, 1777.

men anxiously perceived how feeble, sunk and emaciated the great man was; indeed beneath the ample folds of the enveloping wig little of the stern familiar features could be seen, save the great hook nose and the flashing, deep-set eyes.

Richmond was first to speak; next Weymouth for the Ministers. Then at last Chatham rose—slowly and painfully, as it was observed—and leaning on his crutches and supported on each side, he began to address the peers. At first his voice was low and feeble. "I thank God," he said, "that I have been able to come here this day, to do my duty. I rejoice that the grave has not closed upon me; that I am still alive to lift up my voice against the dismemberment of this ancient and most noble monarchy. I am old and infirm, have one foot, more than one foot in the grave—I am risen from my bed to stand up in the cause of my country—perhaps never again to speak in this House." A stillness of the grave seemed to settle over his auditors, as the greatest of their number spoke to them of the nearness of death. But it was observed that the speaker became confused, that his mind was not master of his thoughts. Yet between these pathetic hesitations, so unlike the Chatham that all men knew, there were sudden flashes of unconnected eloquence that recalled the man as he had been. ". . . My Lords, his Majesty succeeded to an empire as great in extent as its reputation was unsullied. Shall we tarnish the lustre of this nation by an ignominious surrender of its rights and fairest possessions? Shall this great kingdom now fall prostrate before the House of Bourbon? . . . Shall a people that fifteen years ago was the terror of the world now stoop so low as to tell its ancient inveterate enemy, 'Take away all we have; only give us peace.' It is impossible." Then came the final peroration, and his voice filled out to something of its former power. "In God's name," he said, "if it is absolutely necessary to declare either for peace or war, why is not the latter commenced without hesitation? I am not, I confess, well informed of the resources of this Kingdom; but I trust it has still sufficient to maintain its just rights, though I know them not. But, my Lords, any state is better than despair. Let us at least make an effort; and if we must fall, let us fall like men!"[1]

As he sank down exhausted, Temple whispered that he had forgotten something—should he rise to say it? "No, no," said Chatham. "I will do it by and by." The Duke of Richmond replied briefly and with courtesy. Then Chatham made to rise as if to speak again; but he suddenly fell back and seemed in the agonies of death. At once all was confusion, and the House was quickly cleared. But he soon revived and after resting

[1] Chatham, House of Lords, April 7th, 1778.

in the Princes' Chamber for a while they moved him to a house in Downing Street. Two days later he was borne to Hayes. There, for a time, he lingered. But he knew his end was near, for he constantly bade William read from the *Iliad* the account of the death of Hector; and when Lord Pitt, summoned to his regiment at Gibraltar, would have stayed, "Go, my son," he said, "go whither your country calls you: let her engross all your attention; spare not a moment, which is due to her service in weeping over an old man who will soon be no more." So Pitt sailed, never to see his father more. We too take leave of him. His strength slowly ebbed and on the afternoon of May 11th, 1778, he died.

When the news was known Parliament at once voted addresses to the throne that his remains might lie in Westminster Abbey, that he should be interred at the public charge and that a monument should be raised to his memory. Moreover, £20,000 was granted to pay his debts and a permanent annuity of £4,000 was attached to the Chatham Earldom. The King, of course, affected astonishment at all this as "an offensive measure to me personally"[1]—but that was the only unseemly note. On June 7th and 8th the body lay in state; on the 9th with all the pomp and circumstance that he loved so well and in the presence of a great concourse of his countrymen, he was borne to the Abbey. Thus he entered into his rest and is in company with the immortals.

We must return to Ann Pitt, who had been living for some time in a house in Knightsbridge. She had remained on the best of terms with the Butes and if gossiping Walpole is to be believed, had actually tried to persuade her relative, Lord Villiers, into marrying one of their daughters, promising as a reward to procure for him an English peerage through her influence with the Princess of Wales.[2] More recently she had gone to Italy. "Lord Bute desires me to tell you that Mrs. Anne Pitt is going to Pisa, and that I would recommend her to you," Horace Walpole had reported to Mann. "I should do that on my own account, as I am very intimate with her. You know she is Lord Chatham's sister, as well as his very image; but you must take care not to make your court to her on that head, as they are no dear friends. She has excellent parts, a great deal of wit, and not so sweet a temper as to contradict the likeness of her features. She has at times been absolutely *English*, but not in the present style of fashion, and has much too good sense to exhibit any extraordinary scenes. She is

---

[1] George III to Lord North, "Queens House, May 12th., 1778, 5 min. pt. 8 a.m."
[2] Walpole, *Memoirs of George III*, Vol. IV. Lord Villiers was a son of Lady Grandison. Apparently Ann Pitt was unsuccessful as he subsequently married a daughter of Lord Hertford.

extremely well-bred, and knows the world perfectly. In short, she will be much pleased with your attentions, and will please you in a very different way from the generality of our exports. I dread sending you anybody I have not known long, and some that I do; but there is no danger from Mrs. Pitt, who has always lived in the great world, and is not of an age to play the fool—especially on a small theatre. She has not succeeded so well as she intended on a very large one; but you may depend upon it, Tuscany will not tempt her."[1] From Rome, Ann wrote home to Lord Huntingdon, in reply to a letter from him that had "travel'd so far, that I received it after a long delay, from Naples, where I hear the English have had the honour of losing a great deal of money to the King & his subjects. . . ." Then she gives her friend the gossip. "Me de Rochefort had not fail'd to brag to me of your great complisance in describing Pompeii so exactly that she pretends to know it as well as I do, and I believe she is in the right. I was extreamly sensible of your goodness in giving me such an agreeable account of my Lady Bute, not only of her health, but of her looks, her Ladyship may do what she pleases with the outside of her head, provided she keeps the inside exactly as I left it. My Lady Morton is here hoping to set out very soon for England. . . ."[2] On leaving England, Ann had sold her Knightsbridge villa. "I am sorry to tell Mrs. Pitt that her house at Knightsbridge has been led astray, the moment she turned her back; see what it is to live in a bad neighbourhood! Pittsburgh, the Temple of Vesta, is as naughty as Villa Kingstonia. . . ."[3]

But Ann was not the only Pitt to have a partiality for the sunny South, for her nephew, Tom, now something of an invalid, had soon after Chatham's death set out for Italy. "A weakness is fallen on his knees, and makes him a cripple," reported Walpole. "He is, I think, set out for Italy, like Aeneas, with his Creusa, her father of eighty-seven and two sucking babes. Let me give you a caution, he and I have never been on more than civil terms since Mr. Grenville's reign. He now swears by the ghost of his uncle Chatham, whom in those days he detested."[4] But a month later Mrs.

[1] Walpole to Mann, Arlington Street, February 23rd, 1774. By "English" Walpole means "mad."

[2] Ann Pitt to Huntingdon, "Rome, March 11th" [1774 or 1775].

[3] Walpole to Mann, Strawberry Hill, June 8th, 1774. "Villa Kingstonia" refers to the neighbouring house of the celebrated Elizabeth Chudleigh, Duchess of Kingston, who, about this time, was found guilty of bigamy.

[4] Walpole to Mann, Strawberry Hill, September 17th, 1778. Tom had, however, been on better terms with his uncle for some time, and seven years previously Chatham had paid his nephew a visit at Boconnoc. " We were charmed with the kind of beauties abounding at Boconnoc, all of them mild and full of repose, though not wanting spirit: hill, dale, wood and water, happily mingled." Chatham to Calcraft, Burton Pynsent, September 22nd, 1771.

Boscawen was able to report to Mrs. Delany that "Mr. T. Pitt writes from Pisa in perfect health and spirits."[1]

That same year, 1778, we hear more of Ann on her foreign travels. She is getting old and she needs help. "I have writ Mr. Doyly to know if it wou'd be possible for me to be lodged so as not to suffer from the noise and hurry of strangers, in case I shou'd not have pass'd Venice before the Ascension," she wrote from Florence to the wealthy antiquarian John Strange, at this time British Resident in Venice, "but as circumstances are in general, and as I am circumstanced I can not possibly fix my journey at present, neither cou'd I venture to take it alone, I therefore beg Sir you will be so good as to think of me, and to consider for me if you know of any proper Person to keep me company and to take care of the journey which I propose through Germany."[2] Apparently the Stranges were responsible, for we find Ann sending them her hearty thanks. "These baths are particularly recommended for the nerves," she wrote from Schlangenbad, "the water is very like our Bristol as to softness, and little warmer, so that it must be heated for a very moderate bath. The Steel waters of Schwalbuch near this are usually drunk by the bathers, and are less active than those of Spa. These Baths belong to the Landgrave of Hesse Cassel . . . "who is careful to look well after foreign visitors . . . nobody need desire to be better served in every respect, the provisions, and the cook wou'd hardly let you regret your own Table, the Gardens are extremely pleasant with variety of walks, the country very fine and the air perfectly good . . ."[3]

In October Ann returned to England. "Did I tell you that Mrs. Anne Pitt is returned and acts great grief for her brother?" wrote Walpole. "I suppose she was the dupe of the farce acted by the two Houses of the Court, and had not heard that none of them carried on the pantomime even to his burial. Her nephew gave a little into that mummery even to me; forgetting how much I must remember of his aversion to his uncle."[4] Then a few weeks later, he adds significantly, "Mrs. Anne Pitt, I hear, is in a very wild way, and they think must be confined. . . ."[5] But not only to Horace Walpole did Ann cause alarm at this time, for Mrs. Delany's friend, Fred Montagu, thus wrote of "the Virgin" as he called her: "Pitt left London the day that you did; 'the Virgin' arrived that evening from Luton, and Mrs. Pitt escap'd the next morning by break of

<hr />

[1] Walpole to Mann, Strawberry Hill, October 8th, 1778.
[2] Ann Pitt to Strange, "Florence, April 24th, 1778."
[3] Ann Pitt to Strange, "Schlangenbad, July the 4th." (1778).
[4] Walpole to Mann, Strawberry Hill, October 8th, 1778.
[5] Walpole to Mann, Arlington Street, October 30th, 1778.

day. I call'd this morning to enquire after Mrs. Pitt and the children, and had a very good account, but in the midst of my enquiries I was struck with the sign of Mrs. Anne's old coach at the door, upon which I ran immediately away, and *thought* 'the Virgin' was at my heels the whole length of Oxford Street."[1] But the poor "Virgin" was nearing her end and at last it became necessary to place her under restraint. "I had a letter from London yesterday full of ruins and divorces and yᵉ miserable state of Mrs. Ann Pitt," wrote Lady Gower to Mrs. Delany, "who is now mov'd to one of Doctor Duffell's houses."[2] Early in 1781 she died, not, as Horace Walpole wrote, "in a madhouse" but in Dr. Duffell's home for the mentally unbalanced. Poor Ann Pitt! The curse of the Pitts claims you at last.

Meanwhile, poor Tom was having fresh trouble with the Smith family. After the agreement come to at Lord Mansfield's house, John and Mary Smith's three children, Charles Douglas, William Sidney and John Spencer Smith, were, as we have seen, put under their grandfather's care and were received by him with every kindness. Soon after the three boys had been put to school, first at Tunbridge Wells, and later at Bath, their father went abroad and remained away for more than a year. During his absence, his brother, one day to become a general, signified an opportunity of sending the eldest boy to Ireland as page to Lord Harcourt; and though the lad's grandfather was not enthusiastic, the advantages of this introduction to military advancement were so forcibly impressed on him, that at length he reluctantly agreed; so in due course young Charles departed for Dublin, doubtless with his pockets well lined by his indulgent grandparent.

Soon afterwards, John Smith returned from abroad; and it was not long before he was writing to his two younger sons, Sidney and John, a series of hysterical letters in which he did not scruple to let them know his opinion of their mother. "Why do you treat her as if she was your father, instead of an over-bearing arbitrary mother?" he asked Sidney. "Why did you not say, 'I cannot go from Bath without my father's leave?' They cou'dn't tie you neck and heels; if force was attempted, you could have run away: have you not an affectionate father to run to, that is repenting every vein of his heart, that he so mistook your mother's nature, as to consent to the letting her have so much power over my dear boys; but I thought tenderness would bring her to her senses; whereas, I am now convinced, it is the contrary only that will do it."[3] "I think I told you never to call the place

---

[1] Montagu to Mrs. Delany, Hanover Square, September 24th, 1778.

[2] Gower to Mrs. Delany, Bill Hill, December 10th, 1778.

[3] John Smith to Sidney Smith, September, 1774.

your mother lives in your home; though she were in a palace, her home and your home is wherever I live; I never will allow of any other: . . . and when you speak of going to your mama, say, you are going to your mama, or to your mama's lodgings; but take particular care never to call them your home: your school is more your home than your mama's lodgings, as you are there by my approbation, which you never are when you are at the other place. I only consented to it, to try if you will get any money hereafter by my humouring the old grandfather. My love to your untoward mama. O dear! how can she use me so! . . ."[1] "Your mother's unreasonable, abominable treatment of me has, at last, wore me out, and brought things to a conclusion; my sufferings are now near over; I shall very soon have my dear boys, never (till God please) to part any more (as we have done), as long as I live. I will not sell my dear boys, and I am sure they never will sell me; so be comforted, and pray to God to *convict, convince, and forgive your mother's behaviour to us all.*"[2] Then he asks about his allowance. "Can't you find out whether I am to be paid my income by your grandfather, or must I go to law for it?"[3] "I fear your mother has hurt your brother with your grandfather; this is all for the good of the children; it will be your turn next; her plans will all fail, because they are contrary to God's desires, and all her art will never bring them to bear."[4] Then he turns to "My dear little Jack," now in his teens, and writes to him in the same tone. "I have been four weeks in my bed: suffice it to know that I am left still on earth to scourge my unjust, dishonest prosecutors, who I trust soon to bring to publick shame. Mr. Grenville has been with me by my bedside; has changed all his praises of Tom Pitt, in pittying my shocking brutal situation, which your mother has made your grandfather put me in. . . ."[5]

Whilst these letters and many more like them were passing between the querulous parent and the two younger children at Bath, the eldest boy, now a cornet of horse by the gift of Lord Harcourt, returned to London, where he was soon in touch with his father. The result of this contact was unfortunate; for when his mother wrote inviting him to Bath, Charles curtly declined. Nor could he be diverted from this attitude, even when his aunt, Anne Pitt, wrote strongly urging him for his own sake, not to fall out with his wealthy grandfather, and his uncle, Tom Pitt, sent for

[1] John Smith to Sidney Smith, Midgham, March 17th, 1775.
[2] John Smith to Sidney Smith, Margaret Street, July 19th, 1775.
[3] John Smith to Sidney Smith, Midgham Cottage, March 23rd, 1777.
[4] John Smith to Sidney Smith, Midgham Cottage, April 21st, 1777.
[5] John Smith to John Smith, junior, August 19th, 1778.

him to London and in the presence of old Wilkinson vainly endeavoured by every art of persuasion to turn him from his obstinacy. Whereupon they were forced to make it plain to him that in renouncing his mother he was renouncing her family. This extreme attitude seems to have brought young Charles to his senses, for not only did he soon after write dutiful letters to his mother, but he actually paid her a visit in Bath, when he entreated her to exert her influence with his grandfather to continue his allowance. At first old Wilkinson was obdurate, but gradually by the joint pleading of both his daughter and his son-in-law, he was induced to relent to the extent of offering Charles £1,000, to which he afterwards added £350, on the understanding that the money was paid into the hands of an agent and the whole arrangement drawn up by a solicitor in legal form.

Thus matters stood when Mr. Wilkinson was suddenly incapacitated with a paralytic stroke. In this state he remained for the rest of his life,[1] which he spent at Tom Pitt's house. Whilst the old man was in this broken state, Charles Smith wrote to his uncle expressing his particular desire to see his grandfather, a request which, of course, Tom Pitt was bound to decline,[2] whereupon Charles wrote his uncle an angry letter, casting reflections on his probity and demanding a sufficient sum to purchase his commission—"the price demanded will, I fear, be more than £1,350. I cannot name the officers who retire, as I am not certain in what regiment, whether the 20th. or 22nd. the vacancy will fall."[3] At first Tom refused[4] but he subsequently relented and advanced out of his own pocket no less a sum than £1,800. "Having called upon the agent, and finding £1,800 was this day paid into his hands," wrote Charles gratefully, "I cannot refrain taking the earliest opportunity, by Mr. Sewell, to return you my sincerest thanks *for all the trouble you had taken upon this occasion.*"[5] It was not long, however, before the young man was showing his gratitude in curious ways.

Early in the following year, Mr. Wilkinson, being by now entirely incapacitated, Tom Pitt, appointed Committee of his person, made formal application in Chancery to be appointed also Committee of his estate. This was vigorously opposed by his nephew: "Mr. C. Smith said, he had many reasons to give, which would show you was a very improper person.

[1] He died in March, 1784.
[2] Thomas Pitt to Charles Smith, "24th. or 25th. August, 1782."
[3] Charles Smith to Thomas Pitt, London, August 26th, 1782.
[4] Thomas Pitt to Charles Smith, August 27th, 1782.
[5] Charles Smith to Thomas Pitt, London, November 20th, 1782.

I desired him to state them: he said, the first was, that if you was the Committee, you would possess yourself of all the family writings and papers and not permit him or his father to have the inspection of them. . . . The next objection was, that if you was appointed Committee, and it became necessary for them to make any application to you, it could not be done as the families were much at variance; I answered if the family were so, it was the fault of his father and him; and if he would approach you as a nephew, you would receive him as an uncle; that you had done many kind and generous things, and a constant correspondence was kept up between his mother, you and Mrs. Pitt: he said, *he had never received anything from you but justice; and that he did not think himself obliged of.*[1]

Then the worthless John Smith began to give trouble. It will be recalled that when at the meeting at Lord Mansfield's house, the agreement was come to by which Wilkinson was to pay Smith £200 a year, the notes that they exchanged on the subject were not in identical terms; and that, whereas in the paper signed by Smith it was agreed by him to separate from his wife and to give up the children to their grandfather, in return for which Wilkinson would pay Smith the annuity and the future debts of his daughter, in the paper signed by Wilkinson agreeing to the payments, the obligations of the son-in-law were not set forth. This difference in form subsequently led to much confusion, for Wilkinson interpreted the agreement that his financial obligations were dependent on his son-in-law not molesting his wife or communicating with his children; and accordingly when John Smith contrived to set the children's minds against their mother and her family, the old man promptly cut off the allowance. The result was an action at law brought by John Smith against his father-in-law for the recovery of the unpaid allowance, an action which after Wilkinson's incapacitation had to be faced by Tom Pitt as Committee of his estate. The Court decided that the undertaking on the part of Wilkinson was absolute and was in consequence not subject to any other undertaking on the part of John Smith. It therefore became Tom Pitt's duty to hand over to Smith the unpaid annuity and to continue the payment of £200 a year from the Wilkinson estate. Never, perhaps, has vice more singularly triumphed over virtue, for on this sordid note our dismal story ends.

John Smith spent most of the remainder of his days in sullen retirement at Dover in a kind of boathouse, long known as Smith's Folly. Two of his three boys are known to fame and the name of one of them is familiar

[1] Winterbottom to Thomas Pitt, Merchant Taylors Hall, December 8th, 1783.

to every lover of gallantry and adventure; for the second son of John and Mary Smith became Admiral Sir Sidney Smith, the hero of Acre.

During the evening of Tuesday, June 9th, 1778, two young men sat together in a house in Harley Street. It had been a sad day, for they had just returned from the melancholy ceremonial in Westminster Abbey, where with great pomp and circumstance the mighty Chatham had been laid to rest amongst the nation's illustrious dead. The host was Lord Mahon; the guest, his brother-in-law, William Pitt, who, in the absence abroad of his elder brother, had been chief mourner. "The Court did not honour us with their countenance," wrote William to his mother, "nor did they suffer the procession to be as magnificent as it ought . . ." but it had notwithstanding everything essential to the great object, the attendance being most respectable, and the crowd of interested spectators immense. . . . All our relations made their appearance. . . . I will not tell you what I felt on this occasion, to which no words are equal; but I know that you will have a satisfaction in hearing that Lord Mahon as well as myself supported the trial perfectly well, and have not at all suffered from the fatigue. The procession did not separate till four o'clock."[1] The next morning the dutiful son joined his mother at Hayes, and shortly afterwards the whole family left for Somerset, where they remained throughout the summer and early autumn.

Only in October William returned to Pembroke Hall, by which time it was evident that he would have but a very sparse income, for though the generosity of parliament had been sufficient to pay off the more pressing of the father's debts and to provide just enough to enable the second Earl to maintain the family honours, whilst Lady Chatham was comfortably provided for by the pension of £3,000 a year granted in 1761 for three lives,[2] it was clear that there was little for the younger children. James Charles, the sailor, was shortly to depart for the West Indies, so his immediate requirements would be small; but William was designed for the Bar, and soon there arose the question of the purchase of Chambers at Lincoln's Inn. "While I was in town I saw a set that are to be disposed of, and which have no other fault than being too dear and too good. At the same time I heard of none at an inferior price, which were not as much too bad. The whole expense of these will be eleven hundred pounds, which sounds to me a frightful sum. . . ."[3] The "frightful sum" was found by the generosity

[1] William Pitt to Lady Chatham, Harley Street, June 9th, 1778.
[2] She was, however, often gravely embarrassed by the non-payment of arrears on the pension.
[3] William Pitt to Lady Chatham, Pembroke Hall, November 30th, 1778.

of William's uncle, Temple; thus the young man was entered at Lincoln's Inn,[1] and in due course he began to keep his terms.

Of William's career at the Bar, there is nothing of importance to relate. Much of his time was spent at the House of Commons and he was much in Society. He attended the Opera[2] and the Duchess of Bolton's Ball;[3] he stayed with Lord Mahon's parents, the Stanhopes, at Chevening;[4] and at least on one occasion he apparently visited the house of a lady of not quite unblemished reputation: "Harriot went with Lady Williams to Mrs. Weddel's (who is, I believe, a sister of Lady Rockingham's) to see Marks. . . . I was there as well as at a Mr. Broadhead's, to which *some few* ladies did not like to go, from little histories relative to the lady of the house. These did not prevent its being the most crowded place I ever was in."[5] Later he hastened to join his mother in Somerset and comfort her in the loss of her brother, Temple, who died on September 11th, after having been thrown from his chaise in Stowe Park. He was succeeded in the Earldom by his nephew, George, eldest son of his late brother, George Grenville. Of the three brothers, first cousins of William Pitt—George, now Earl Temple and later Marquess of Buckingham, Thomas who succeeded George as Member of Parliament for the county of Buckingham, and William Wyndham, afterwards Lord Grenville—more will be heard as our narrative unfolds.

On June 12th, 1780, young Pitt was called to the Bar, and a few weeks later the family had to mourn another death more poignant than the loss of Lady Chatham's pompous brother. For some time now, Hester Mahon had been in poor health; she had borne her husband three children[6] and though only twenty-five, she had never completely rallied from the birth of the youngest child. As the winter passed to spring and the spring unfolded into summer, the poor mother's strength gradually ebbed until at last on July 10th she died at Chevening. "Poor Charles had passed a melancholy day," wrote his mother. "I keep him amused as much as I can, and nothing but hindering him to think is of service. Alas! when he

---

[1] "On the north side of the attic of staircase number 4 of Stone Buildings (the nearest to Holborn)." Holland Rose, *William Pitt and National Revival.*

[2] William Pitt to Lady Chatham, "Hotel, King Street, Feb. 11th., 1778."

[3] William Pitt to Lady Chatham, "Nerot's Hotel, King Street, Tuesday Halfpast two," 1779.

[4] William Pitt to Lady Chatham, "Nerots Hotel, King Street, Saturday, Aug. 21st., 1779."

[5] William Pitt to Lady Chatham, Grafton Street, April 4th, 1780. This was Lady Williams' house, at which Lady Harriot Pitt was staying at this time.

[6] The Ladies Hester, Griselda, and Lucy Stanhope.

does—but I will not dwell on that subject that must be heart-breaking to us all. . . ."[1] In March of the ensuing year, Lord Mahon married again. His second wife was Louisa, the only child of Lady Chatham's youngest brother, Henry Grenville, and of the gay, beautiful and witty Peggy Banks of long ago. This was no love match, and the couple proved an ill-assorted pair. Louisa was "a worthy well-meaning woman, but stiff and frigid with a chilling, conventional air,"[2] who thought of nothing but her toilette. "She got up at ten o'clock," wrote her step-daughter, Lady Hester Stanhope, "Went out and then returned to be dressed, if in London, by the hairdresser; and there are only two in London, both Frenchmen, who could dress her. Then she went out to dinner, and from dinner to the Opera, and from the Opera to Parties, seldom returning until just before daylight."[3] A more unsuitable wife for Mahon it would have been difficult to find!

Though Pitt had become a practising barrister, his constant attendances at the House of Commons had made him long to follow in his father's footsteps. We shall not be surprised, then, to find him on the dissolution of parliament hastening down to Cambridge, where he hoped to be elected member. But youth's ambitions are often unrealized and after an arduous contest he found himself at the bottom of the poll. "The struggle has not been dishonourable," he reported to his mother, and he added that he was just off to Cheveley, the Duke of Rutland's Cambridgeshire seat.[4] The Duke, son of the gallant Granby, was an old friend of Pitt's, and was therefore anxious to help him. Consequently William could soon write, "Appleby is the place I am to represent, and the election will be made (probably in a week or ten days) without my having any trouble or even visiting my constituents."[5] But no sooner did he report this joyful news than the family had to mourn another death, for tidings came that James Charles had died in the West Indies. Only in the previous autumn the Alec. Hoods had received a letter from the young sailor recounting at length our successful action at Pinobscot and containing "A List of the Fleet taken & Destroyed at Pinobscot the 14 and 15 of August by his Majesty's ships under the command of Sir George Collier." "I have wrote to my mother

[1] Lady Stanhope to Lady Chatham, August 6th, 1780.

[2] Cleveland, *Life and Letters of Lady Hester Stanhope.*

[3] *Memoirs of Lady Hester Stanhope*—as related by herself in Conversation with her Physician.

[4] William Pitt to Lady Chatham, Pembroke Hall, September 16th, 1780.

[5] William Pitt to Lady Chatham, "Lincoln's Inn, Thursday night, November 1780."

by this Post," states James Charles, "and mentioned to her that as I am first Lieut. and as Promotion is frequently given in the case of a ship bringing home despatches of good news, whether she would not think it advisable to apply in the present circumstance for Promotion for me, and as you have been always so good as to interest yourself warmly in any thing that might be advantageous to me, which I shall ever be truly sensible of, I trouble you with asking your advice upon this subject."[1]   And now they had to mourn his loss !   William hurried down to Somerset to comfort his mother and then persuaded her to move to Hayes, so that she might be more accessible from London.

It was on January 23rd, 1781, that Mr. Pitt, aged twenty-one, took his seat as Member of Parliament for Appleby.   That date was to prove a notable one for the new member, marking as it did the commencement of a great career and the conclusion of a noble life, for it was on that very day a quarter of a century later, when the fortunes of England seemed at their lowest ebb, that the eyes of the exhausted statesman were closed in death.

[1] James Charles Pitt to Hood, "Greyhound, Spithead, Sep^t 23rd 1779."

CHAPTER V

Pitt and Fox

WHEN young Mr. Pitt first took his seat in the House of Commons in January 1781, Lord North was still at the head of his weak Administration and, yielding his better judgment to the obstinacy of the King, was continuing to wage the fatal war against the revolted American colonies. The Opposition was composed of two parties which, united in their common desire to overthrow the Ministry, were usually found voting together against the Government. Of these two factions, by far the larger was that of the old Whig Houses or "Revolution Families", led by Lord Rockingham; the smaller consisting of the old adherents of Lord Chatham, was led by Shelburne and Camden. But it was not from their leaders that these parties derived their effectiveness, for in the ranks of the latter were to be found such men as Dunning, the great lawyer; Barré, a much-lauded debater; and Tommy Townshend, an active and popular House of Commons man; whilst followers of Rockingham numbered Burke, the philosophical Irishman; and before and above them all, the clumsy, uncouth, unwashed form of Charles James Fox, a younger son of the late Lord Holland.

With his short, squalid, heavy figure, destitute of elegance or grace, his harsh, inharmonious voice, his dark, saturnine, Judaic features, not unlike those of Charles II, from whom of course he was descended in the female line; with his negligent dress, for he was usually seen in an old blue frock-coat and a threadbare buff waistcoat; with his evil reputation for vice and gambling, there was little to recommend Charles Fox as a popular leader. "I am much surprised," said the Abbé de Lageard to Pitt during his continental tour in 1783, "that a country so moral as England can submit to be governed by such a spendthrift and such a rake as Fox; it seems to show that you are less moral than you claim to be." "The remark is just," was the generous answer, "but you have not been under the wand of the magician." And what a wand it must have been! His remarkable powers of oratory, his unrivalled skill as a debater, never bettered—scarce ever challenged—in any age or in any land, his charm of manner, that overcame the shortcomings of his personal appearance and the hopeless follies of his private life, his open-handed generosity, his philosophic calm in the face of public disappointment and private disaster assured Fox a host of friends, both personal and political, ever ready to lend a helping hand. This was the man who was to prove for so long the opponent—alas! the bitter opponent—of William Pitt.

How different was the younger man, now entering for the first time the portals of the House of Commons, from his great rival, how different in appearance, temperament and spirit! Pitt was tall and slightly built, with the proud, haughty, turned-up Grenville nose of his mother, and with all the transcendent brilliance with which his father had amazed and awed the world. But, whereas the unsurpassed gifts of Chatham had flowed from him like a mighty current of a torrid stream, the more tranquil talents of his son were akin rather to the limpid waters of a cooling brook or the brittle brilliance of a well-cut stone. His voice was soft and sonorous, his manner frigid, contemptuous, detached, dignified and perfectly self-controlled. Indeed, there was something repellently unnatural in such awful self-possession in a youth of twenty-one. Yet his extraordinary wit and conversational powers secured him friends and he, Wilberforce, the Hull banker's son who was to make a noble and humane cause his own, Mahon, his brother-in-law, recently returned for the borough of High Wycombe, Edward Eliot, soon to marry his younger sister, and other young men of the day, formed an intimate club or society known as Goostree's. There Pitt used to dine almost every night. "He was the wittiest man I ever knew," attested Wilberforce, "and what was quite peculiar to himself, had at all times his wit under control."[1] And all the world knows of his celebrated encounter with the oracular Gibbon when the genius of the young politician overwhelmed the great historian.[2] With these talents and this nature it was not surprising that the son of Chatham should take an early opportunity to make his maiden speech in the House of Commons. Nor was his chance long in coming. Pitt, in common with nearly all his friends, had joined the smaller of the Opposition parties, and as a member of this group he rose to speak to a crowded and expectant House on the motion for the second reading of Burke's famous Bill for Economical Reform.[3] North pronounced it the best maiden speech he had ever heard.[4] Another member dubbed Pitt "a chip of the old block." "He is not merely a chip of the old block," was Burke's generous retort;

[1] *Life of William Wilberforce*, by his sons, Vol. I.

[2] Bland Burgess, *Letters and Correspondence*.

[3] William Pitt, House of Commons, February 26th, 1781.

[4] "This young man, Mr. Pitt, gained an universal applause. I heard Lord N. say it was the best first speech of a young man that he had ever heard." Selwyn to Carlisle, Tuesday, February 27th (1781).

"he is the old block itself." A few weeks later Pitt made a second speech that was no less successful.[1] "The young William Pitt has again displayed paternal oratory," wrote Horace Walpole. "The other day on the Commission of Accounts, he answered Lord North, and tore him limb from limb. If Charles Fox could feel, one should think such a rival with an unspotted character, would rouse him. What if a Pitt and Fox should again be rivals!"[2]

On Sunday, November 25th, terrible tidings reached us from across the Atlantic. On October 19th, Lord Cornwallis had been compelled to surrender at Yorktown. Even the phlegmatic North was alarmed; he took it "as he would have taken a ball in his breast," a friend told Wraxall, "for he opened his arms, exclaiming wildly, as he paced up and down the apartment during a few minutes, 'O God! it is all over!' Words which he repeated many times under emotions of the deepest consternation and distress."[3]

The receipt of these tidings was an obvious signal for renewed onslaughts on the government. Fox advocated an appeal to the country, and he was ardently supported by Thomas Pitt, who went so far as to advise the withholding of supply until the result of the appeal to the electors was known. The attack was taken up by Burke, while Tom Pitt, in gloomy despondency seemed unable to envisage any remedy under such a Parliament and such a king. "It is no longer a matter of importance what set of puppets work the dismal scene," he cried. "While the fatal system remains, and the deadly secret influence which has continued throughout the present reign pervades every measure and every department, it signifies little what ostensible agents are placed at the head of affairs."[4] On the following day, his cousin also spoke.[5] Early in the New Year, when Parliament reassembled, the vigorous attacks were renewed: and in these debates, the two Pitts played prominent parts—William "dignified, impressive, collected, was always heard with a sort of veneration, as the living substitute of him who under two successive reigns had subjected our foreign enemies while he trampled opposition under his feet"; Thomas, "solemn and declamatory, if not theatrical; sometimes whining, yet often appealing with great effect to the passion or to the understanding of the House. . . . Their joint co-operation unquestionably conduced the success which crowned the party at the conclusion of the debate."[6] The Ministers were totally incapable of withstanding the

[1] William Pitt, House of Commons, May 31st, 1781.
[2] Walpole to Conway, Strawberry Hill, June 3rd, 1781.
[3] Wraxall, *Historical and Posthumous Memoirs*, Vol. II.
[4] Thomas Pitt, House of Commons, November 27th, 1781.
[5] William Pitt, House of Commons, November 28th, 1781.
[6] Wraxall, *Historical and Posthumous Memoirs*, Vol. II.

attack; and it was not long before North resigned and George III was forced to receive Lord Rockingham as his new Prime Minister.

In this Government, in which an attempt was made to apportion offices between the two opposition parties, no place was found for the son of Chatham, though the minor but lucrative post of Vice Treasurer of Ireland was pressed upon him. As the situation carried a salary of £5,000 a year, a penniless barrister of not quite twenty-three need not have thought it beneath his dignity; but ten days before North's resignation Pitt, with superb presumption, had declared in the House of Commons, "For myself, I could not expect to form part of a new administration, but were my doing so more within my reach, I feel myself bound to declare that I never would accept a subordinate situation."[1]

The first matter that came before the new government was the vexed question of Parliamentary Reform, and on May 7th Pitt brought it forward in a lengthy speech in which he moved for a Select Committee to enquire into the state of the representation of the people. He vehemently attacked "the corrupt influence of the Crown, an influence of the most pernicious kind . . . of which it has been said 'that it has grown with our growth, and strengthened with our strength.' Unhappily, however, for this country, it has not decayed with our decay; nor diminished with our decrease." He declared himself the unrelenting enemy of close boroughs, and he reminded members of the views expressed by his father that, unless some equitable system of representation could be established, the nation "must be confounded in the mass of those whose liberties were lost in the corruption of the people."[2] But the Government and the House were by no means unanimous on this point, and strangely enough Pitt found himself opposed by his cousin, Thomas, who was clearly on delicate ground, seeing that he had elected himself, and his father-in-law, old Pinckney Wilkinson, as members for Old Sarum. With great address, therefore, he demonstrated from his own conduct in successive Parliaments, that a man who sat for a close borough might be as honest, as high-minded, as free from corruption as he who took his seat for a county constituency or for the City of London. Equality of representation, he contended, could not have been the basis on which our ancestors intended to erect the liberties of England, for did they not allow the little county of Rutland to send as many members to Parliament as the greatest counties in the country? To one suggested reform only would he agree, and that one had been recommended by the great Earl of Chatham, that an additional knight of the Shire or member should

[1] William Pitt, House of Commons, March 10th, 1781.
[2] William Pitt, House of Commons, May 7th, 1782.

be granted to every county throughout England. On dividing, the motion was lost by only twenty votes in a House of more than three hundred members.

Meanwhile, the war dragged on in America without any momentous developments, and in the summer of 1782, it was decided to send over to Paris two representatives—Richard Oswald, a London merchant with experience of American affairs, to treat with Dr. Franklin, and Thomas Grenville, second son of George Grenville of unhappy memory and the intimate friend of Charles Fox, to treat with Vergennes.

Thomas Grenville was a man of great charm but of no more than average ability—though he acquired one of the most splendid libraries in the kingdom which with rare nobility he bequeathed in its entirety to the British Museum—but in the days of the Georges the Grenvilles, it seems, had always to be found lucrative posts in the public service. At this time, there flourished three members of this self-important family—Thomas and his elder and younger brothers, George, Lord Temple and William Wyndham Grenville. The eldest, afterwards Marquess of Buckingham and father of the first Duke of Buckingham and Chandos, was as like in temper as he was unlike in build to the uncle whose earldom he had inherited. Whilst the late Lord Temple was tall, gawky and angular, his nephew was portly, sleek and comfortable; but in character they were the same, masses of insufferable pride, conceit and self-importance. The youngest of the brothers, afterwards Lord Grenville, far the ablest of the three, lacked the pride of George and the charm of Thomas; indeed, this cold, heavy, formal, calculating man has suffered a like fate to his father, for whereas in his lifetime he occupied a considerable place upon the public stage, to-day he is forgotten; he has dropped out of history from the sheer lack of that warm humanity that enables a man to live long after his body has mouldered in the grave.

Not unnaturally, our affairs in Paris, conducted by two independent negotiators, did not prosper, and the letters that Grenville sent home are full of complaints of chaos and confusion.[1] But it was not long before the negotiations were brought to an abrupt finale by the unexpected termination of the Government. Already fissures were to be seen in the Government façade. The Chancellor, the quarrelsome Thurlow, was on ill terms with most of his colleagues; the joint Secretaries of State, Fox and Shelburne, in jealous dislike of one another were constantly bickering; the negotiations for peace were not prospering. To quell these disturbances, a strong leader was required, and the leader of the Government was weak, timid and vacillating. In any case then, these discordant elements could hardly have been kept together very much longer, but their dissolution was

[1] Grenville to Fox, June 4th, 16th, and 21st, 1782.

hastened by an event totally unexpected. Lord Rockingham suddenly died; whereupon the whole edifice of his government collapsed.

As soon as the news was known, the King sent for Shelburne; and Fox, chagrined at not having been summoned, promptly resigned. He was followed into retirement by other malcontents. Thomas Grenville, too, begged to be recalled from his untenable position in Paris.[1] The offices thus vacated were soon filled. The two retiring Secretaries of State were succeeded by Tommy Townshend and Lord Grantham; Pitt's two cousins, Lord Temple and William Grenville were appointed Lord-Lieutenant of Ireland and Chief Secretary respectively; and Pitt himself accepted the great position of Chancellor of the Exchequer. A few days previously he had written to his mother to report Lord Rockingham's death; and he added with sublime self-confidence: "With regard to myself, I believe the arrangement may be of a sort in which I *may* and probably *ought* to take a part. If I do, I think I need not say you pretty well know the principles on which I shall do it. In this short time nothing is settled, and I only saw what were the strong wishes of *some* who foresaw the event. But how different pretensions will be adjusted is a matter of great uncertainty."[2] So the very day after Rockingham's death this stripling of twenty-three could write to his mother with serene simplicity of his advent to high office as a thing inevitable and already settled. And a few days later he wrote again with the same studied calm: "My lot will be either at the Treasury as Chancellor of the Exchequer, or in the Home department as Secretary of State."[3] One wonders what words Lady Chatham found to express her feelings towards her amazing son!

The new Government hastened to come to terms with America, France and Spain, and before the end of January 1783, preliminary treaties with both were signed in Paris. The conditions obtained were not unfavourable: to the Americans we conceded that independence that in fact they had already won by their arms; to the French we restored Pondicherry and Chandernagore, the settlement of Senegal and St. Lucia island; and to Spain we gave back Minorca and both the Floridas. But the Cabinet was much divided, and it was soon evident that if the Government was to continue it must obtain renewed strength; and at last after some hesitation Shelburne agreed that Fox and his friends should be invited to join it. In an effort to facilitate these arrangements, Pitt called upon Fox, but the interview was short. "It is impossible for me to belong to any administration of which Lord Shelburne is the head," declared Fox. "Then we need discuss the

[1] Grenville to Temple, Paris, July 9th, 1782.
[2] William Pitt to Lady Chatham, Tuesday, July 2nd, 1782.
[3] William Pitt to Lady Chatham, Friday, July 5th, 1782.

matter no further," was Pitt's curt reply. "I did not come here to betray Lord Shelburne." Pitt saw his cousin, William Grenville, later in the day and related to him all that had passed. "The one must be very desperate, the other very confident, before such a question could be so put and so answered," was Grenville's sage comment.[1]

But this rather half-hearted approach to Fox was ere long put in the shade by far more sinister negotiations, for it was soon known that efforts were being made to bring North and Fox together at a private interview. At length on February 14th the meeting duly took place, and the two statesmen quickly came to terms. They would lay aside their former animosity, or, in other words, no longer abuse each other in public; they would treat as an open matter the vexed question of Reform; they would oppose the Address on the Peace. Three days later this was moved in both Houses of Parliament: in the Lords it was carried, but in the Commons, where it was proposed by Thomas Pitt and seconded by Wilberforce, the combined opposition prevailed. Tom Pitt, who, according to Walpole, was intensely jealous of his cousin,[2] delivered a vehement and witty philippic against North for his unholy alliance. Not only had he by his persistence in the war inflicted cruel wounds on his country, alleged Tom, but now, by opposing the peace, he was doing his utmost to prevent a healing salve being applied to them. He likened the case to that of the man of Bury, who, learning that a brother-in-law whom he had attacked was in a fair way of recovering, had visited him in his sick-room and torn away the bandages.[3] William Pitt, who did not rise till four o'clock, made perhaps the worst speech of his career, and even had the bad taste to sneer at Sheridan's connection with the stage. "No man admires more than I do," he declared, "the abilities of that right honourable gentleman, the elegant sallies of his thought, the gay effusions of his fancy, his dramatic turns, and his epigrammatic points; and if they were reserved for the proper stage, they would no doubt receive, what the honourable gentleman's abilities always did receive, the plaudits of the audience; and it will be my fortune, 'sui plausa gaudere theatri.' But this is not the proper scene for the exhibition of these elegancies; and I therefore must beg leave to call the attention of the House to the serious consideration of the very important question now before us."[4] "If ever I again engage in those compensations to which the Right Hon. gentleman has in such flattering terms referred," was Sheridan's withering retort, "I may be tempted to an act of presumption. I may be encouraged

[1] Grenville to Temple, February 11th, 1783.
[2] Walpole, *Last Journals*, Vol. II.
[3] Walpole, *Last Journals*, Vol. II.
[4] William Pitt, House of Commons, February 17th, 1783.

by his praises to try an improvement on one of Ben Jonson's best characters in the play—the Angry Boy in 'The Alchymist.'"[1]

Though he recognized that his Ministry was doomed, Shelburne did not at once resign, and a few days later the battle was renewed. Whilst Fox was delivering his attack on the Ministry, the Chancellor of the Exchequer, whose stomach was disordered, could be seen holding open with one hand Solomon's Porch, the door behind the Speaker's chair, whilst in the other he grasped the basin into which at intervals he vomited. But when Fox sat down, Pitt at once rose, and he replied in a great speech that lasted nearly three hours. He deplored the sorry state first of the navy and then of the army. He deplored the sorry state of the national finances— an unfounded debt of thirty million pounds. He recalled the happier days of his father's glory. "I feel, Sir, at this instant, how much I had been animated in my childhood by a recital of England's victories," he declared. "I was taught, Sir, by one whose memory I shall ever revere, that at the close of a war, far different indeed from this, she had dictated the terms of peace to submissive nations. This, in which I place something more than common interest, was the memorable era of England's glory. But that era is past: she is under the awful and mortifying necessity of employing a language that corresponds with her true conditions, the vision of her power and pre-eminence are passed away." In these melancholy circumstances he had no alternative to defending the Ministers and the terms of the peace. But it was all very distasteful, and with arrogant pride, he declared that his one interest was his country's good. "On these principles alone I came into parliament, and into place," he pleaded, "and now I take the whole House to witness, that I have not been under the necessity of contradicting one public declaration I have ever made. . . . You may take from me, Sir, the privileges and emoluments of place," he trumpeted, "but you cannot, you shall not, take from me those habitual and warm regards for the prosperity of Great Britain, which constitute the honour, the happiness, the pride of my life; and which, I trust, death alone can extinguish. And, with this consolation, the loss of power, Sir, and the loss of fortune, though I affect not to despise them, I hope I soon shall be able to forget.

> "*Laudo manentem; si celeres quatit*
> *Pennas, resigno quae dedit—*
> ——————————*probamque*
> *Pauperiem sine dote quaero.*"[2]

[1] Sheridan, House of Commons, February 17th, 1783.
[2] William Pitt, House of Commons, February 21st, 1783.

But all this eloquence was vain. At half-past three in the morning of February 22nd, the House divided. The Opposition again triumphed, and on the morning of February 24th, Lord Shelburne resigned; whereupon the King hastened to send for Pitt. But he was wise enough to refuse the tempting bait. "The good judgment of so young a man," wrote the Duke of Grafton in his Diary, ". . . adds much to the lustre of the character he had acquired, for it was a temptation sufficient to have offset the resolution of most men." Such was it thought at the time, but we now know differently. What he then declined he accepted a few months later; thus he demonstrated himself to be not quite the glorious youth depicted by Stanhope and Holland Rose, but rather a wise tactician in the parliamentary fray.

On the refusal of Pitt, the King was in despair. He turned to North and implored him to undertake the Government without Fox, but he persistently refused. He then besought Lord Gower, and when he declined he even approached Tom Pitt, though the latter had barely recovered from a grave domestic anxiety. "T. Pitt's daughter is either dying or actually dead," wrote Grenville to his brother, "I pity them exceedingly, for no people dote more on their children."[1] And though he was three days later able to report, "T. Pitt's child is recovering very fast,"[2] it was unlikely that the not too robust Tom could be thus tempted. But the king in his extremity certainly sent for him, for William Grenville, who had audiences on March 16th, and 20th, thus reports his conversation with the Sovereign on the latter occasion. "He mentioned his having sent yesterday again to Tom Pitt, to endeavour to persuade him to stand forward, and his having declined it. He then went a good deal into T. Pitt's character, speaking very highly of his good sense and integrity, but expressing his doubt whether his health would ever allow him to take an active part; that, however, he had received this satisfaction from his conversation, that he had the pleasure of seeing that he approved of the conduct which he had held."[3]

Thus there was no avoiding the hated Fox-North coalition, and on April 2nd the new Ministers—the Duke of Portland, a figure-head Premier; Fox and

[1] Grenville to Temple, "Pall Mall, March 24th., 1783."

[2] Grenville to Temple, "Pall Mall, March 27th., 1783."

[3] Grenville to Temple, "Pall Mall, March 28th., 1783, Half-past Seven, p.m." In the royal archives at Windsor there are copies in the King's hand of two memoranda on these negotiations, drawn up by Thomas Pitt. Neither is dated, but one is headed "Minutes of a conversation with Ld. Gower at Whitehall, March 7th., 1783," and the other is endorsed by the King "Mr. Thos. Pitt's first paper." George III also drew up a paper with a very full description of the negotiations. This undated memorandum is also at Windsor.

North, joint Secretaries of State, and the rest—kissed their Sovereign's hand. Some measure of George's mortification may be gathered from his letter to Temple, written the previous day: "Since the conversation I had with Mr. William Grenville on the 16th. of last month, I have continued every possible means of forming an Administration. . . . Judge, therefore, of the uneasiness of my mind at having been thwarted in every attempt to keep the administration of public affairs out of the hands of the most unprincipled coalition the annals of this or any other nation can equal. I have withstood it till not a single man is willing to come to my assistance, and till the House of Commons has taken every step, but insisting on this faction being by name elected Ministers. . . . I trust the eyes of the nation will soon be opened, as my sorrow may prove fatal to my health if I remain long in this thraldom . . . and I hope many months will not elapse before the Grenvilles, the Pitts, and other men of abilities and character will relieve me from a situation that nothing could have compelled me to submit to, but the supposition that no other means remained of preventing the public finances from being materially affected."[1] Lord Townshend, who was present when Fox kissed hands, humorously reported that the King "turned back his ears and eyes, just like the horse at Astley's when the tailor he had determined to throw was getting on him."[2]

But there was at least one member who heartily disapproved of the Coalition. "I desire to declare that I am unconnected with any party whatever," Pitt declared. "I shall keep myself reserved, and act with whichever side I think is acting right."[3] On May 7th he brought forward once again the question of Parliamentary Reform, and now he was supported by his cousin, who expressed himself as willing "to surrender his borough of Old Sarum into the hands of Parliament as a free sacrifice, as a victim to be offered up at the shrine of the British Constitution. Should the victim be accepted, he would suggest that the power of returning two members might be transferred to the Bank of England."[4] A month later Pitt introduced a Bill for the reform of abuses in Public Offices;[5] and though he was unsuccessful, the weakness of the Ministry was vividly shown. "To rub through the remains of the Session," reported William to his mother, "seems almost as much as they can expect, all things considered."[6]

[1] George III to Temple, Queen's House, April 1st, 1783.
[2] Russell, *Memorials of Fox,* Vol. II.
[3] William Pitt, House of Commons, March 31st, 1783.
[4] Stanhope, *Life of William Pitt,* Vol. I.
[5] William Pitt, House of Commons, June 17th, 1783.
[6] William Pitt to Lady Chatham, May 24th, 1783.

In the summer of 1783 a domestic event brought great happiness to the Pitt family. Lord Chatham became engaged to Mary Elizabeth Townshend, daughter of Tommy Townshend, who had recently been created Lord Sydney. "I will only add," wrote the happy bridegroom-to-be, announcing his engagement, to Alec Hood, "that all who know her agree I have every reason to feel the most real happiness in the union, and your friendship will I know lead you to participate sincerely in it."[1] "You have, I am sure, easily imagined, though not so near a spectator, how much joy the long-expected declaration produced," wrote William to his mother. "Lord Sydney is the happiest person in the world—at least two excepted—and is delighted with your answer to his letter. I cannot learn with any certainty when the union is likely to be completed; but as there are not many materials for the law's delay, I imagine it cannot be long."[2] The young couple were married on July 10th, and went to Hayes for the honeymoon. There, shortly afterwards, they were visited by William, who went thence to Stowe. "My excursion to Stowe was a very short one—the pleasantest, however, that could be. I found more beauties in the place than I expected; and the house, though not half finished in the inside, the most magnificent by far that I ever saw."[3] From Stowe he went to Brighton, and towards the middle of August he joined his mother at Burton Pynsent.

In September, Pitt, accompanied by his friends, Wilberforce and Eliot, paid his one and only visit to the Continent. From Calais they went to Rheims. "We are going to-day to dine at a country-house in the midst of vineyards, which, as this is the height of the vintage, will furnish a very pleasant scene," wrote William to his sister. "Tomorrow we are to dine at a magnificent palace of the Archbishop's, who lives about five miles off, and is a sort of prince of this country."[4] Here the travellers made the acquaintance of a young priest, nephew of their host, soon to become Bishop of Autun, and one day world famous as Prince Talleyrand. Not many years later Pitt was to meet this remarkable man again and under very different circumstances. From Rheims the friends travelled to Paris, where the son of Chatham was assured of a warm welcome at Court. "I am just setting out to Fontainbleau for two or three days," he reported to Lady Chatham, "where I shall find the Court and all the magnificence

[1] Chatham to Hood, "Saville Street, June 11th, 1783."

[2] William Pitt to Lady Chatham, Saturday, June 14th, 1783.

[3] William Pitt to Lady Chatham, "Savile Street, July 22nd., 1783."

[4] William Pitt to Lady Harriot Pitt, Rheims, October 1st, 1783.

of France, and with this expedition I shall finish my career here."[1]   At Fontainebleau Pitt apparently took part in the chase, for Wilberforce noted in his diary: "October 17th. morning: Pitt stag-hunting, Eliot and I in chaise to see king.   Clumsy, strange figure in immense boots.   Dined at home; then play."   The son of Chatham was clearly a figure of interest at the French Court, and it appears that Marie Antoinette and many of her circle took favourable notice of the tall, good-looking young man.   "They all, men and women, crowded round Pitt in shoals; and he behaved with great spirit, though he was sometimes a little bored when they talked to him of Parliamentary Reform."[2]

It was during this tour that Monsieur and Madame Necker are supposed to have offered Pitt the hand of their daughter with a fortune of £14,000 a year, to which proposal Pitt is said to have replied, "I am already married to my country."   Lord Stanhope gives no credence to this story,[3] and certainly the answer does not sound like the words of Pitt.   But whether the proposal was made or not, the parents of the future Madame de Staël certainly wished for the union; for a year or so later when Madame Necker was seriously ill, she wrote her daughter, Germaine, in unmistakable terms: "I did desire that you should marry Mr. Pitt.   I wished to confide you to the care of a husband who had made for himself a great name; I would also wish for a son-in-law into whose care I could recommend your poor father, and who would feel the full weight of his charge.   You were not disposed to give me this satisfaction.   Well, all is now forgiven. . . ."[4]

The three friends returned to England on October 24th, and on November 18th Fox introduced into the House of Commons his famous plan for the better government of India.   This controversial measure was vigorously attacked by Wilberforce and by Pitt, who twice spoke against it[5] and who dubbed it "the boldest and most unconstitutional measure ever attempted, transferring, at one stroke, in spite of all charters and compacts, the immense influence and patronage of the East to Charles Fox, in or out of office."[6] But their efforts were vain; the Bill was carried by a large majority, and on December 9th Fox with the body of his followers, triumphantly presented the Bill at the bar of the House of Lords.

---

[1] William Pitt to Lady Chatham, "Hotel de Grande Bretagne, Paris, Wednesday October 15th." (1783).

[2] Wilberforce to Bankes, October 1783.

[3] Stanhope, *Life of William Pitt,* Vol. I.

[4] Hansonville, *The Salon of Madame Necker,* Vol. II.

[5] William Pitt, House of Commons, November 18th and 27th, 1783.

[6] William Pitt to Rutland, November 22nd, 1783.

In the Upper House, the measure was vehemently attacked by Lord Temple, recently returned from the Vice-royalty of Ireland, and by Thurlow. But they did not confine themselves to passionate rhetoric; they had in fact for some time been acting in concert, and had drawn up a memorandum, still extant in Lord Temple's hand, in which the Bill is spoken of as "a plan to take more than half the royal power and by that means disable His Majesty for the rest of the reign." This document, long a secret, was found amidst the papers of Stowe and in 1853 was published together with many other materials from that source.[1] But the King needed no such goading. According to a manuscript preserved at Chevening, it appears that during the night of December 11th the Sovereign sent for Temple and presented him with a written sheet, apparently in his own hand, which stated that "His Majesty allowed Earl Temple to say that whoever voted for the India Bill was not only not his friend, but would be considered by him as his enemy; and if these words are not strong enough, Earl Temple might use whatever words he might deem stronger and more to the purpose."[2] Temple's commission from the King could not, of course, long remain secret, and a few days later the many rumours that were rife were referred to in the Lords by the Dukes of Portland and Richmond. Lord Temple at once rose to reply. He readily admitted having had his audience. "It is the privilege of the Peers, as the hereditary Counsellors of the Crown, either individually or collectively to advise His Majesty," he declared. "I did give my advice; what it was, I shall not now declare; it is lodged in His Majesty's breast. But though I will not declare what my advice to my Sovereign was, I will tell your Lordships negatively what it was not: it was not friendly to the principle and object of the Bill."[3]

The effect of this pronouncement was inevitable; the Lords tumbled over themselves to vote against the Bill. Thus the two Houses were at variance and the King naturally anticipated his minister's resignation. But Fox and his colleagues, sustained as they were by a vast majority in the Commons, determined to stand their ground. The King, however, would have none of this, and late on December 18th, a royal messenger was

[1] Buckingham and Chandos, *Court and Cabinets of George III*, Vol. I.

[2] I have quoted from Lord Stanhope's biography of Pitt, where he is careful to point out that there may be some doubt as to the precise words as the original paper has not been found. Stanhope, *Life of Pitt,* Vol. I. See also Buckingham and Chandos, *Courts and Cabinets of George III,* Vol. I.

[3] Temple, House of Lords, December 15th, 1783.

despatched to North requiring the resignation of the ministers.[1] North complied instantly,[2] and thus the hated coalition fell.

On the following day, a remarkable scene was enacted in the House of Commons. Whilst Fox and North took their seats on the front Opposition benches, a young barrister, Richard Pepper Arden by name, rose in his place holding an open paper in his hand: in solemn words he moved that a new writ be issued for the borough of Appleby "in the room of the Right Honourable William Pitt, who, since his election, has accepted the office of the First Lord of the Treasury and Chancellor of the Exchequer." The news that this young man of twenty-four had consented to form a Government was received with a great shout of derision from the crowded benches of the Opposition. Thus was heralded the first Administration of William Pitt. It was destined to survive for seventeen years.

On April 30th, 1784, John Pitt of Encombe sat down at his desk in London to write to his son, giving him a summary of events at home. The reader will recall meeting the Great Commoner of the West in the days when he accompanied his celebrated cousin to Bath and welcomed him to his princely seat in Dorset. He will remember, too, the happy day in 1754, when his son, William Morton, was born. That child was now a man. He had sat in the House of Commons as member for the County of Dorset since 1778, and was already in 1784 becoming known for his efforts on behalf of the poor and to ameliorate the condition of prisons. He had had much correspondence with Lord Pelham on this subject. "If I am permitted to remain a little in Dorsetshire this Autumn," he had written a few years back, "I hope to finish a Book which I have had some time in hand, the matter of which I think I may promise myself will please you. It is a short account, to the present time as far as can be traced, of every Felon who has been within our Walls for 14 years, and I believe you will be surprised to find *how many* are *now* behaving well, and maintaining themselves and families by their own industry. . . ."[3] He had consulted the Lord Chancellor, Lord Eldon, to whom he had submitted a plan for an enquiry into the state of the Prisons. "He made several objections, some of which I admit to have considerable force, yet I cannot but flatter

---

[1] George III to North, "Queen's House, Dec. 18th., 1783, m. 43 past 10 p.m."

[2] North to George III, December 18th, 1783. The story of Lord North receiving the King's messenger in bed at 1 o'clock in the morning is apparently without foundation. Massey, *Reign of George III.*

[3] William Morton Pitt to Pelham, "Fort Monckton, 13th. Sept. 1801" Endorsed "Answered Sept. 16th."

myself that *something* is practicable."[1] "The Lord Chancellor objects decidedly to *my plan*" he wrote a month later, "but I mean to submit something else to give to him next winter, which I hope may be thought less objectionable."[2] In 1784, William Morton was touring on the Continent, and his father had long wished to give his son a résumé of the news from home, but hitherto affairs had been in too confused a state for this to be possible. He utterly condemned Fox's India Bill, and Fox and Burke he treated with withering scorn. Then he turned to the elevation of Pitt to power, and he continued in a happier strain. "But the King, galled by the shackles in which Fox had, without the least regard to the common rules of decency, always kept him, happily thought fit to embrace a proposition to emancipate himself, and soon settled a plan of placing William Pitt at the head of affairs. A new administration was immediately appointed, and by their firmness and steadiness, which I am sure will be lasting, the coalition is excluded and totally defeated."[3]

How came it that Pitt now accepted the glittering prize that he had rejected a few months earlier? The researches of Professor W. T. Laprade supply a partial key to that riddle. There was at that time at the Treasury Board a senior secretary by name Robinson, whose parliamentary business was largely analogous to the work of the present-day "Whip"; thus it was his duty to see that a sufficient number of the supporters of the administration were present in the division lobby on important occasions and at election time so to manage the constituencies that a favourable majority could be counted upon. Fortunately, the papers of this ingenious official are now available to us;[4] and these interesting documents show that somewhere about mid-December, 1783, probably on instructions from the King, Robinson compiled a complete estimate of what support Pitt could count upon in the existing House of Commons and what support he would probably be able to rely on in a new parliament elected after a dissolution. Robinson divided his columns into "pro," "hopeful," "doubtful" and "con" and his estimates worked out in this manner. In the old parliament, Pitt could count on the support of 149 certainly *pro* and 104 hopeful, whilst the coalition could muster 231 *con* and 74 doubtful, that is, probable coalition supporters. After a dissolution and a general election, however, things looked very different. Pitt then would have 253 *pro* and 116 hopeful, whilst the opposition could count only on 123 certain and 66 doubtful

---

[1] William Morton Pitt to Pelham, "Kingston, Sept. 19. 1802."

[2] William Morton Pitt to Pelham, "Kingston, Oct. 15th. 1802."

[3] John Pitt to William Morton Pitt, London, April 30th, 1784.

[4] *The Parliamentary Papers of John Robinson, 1774-1784.* (Ed. Laprade.)

supporters. By the middle of December these lists were complete, and though Robinson's estimates were in many details far from accurate, his broad conclusions proved to be surprisingly correct;[1] accordingly, Dundas, relying on the accuracy of the forecast, arranged a meeting at his house of those anxious for Pitt to take office. "The Lord Advocate wishes to get an appointment made for you and he and Mr. Pitt and myself to meet as soon as possible in the most secret way," wrote Richard Atkinson to his friend Robinson, "not," he added cautiously, "from any improper desire of secrecy but lest the measure in agitation should be guessed at if an interview was known. It has ended in appointing this evening at seven o'clock at the Advocat's house in Leicester Fields, when he will have some dinner for us. . . . I understand in general all goes right."[2] With this secret information, the King felt safe in dismissing his hated ministers and, to the relief of many, the cautious Pitt hesitated no longer. "I believe we all feel equaly interest'd in the late change of public men," was the acid comment of Lord Camelford, "which may I hope secure us from such public measures as we have lately seen brought forward, and which threaten'd no less than the transferring the Crown from the head that wears it to that of Mr. Ch. Fox."[3]

But though young Mr. Pitt might be called to the head of affairs, it proved no easy task for him to form a government. In the Upper House, where there was no orator to match Thurlow, now again Chancellor, or Camden, the friend of Chatham and the cordial supporter of his son, his position was fairly secure. But in the Lower House he was so woefully weak that he took the surprising initial step of attempting a coalition with Fox. He was led to make this approach by the report that reached him of a conversation between Lord Beauchamp and James Grenville, when the former "though not pretending to be authorized, had very strenuously urged the possibility of a measure of this nature succeeding particularly from an idea that Lord North might be easily prevailed on to give up a seat in the Cabinet."[4] Temple, too, reported to the King that Pitt had taken

[1] Mrs. Eric George in an address entitled "Fox's Martyrs; the General Election of 1784," delivered before the Royal Historical Society in 1937, proved that, though Robinson's conclusions were in the main right, he erred in expecting to win a number of pocket boroughs which in fact he lost, and in not knowing he would win some "popular" constituencies, which in fact he did win. See *Transactions of the Royal Historical Society*, 4th Series, Vol. xxi. I am much indebted to Professor Richard Pares for having brought this interesting address to my notice.
[2] Atkinson to Robinson, December 15th, 1783. The note was endorsed in Robinson's hand, "answered immediately and went accordingly."
[3] Camelford to Hood, "Dec. 30th, 1783."
[4] Spencer to Dowager Lady Spencer, December 21st and 22nd, 1783.

advantage of His Majesty's permission to discuss with Lord Spencer the "general idea of an accommodation."[1] The reply came later the same day: "Mr. Fox, the D. of Portland, and L. John Cavendish have determined that they cannot consider this as a proper moment for a negociation in general; besides the particular objections there might be to a negociation such as was proposed one of them in particular (viz. that relating to L. North) would from their present situation with respect to him be absolutely insuperable." So the matter ended, much to the relief of the King: "Lord Temple's note is only a confirmation of what He must remember I suspected when He the last night first broached the idea of a willingness in Mr. Fox to negotiate."[2]

Then again he was to suffer almost immediately a further set-back that must have touched him nearly. His kinsman, Lord Temple, had on the morning of Friday, December 19th, accepted the Seals as Secretary of State, and Pitt was relying on him to lead the House of Lords. Yet sometime between Monday, December 22nd and Tuesday, December 23rd the imperious Temple resigned his office. This was indeed grievous news; poor Pitt could not sleep a moment the whole night through and to Tomline the next morning he expressed great uneasiness at the state of affairs.[3] The cause of Temple's sudden retirement is not certainly known. The explanation given by William Grenville in the House of Commons next day that Temple had resigned so that the protection of office should not shelter him from an enquiry into his conduct in circulating the opinions of the Sovereign on Fox's India Bill, was not generally considered adequate. That the overbearing and truculent head of the Grenvilles expected some high honour—perhaps a dukedom—and was furious when he realized that no such honour was intended, seems the most likely explanation. As it was, the outraged nobleman retired in high dudgeon to Stowe, whence he wrote to Pitt a letter that exudes resentment from every line.[4] But in spite of all

[1] William Pitt to Spencer, "Sunday night, Decr. 21st, 1783."

[2] It must be admitted that it is most strange that no mention of this approach to Fox is made in his memorials, in the Buckingham and Chandos memoirs or in the Fortescue papers from Dropmore; nor is it recorded in the lives of Pitt by Tomline, Stanhope or Holland Rose. But see Barnes, *George III and William Pitt, 1783–1806* and Feiling, "The Second Tory Party, 1714–1832," Appendix I. Professor D. G. Barnes quotes from the transcripts in the W. L. Clements library in Ann Arbor, Michigan. The originals are in the Royal Archives at Windsor. Mr. Keith Feiling gives the correspondence between Spencer and his mother and Pitt and Spencer. The originals are at Althorp.

[3] Tomline, *Life of Pitt,* Vol. I.

[4] Temple to William Pitt, "Stowe, December 29th., half-past one" (1783).

WILLIAM PITT, son of William Pitt, Earl of Chatham
Hoppner

difficulties the Cabinet at length was formed; Gower, Lord President of the Council; Rutland, Privy Seal; Thurlow, Lord Chancellor; Sydney and Carmarthen, Secretaries of State; and Howe, First Lord of the Admiralty. These six peers, with Pitt, formed the Cabinet, and of them Pitt alone sat in the House of Commons. The Prime Minister had no illusions as to the weakness of his Ministry. "What if they withhold supplies?" he asked. "They will not stop them," replied Mahon with rare penetration; "it is the very thing which they will not venture to do."[1]

No sooner was the new Government formed than the onslaught of the Opposition began, and on the very day of his re-election for Appleby Pitt found himself defeated on five successive motions. The Coalition affected to look upon the Premier as an inexperienced boy who could not be expected to retain his place for more than a few days. They laughed, they jeered, they stormed, they ranted. Day after day the pitiless attack was remorselessly pressed home and on not less than sixteen occasions between December 17th, 1783, and March 8th, 1784, the Opposition triumphed. But the young Prime Minister would not give in; his spirit never wavered; and his high resolve was buoyed up by the conviction that the great body of the nation was with him in the battle. He was bidden to come in state to receive the highest civic honour, the freedom of the city of London, at the hands of the Lord Mayor, and he was sumptuously feasted by the city fathers in Grocers' Hall. Meanwhile, the King looked on with sympathetic interest and when, on his return, Lord Chatham's coach, in which were Chatham, Pitt and Mahon, was attacked by roughs outside Brooks's and the life of the Premier was for a time in danger, George III wrote a note of encouragement to his minister the very next day.[2] It is some indication of the low state into which Fox's credit had fallen that it was popularly believed that he himself was implicated in the dastardly assault on his rival; though he indignantly denied the offence, pleading as an alibi that he was at the time in bed with his mistress, Mrs. Armistead, who, if required, was prepared to substantiate the fact on oath. The previous month, George III had shown his regard for Pitt by conferring at his request no less than four peerages, one of which was bestowed on Tom Pitt, who now became Lord Camelford; and he was most anxious to do all in his power to sustain his courageous Premier. "If you resign, Mr. Pitt," he is reported to have said, "I must resign also."[3]

[1] Wilberforce, *Recollections*. But Mahon had refused a place in his brother-in-law's Ministry.

[2] George III to William Pitt, February 29th, 1784.

[3] Dutens, *Memoirs of a Traveller now in Retirement,* Vol. V.

And so the great struggle between Pitt and Fox continued. Again and again the Government were defeated, but it gradually became clear that the Coalition majorities were shrinking until on an ever-memorable day, March 8th, 1784, that "virtuous and respectable majority," as Fox had once called it, was reduced to one. It was this moment that the wily Pitt chose for an appeal to the country. The king, who had been in favour of an earlier dissolution, was overjoyed. The Prime Minister's forbearance was soon rewarded, for the result of the General Election answered King George's most sanguine hopes. The Coalition was routed. Altogether, one hundred and sixty Opposition supporters—Fox's martyrs, as they were called—lost their seats; and even Fox himself was hard put to it to obtain election at Westminister. Indeed, he would probably have failed but for the active partisanship of the Prince of Wales and the persuasive fascination of the bewitching Georgiana, Duchess of Devonshire, who, with her sister, Lady Duncannon, canvassed the humblest homes, dazzling and enchanting the electors with her great beauty and charm. "I could light my pipe at your eyes," was said to be the ecstatic boast of an Irish mechanic to the lovely duchess; but the comment of the hesitant butcher, whose vote her grace purchased with a kiss, is unhappily not recorded. "Westminster goes well," Pitt caustically reported, "in spite of the Duchess of Devonshire and other *women of the people*."[1] Very true was this appraisal for, even after all these extraordinary exertions, Fox was only just elected, being no higher than third on the poll for the constituency; and when parliament met on May 18th the party of William Pitt had a clear majority over all those adversaries who had struggled so long and fought so strenuously to pull him down.

There stood the young Prime Minister in the midst of his triumphs, tall, cool, imperturbable, a little scornful perhaps, and certainly very sure of himself. "I came up no back stairs," he had recently declared in a noble speech. "When I was sent for by my Sovereign to know whether I could accept of office, I necessarily went to the royal closet. I know of no secret influence, and my integrity shall be my guardian against that danger. . . . I will never have the meanness to act upon the advice of others, nor the hypocrisy to pretend, when the measures of an administration in which I have a share are deserving of censure, that they were measures not of my advising. If any former ministers take these charges to themselves, to them be the sting. Little did I think to be ever charged in this house with being the tool and abettor of secret influence. . . . This is the only answer I shall ever deign to make on the subject, and I wish the House to bear it in their

[1] William Pitt to Wilberforce, April 3rd, 1784.

232

mind, and judge of my future conduct by my present declaration: the integrity of my own heart, and the probity of all my public as well as my private principles, shall always be my sources of action. I will never condescend to be the instrument of any secret advisers whatever, nor in one instance, while I have the honour to act as Minister of the Crown in this House, will I be responsible for measures not my own, or at least in which my heart and judgment do not cordially acquiesce."[1] He was the favourite of his Sovereign, the darling of the people; and he dominated over his colleagues as mighty Everest would dominate over a tender hill of the Scottish Highlands. He had already shown himself, as Macaulay tells us, the greatest master of the art of parliamentary government, and was destined ere long to show himself a greater than Walpole, or Chatham, or Fox, or Canning, or Peel.[2] He was by far the most illustrious subject of King George III; his was perhaps the most brilliant reputation in all Europe. And he had just completed his twenty-fifth year.

[1] William Pitt, House of Commons, January 12th, 1784.
[2] Macaulay, *William Pitt* (Biographies).

CHAPTER VI

The Young Prime Minister and the King

ONE day during the autumn of 1784, a little pot-bellied man with a round fat face and a double chin sat down in his villa at Lausanne to write a letter. Most of his time was employed in writing a history—a history which to-day is esteemed one of the crowning masterpieces of the English tongue—but on this occasion he was writing to a friend at home. "Since my leaving England," wrote Edward Gibbon, for it was he, "in the short period of last winter, what strange events have fallen out in your political world! It is probable, from your present connections, that we see them with very different eyes; and, on this occasion, I very much distrust my own judgment. I am far too distant to have a perfect knowledge of the revolution, and am too recently absent to judge of it with impartiality. Yet let me soberly ask you on Whig principles, whether it be not a dangerous discovery that the King can keep his favourite Minister against a majority of the House of Commons? Here indeed (for even here we are politicians), the people were violent against Fox, but I think it was chiefly those who have imbibed in the French service a high reverence for the person and authority of Kings. They are likewise biassed by the splendour of young Pitt, and it is a fair and honourable prejudice. A youth of five-and-twenty, who raises himself to the government of an empire by the power of genius and the reputation of virtue, is a circumstance unparalleled in history, and, in a general view, is not less glorious to the country than to himself."[1] When these words were penned, be it noted, Pitt had not only raised himself to a supreme position in the State; he had brought to order the country's finances, and he had settled for seventy years the perplexing question of the Government of India.

It was in dealing with the nation's disordered finances that the new Minister found his true bent. Our credit was low; the national debt had risen; the heavy expenses of the late war had left us with a deficit of six million and a floating debt of some fifteen millions, besides a debt to the Bank of England and sundry deficiencies on the Civil List. Moreover, revenue was drastically diminished by smuggling, mainly in tea. To cope with

[1] Gibbon to Eliot, Lausanne, October 27th, 1784.

this serious state of affairs Pitt imposed more stringent regulations as to the rights of search, at the same time taking away much of the smuggler's profit by lowering and varying the tea duty. The deficit thus caused was partly met by the doubtful expedient of increasing the window tax and by a loan open for the first time to public competition. He also introduced a number of imposts on race-horses, hats, bricks and tiles, candles, linens and calicoes, ale licences, shooting licences, paper, hackney coaches, lead for export, imported silk, and postage. On June 30th, 1784, he introduced his budget into the House of Commons, moving 133 financial resolutions in connection with it. He calculated that these imposts would yield to the Exchequer about £900,000. Early the following year, though Pitt was able to show a vast improvement in the country's financial position, he was compelled nevertheless to levy fresh taxes, calculated to produce £400,000. Among these were an increased duty on men-servants, graduated according to the number employed, a duty, also graduated, on maid-servants—a measure that evoked an infinite variety of jests that were perhaps neither very diverting nor very seemly!—and a tax on shops. The second and third of these proposals were extremely unpopular and were ultimately repealed.

During the course of 1784 Pitt introduced a measure for the better management of the East India Company, which provided that the political power hitherto enjoyed by the directors was to be transferred to a Board of Control.[1] The Bill, though violently assailed by Fox, Burke, Sheridan and Francis, finally passed both Houses with some amendments but without a division. The somewhat complex system of double government instituted by this measure lasted until the Act of 1858. In the following year, Pitt brought before the House of Commons two measures of the highest importance, one for regulating and improving our commercial relations with Ireland[2] and the other for the reform of parliament.[3] To parliamentary reform the King was known to be opposed; and Pitt felt it wise to set out in writing the detailed heads of his proposals, at the same time tactfully warning George III of the inadvisability of the King's Friends proclaiming to the world by their opposition that a breach existed between the King and his Minister.[4] The Sovereign promised not to exercise any influence against the measure,[5] but his true views on the subject are expressed in a

[1] William Pitt, House of Commons, July 6th, 1784.
[2] William Pitt, House of Commons, February 22nd and May 12th, 1785.
[3] William Pitt, House of Commons, April 18th, 1785.
[4] George III to William Pitt, March 19th, 1785.
[5] William Pitt to George III, March 20th, 1785.

little-known letter to Lord Sydney: "Undoubtedly I am not obliged to take any notice of it till I see Him on Monday; but there are some expressions which seem to require being properly understood between us; I have therefore drawn up the enclosed answer which if Lord Sydney sees no objection to, I mean either to night or early in the morning to send to Mr. Pitt, for though out of attention to Mr. Pitt, I carefully avoid expressing my unalterable Sentiments in any change in the Constitution, yet more must not be expected from me."[1] The position between Pitt and his Sovereign was thus made quite clear. For Pitt's own sake George would not openly oppose him. But as his views were well known it was obvious what effect his silence or neutrality would have on the measure. It is strange that the astute Pitt does not seem to have perceived this; at any rate he showed the greatest zeal in promoting the Bill, even persuading his friend Wilberforce to hurry back from the Riviera to support it; and when, on April 18th, the House of Commons made it plain that neither his oratory nor his blandishments had persuaded them, the shock to his pride was such that he never again made an attempt to promote parliamentary reform.

Nor did Pitt's effort to establish free trade with Ireland fare better, though in a great speech explaining his policy, he denounced England's past treatment of Ireland, and made a powerful plea for better future relations through the medium of his proposals. "Adopt them," he cried, "adopt that system of trade with Ireland that will have tended to enrich one part of the Empire without impoverishing the other, while it gives strength to both; that like mercy, the favourite attribute of Heaven:

"'is twice blessed,
It blesseth him that gives and him that takes.'"[2]

Unfortunately, others in the House of Commons were less far-seeing, with the result that in July the Premier was forced so to remould his resolutions, swollen to the number of twenty, that they little resembled those he had originally introduced.[3] These amendments, forced upon Pitt to secure English support, were restrictive of Irish trade; and Fox was not slow to see his chance. With consummate ability and impassioned eloquence, he thundered against the proposals. "I will not barter English commerce for Irish slavery," he cried; "that is not the price I would pay, nor is this the

[1] George III to Sydney, March 19th, 1785.
[2] William Pitt, House of Commons, May 12th, 1785.
[3] William Pitt, House of Commons, July 22nd, 1785.

thing I would purchase." This trumpet call resounded throughout the length and breadth of Ireland. Grattan condemned the resolutions with fiery eloquence, and they only passed the Commons by a narrow majority. Such an expression of hostility could not be ignored, and Pitt was forced to abandon his scheme. Thus was lost for ever one of the rare opportunities of uniting in friendship the two neighbouring countries, whose relations down the years have been so sad and so dour.

Whilst these and other public affairs were moving, happiness in several forms was coming the way of the Pitts. In the first place, William's sister, Lady Harriot, was on September 21st, 1785, married to his old friend, Edward Eliot, son of the recently ennobled Lord Eliot, and since the beginning of the previous year one of the Lords of the Treasury. To his mother, whom he is to visit in Somerset shortly, William wrote that he is "to meet the bride and bridegroom in my way at Salisbury. You will have heard from my sister since the union was completed, which I trust furnishes a just prospect of increasing happiness to both."[1] During the ensuing autumn, Pitt bought a country home: this was Holwood, or as he always spelt it, Hollwood, just beyond his birthplace at Hayes, in Kent. The house was small but well placed, commanding extensive views from the heights of Sydenham on the one side to the heights of Knockholt Beeches on the other. This purchase, together with Pitt's complete neglect of his private affairs, started that embarrassment which was to become so marked before his day was done. Even at this time, his friend, Robert Smith, asked to investigate matters, warned William of the ruinous waste that he was suffering at the hands of domestics; but no effectual supervision seems to have been applied, and things gradually deteriorated into a truly hopeless state of ruin and disorder.

The happiness afforded to the Pitts by the Eliot marriage was shortlived. In August, 1786—but eleven months after the wedding—the young couple came to London for Harriot's confinement. "I am *obliged* to approve of your plan for the time of your confinement at the same moment that it distresses me that my scheme is put out of the question and my wish disappointed," wrote Harriot's mother. "The reasons you give against what I proposed," she adds, "are quite sufficient, and the happy circumstance of your being provided in your Friend of so amiable and sensible a Nurse is most comfortable and pleasant. God knows, however strong my Desire to have been in that place myself, my bodily abilities would by no means have answered to it. Everything I have heard of Mrs. Pretyman makes me quite overjoy'd with the Thought of your having her with you."

[1] William Pitt to Lady Chatham, "Brighthelmstone, September 28th, 1785."

She would like to meet her, "... but I am now, my dearest Harriot, an old Woman for *new Aquaintance*, and out of her date. I am flatter'd however with her wish to know me. ...."[1] At first all went well, and towards the end of September William was enabled to announce to his mother the birth of a daughter.[2] But this state of affairs did not last. "The disorder under which my poor sister has suffered since Friday morning appears, I am grieved to say, to have taken so deep a root, that all the efforts of medicine have served only in some degree to abate it. ...." wrote William to Mrs. Stapleton, his mother's faithful companion and friend. "This circumstance and the loss of strength render her case now so alarming, that although hope is not entirely extinguished, I cannot help very much fearing the worst. ...." And in a postscript he adds the melancholy news: "Since writing this the symptoms are become decided; and though the sad event has not actually taken place, it is inevitable. ...."[3] Later the same day, Lady Harriot died.

To the poor widow in Somerset this was a crushing blow. "I did not fail to write my congratulations to my friend on her daughter's safety," wrote Mrs. Boscawen to Mrs. Delany—"Alass! how short was that suppos'd safety; and I wrote no more; yet this day I have received a letter from Mrs. Stapleton, who knowing how truly concern'd I should be for my friend, most kindly gives me more consolation than she thinks I could have hop'd for, even from her fortitude and exemplary resignation, so often try'd. She tells me she weeps inconstrain'd and speaks continually of this beloved daughter, and by this vent of her sorrow and humble submission to the divine will, her friend hopes she will not find her feeble state of health much impair'd. I am sure she has an excellent cordial in the friendship and affection of Mrs. Stapleton."[4] Poor mourning Hester! But she was soon to have some consolation in her sorrow, for the orphaned child, christened Harriot, made a home with her grandmother at Burton Pynsent, whence came periodic reports to the widower-father. Three months after the mother's death, Hester wrote that Lady Fortescue, on a visit to Burton, "said over and over that she never had seen a more lovely Babe. The little Creature seem'd as if she had determin'd not to be outdone, in proportion to her Age, by her young visitor" (Lady Fortescue's boy), "for she received the whole Assembly that attended her undressing with the most

[1] Lady Chatham to Lady Harriot Eliot, Burton Pynsent, May 3rd, 1786.

[2] William Pitt to Lady Chatham, September 20th, 1786.

[3] William Pitt to Mrs. Stapleton, "Downing Street, Sunday, September 25th., 1786, 11 o'clock." Mrs. Stapleton was an aunt of the 1st Lord Combermere.

[4] Mrs. Boscawen to Mrs. Delany, Glan Villa, October 3rd, 1786.

perfect good Humor, and went through all her ceremonies in the most agreeable manner, so as to be greatly flatter'd."[1]

The following spring, we hear of a new tooth having made its appearance, "being come perfectly out of the Gum, and that without having occasion'd the smallest uneasiness, and being so visible that it show'd itself, which saved little Poppet from being affronted by any troublesome curiosity from her *Nurses*. . . ." But clearly she was a child of character, for we are told in the same letter that when she is angry "she expresses it in a new way, not by crying, but by *scolding* so ridiculously that it is impossible not to laugh. We think her much improved in Beauty, but I cannot say as yet, that any share of it is owing to an increase of Hair, tho' it certainly is thicker than it was. I must not forget to mention, what I ought to have added when I was upon the Article of Teeth, that the *three* which I gave an account of having not advanced, *perceptibly at least*, but seem, as before, very near breaking the skin. Notwithstanding which if there is such a Thing as being better than well, it is her Case."[2] Later in the same year, Lady Chatham reports on the weaning. "The Business," she assures him, "has been accomplish'd with the greatest success possible. She has been neither *sick*, nor *sorry*, which last extraordinary circumstance is only to be accounted for by her great indifference to the Nurse. We brought in Cooking's wife as an Assistant in the place by her, being a knowing experienced Person having weaned and brought up five children of her own. Favourite Nanny has had the Honour of Sleeping in the bed with her young Mistress and of performing all necessary offices of washing, pumping, dressing etc." "I wish you cou'd see how pretty the little creature looks," concludes the fond grandmother, "and how lively and merry."[3]

In the following year there is more news of baby Harriot, "the most enchanting little Thing that ever was." "You know, she is a Lady of *great order*. The other day she observed that in oiling the Hinges of one of the little Doors in the Nursery, the oil had got through, and stain'd the Paper. She called in a great Hurry for Betty (who was in the Bedchamber) and upon Capper's asking her what she wanted Betty for, she said she wanted 'to *talk* to her about Greasing the Doors, and being so dirty.'"[4] So, tended by a grandmother's loving care, the child grew up. A few years later, her father died—a loss which much distressed Lady Chatham. "I am happy to be able to tell you that my Mother, tho' much afflicted, bore

[1] Lady Chatham to Eliot, Burton Pynsent, Saturday, December 23rd, 1786.
[2] Lady Chatham to Eliot, Burton Pynsent, April 15th, 1787.
[3] Lady Chatham to Eliot, Burton Pynsent, April 30th, 1787.
[4] Lady Chatham to Eliot, Burton Pynsent, December 13th, 1788.

the shock as well as cou'd be expected," reported her son to Alec Hood, "and is upon the whole tolerably well. She suffered, as we all did, for some time a good deal of anxiety about my Niece, as no *Will*, leaving any directions about her, was for many days found. Fortunately, in searching among his papers in Downing Street it was found, and he has left my Mother, myself, my Brother, and the Bishop of Lincoln her guardians, and her fortune will be considerable."[1] In 1806 Harriot married Colonel, subsequently Sir William, Pringle, and became the mother of a son and four daughters. She died in 1842.

In the midst of the sadness caused by his sister's death, Pitt received the longed-for tidings from across the Channel. On September 26th, the day following the death of Lady Harriot Eliot, William Eden, our special envoy to the French Government, signed a Treaty of Commerce with de Rayneval, the French Minister. Other matters not dealt with in this treaty were settled in a subsequent Convention, which Eden signed with Vergennes on January 15th of the following year. Thus was brought to fruition one of the projects that was dearest to Pitt's heart.

Perhaps the most stirring event of the time, however, was the trial of Warren Hastings. In two of the charges brought against the great pro-consul—those referring to Hastings' treatment of Cheyte Sing, Rajah of Benares, and to the Begums of Oudh—Pitt cast his vote against the accused. The Session of 1788, memorable for the opening of this great trial, is memorable also for the first steps taken in parliament for the abolition of the Slave Trade, a cause that has rendered immortal the name of Pitt's friend, William Wilberforce. Earlier in the century, the trade had been regarded as sound commercial enterprise; but the case of James Somersett in 1772, which was concerned with the status of slaves brought from the Colonies to Great Britain and their liability to be sent back whence they had come, had focused attention on the trade in general and aroused the consciences of honourable men throughout the land. From this date enquiries into the trade in slaves began to be made, largely through the efforts of the Quakers, and at last in May 1787 a Committee was formed to work for its abolition. Of this Committee of twelve, all but two were members of the Society of Friends, and the Chairman was that great and good man, Granville Sharp. But strenuous as were the exertions of men like Sharpe and Thomas Clarkson, by far the largest share of praise must be awarded to Wilberforce, who in his memoirs has thus described his efforts at this time: "I got together at my house, from time to time, persons who knew anything about the matter. . . . When I had acquired so much information, I began to talk the matter

[1] Chatham to Hood, "Hyde Park Corner, October 6th, 1797."

over with Pitt and Grenville. Pitt recommended me to undertake its conduct as a subject suited to my character and talents. At length I well remember, after a conversation in the open air, at the root of an old tree at Holwood,
just above the steep descent into the vale of Keston, I resolved to give notice,
on a fit occasion, in the House of Commons, of my intention to bring the
subject forward." The gnarled old tree under which the friends sat to
discuss their schemes became known as "Wilberforce's oak." Thus began
the great and honourable movement that led to so much controversy and
so much bitterness before the horrors of an infamous traffic were at last
eradicated from the civilized world.

At this time Pitt was at the height of his power and influence, and it
could not be justly said that in rising he had omitted to raise his relatives
with him. In 1784 he had persuaded the King to create the proud Temple
Marquess of Buckingham, a dignity which that self-opinioned nobleman
somewhat grudgingly accepted. "In the contingency of the garter being
clearly promised . . . I shall with great satisfaction, accept the Marquisate,
though the value is a little sunk by the accession of Lord T. to the number."[1]
In the autumn of 1787, on the death of the Duke of Rutland, Pitt pressed
upon Lord Buckingham the Lord-Lieutenancy of Ireland.[2] In the summer
of 1788, Pitt was enabled to elevate a relative much nearer and dearer to him
than Buckingham, and he hastened to announce the news to his mother.
"It is no other than this, that a new arrangement in the Admiralty is, from
various circumstances, become unavoidable, that Lord Howe must be
succeeded by a landsman, and that landsman is my brother. I have some
doubts whether the public may not think this too much like monopoly,
but that doubt is not sufficient to counterbalance the personal comfort which
will result from it and the general advantage to the whole of our system."[3]
As it happened the appointment was not ill received; but it proved an
unhappy choice, and ere long fraternal affection could not blind William
to the fact that his brother John was very ill fitted for so great a post.

Early in September, Pitt is at last able to pay his mother a visit at Burton
Pynsent, returning in a few weeks to Holwood for the remainder of the
long recess. Never did the political horizon seem more bright, more free
from clouds, more promising for a serene to-morrow, So hopeless appeared
the prospects of the Opposition that Charles Fox set out on a tour of Italy,
accompanied by his mistress, Mrs. Armistead. But appearances were
deceptive. Already, there was a little cloud, no bigger than a man's hand.

[1] Temple to Grenville, October 3rd, 1784.
[2] William Pitt to Buckingham, "Downing Street, Oct. 29th, 1787, ½ past 12."
[3] William Pitt to Lady Chatham, "Downing Street, June 19th., 1788."

Early in the autumn the storm broke with all its fury and the nation stood aghast to witness an appalling tragedy enacted before its eyes.

The health of the King had never been robust, and ever since his accession to the throne some dark, nameless fate, ominous and dreadful, had seemed to hover over him. His first serious illness had occurred in January 1765, when he was twenty-six, and it had lasted rather more than three months. But less than a year later he was suffering from what was probably the same complaint. The attacks were termed fevers, but they were accompanied by a condition of nervous excitement and incoherence amounting to dementia. The King, whose regular manner of talking was rapid and staccato, became more garrulous, rambling and incoherent than ever; and he complained of tormenting headaches that nothing would relieve. At the time of these attacks he could not sit quietly in the house, but sought release from his dark thoughts in riding and other forms of outdoor exercise. Soothing music, preferably of an ecclesiastical nature, afforded relief from his neurosis. At times of crisis, he dreaded the appearance at Court of new faces; he could not bear unfamiliar scenes; so the greater part of his life was passed in London, Windsor or Kew, where life was regulated, ordered, unchanging, where there were no surprises, where he could be protected from himself by his devoted Queen.

After this second attack, George III seemed better in health, and it was hoped that he had grown out of his malady. Thus, early in the year 1788, he was reported to be in excellent health. "The king walks twelve miles in his way from Windsor to London, which is more than the Prince of Wales can do *a l'heure qu'il est.*"[1] But as the spring unfolded into summer, those around him were disturbed to notice some of the old fatal signs returning. The King was observed to gabble even more than usual in his speech and these moods of confused hilarity were apt to be swiftly succeeded by moods of blank dejection. He was becoming fat and florid. His eyes goggled in an alarming manner. He swayed from side to side as he walked. The symptoms were evidently disturbing and a change of scene was prescribed. "Having had rather a smart bilious attack, which by the goodness of Divine Providence, is quite removed," wrote the King to Bishop Hurd, "Sir George Baker has strongly recommended to me the going for a month to Cheltenham, as he thinks that water efficacious on such occasions, and that an absence from London will keep me free from certain fatigues, that attend long audiences. . . ."[2] So the Court duly set

---

[1] Storer to Eden, Golden Square, January 18th, 1788.

[2] George III to Bishop of Worcester, Windsor, June 8th, 1788.

out from Windsor and took up residence at Bays' Hill Lodge, a small and uncomfortable house belonging to Lord Fauconberg on the outskirts of Cheltenham.

This visit was not unsuccessful. The King drank the waters, and he and the Queen paid a number of visits in the neighbourhood. They honoured Lord and Lady Bathurst with their company at Oakley Grove, and the Coventrys at Croome; they paid a visit to Bishop Hurd at Hartlebury Castle, thirty-three miles away, for the Three Choirs Festival. But it was clear that the King's health was not normal. Ugly and disconcerting stories got about of his having slipped out of the bishop's palace at five o'clock in the morning and of having gone to the house where his equerries were lodged to rout them out of bed—not apparently because he required their services, but just for the fun of the thing. They, strangely enough, never saw the joke! Another morning, it was said, he stood on Worcester Bridge, a mob of townsfolk eyeing him curiously. "This, I suppose, is Worcester New Bridge, hey?" he suddenly ejaculated. "Yes, please your Majesty." "Then, boys," he suddenly cried, "let's have a huzza!" Whisking his great cocked hat off his head, he set the example; and was followed by a cheering though astonished rabble all the way back to the palace."[1]

On the Court's return to Windsor, things did not mend. Soon after their arrival at the Castle, Mrs. Siddons was summoned to play before the King and Queen. When alone with the King during her visit, his Majesty portentously handed the great actress a sheet of paper, which she was astonished to find completely blank, save for the royal signature. This was clearly very odd; but fortunately Mrs. Siddons, knowing her duty, promptly carried the sheet to the Queen, who gratefully thanked her for her discretion.[2] By now the royal doctors began to take alarm and tried unsuccessfully to dissuade the King from attending the Levee fixed for October 24th at St. James's Palace. "Mr. Pitt really seemed distressed at seeing my bodily stiffness yesterday," wrote George III the next day, "which I alone exhibited to stop further lies and any fall of the Stocks. . . . I am certainly weak and stiff, but no wonder. I am certain air and relaxation are the quickest restoratives."[3] Yet the King's behaviour at the Levee had been noticeably odd.

The next day the Court moved from Kew to Windsor, where it became increasingly apparent that the King was seriously ill; but the patient strove

[1] Vulliamy, *Royal George.*

[2] Campbell, *Life of Mrs. Siddons*, Vol. II.

[3] George III to William Pitt, Kew, October 25th, 1788.

gallantly to make light of it. "He attempts reading the despatches daily, but as yet without success," he wrote Pitt, "but he eats well, sleeps well, and is not in the least fatigued with riding, though he cannot yet stand long and is fatigued if he walks. Having gained so much, the rest will soon follow."[1] Perhaps he pretended this optimistic view because he suspected the awful truth, for on one occasion he burst out to his old friend, Lady Effingham, a Lady of the Bedchamber to the Queen, "My dear Effie, you see me, all at once, an old man";[2] whilst on another occasion after returning from his ride he suddenly broke down whilst talking to the Duke of York and without warning blurted forth, "I wish to God I might die, for I am going mad."[3]

And then one day a terrible thing happened. King George was out driving with the Queen in Windsor Great Park when, suddenly exclaiming "Oh! there he is!" he sprang out of the phaeton and walked over to one of the giant oaks that adorn and beautify the district. Doffing his hat and bowing respectfully, his Majesty cordially shook one of the lower branches of the great tree. In a moment he was gabbling incoherently. The page in attendance hurried up to the King who was conveying to the King of Prussia his views on public affairs. "May it please your Majesty . . ." "Go away. Don't you see I'm engaged?" came the angry answer. But the page was ordered to persist. "I beg your Majesty's pardon, but . . ." "Hey? What, what is it?" "May I be permitted to inform your Majesty that . . ." "Hey? Why? What, what's the matter?" asked the King testily. "May it please your Majesty. Her Majesty is in the carriage and I am commanded to intimate her Majesty's desire for your Majesty's company." "Lack a day! Lack a day!" cried the King, "that's true, that's true. So she is!" and apologizing profusely to his Majesty of Prussia, he trotted back to the phaeton and his anxious Queen.[4]

It was clear that things were serious, and the Prince of Wales and the Duke of York hastened to Windsor. So desperately ill was the King considered that on the night of November 6th to 7th, the two princes, the doctors, the equerries-in-waiting and others in attendance spent the night together in one of the rooms near the King's chamber. In the silent

---

[1] George III to William Pitt, Windsor, November 3rd, 1788.

[2] Frances Burney, Madame d'Arblay, Saturday, November 1st, 1788. *Diary and Letters*, Vol. IV. Lady Effingham was Elizabeth, daughter of Peter Beckford and Louisa Pitt, daughter of Lord Rivers, and sister of Penelope Ligonier of unhappy memory. She was the widow of Thomas, 2nd Earl of Effingham, and in 1776 had married Sir George Howard.

[3] Moore, *Life of Sheridan*, Vol. II.

[4] A Page of the Presence, *A History of the Royal Malady* (1789). A rare pamphlet.

watches towards dawn the awkward swaying figure of the King was observed to enter the apartment. Amazed to encounter so large a company, he angrily asked them what they did there at such an hour; then he began muttering pathetically of his favourite son. "Yes, Frederick is my friend . . . my friend. Hey? Frederick is my friend." The watchers stood rooted to the spot, and even Sir George Baker was unable to summon sufficient courage to lead the poor invalid back to his room. Suddenly the King recognized his doctor; and standing in front of him for a moment, he laid his hands on his shoulders, pinned him against the wall, and told him with some truth that he was nothing but a feeble old woman! At this point, Colonel Digby, Chamberlain to the Queen, at last bestirred himself. He boldly went up to the King and taking him by the arm, said in a tone of respectful authority that he must go back to bed. "I will not go," exclaimed King George peevishly. "Who are you?" "I am Colonel Digby, Sir," came the reply. "Your Majesty has been very good to me often, and now I am going to be very good to you; for you must come to bed. It is necessary to your life." Whereupon, Digby took hold of the astonished King, who suffered himself to be led to his room as passively as if he had been a child.[1]

During November, the King's condition alternated between slight recovery and extreme eccentricity, until one dreadful evening at dinner soon after the Prince of Wales' arrival from Brighton, when the unhappy patient broke forth into delirium. The poor Queen, now in hysterics, begged that her husband might sleep in a dressing-room, and declared that in the middle of the night he gave her a horrible fright by suddenly invading her bedroom with a lighted candle in his hand just to see, as he said, that she was still there.[2] At dawn the next day, the hoarse, babbling voice could be heard all over the Castle, sometimes muttering, sometimes shouting in raucous, rasping tones, "I am not ill. I'm nervous. I'm nervous. . . . But I love you all very well, if you would but tell me the truth. I love Dr. Heberden best, for he has not told me a lie. Sir George has told me a lie . . . a white lie, he says. If you must tell me a lie, let it be a black lie. I am nervous . . . that's what's wrong. . . . I'm nervous. . . . I'm dreadfully nervous . . . only tell me the truth. . . . I'm nervous. . . . I'm . . ." So it rambled on and on as if till eternity, the dreadful reiterations of the disordered mind echoing and reverberating down the draughty, comfortless

[1] Frances Burney, Madame d'Arblay, Friday, November 7th, 1788. *Diary and Letters*, Vol. IV.

[2] Frances Burney, Madame d'Arblay, Wednesday, November 5th, 1788. *Diary and Letters*, Vol. IV.

corridors of the Castle. It was obvious, painfully obvious, that his Majesty King George III was insane.

While these terrible happenings were taking place in the inner circle of the royal family, a great celebration was being held to commemorate the advent in England of King William of glorious memory. The Society for Commemorating the Revolution in Great Britain had existed ever since 1688, and its annual meeting was invariably held on November 4th, the date of King William's birthday. The celebrations held in the year of King George's illness were particularly noteworthy for they commemorated the centenary of the Revolution under which the now afflicted House of Hanover had come to the English Throne. On this occasion, a company of some four hundred persons attended a service at the Nonconformist Meeting-house in Old Jewry, and afterwards adjourned to the London Tavern for a sumptuous repast. The Chairman of this noteworthy gathering was Charles Mahon, now Lord Stanhope,[1] and he paraded in procession down the room preceded by the stewards bearing the colours that King William had displayed on his march from Torbay. After the meal the Company turned to business; and resolutions were promptly passed that a perpetual anniversary of thanksgiving for the blessings afforded by the glorious Revolution should be held annually on December 16th, the day of the passing of the Bill of Rights, and that Henry Beaufoy, one of those present, should move for leave to bring in a Bill for this purpose in the House of Commons. It was then decided, under Stanhope's guidance, that "Three Fundamental Principles" should be asserted to the effect that authority, both civil and political, is derived from the people, that the abuse of power justifies resistance, and that the fundamental rights of Private Judgment, Liberty of Conscience, Trial by Jury, Freedom of the Press and Freedom of Election are and must ever be held sacred and inviolable. Some forty-one toasts in all were drunk that day, and the convivial gathering was concluded with music and singing. After dark, the Monument was illuminated, and in front of the London Tavern was displayed a transparent painting emblematic of the Glorious Revolution, bearing the inscription "A Tyrant Deposed and Liberty Restored, 1688."[2] In accordance with the Society's resolution, Beaufoy in due course introduced into the House of Commons a Bill for fixing a date each year for national thanksgiving. All went well in the lower House, but when Lord Stanhope introduced the Bill into the Lords, it was decisively rejected.

[1] He had succeeded his father on March 7th, 1786.

[2] "An Abstract of the History and Proceedings of the Revolution Society in London. Printed by Order of the Committee, 1789."

Meanwhile, the King's desperate state brought into inevitable prominence the question of a regency, and during the last months of 1788 and the opening months of the following year this was debated very fully in parliament. It was well known that Pitt, who had neither regard nor respect for the heir to the throne, was in favour of a limited regency, and this had alarmed the Prince and his friends. Charles Fox, travelling abroad, was sent an urgent summons to return. He left for home immediately, and on November 24th reached his lodgings in St. James's Street, but it was some days before he could recover from the effects of the journey. It was not only ill health, however, that worried Fox; for he was troubled also by the pushing antics of Sheridan, who had entered into secret negotiations with the Chancellor, the surly, overbearing Thurlow, with the object of bribing him to forsake his party for the opposition on the understanding that he should retain the woolsack in the anticipated change of Government. Fox was furious. He detested Thurlow; moreover, he had promised the Great Seal to Wedder-burn. Judge then of his chagrin on finding that negotiations had gone too far to be broken off, and that he must bow to the inevitable.

At the end of November it was decided to remove the King to Kew, for those at Windsor whose duty it was to tend the poor invalid were well-nigh exhausted. Indeed, Mr. Fortnum, one of the footmen, was so worn out that he begged to be allowed to retire from the royal service, and in due course he started a grocery business in Piccadilly. But there was another object in the move, for at Kew there was a large garden where the patient might exercise himself without being spied on, as at Windsor, by the prying eyes of an inquisitive crowd. Another step was taken at about this time, for Dr. Francis Willis, rector of St. John's, Wapping, an expert in mental diseases who had for some twenty-eight years run a private asylum near Boston, in Lincolnshire, was summoned to attend the King.

Meanwhile, debates on the regency were held in both Houses of Parliament. On December 10th, Pitt in the Commons and Camden in the Lords produced the doctors' evidence as to the prospects of the King's recovery. The general view seemed to be that ultimate recovery was probable but that it would not be rapid. Therefore, a regency was inevitable. But, as the King was likely sometime to be in a position to reassume the royal authority, the regency should, Pitt suggested, be of a limited nature, and the care of the royal person and household should be invested in the Queen. Such a limited authority was, however, very far from the aspirations of the Prince of Wales and the Opposition, and a memorable contest took place in the House of Commons between Pitt and Fox on the regency question. Pitt moved on December 10th for a Committee to be formed to search for precedents; whereupon Fox rose instantly to attack the proposition. Why search for precedents? he asked. All knew that no precedents existed. There was then a person in the kingdom different from any other person—an Heir Apparent of full age and capacity to exercise the royal power. Therefore, declared Fox, the Prince had as clear, as express a right to assume the reins of Government during the King's incapacity as in the case of the King's demise. This was his right, and it was for the House to pronounce when he ought to take possession of and to exercise that right. Such language was certain to offend many on both sides of the House, and Pitt was not slow to see his chance. "I'll *un-Whig* the gentleman for the rest of his life," he is alleged to have declared delightedly to a neighbour on the Treasury Bench, at the same time slapping his thigh energetically with his hands.[1] The doctrine just expounded was sufficient in itself, he declared, for the appointment of the Committee he proposed, and he would continue to maintain that "it was little less than treason to the Constitution to assert that the Prince of Wales had a claim to the exercise of the Sovereign power during the interruption of the personal authority of his Majesty by infirmity and in his life time."[2] Treason! An ugly word. "Thus the gauntlet was fairly and on both sides cast down."[3]

But if Fox had given Pitt his chance, the indiscreet Burke was to give him another by terming the Prime Minister "one of the Prince's competitors." Pitt rose at once and with lofty scorn, "At that period of our history, when the constitution was settled on that foundation on which it now existed," he asked, "when Mr. Somers and other great men declared that no person had a right to the crown independent of the consent of the two Houses, would it have been thought either fair or decent for any member of either House to have pronounced Mr. Somers a personal competitor of William III?" Fox was quick to see his blunder, and two days later in the House of Commons attempted to repair the damage, but apparently to very little effect. "Pitt stands higher and higher in general estimation," wrote Sir William Young excitedly to Lord Buckingham. "As I passed the gallery to write this, Marquis of Townshend caught my arm and said, 'A glorious fellow, by G——, Young! His speech is that of an angel.'"[4] But if Fox's and Burke's contributions to the debate had been unfortunate, they were nothing to the egregious folly of the volatile Sheridan, who was

---

[1] Moore, *Life of Sheridan*, Vol. II.

[2] William Pitt, House of Commons, December 10th, 1788.

[3] Stanhope, *Life of Pitt*, Vol. II.

[4] Young to Buckingham, "House of Commons, Friday, Half-past five, December 12th., 1788."

actually guilty of the appalling indiscretion of warning the House against "the danger of provoking the Prince to assert his right."[1] "Only think of Fox's want of judgment," wrote William Grenville to his brother, "to bring himself and them into such a scrape as he has done, by maintaining a doctrine of higher Tory principle than could have been found anywhere, since Sir Robert Sawyer's speeches."[2] "The day was closed," he wrote two days later, "by such a blunder of Sheridan's as I never knew any man of the meanest talents guilty of before. During the whole time that I have sat in Parliament, in pretty warm times, I never remember such an uproar as was raised by his threatening us with *the danger of provoking the Prince to assert his right*, which were the exact words he used."[3]

In the House of Lords, the Chancellor, who had probably received private intelligence of the views of Dr. Willis as to the probability of the King's speedy and complete recovery, was showing signs of wavering. On December 10th he made a cautious speech, but some days later the climax of his effrontery was exposed. The House was full because it was known that the Duke of York intended to speak on the regency question, and Pitt, Burke and Wilkes, all sat on the steps of the throne. The Duke of York for once in his life spoke with sense and moderation, expressly disavowing on his brother's behalf the slightest intention of raising any claim not derived from the will of the people.[4] No sooner had the prince sat down than Thurlow addressed the peers. In a manner solemn and portentous, with much show of emotion and amid the shedding of many tears, he dilated on the unhappy state of the King. It was, he assured the House, his fixed and unalterable determination to stand by his afflicted Sovereign. With much elevated talk of personal gratitude, he declared that the first duty before them was to preserve the rights of the Sovereign entire so that upon his recovery he might find his situation unaltered: and so mounting steadily by such steps to the pinnacle of his peroration, he burst forth with the famous words: "When I forget my Sovereign, may God forget me."[5] The House, knowing the character of the speaker, was horrified. "God forget you?" muttered Wilkes, eyeing him with his famous squint, "He'll see you d——d first!" "Forget you?" muttered Burke, "the best thing that can happen to you." "Oh, the rascal," exclaimed Pitt, as he dashed from the Chamber.

[1] Sheridan, House of Commons, December 12th, 1788.
[2] Grenville to Buckingham, Whitehall, December 11th, 1788.
[3] Grenville to Buckingham, Whitehall, December 13th, 1788.
[4] Duke of York, House of Lords, December 15th, 1788.
[5] Thurlow, House of Lords, December 15th, 1788.

But if the Chancellor's conduct at this time was reprehensible, it was as nothing compared with the discreditable behaviour of the Prince of Wales and the Duke of York. At this dreadful time these two deplorable young men were indulging in every form of orgy and vice. "What do you think of the Duke of York's having a meeting of the Opposition at his house on Thursday, before the House of Lords met, and then going down there to hear the examinations read?" asked William Grenville. "After that, they closed the day by both going in the evening to Brooks's."[1] Whilst on the subject of their gambling, Lord Bulkeley has some cutting things to say: "The Princes go on in their usual style, both keeping open houses, and employing every means in their power to gain proselytes, attending the Beefsteak Clubs, Freemasons' meetings, etc. . . . The Duke of York never misses a night at Brooks's, where the hawks pluck his feathers unmercifully, and have reduced him to the vowels I.O.U. The prince likewise attends very often, and has taken kindly to play."[2] At Brooks's of course, they indulged in the most shocking indecencies on the topic of the king's madness. They scoffed at their parents, mocking their misfortunes, and it is even alleged that George employed his talents for mimicry, which were remarkable, in imitating the sufferings and ravings of his afflicted father. Indeed, even in that fashionable den of vice, the brutality of these revolting princes disgusted the most profligate of their associates. "If we were together," wrote Grenville to his brother at Dublin Castle, "I could give you some particulars of the Prince of Wales's behaviour towards the king and her, within the last few days, that would make your blood run cold."[3] We hear much, too, of the Prince of Wales's drunkenness—"The Prince, being very drunk the other night, promised a regiment to Captain Macdonald, who has not the smallest pretensions to one; but he keeps him to his promise,"[4]—and of his personal canvasses for support— "Lord Lonsdale's people were against us in consequence of a letter, written by the Prince of Wales himself, soliciting it, as a personal favour;"[5] whilst Lord Bulkeley writes of "the open and undisguised canvass of the Prince and the Duke of York, and the very liberal distribution of promises from both."[6] No wonder that General Grenville should write to Lord Cornwallis: "I see nothing but anarchy and confusion staring us in the face,

---

[1] Grenville to Buckingham, Whitehall, December 7th, 1788.

[2] Bulkeley to Buckingham, January 1789.

[3] Grenville to Buckingham, Whitehall, December 21st, 1788.

[4] Huber to Eden, Saturday, February 21st (1789).

[5] Grenville to Buckingham, Whitehall, December 17th, 1788.

[6] Bulkeley to Buckingham, Stanhope Street, December 29th, 1788.

unless it should please Providence to restore H.M. to his former sound state of body and mind, which I believe is the universal and most sincere prayer of every well-meaning subject."[1]

And so amid an atmosphere of hatred and suspicion the regency debates were continued in both Houses of Parliament. It was, of course, recognized that the Regent would not keep Pitt in office for a moment; and as the latter had practically no means and many debts, he made arrangements to return to his old practice at the Bar. On hearing of this, however, the principal merchants and bankers of the City of London clubbed together to raise a sum of £50,000 to ease his position, but so popular was the cause that twice that sum was quickly promised. They then requested George Rose, Secretary of the Treasury, to press upon him this free gift of £100,000. But Pitt was adamant, and he assured his friend that "No consideration upon earth shall ever induce me to accept it." And so the debates continued. And as they did so, the health of the King fluctuated: sometimes he seemed mending; at others his malady appeared to have as strong a hold as ever. But as the leaves fell that autumn of 1788, and the weeks passed on and the old year died, and the new year was born, it was observed by the observant about the throne that the periods of improvement became more frequent and more marked. And as the debates continued and became more heated, the King's illness gradually became a party question, the followers of Pitt longing for, and the followers of the Prince and Fox dreading the patient's recovery, and in this appalling controversy even the doctors joined. "The opposition physicians about his Majesty," wrote Sidney Smith, son of John and Mary Smith of unhappy memory "(and however odd it may sound such there have been) say everything they can to invalidate the daily testimonies of the others, so between both, the public are strangely divided in doubts, hopes and fears." [2]

But whether men liked it or not, the King's health was clearly improving; and about the middle of February, Dr. Willis reported to the Chancellor that the King had recovered. The Prime Minister, who had an audience on the 14th, hastened to convey the good tidings to his mother. "The public account this morning is that the King continues advancing in recovery. The private one is that he is to all appearances perfectly well, and if it were the case of a private man, would be immediately declared so."[3] On February 23rd the two Princes, for whom, of course, their father's recovery

<hr>

[1] Grenville to Cornwallis, Sackville Street, December 27th, 1788.

[2] Smith to Eden, 31, Little Marylebone Street, Cavendish Square, London, December 30th, 1788.

[3] William Pitt to Lady Chatham, Thursday, February 19th, 1789.

was the worst possible news, saw the King in presence of the Queen. "They kept him waiting a considerable time before they arrived," reported Grenville, "and after they left him, drove immediately to Mrs. Armstead's, in Park Street, in hope of finding Fox there, to give him an account of what had passed. He not being in town, they amused themselves yesterday evening with spreading about a report that the King was still out of his mind, and in quoting phrases of his to which they gave that turn. It is certainly a decent and becoming thing, that when all the King's physicians, all his attendants, and his two principal Ministers, agree in pronouncing him well, his two sons should deny it. . . . I bless God it is yet some time before these *matured and ripened virtues* will be *visited upon us* in the form of a Government."[1] "The truth is," commented Lord Bulkeley on the princes' behaviour, "that they are quite desperate, and endeavour to drown their cares, disappointments, and internal chagrin in wine and dissipation."[2] "It is with infinite satisfaction I renew my correspondence with Mr. Pitt by acquainting him of my having seen the Prince of Wales and my second son," wrote the King. "Care was taken that the conversation should be general and cordial: they seemed perfectly satisfied. I chose the meeting should be in the Queen's apartment, that all parties might have that caution which at the present hour could but be judicious."[3] One can only be thankful that the poor man did not know the truth.

The King's recovery was a signal for wild rejoicing. On March 10th all London was illuminated; on March 13th George received the congratulations of the *Corps Diplomatique*; on March 14th the Court quitted Kew, the palace of sorrows, and returned to Windsor. Not only in London and Windsor was there rejoicing, however, but in every village in the kingdom. Of the festivities at Stowe we have an amusing glimpse from Lady Buckingham, who, unlike her lord, had a sense of humour. "The loyal town of Buckingham has been beforehand with your wishes," she wrote banteringly to her brother-in-law. "As the Mayor and Corporation all wear wigs, of course they foresee events long before other people, and therefore never act but upon grave and mature deliberation. They have been planning an illumination for some time, as also the roasting a cow. . . ."[4] "Our ox, accompanied by loaves, was divided *regularly* to above two thousand people; the rest was a scramble, as you may imagine, though, considering that we were not sparing of our beer, there was very little riot.

[1] Grenville to Buckingham, Whitehall, February 24th, 1789.
[2] Bulkeley to Buckingham, February 24th, 1789.
[3] George III to William Pitt, Kew, February 23rd, 1789.
[4] Lady Buckingham to Grenville, undated but March 1789.

The north front was very thoroughly illuminated; that, with the ox roasting in front, made a grand show, and all the quality of Buckingham came to see it. As I had a hint that might be the case, I had provided accordingly; we had a supper in the hall, and made a Ranelagh of the saloon, which all ended with an impromptu dance in the dining-room. All the fat, would, however, have been in the fire if old Woodward and Parrot had not perceived that the Corporation (who mean to give a fête on Tuesday next) had cast an eye of envy on our ox, who happened to be double the size of the one they had provided. It has therefore been decided in our privy council that an ox of the proper size should be given to them. All that I am anxious for is that whatever fault I commit in my regency may be of the right side."[1] One wonders if grave Mr. Speaker Grenville smiled at his sister-in-law's gay nonsense! A month later, Sidney Smith saw the King at Windsor, and could assure Eden of his complete restoration. "You will say you had rather hear of his mind than his body," he continued, "in answer to which I can assure you of the goodness of his memory and the composure of his manner, for I put myself in his way a few days ago, at Windsor, and got near enough to be spoken to. He alluded to the intention I had expressed of going to Spain, when I took leave to go abroad two years ago, and was more accurate as to the exact month in which I returned than I could be at a moment's warning, for I mistook it, and he corrected me, remembering my having kissed hands on my arrival before *his illness*, which he alluded to as the circumstance that made him remember my being at the levee on my return. . . ."[2]

And so for a time we take leave of him, thin, frail and feeble still, but sane and sensible once more.

On a sweltering July day in 1789, the fevered Paris mob burst into the Bastille. With the fall of the "bogey fortress"[3] the French Revolution had begun. On July 14th, 1790, the first anniversary of this event, some six hundred and fifty gentlemen, each wearing a revolutionary cockade, sat down to dinner at the Crown and Anchor Tavern, prepared to enjoy themselves. The table was beautifully decorated and the centre-piece, appropriately enough, was a piece of stone taken from the ruins of the fallen fortress. The chairman of the gathering was Lord Stanhope, whose attitude to France is thus amusingly described by his friend, Lord Holland. "My little sister in her patriotic anxiety about the climate of her country

[1] Lady Buckingham to Grenville, Stowe (March) 15. (1789.)

[2] Smith to Eden, London, April 24th, 1789.

[3] Madelin, *The French Revolution*.

follows Lord Stanhope's rule about the French Republic. . . . When they are right I praise them and when they are wrong I hold my tongue, and that you know is candid."[1] On this occasion Lord Stanhope did not hold his tongue but made an animated speech in favour of the revolution. "The French have even improved on our Constitution," he declared, "for they have not only civil but religious liberty." They had no laws to complain of such as disgraced our Statute Book. They did not restrain their women from going out of the kingdom lest they should be converted from their religion, nor had they a law by which their clergy by fasting and praying were enabled to cast out devils. They had abolished tithes, and they had made a provision that no description of men should be driven from offices of trust because they had the bad or good fortune to differ from the Established Church. . . . There was much more on these surprising lines, and the speaker concluded with the toast, "To the extinction of all jealousy between France and England, and may they vie with each other in seeking to extend the benefits of peace, liberty and virtue throughout the world." These admirable sentiments were echoed and endorsed by Sheridan, who moved, "That it be resolved that this meeting does most cordially rejoice in the establishment and confirmation of liberty in France, and that it behold with peculiar satisfaction the sentiments of amity and good will which appear to pervade that country towards this." After the passing of a variety of resolutions and some inharmonious observations from the fiery Horne Tooke, the meeting concluded with the toast, "Earl Stanhope," proposed by Sheridan and very heartily drunk to by all the company. The resolution thus passed was forwarded to France by Lord Stanhope in a letter to the Duc de la Rochefoucauld. "It is with extreme satisfaction that I have the honour to inform you that yesterday, July 14th, we, to the number of 652 friends of liberty, celebrated your glorious Revolution and the establishment and confirmation of your free constitution. Mr. Sheridan proposed the enclosed resolution, which was received with repeated acclamations and with all the warmth which characterizes free and independent men. May I ask you, on behalf of this assembly, to present it to the National Assembly of France? It is as their President of the day that I ask this favour. Soon we hope that men will cease to regard themselves under the odious aspect of tyrant and slaves, and that, following your example, they will look on each other as equals and learn to love one another as free men, friends, and brothers."[2]

The reply to this courteous letter was not long in coming: it was

[1] Holland to Caroline Fox, 1803.

[2] Stanhope to Rochefoucauld, July 15th, 1790.

addressed to Stanhope by the President of the National Assembly himself. "It is fitting, my Lord, in a country in which liberty may be said to be naturalised that the French Revolution should be rightly judged," he wrote. "When shall we see that happy day in which governments will be distinguished only by their humility and good faith? It is to men like you, my Lord, and to the worthy members of your Society that it is reserved to hasten this new revolution. Your benevolence will then encircle the whole surface of the globe."[1] By such complimentary exchanges was the upheaval in France welcomed by Lord Stanhope and his associates of the Society for Commemorating the Revolution in Great Britain. Thus as "the Jacobin Earl" and "Citizen Stanhope" he became known; and in these appellations the lord of Chevening assuredly rejoiced.

[1] Treilhard, President of the National Assembly, to Stanhope, July 28th, 1790.

CHAPTER VII

The Pitts, the Grenvilles, and the French Revolution

WHEN William Pitt came to power in December 1783, England was completely isolated, for there had been of recent years many surprising changes in international affairs. Prussia, under the leadership of Frederick the Great, had assumed a dominant place among the States of Europe. Russia, torn by internal factions and dynastic revolutions for forty years following the death of Peter the Great, had become one of the most important and influential peoples of the world, and had achieved this remarkable position under the rule of a female sovereign who was a Russian neither by birth nor by breeding, but the daughter of a petty German prince. These two supreme rulers, as if drawn to each other by mutual affinity, concluded a defensive treaty in 1764. Another noteworthy political change had been the Franco-Austrian alliance, followed by the marriage of the Dauphin and Marie Antoinette. This was effected through the influence of Marie Antoinette's mother, the Empress Maria Theresa, who since the death of her husband in 1765 had been joint ruler with her son, Joseph II, of the Austrian dominions. But mother and son had not agreed, and Joseph had early conceived a great admiration for Catharine, whose court and country he visited in the summer of 1780. That autumn Maria Theresa had died, and her cautious policy was soon reversed. In May 1781, Joseph and Catharine exchanged formal letters undertaking that in case of Russia being involved in war with Turkey, Austria should come to her aid, and that Russia should maintain the Pragmatic Sanction and defend the Austrian States against aggression.

In 1783, Catharine having thus gained a secure footing on the Black Sea, soon commenced to fortify the great port of Sevastopol. Before long she was hard at work building a fleet in that harbour. Whilst the senior partner in this unholy alliance was thus gaining successes at the expense of Islam, the junior was seeking for easily gained plunder from weaker neighbours. First, he attempted to induce the Elector of Bavaria to agree to the exchange of Bavaria and the Upper Palatinate for the Austrian Netherlands; and when Charles Theodore did not respond, Joseph hastened to increase the bribe by advancing a claim to Maestricht and by announcing his intention of opening the Scheldt to commerce. But he was soon in trouble, for France decisively intervened to thwart Austrian ambition; so Joseph must give way and by the Treaty of Fontainebleau of 1785 was forced to withdraw his claim to Maestricht and to renew his treaty obligation to close the Scheldt. Indeed, so unsuccessful was this imperial free-booter in his schemes for easy pillage that but for the death of Frederick the Great in August 1786 and of Vergennes, the able Foreign Minister of France, in February of the following year, he might have brought them to a timely end. But these events put a somewhat different complexion on affairs. The new King of Prussia, Frederick William II, and the new French Foreign Minister, Montmorin, were not the men to command the respect enjoyed by their predecessors. So the Emperor decided to remain, at least for a time, at the side of his powerful ally, and continued to hope that he might eke out from this pirates' partnership some pickings from his mistress's table.

It did not, however, take Joseph's successor, Leopold II, long to reverse his policy, and though he lived to rule Austria for only two years, he was successful in rescuing her from the imbroglio into which Joseph had driven her, and before he died the Austro-Russian alliance had been abruptly terminated. Catharine, thus deserted, soon saw the necessity for freeing herself from other entanglements. She accordingly found speedy means of composing her differences with Gustavus III of Sweden, thus leaving herself free to pursue with relentless fury her attack on the Ottomans, and Suvoroff's famous storming of Ismail towards the close of 1790, gave her heart to receive with comparative equanimity the urgent representation from England and Prussia that she should forthwith conclude peace with the Turks. Bowing to the inevitable, the proud Empress let it be known that she would come to terms; but she insisted on retaining Oczakoff, near the mouth of the Dniester, which two years previously had been captured by Potemkin at heavy cost. Her haughty temper would not suffer her to emerge empty-handed from a bloody, expensive, but successful conflict.

Faced with these events, Pitt's first task was to restore his country's finances, ruined by the disastrous war with America, and to recover for her once again a prominent place in the councils of Europe. He commenced his activities by concluding with our hereditary enemy, France, a treaty of Commerce, which however was nullified by the revolution. But his most remarkable success was the formation of a triple alliance between England, Prussia and Holland, the treaty for which was signed on April 15th, 1788. This was a truly sensational triumph for the young Minister, for after no more than five short years of office, he had restored to his country her rightful place amongst the great powers of Europe.

The settlement of these affairs was swiftly followed by an unfortunate dispute with Spain over the settlement at Nootka Sound, as the result of which on May 5th, 1790, a message from the king was presented to the Commons by Pitt and to the Lords by Leeds,[1] announcing the imminent prospect of war. The result was a vote of Credit for £1,000,000 for expenses. For a time Spain continued her preparations, calling upon France to honour her pledge of assistance under the Family Compact. But France had no taste for this rôle; so Spain, disappointed in her hopes of French assistance, soon changed her tone and strove henceforth to gain security by compliance with our demands. Thus the Family Compact was broken and isolated France exhibited her weakness for all to see.

To the triumphant Pitt, the King offered a splendid reward, which, however, he respectfully declined.[2] But the honour was eagerly sought for by Chatham. "Nothing can be more delicate than the manner Lord Chatham has laid before me, his application for one of the vacant Garters; I assure him that I shall with pleasure confer this mark of my approbation on him to-morrow. . . ."[3] But George III's letter of the same date to William does not sound quite the same tone. "Mr. Pitt's note is just arrived, intimating a wish that I would confer the third vacant Garter on his brother, Lord Chatham," he wrote. "I trust he is too well convinced of my sentiments to doubt that I with pleasure shall tomorrow give this public testimony of approbation, which will be understood as meant to the whole family."[4]

A few weeks before this offer was made, Pitt had determined to strengthen his administration in the Upper House by the elevation of his cousin, William Grenville, the recently appointed Secretary of State, to the peerage. "By the help of this arrangement," he wrote eagerly to his mother, "I think we shall open the new Parliament with more strength than has belonged to us since the beginning of the Government, and it is a very pleasant circumstance in the business that all parts of Government are highly satisfied with the measure, and that those who please themselves with the reports which you will see of divisions among us will find themselves complete disappointed."[5] Within a short time, Grenville received further promotion, for on the resignation of Leeds, he was given the Seals of the Foreign Office. This arrangement had the hearty approval of the king;[6] moreover it gave the ablest member of the Grenville family a wide

---

[1] Carmarthen had succeeded his father in the dukedom in the previous year.
[2] George III to William Pitt, December 12th and 13th, 1790.
[3] George III to Chatham, Windsor, December 14th, 1790.
[4] George III to William Pitt, December 14th, 1790.
[5] William Pitt to Lady Chatham, Downing Street, November 24th, 1790.
[6] George III to William Pitt, Windsor, November 21st, 1790.

field for the exercise of his undoubted talents. The new Home Secretary was that dour Scot, Pitt's hard-drinking friend, Henry Dundas.

The successes which Pitt had thus far obtained were remarkable. Europe was pacified; England dominant. But in a moment all was changed. No longer was he the great peace Minister. His character and reputation were tarnished. "He lived to be held up to obloquy as the stern oppressor of England and the indefatigable disturber of Europe."[1]

The capture of the Bastille has become symbolical. To popular feeling the grim fortress had come to represent all that is most loathsome in arbitrary power; its fall seemed to herald the dawn of a new age of freedom and of justice. In England men looked upon the events in France with a sympathetic detachment that perhaps is only possible in a country separated from the scene by the protecting shield of blue water, so that without perceiving or understanding what we witnessed, we saw the National Assembly at its meeting in Paris on August 4th—no more than some three weeks after the fall of the Bastille—sweep away in one single vote without thought or deliberation "the complicated privileges of a thousand years."[2] It all happened in a flash. About eight o'clock in the evening, just as the sitting of the Assembly was terminating, the Vicomte de Noailles rose. What, he asked, had caused the people to pillage the estates of the rich? It was, he declared, the heavy burden of the seignorial rights and dues—the hated remnant of the feudal system! This odious tyranny must be swept away. The Third Estate could hardly believe their ears. Here was a sprig of the nobility voluntarily putting his head in the noose: that was a solution of all their problems. Nobody troubled to recall that de Noailles was but a cadet of his House, a ruined man, "Jean sans Terre" to his friends, with nothing to lose. Deputies went wild with joy; and when de Noailles was supported by the Duc d'Aiguillon and the Duc du Chatelet, the applause was thunderous. Thus a torrent of wild magnanimity was undammed. Every man competed in generosity with his neighbour—to give away his own? Not at all. "Every man," wrote a witness of the scene, "most generously gave away that which he did not own." By eight o'clock in the morning, some thirty decrees had legalized the most complete social upheaval any nation has ever known. The rights of the clergy, of the nobles, of the Parliament, of the provinces—all were thrown away in this ecstasy of abnegation. The feudal system was abolished: all French citizens were equal at last.

But all this revolutionary ardour was insufficient to satisfy the mob of

[1] *The Cambridge Modern History*, Vol. VIII.
[2] Stanhope, *Life of Pitt*, Vol. II.

Paris, who, urged on by secret agitators soon to be known as Jacobins, once more took to arms. On October 5th, yelling "To Versailles! To Versailles!" they surged thither in procession, burst into the palace, penetrating even to the Queen's bedchamber, clamoured vociferously for the seizure of the Royal Family—"the baker," "the baker's wife," and "the baker's little boy"—butchered those of the royal guard who attempted to oppose them, and bore back the unhappy Sovereigns in triumph to the Capital. It was clear that the King, the Assembly, the people had all lost control: the true direction of affairs was in the hands of the mob.

How differently were the events regarded by the two great leaders of the Whig Opposition in the House of Commons! To Fox, the lover of liberty, they were the glorious heralds of a golden age. "How much it is the greatest event that ever happened in the world!" he declared of the taking of the Bastille, "and how much the best!" To Burke, on the other hand, they were the foreboders of the awful events to come, and in his immortal *Reflections*, with rare intuition he prognosticated their future course; indeed, in spite of the crude but forceful counterblast of Paine's *Rights of Man* and the cultural excellence of Mackintosh's *Vindiciae Gallicae*, the triumph of the brilliant Irishman was complete.

Whilst the Whig chiefs were allowing their emotions to cloud their judgment, the cool, impenetrable Prime Minister made a more balanced estimate of events. "The present convulsions in France," he declared, "must sooner or later terminate in general harmony and regular order; and though such a situation might make her more formidable, it might also make her less obnoxious as a neighbour. I wish for the restoration of tranquillity in that country, although it appears to me distant. Whenever her system shall become restored, if it should prove freedom rightly understood, freedom resulting from good order and good government, France would stand forward as one of the most brilliant powers in Europe. Nor can I regard with envious eyes any approximation in neighbouring States to these sentiments which are the characteristic of every British subject."[1]

Meanwhile, the revolution progressed in a delusively peaceful manner. This was largely due to the wisdom of a strange, hideous, pock-marked, thick-set man of outstanding ability and eloquence, Mirabeau by name. This genius fully understood how essential it was that, if the revolution in France was to be successful, the fears of her neighbours must be allayed. The revolution, he declared, is for home consumption, not for export. There is a modern ring about these phrases; and in truth Mirabeau did not so express himself, but that was the meaning of his words. The King,

[1] William Pitt, House of Commons, February 9th, 1790.

he said, must leave Paris, must set up his court in a provincial capital, and must there summon a Convention and appeal to the people. To the Convention and the people the King must acknowledge that feudalism and absolutism are dead, and that henceforth a new relationship exists between him and his subjects. The same sentiment was lisped forth by a little lawyer from Arras, whose sallow cheeks and green, deep-set eyes, partly hidden behind dark spectacles, were soon to earn him a sinister notoriety. "We must declare that France renounces all thoughts of any conquests, that she considers her limits to be fixed by an eternal destiny." These words, too, have a modern sound, but they are from the lips of no twentieth century ruler. Strange how these two men, differing in so much, should so agree—Mirabeau "the torch of Provence," Robespierre "the candle of Arras!"

The nobility of France greeted the advent of the revolution either with a sort of resigned apathy or as a rather indifferent joke. Indeed, it was only when the next class, the Clergy, came to be attacked that matters began to look serious. It was on October 10th that the Bishop of Autun, whom Pitt had met at the palace of the Archbishop of Rheims in 1783, with his still, small voice, moved from the rostrum of the Assembly that the property of the Church should be placed at the disposal of the State. The clergy were horrified. They had already forfeited their tithes worth eighty millions a year; were they now to sacrifice the Church property in addition? They fought fanatically against this proposal, but the scales were heavily weighted against them. The effect of the confiscation of the property of the Church was profound. It alienated the clergy; it alienated the King, who was horrified at what he could only regard as the sinful seizure of the property of God. And though Louis' views were of small direct consequence, the action of the State served to widen the breach between the throne and the people and thereby to give the revolution a less peaceful impulse.

And now things were deteriorating fast. All France outside Paris was in a state of wild excitement. Riots broke out in many towns, mainly in the south, and the Assembly did not dare to resort to repressive measures. Thus encouraged, the army become restive, and constant outbreaks culminated in a serious mutiny at Nancy. This insubordination led many to advocate war so as to give the men an outlet for their passions. Wiser heads counselled caution; how could such a rabble fight the country's enemies? they asked. Ere long the army was to show its mettle, but the time was not yet.

Meanwhile, the refugees, seeking to stir up strife against their country, were bringing discredit upon themselves and increased danger to their Sovereigns. It was at this critical hour that a great misfortune overtook the Royal House. Mirabeau, the only man who might have saved the King, was taken ill. As he lay dying in his house in the Chaussée d'Antin, all Paris, overwhelmed with grief and alarm, surged around the doors. Though near his end, he sensed what no one knew, that Louis and the Queen meditated flight, and the very night before he died he vehemently advised against it. "I carry the last rays of the Monarchy away with me," he muttered. Even at the portal of death, how clear-sighted he was! His genius was recognized : with the greatest pomp he was borne to the Pantheon, and all Paris, weeping, followed him to the tomb.

Only Louis would not accept his counsel. At 7 o'clock in the morning of June 21st, 1791, the King's *valet de chambre*, entering the royal bedchamber found the bed unoccupied. He at once gave the alarm. By eight o'clock the tocsin announced to a distracted Paris that the birds had flown. The mad escapade of the royal family was thwarted at Varennes, near the Belgian frontier, whence they were conducted back to Paris by immense crowds in sullen, scornful, terrible silence. The next morning, when the Queen doffed her cap, her waiting woman perceived that her hair had blanched overnight. She seemed to have aged by twenty years.

In England, the disgust caused by these events was widespread, and King George was profoundly shocked at the treatment meted out to the French Sovereigns.[1] But not the English Sovereign alone was disturbed at these events, for Marie Antoinette's brother, Leopold, could hardly turn a deaf ear to his sister's appeals for help. Yet he was unwilling to take any positive action save in concert with other Powers. He had already sought the co-operation of England, and without success. He had then turned to Prussia, whose King, Frederick William, seemed genuinely anxious to assist the French Sovereigns. In August the two monarchs held a conference at Pilnitz, a country palace of the Elector of Saxony, whence they published the celebrated Declaration that the present unhappy situation of the King of France was a matter of common concern and that they intended to invoke the consent and assistance of other powers with a view to setting right that situation, even if necessary by force of arms. Negotiations were rapidly set on foot with other States, and both the Empress of Russia and the King of Sweden showed a disposition to stand to arms. But in truth, neither Leopold nor Frederick William was prepared to make any move without the entire co-operation of England, and this they knew full well they could not obtain. At the same time, de Calonne, acting on behalf of the emigrant princes, implored Pitt for a loan, but to this request he received a blank refusal. On September 13th Louis found himself compelled to

---

[1] George III to Grenville, Windsor, June 27th, 1791.

accept the new French Constitution and Leopold, thankful to escape from his dilemma, declared that this acquiescence put an end to all need for interference in the affairs of France.

It is not surprising that, with Pitt at the helm, England declined to listen to Leopold's blandishments. To Pitt peace was an essential of national prosperity, and as he pointed out to the House of Commons in his Budget Speech in February, 1792, during the past four years there had been an average annual surplus of £400,000, which sum he proposed to utilize as to half by adding £200,000 yearly to the Sinking Fund, and as to the other half by the repeal of the additional tax on malt only recently levied, and of the taxes on houses having less than seven windows, on carts, on wagons, on female servants, and of the last half-penny per pound on candles. With strange lack of vision, he expressed the surprising view that peace was likely for at least fifteen years. "I am not, indeed, presumptuous enough to suppose," he said, "that when I name fifteen years, I am not naming a period in which events may arise, which human foresight cannot reach, and which may baffle all our conjectures. We must not count with certainty on a continuance of our present prosperity during such an interval; but unquestionably there never was a time in the history of this country, when, from the situation of Europe, we might more reasonably expect fifteen years of peace, than we may at the present moment."[1] In support of this view he asked the House to vote only 16,000 seamen, being 2,000 less than the previous year, and he planned to reduce the cost of the military establishments by £200,000 a year. Never, perhaps, has so great a minister so sadly misread the signs of the times!

When the Bill came before Committee in the House of Lords, it was attacked with rare vituperation by the surly Thurlow, who declared that "the scheme is nugatory and impracticable; the inaptness of the project is equal to the vanity of the attempt."[2] Pitt was not the man to suffer such language and he promptly begged the King to choose between them. George, on being presented with this ultimatum, could not hesitate; and the Chancellor was instructed to deliver up the Great Seal.[3] So fell gruff Thurlow, victim of his own arrogance. "I did not think," he growled forth to Sir John Scott, the future Lord Eldon, "I did not think that the King would have parted with me so easily. As to that other man," he spat forth in his impotent rage, "he has done to me just what I should have done to him, if I could."[4]

[1] William Pitt, House of Commons, February 17th, 1792.
[2] Thurlow, House of Lords, May 15th, 1792.
[3] George III to Dundas, "Queen's House, May 16th., 1792. 40m. past 6 p.m."
[4] Twiss, *Life of Lord Eldon*, Vol. I.

Meanwhile, affairs in France were moving fast. Early in 1792, war between France and Austria and Prussia seemed inevitable. French ministers, anxious for England's help or neutrality, sent Talleyrand to London with spacious promises. He was soon given to understand how matters stood. At Court King George treated him with the utmost coldness, and the Queen turned her back. He was received by Pitt and Grenville: the former condescended to remember their earlier acquaintanceship; the latter listened in stony silence to all his arguments. In March he returned empty-handed to his own people. Yet war did not break out immediately. On March 1st the Emperor Leopold died suddenly in Vienna and his eldest son was believed to be a far less formidable opponent. At almost the same time the assassin's blow removed Gustavus from the scene, and Sweden declared a neutral policy. At these seemingly favourable turns of events, France became more warlike. In Paris a new Ministry had been formed, and its ablest member, Dumouriez, Minister for Foreign Affairs, was anxious for a war with Austria which he hoped would make him the arbiter of France. His plan was for an invasion of the Austrian Netherlands, and as this would certainly inflame England, he sent Talleyrand to accompany Chauvelin, the accredited ambassador to the Court of St. James's, with assurances and with a letter for George III, supposed to have been written by Louis, expressing his thanks for our neutrality and a desire to increase the friendship of the two countries by a formal alliance.[1] Fully aware of the unhappy position of Louis XVI, both Pitt and Grenville knew what value to put on these assurances. On April 20th France declared war.

Within a few days, terrible rumours began to permeate the French capital. The whole plan of the war had gone awry. Three French armies were to invade the Netherlands, one under Dillon against Tournay, another under Biron against Mons, and a third under Lafayette was to march on Namur. But the first movement was sufficient to show of what stuff the French army was made. Dillon's forces at the first sight of bloodshed, were so smitten with panic that they fled in confusion; and the general, attempting to stem the flight, was cut to pieces by his own men. The force under Biron was completely routed before Mons. Lafayette was forced to beat a precipitate retreat. At this point Prussia determined to join her ally. She accordingly declared war on France, and the Duke of Brunswick, chosen to command the combined forces, issued the ill-starred manifesto that was to do such irretrievable damage to the royal cause. If Louis and Marie Antoinette were exposed to the smallest violence, if they were not immediately set free and placed in safety, it declared, the city of Paris was to

---

[1] Grenville to George III, Whitehall, April 28th, 1792.

be sacked and the population murdered. Empty threats that served only to inflame the capital. Mob law was almost supreme. The Tuileries was assailed, the guard massacred. The terrified prisoners sought safety in the hall of the Assembly, only to hear the passing of decrees suspending the royal functions and summoning a new body to be known as the Convention, a fresh milestone on the road to liberty. From this humiliation they were removed under close guard to the ancient stronghold of the Knights Templars. To such depths of ignominy had fallen the once proud inheritance of the Grand Monarque.

Thus the grim events relentlessly moved on to the final tragedy. As the Duke of Brunswick crossed the French frontier, seized Longwy, invested Verdun, and marched on Paris, the tocsin rang out and all able-bodied citizens, eager to enrol themselves as volunteers for the defence of their country, converged on the Champs de Mars. Meanwhile, gangs of murderers were sent to the jails to massacre the prisoners. They set to work with relish. In four days, it is said, no fewer than six thousand innocent persons were butchered, and the blood of the fallen was eagerly smeared on the faces of their assassins, anxious to show by these awful signs that they had done their duty. Not sex, not youth, not beauty, served as a shield. Dead bodies were a beauteous sight to these abandoned men; bodies writhing in death-throes were even more exquisite, and especially did they gloat over the pangs of Catholic priests praying in their last agonies for the souls of their murderers.

The position of France seemed hopeless, yet she was not to perish. Thanks to the lethargy of the enemy, Dumouriez, her new commander, had been given opportunity to reorganize his army. At the same time, Servan, the War Minister, had recalled the General of the Army of the Centre and had replaced him with Kellerman, a brave soldier and inspiring leader, but no strategist. These two forces united, and at Valmy they barred the way to Paris. At first the attackers gained some advantage, but when the Prussians discharged their heavy artillery, the French did not flinch. That was a great surprise. The Prussian infantry pressed forward. The French did not give way. On the contrary, they began to sing "Ça ira" and the "Marseillaise," to wave their hats in the air and to shout "Long Live the Nation." Moreover, the French guns, well placed on the heights of Valmy and Mont Yvron, began to send a hail of shot upon the advancing Germans. This was not at all the reception the forces of the Duke of Brunswick had expected: they paused; they wavered. Suddenly the Commanding Officer, seeing that they had had enough, turned to the king at his side and, pointing out that it was pouring with rain, suggested that the fight should cease. The king agreed; and lo and behold! within ten days the armies of the invaders were in full retreat. In truth, Valmy was little more than a cannonade, but the republican army rejoiced as at a great victory. France was a mighty nation, they declared; she could conquer the world. And voicing the cheerful cry of "Vive la France!" they set forth in pursuit of the enemy. In the south, French forces had repelled the Piedmontese and had conquered Savoy and Nice. Another force from Alsace under the gallant Custine advanced into Germany, captured Metz and marched on Frankfort. In the north, Dumouriez invaded the Netherlands, won the great victory of Jemappes near Mons, and within a month overran the whole country from Namur to Antwerp.

Amid such violence, the discredited Monarchy of France could not stand, and towards the end of 1792 a Committee was formed to try the unhappy king. The result was never in doubt, though the majority was narrow and included the dishonoured name of Philippe Égalité himself. On January 21st, 1793 the last act of the dismal tragedy was enacted in the Place de la Révolution, and the executioner, having performed his awful duty, held aloft the dripping head for all to see; unhappy head, so feeble in life, so pathetic in death, yet but one of so many that fell in France that year like leaves before an autumn wind. What should happen to such heads as this? "The coalesced kings threaten us," boomed the great voice of Danton in the Convention, "let us hurl at their feet as gage of battle the head of a king."[1]

In the House of Commons, a calm, cool voice was addressing an anxious and expectant Chamber. "Whenever they obtain a temporary success, whatever be the situation of the country in which they come, whatever may have been its antecedent conduct, whatever may be its political connections, they have determined not to abandon the possession of it, till they have effected the utter and absolute subversion of its form of government, of every ancient, every established usage, however long they have existed, and however much they may have been revered. They will not accept, under the name of liberty, any model of government, but that which is conformable to their own opinions and ideas; and all men must learn from the mouth of their cannon the propagation of their system in every part of the world." So much for such catchpenny phrases as the revolution not being for export. England must face the issues. "I take the conduct of France to be inconsistent with the peace and liberty of Europe. . . . They have neither withdrawn their armies from the neighbouring nations, nor shewn the least disposition to withdraw them. If France is really desirous of maintaining friendship and peace with England

[1] Danton, The Convention, January 31st, 1793.

she must show herself disposed to renounce her views of aggression and aggrandisement, and to confine herself within her own territory, without insulting other governments, without disturbing their tranquillity, without violating their rights. And unless she consent to these terms, whatever may be our wishes for peace, the final issue must be war. . . . This country has always been desirous of peace. We desire it still, but such as may be real and solid, and consistent with the interests and dignity of Britain, and with the general security of Europe."[1]

On the day these words were uttered, the French Republic declared war on Great Britain and Holland.

When we last encountered the Camelfords they were travelling abroad. Not by any means all of their time, however, had been spent out of England, and we have already encountered Mr. Pitt, M.P., in the House of Commons before his elevation to the peerage. On the death of Lord Harrington in 1779 he bought from the executors the lease of Petersham Lodge by Richmond Park the fee simple of which he subsequently purchased from the Crown,[2] and here and at Camelford House, the home he built for himself at the top of Park Lane fronting Oxford Street, the Camelfords were wont to entertain their friends. "I dined yesterday at Petersham," wrote Anthony Storer to his bosom friend, Lord Carlisle, "You know it now belongs to Tom Pitt. Lady Pembroke dined there; she has a small lodging just on the other side of Tom Pitt's pale at a keeper's house in Richmond Park, to which she has built four rooms out of her pin money."[3] Amid these pleasing surroundings the two children had grown up, Anne into a lovely girl, charming and accomplished, and Thomas into a big, headstrong lad, bursting with energy. "The Cornish Hercules," Lady Chatham had once called him,[4] and he did not belie the compliment. The reader will recall the anxious solicitude that Lord Grenville, ever a friend of the Camelfords, took in Anne Pitt's health when as a child her life was despaired of, and that solicitude had not diminished now that she had grown to woman's estate. Indeed, he had watched with interest her growth to maturity and he early determined to claim her as his bride. "Lord Camelford is full of you, and of the most sanguine and flattering accounts of his daughter's

[1] William Pitt, House of Commons, February 1st, 1793.

[2] In 1790 Camelford sold Petersham Lodge to the Duke of Clarence, afterwards William IV.

[3] Storer to Carlisle, Portugal Street, June 18th, 1781.

[4] "Many congratulations to you and Mrs. Pitt on the health and promising state of the young Cornish Hercules and his sweet sister." Lady Chatham to Thomas Pitt, Hayes, April 18th, 1777.

mind," wrote Lord Buckingham to his brother in the summer of 1791, "and Lady Camelford told me last night that she was perfectly satisfied that Annette preferred you, *at present*, to every other man, and liked the prospect of marrying you."[1]   But though the fair Anne appears to have made up her mind to wed her ponderous and somewhat elderly suitor,[2] she was not to be hurried.   "We sent you back your Annette in high good humour, and with a very decided wish, *explained to Mary and to me*, that she was to remain in England, *with all its consequences*, rather than to go abroad. Papa and mamma are greatly satisfied that her preference is now decided. Perhaps I might be permitted to ask a question or two upon that subject if I thought it could assist you; but, in trying it, I found so little encouragement from him, that I dropped it; and I fear I have nothing to recommend to you but patience."[3]

Patience was certainly required, for a year later they were not wed; but the courtship seems to have gone smoothly.   "I have not told you all that I have felt for you in seeing your prospects crowd upon you faster than we had expected," his brother wrote him the following summer, "but you know the anxious wishes I entertain for your happiness, and I will say no more upon the subject, except that I shall lay in my claim very early with Lord Camelford to transfer your Arcadia and your courtship to the cooler climate of Stowe (where, by the bye, I am writing by a fireside) for the remainder of the dog-days; for I fancy you would not choose to run backwards and forwards from Boconnoc, and I am persuaded he will not continue in London."[4]   And a week later, "A thousand joys upon the arrivals in your Deal list," he wrote.   "I write a few words to him, but purposely avoid every thing that can interfere with the arrangements which you may have made for planting your arcadian bower in the secluded and solitary angle formed by Oxford Street and Park Lane."[5]   Nothing did interfere with the arrangements, and on July 18th, William Grenville and Anne Pitt became man and wife.   Within a few weeks of the marriage, the bride's father was forced abroad again by his health.   "We left Lord Camelford far from well, and in the intention of coming immediately to town, in order to set out again for the Continent," wrote the bridegroom to his brother.   "It is a melancholy reflection to think that he should again so

[1] Buckingham to Grenville, June 23rd, 1791.

[2] In 1791 Lord Grenville was 32 years of age, and Anne Pitt about eighteen.

[3] Buckingham to Grenville, June 30th, 1791.

[4] Buckingham to Grenville, June 20th, 1792.

[5] Buckingham to Grenville, June 22nd, 1792.

THOMAS PITT, Lord Camelford, son of Thomas Pitt

Reynolds

ANNE WILKINSON, Lady Camelford

Artist unknown

soon be obliged to leave us."[1]   Very soon he was to leave them for good;
already the dew of death was gathering on his brow.

Lord Buckingham was wrong in saying that his brother planned to
"plant his arcadian bower" in London, for as far back as a year before the
marriage he had been corresponding with him about the purchase of a
country property at Burnham. "As to your purchase," he wrote in the
summer of 1791, "it is impossible to think of it as a money transaction, for,
in that point of view, it cannot be entertained.   But I think you fully justified to yourself in determining to pay largely (on the Scale of your property)
for your comfort; and it would seem impossible, if you determine to pay
£2,000 for the *place and your comfort* over and above the £2,000 which you
allow me to add to the same object, that the remaining part of the purchase
money can be very ill laid out; though I think that it probably will not be
very advantageously expended. Still, however, if the purchase pays you
3½ per cent. for your money, it cannot be said to be a very ruinous undertaking."[2] "I had heard from Tom of your Burnham purchase," he wrote
late the same year. "I fear from your account of it, that it is hardly extensive enough in land, which I hold to be an object to you, as £3,000 will
hardly give you there more than about 70 acres; and I should fear that,
whenever you resided there *permanently* you would feel cramped with a
domain so small. As to a house, I am sure that you will do better by
adding occasionally (though upon a regular plan) *as you want room*, than by
purchasing a large and perhaps ill-arranged house."[3]   Thus Dropmore was
purchased, and there the Grenvilles took up their residence soon after their
marriage.

The honeymoon was spent at Pitt's home. "I hope you have found
Hollwood habitable.   Lord Buckingham presses me so much to meet you
at Stowe, that I think our rendezvous must be there instead of Burton"[4]—
and a cordial invitation came from Lord Auckland, then at the Hague, to
visit Eden Farm—"I understand that you are passing some weeks at Holwood," he wrote, "I wish to remind you that I have a good garden in tolerable condition at Beckenham, and that my steward has directions, and will
be glad to obey any orders from you relative to its produce.   It will give us
pleasure to hear that Lady Grenville and you take occasion in your airings
to walk round the place."[5] Thence the Grenvilles went to visit Lady

[1] Grenville to Buckingham, St. James's Square, September 20th, 1792.
[2] Buckingham to Grenville, Wotton, August 28th, 1791.
[3] Buckingham to Grenville, December 6th, 1791.
[4] William Pitt to Grenville, The Grainge, July 22nd (1792).
[5] Auckland to Grenville, Hague, July 24th, 1792.

Chatham at Burton Pynsent, and to Weymouth for the sea air; but in the autumn they were able to move into their new home, for which the Buckinghams sent supplies from Stowe. "I gave up the hopes of the autumnal visit which you promised me when I saw you forced up to London after the 10th August, but, as I conclude that you will be at Dropmore as soon as you can put up your bed, I shall give you notice of your cargo of plants as soon as the season serves for it."[1] "I forgot to ask you whether your good woman has any room for birds which we promised to supply? If she has place for them my chaise is a good higler's cart to bring them, and some poultry if she likes them."[2] And again a few years later, "Ten ewes of my best breed to whom a very fine ram has been very properly attentive, together with ten more of this year's breed and a young gentleman, who will all be forward for next year's marriage, are ready for you; and will set out as soon as you please.   They will be three days on the road, and will be overtaken on the third by my cart with 7,000 three-year-old beech, and a number of odds and ends of other plants, including 1,500 two-year-old oaks, together with some pigeons and poultry for Madam. . . . ."[3] It is not to be supposed that Anne Grenville declined these offers, so that the Stowe chaise must often have trundled over to Dropmore laden with supplies.   At Dropmore the Grenvilles were soon visited by Lord Mornington, who wrote delightedly on his friend's new-found happiness. "I told Pitt that matrimony had made three very important changes in you, which could not but affect your old friends.   1st., a brown lapelled instead of the eternal blue single-breasted; 2nd., strings in your shoes; 3rd., very good perfume in your hair powder.   All the rest remained the same, particularly quiz drawing, which Lady Grenville seemed to be studying with great application."[4]

Whilst Anne Pitt was marrying the future Prime Minister and settling down to a long life of placid contentment, her brother was embarking on his wild life of extravagant folly that was so soon to end in grave disaster. His early education had been received at Berne in Switzerland, the grandeur and stillness of which seem to have had a strange fascination for his restless soul, and at Charterhouse.   But when he was approaching manhood, he showed such a predilection for the sea that his parents were constrained to allow him to enter the Royal Navy, and in 1789, when no more than fourteen, he sailed as a midshipman in the *Guardian* frigate laden with

[1] Buckingham to Grenville, September 23rd, 1792.

[2] Buckingham to Grenville, November 25th, 1792.

[3] Buckingham to Grenville, November 5th, 1797.

[4] Mornington to Grenville, Ramsgate, October 24th, 1792.

stores for the new convict colony settled at Botany Bay. During the voyage disaster overtook them and the unfortunate ship was almost lost. On Christmas Eve, then in latitude 44° S. and longitude 41° E., they approached a vast iceberg, from which the captain resolved to replenish his water supply. Unfortunately, however, a point of the berg, extending some way under the water, struck the ship heavily so that in a few moments she was evidently sinking. That day, anxious for the safety of his crew, Captain Riou called for volunteers to stay aboard and try to bring her safely to port. "Poor Riou was determined to share the fate of the *Guardian* and resisted all persuasion to take to a boat . . . Lord and Lady Camelford are in the deepest distress upon the melancholy catastrophe; their only son being in the *Guardian* and would not quit Riou."[1] The remainder filled the boats and after nine days in this plight they were picked up by a French merchant ship and on January 18th, 1790, were landed at the Cape of Good Hope. For Riou and his men there seemed small hope, and their fate was long in doubt. "Lord Chatham's account of the loss of the *Guardian* is one of those events that cannot but be deplored," wrote the King, "in addition to which I fear Lord Camelford's only son was one of the Midshipmen."[2] But rare courage and wonderful seamanship overcame all perils, and after a passage little short of miraculous these brave and enterprising men succeeded in bringing their ship to the Cape. "I have never received more real joy than on reading Lord Chatham's note enclosing the letter from Capt. Riou with the account of the safe arrival of the *Guardian* at the Cape of Good Hope; I desire Lord Camelford may be acquainted how sincerely I rejoice at the change of his situation."[3] In September, 1790, Tom Pitt landed at Harwich, having made the voyage home in the packet *Prince of Orange*. He was then fifteen and a half years old.

Such an adventure might well have daunted young Pitt's tender years, but he was soon at sea again. Shortly after his return, a voyage round the world was being fitted out under the command of Captain George Vancouver, and Thomas solicited an appointment in the commander's ship, the *Discovery*, soon due to leave these shores. On April 1st they sailed, and for some three years Lord Camelford's son remained under Captain Vancouver's command. Rounding the Cape of Good Hope, they surveyed the south-west coast of Australia; thence they steered to New Zealand, explored Dusky Bay and turned north for Tahiti. For some time nothing was heard of the traveller. "We have had no letter since the arriving at

[1] Hood to Cornwallis, Admiralty, April 26th, 1790.
[2] George III to Chatham, "Windsor, April 24th., 1790, $\frac{m}{25}$ pt. 6 p.m."
[3] George III to Chatham, "Queen's House, April 28th, 1790 $\frac{m}{10}$ pt. 6 P.M."

the Cape," wrote his father to an unknown correspondent, "one came to me that gave me a false hope, but it was an old one written when he was going from the Cape towards Botany Bay."[1]   Then what exactly happened is not known, all that is certain is that Captain Vancouver was constrained to flog the young man three times, to thrust him in the bilboes and finally to put him ashore at Hawaii, in the Indian seas.   Thence he made his way to Malacca, where on December 8th he had entered as an able seaman on board the *Resistance*, whose commander, Sir Edward Pakenham, three weeks later appointed him lieutenant.   At first it seemed as if Thomas had learnt his lesson, for under Pakenham he gave no trouble.   But after less than a year's service he was suddenly discharged, and was suffered to find his way back home as best he could.   After further adventures, of which we have no very precise details, he at last succeeded in reaching England once more. He still nursed a grudge against Vancouver, however, for the treatment he had received at his hands, and on his return home in October 1796, he sent him a challenge.   But the Captain declined to receive it; Pitt had himself to thank for the trouble had been brought on by his misbehaviour, and the Commander had only done what was necessary for the maintenance of discipline and order.   At the same time, Captain Vancouver offered to submit the affair to the judgment of any flag-officer in his Majesty's navy and if such officer should adjudge that he was liable by the laws of honour to be called out, he would willingly give the satisfaction required.   Such a tame solution of the dispute was not at all congenial to the fiery Tom Pitt, who now threatened Vancouver with personal chastisement.   As ill-luck would have it, he not long afterwards encountered the Captain in Bond Street, when he immediately attempted to put his threats into action and was only prevented by the activities of the bystanders and by Vancouver's brother warding off the blows.   Shortly afterwards Vancouver died— from chagrin, as some say, at the unmerited disgrace of this unworthy scene.

Whilst their son was experiencing these adventures on the high seas, Lord and Lady Camelford were attempting to recruit the former's failing health by wintering in the sunny climate of Italy.   "I enclose to you a letter (probably written to me for your perusal) from Lord Camelford," wrote Lord Buckingham to his brother, "it smells most violently of his emigrant society, but much of it is alas! too true.   I am uneasy about his motions, both from the time of year and the peculiar difficulties of a winter journey at this time to Rome; and from the chance of his finding a flame in every corner of Italy as fierce and as unexpected as that from which he is

[1] Camelford to ——, July 1st, 1790.   The original of this letter is in the author's possession.

running in the Netherlands."[1] The Camelfords never made the journey to Rome. In December Lord Camelford wrote to Pitt from Florence, and on a curious subject. Recent events in France having driven from that distracted country the Countess of Albany, widow of the Pretender, and her constant companion, Count Alfieri, who has been already met with in these pages, they had settled in Italy. There Camelford found them in serious need. "I write to acquit myself of a commission I have received from the Comtesse Albany," he wrote to Pitt, "who desires to assure you that the kind part you were so good as to take in her business, both when she left England and since, lays her under obligations that she shall never forget. After what is past, I conclude it is in vain to hope the subject can be renewed in any shape hereafter. It is impossible for me, however, to be witness to the situation of that unfortunate lady without reflecting upon the effect her present distress must produce upon every feeling mind in Europe. By her flight from France, where, had she remained two days longer, her certain imprisonment had been the consequence, and she would have been included in the general massacre, she has lost every resource from that country. Driven afterwards from her family at Brussels, from the apprehensions of what has actually taken place immediately after, she has taken refuge here as the only asylum that could afford her any promise of safety; and here she lives upon the debris of what she could save out of her fortune at a sequin a day. I need make no comments—your generous mind will supply them. If she had a pension of £1,000 she would be happy. Pardon me, my dear Sir, if I cannot resist the impulse that has made me state this to you, having no means of laying it before the person whose good heart would, I am sure, be not insensible to it, if he could be witness to it as I am. It is a strange world, and the vicissitudes of it are striking in a manner never before experienced."[2] The vicissitudes of life were soon to demonstrate themselves to Lord Camelford, for on January 19th, 1793, he died in Florence,[3] and his appeal only reached Pitt by the hand of Lord Hervey after his death. Thus the adventurous boy in the far-off seas succeeded to his father's peerage and great estate.

News of Louis' execution reached London on January 23rd; on the next day, to the King's great satisfaction,[4] Chauvelin and Talleyrand were

---

[1] Buckingham to Grenville, November 18th, 1792.

[2] Camelford to William Pitt, Florence, December 14th, 1792.

[3] Peter Beckford states that Camelford died at Pisa, but the *Gentleman's Magazine* records his death at Florence, and that is generally accepted as correct.

[4] George III to Grenville, Queen's House, January 24th, 1793.

peremptorily bidden to leave the kingdom within eight days, and though the latter wrote dignified letters of protest to the King, Pitt and Grenville, not one of them returned him any answer. In Parliament, Pitt did not moderate his language. He denounced the King's execution as "that dreadful outrage against every principle of religion, of justice and of humanity, which has created our general sentiment of indignation and abhorrence in every part of this island and most undoubtedly has produced the same effect in every civilised country . . . the foulest and most atrocious deed which the history of the world has yet had occasion to attest." He contrasted the ruin and anarchy of France with the freedom and propriety of England. "In this country," he declared, "no man in consequence of his riches or rank is so high as to be above the reach of the laws, and no man is so poor or inconsiderable as not to be within their protection."[1] This was the popular view. In the Commons, Fox could not muster fifty votes in favour of his two motions for peace; in the Lords, only Stanhope and some three other peers registered protests. The will of the people was not in doubt.

As soon as war was declared Pitt determined upon forming a vast coalition of European Powers to meet the aggressions of France, and so successful was his diplomacy that between the spring and the autumn of 1793 he had concluded alliances with Russia, Prussia, Austria, Spain, Sardinia, Naples, Portugal, Holland, and certain minor German princes and had agreed to grant subsidies totalling £832,000 for the hire of foreign troops. At first the Allies were successful. On February 17th Dumouriez at the head of a powerful French force crossed the Dutch frontier. His plan was to capture Maestricht, for Miranda to capture Venloo, and for these two victorious armies then to combine and march on Nymegen. Unfortunately for these plans, the Prussians reached Maestricht first; whereupon Dumouriez ordered Miranda to lay siege to the town. But the French generals were soon in difficulties. The Austrians pressed forward, forcing Miranda to raise the siege and fall back in disorder. At Saint-Trond he effected a junction with Valence and turned at bay. A few days later the Convention declared the country in danger and recalled Dumouriez to defend Brussels. Back came the General, breathing fire and slaughter against his Government. "See how these fools neglect my requisitions and control my plans," he roared; and in his fury he despatched a letter to Paris that horrified the Convention. After a hurried meeting they determined to suppress the offending document and to send commissioners to bring the General to his senses. Meanwhile the French forces, having suffered

[1] William Pitt, House of Commons, February 1st, 1793.

another reverse, this time at Neerwinden, retired in confusion to the strong line of border fortresses erected by Louis XIV and Vauban, and in little more than a month's fighting the Austrians had recovered the whole of Belgium. The effect of this new reverse on Dumouriez was disastrous. Furious with the politicians whom he blamed for all his troubles, chagrined at his lack of military success, he entered into treacherous communication with the Commanders of the Austrian army, the Prince of Saxe-Coburg and General Mack, with a view to evacuating the Netherlands and marching against the Convention in the guise of saving his country; and when, late in the evening of April 1st, the commission from the Convention arrived at his headquarters, he promptly seized and handed them over to the enemy. His next few days were spent in attempting to suborn the army, and when this proved impossible, for the bulk remained loyal, the General, attended only by a single regiment of hussars and certain members of his personal staff, rode over to the Austrian lines.

The treachery of the French general coupled with the serious revolt which took place in the provinces during the summer of this hectic year, 1793, led to the fall of the moderate party in Paris. A Republic had been proclaimed shortly before the death of the King and three main parties had been formed in the Convention. The Gironde were the moderate republicans; the Plain, or Marais, consisted of a few hundred undistinguished deputies who moved to and fro following like sheep without a shepherd and at the whim of any one of their number who might summon sufficient courage to declare himself; and the Mountain, the real force of the Assembly. The chief members of this fiery and subversive minority were Danton, Marat and Robespierre, and it included men like Camille Desmoulins, Collot d'Herbois, Fabre d'Eglantine, the most violent of the Jacobins. Thus the most subversive and most powerful of the parties had in its ranks the ablest men of the revolution; and additional power was given to it by the disasters of the war. These misfortunes which seemed to endanger the very existence of the State were responsible for the establishment of the two dreadful and sanguinary committees of the Terror which was so soon to follow, the Committee of Public Safety and the Comité de Sureté Générale, both of which had hitherto been restrained to some extent by the moderation of the Girondists. But these anxious days were no time for moderation and the ruthless Mountain set about its work of destruction. Soon the chief place on the Committee of Public Safety was occupied by the sinister Robespierre, shortly to become virtual dictator of France. Henceforth the terrible drama moves inevitably towards its climax like some sombre Greek tragedy at the close of which no leading character survives.

The weapon of the dictator was the Terror. "Terror, apart from which virtue is powerless." Thus the more he desired the establishment of virtue, the fiercer must become the Terror under his sway. This was the great theory of this terrible little Arras lawyer, this lover of words—this man of theories, of virtue, and of blood. "In times of peace the springs of popular government are in peace," he declared, "but in times of revolution, they are both in virtue and in terror." But Barras, the realist, was more concise. "We must guillotine others," he said, "or expect to be guillotined ourselves." In the Public Prosecutor, Fouquier-Tinville, the unsuccessful financier soured by poverty—dark, sallow, pock-marked, with bushy eyebrows and glistening, beady eyes—the dictator had a helpmate worthy of the times. "Heads are falling like slates," declared Fouquier delightedly in the midst of this holocaust, but he was far from satisfied. "Next week I'll take the tops off three or four hundred!"

Heads fell like slates. Among the first to suffer was the noble Caen maiden whose great knife had terminated so suddenly the hideous life of the dreadful dwarf of the Rue des Cordeliers. Next came the Queen. During the night of July 3rd her little son, the Dauphin, had been snatched from her, and on August 1st she was removed to the Conciergerie, a noisome place where she was so closely watched that she could not change her linen. Yet amid unimaginable misfortunes this unhappy woman, so foolish in her days of power, so noble in her days of captivity, never wavered. With steady tread and majestic mien she went to her doom, and the vile Hébert rejoiced at seeing the head of the "female Veto cut off her harlot's neck." Six months later his own summons came. When the sentence that he rejoiced in for others was delivered upon himself, he whimpered with fright and was carried from the Court in a dead faint. On the scaffold, too, he made a sorry figure and all Paris gaped at the dread form of Père Duchesne, whom for the first time they perceived to be only a little pale-faced man shivering and trembling ignobly at the prospect of death.

In October most of the leaders of the Gironde were sent to their doom. In November, within a month of the Queen's death, the greatest of her enemies, the ignoble Philippe Égalité, met his well-deserved end. Two days later perished Madame Roland, another of the Queen's most bitter enemies. Calm and smiling she set forth to perish on the scaffold at the age of thirty-one. "O Liberty," she exclaimed, "what crimes are committed in thy name!" Brave, noble words that come down to us through the years. Within a short time of her death the two men she had loved followed her to the grave. Poor old Roland, in hiding in a back street of Rouen, heard from the cries of the newsvendors of the death of the wife who had long tired of him. Without a word he went out into a wood some leagues from the city and passed his sword-cane through his heart. The other was Buzot, now known to have been her lover. He, at St. Emilion, took leave of his senses, wandered into the country and disappeared. His pursuers tracked him from place to place. At last they found him lying in a cornfield near Castillon: he was not a pleasant sight for he had been half devoured by the wolves.

Meanwhile the war continued. Our forces under the Duke of York joined those of the Prince of Coburg. They were opposed before Valenciennes by a considerable army under a new commander, Dampierre, a brave but irresolute General of the old school, who promptly attacked on May 1st and 7th, suffering repulses on both occasions, losing his life on the second. The French troops, dangerously weakened by these set-backs, retired in some disorder first to Valenciennes and then to Bouchain. The Duke of York was anxious to advance immediately on Paris, but Coburg, supported by Mack, urged the more cautious policy of securing the border fortresses. It was accordingly decided to besiege Condé and Valenciennes, and the Duke of York was given the task of reducing the latter stronghold. The bombardment was long and vigorous. For forty-one days it was strenuously defended by the French garrison under Ferrand, and did not surrender until the greater part of the town had been destroyed and half the troops within had perished. On July 10th, Condé fell; on July 26th the town and fortress of Valenciennes at last submitted.

The French Army was now in deadly peril and doubtless a determined advance would have brought the invaders to the gates of Paris. But determination was lacking in the allies' councils, and this saved France from irreparable disaster. In November, the Duke of York turned aside to lay unsuccessful siege to Dunkirk. Nor were expeditions sent to Normandy to aid the Vendeans and to Toulon to occupy that harbour any more fortunate. The former arrived too late to be of any use; the latter, under Hood, after an initial success in June, was forced, largely by the young Corsican, Napoleon Bonaparte, to abandon the port in December. The baneful effects of this evacuation were, however, to some slight degree mitigated by an act of enterprise and daring that wrought havoc on the enemy's ships in that harbour. Young Sidney Smith, who, though not yet thirty years of age, had recently been knighted for his services to Gustavus III, had been out to Constantinople on a visit to his brother, Spencer Smith, our Ambassador to the Porte. On arrival at Constantinople, however, he learnt of the breaking out of hostilities against England and he received immediate orders to sail for home. Calling at Smyrna, he found there many seamen awaiting passages and on his own responsibility he purchased a small vessel, and with forty sailors aboard he joined Lord Hood at Toulon.

No sooner had he arrived than the evacuation began, and the impetuous Smith at once volunteered to the Admiral to fire the French ships left in the harbour. Hood promptly took him at his word. "You *must* burn every French ship you possibly can," he wrote,[1] and when Smith, perhaps repenting of his rashness, began to enumerate the difficulties, Hood was the more insistent. "It *must* be undertaken," he wrote three hours later . . . "the conflagration may be advantageous to us—no enterprise of war is void of danger and difficulty—both must be submitted to."[2] Thus admonished, Smith set about him with a will and, though the difficulties inherent in the enterprise prevented him from destroying all the hostile ships in the harbour, he did succeed in firing nine of the twenty-seven ships of the line, together with much smaller craft; and even if his many detractors were to point out that some of the ships which the loquacious seaman boasted of having destroyed—for he put the number at far higher than nine—were ere long to be encountered afresh in many a hard-fought encounter with the British fleet, the services he rendered his country that day were not to be minimized. Lord Hood for one was delighted and sent the gay Sir Sidney home with despatches.

In 1794 the French succeeded in reconquering the whole of Belgium. Towards the end of the year the Duke of York was thrown out of Holland and the Prince of Orange obliged to fly for his life to seek safety in England. The occupation of the island of Corsica, mainly through the determined efforts of a young Norfolk sea captain, Nelson by name, the occupation of the Cape of Good Hope, the conquest of a number of West Indian islands, and Lord Howe's great victory off Ushant over the French fleet under Admiral Villaret-Joyeuse on the glorious first of June, were only partial compensations for the allies' poor success on land.

Meanwhile, whilst France was being saved by the stupidity of her enemies, in Paris heads continued to fall. "We must guillotine others or expect to be guillotined ourselves." The words of Barras were ever present in the mind of the dictator, and he urged on his henchmen to renewed efforts until at last only Danton and his followers survived as possible rivals to his power. And Danton, away at his chateau in Arcis-sur-Aube, seemed not the man he had been. Was it the death of Orleans, or was it the society of his new girl wife that had moderated his revolutionary ardour? Was he disturbed for his own safety? Was he suffering from neurasthenia, as Madelin suggests?[3] None can say. One thing only is

---

[1] Hood to Smith, "*Victory*, December 16th, 3 p.m."

[2] Hood to Smith, "December 18th, 6 p.m."

[3] Madelin, *The French Revolution.*

certain. When Danton returned to Paris at the end of November 1793, he had evidently sickened of bloodshed. At times, as if beside himself, he would exclaim to all and sundry that he would "eat Robespierre's entrails"; but the mood would quickly pass, and then he would tearfully protest that he was "a good friend, a good citizen." "We must guillotine others or expect to be guillotined ourselves." Robespierre, half pitying, half contemptuous, looked askance at this wreck of a man. Clearly he was not safe in his present mood. A well-wisher warned Danton. Yet he continued to sit by the fire and took no measures to secure his safety. The result of this inaction was inevitable. At six o'clock one spring morning he was arrested in his own house: the same day Desmoulins and all his most prominent adherents were also seized. On April 2nd (12th Germinal) the trial opened. Danton resolutely defended himself, but the result was never in doubt. "Vile Robespierre!" he cried, "the scaffold claims you too. You will follow me!" On the scaffold, he momentarily faltered. "My beloved," he murmured, "shall I never see thee more?" Quickly pulling himself together: "Come, Danton, no weakness!" he declared. Then to the executioner, with a touch of his old arrogance, "Show my head to the people," he commanded, "it is worth it!" A moment later, just as darkness fell, Sanson held aloft that large, that fine, that formidable head; then he dropped it and with a thud it fell into the basket.

"Vile Robespierre! The scaffold claims you too. You will follow me!" The tyrant had overreached himself, and within three months, the scaffold claimed him. A ghastly figure drenched in blood, his mouth gaping, his jaw sagging, in company with his closest followers, he was dragged to his doom. As the tumbrils bearing their ghastly cargo of human wreckage rumbled slowly along the Rue Saint Honoré to their final destination at the Place de la Révolution, a grief-racked, half-demented hag sprang on the back of the cart that held what was left of the great dictator, and spat forth in a voice of agony, "Monster, vomited by Hell, thy torment intoxicates me with joy! I have only one regret—that thou hast not a thousand lives, so that I might enjoy the spectacle of seeing them torn from thee one by one! Go scoundrel, go down to the tomb with the curses of all wives and of all mothers!" That dreadful malediction, the curse of all wives and of all mothers, has been amply and terribly fulfilled.

CHAPTER VIII

In the Days of General Bonaparte

TOWARDS the close of the month of March 1796, a young, untried general arrived in Nice to assume the command of the French troops in Italy. He was not quite twenty-seven and he did not look of much consequence, for he was small, shabby and insignificant. But General Bonaparte had already shown his mettle in Paris; and the Directory, the new Government of France, required a vigorous commander to lead their troops to victory beyond the Alps, and by rapine and plunder to fill the void coffer of the State. In this young Corsican, so they believed, they had found the man best fitted to do their bidding. And so it seemed. Within a few weeks he overwhelmed the Austrians in the wild gorges between the Alps and the Apennines; before the end of April he forced the Piedmontese to sue for peace, thus forcing open to the victors the road to Turin. "Soldiers! In the space of a fortnight you have won six victories, taken twenty-one standards, fifty-five pieces of ordnance, several fortified towns, and conquered the richest part of Piedmont: you have made 15,000 prisoners and killed or wounded 10,000 men. . . ." Thus the victorious commander scattered his laurels. "But, soldiers," he was quick to add, "you have done nothing, for you still have work to do!" Whereupon "the little corporal" hurled his troops across the Po at Piacenza, drove the enemy under Marshal Beaulieu behind the Adda, and at the Bridge of Lodi, amid a hail of grape-shot, urged on his wavering men, shattered the ranks of the enemy and drove them in hideous rout and confusion back to the Mincio. The great fortresses of Legnano, Peschiera and Verona fell. The victor laid siege to Mantua. Wurmser, appearing with 70,000 men to raise the blockade, was defeated first at Lonato, then at Castiglione, and with the remnants of his mauled army was hurled back to the upper Adige. No sooner had he returned to the attack than, again overwhelmed three times in quick succession—at Primolano, at Bessano, and at San Giorgio—he was obliged to take refuge in the beleagured fortress of Mantua. Next, Alvinzi appeared at the head of 50,000 men, and a fierce struggle ensued amid the marshlands of Arcola. For three days the issue was in doubt, three days in which the intrepid Corsican constantly exposed himself at the post of danger, three days of the swaying fortunes of armies locked in the grip of mortal combat. At last the Austrians began to retreat; the victory was won.

But as the old year died, weary and bloodstained, and the new year was born, fresh and full of hope, the dauntless Alvinzi returned with 70,000 men at his back. To the soldiers of France this was nothing. By now their belief in the star of their leader was fanatical. Under him, the armies of the Republic were invincible; forward to victory! At Rivoli on January 12th Joubert's men wavered; but as if by magic Bonaparte appeared, rallied the faltering troops, gave battle anew, and hurled back the foe, reeling and staggering into the neighbouring ravines. On February 20th Mantua threw open her gates. Cremona and Pavia were taken, and in a few weeks the conquerors made their victorious entry into Milan. "People of Italy!" trumpeted Bonaparte, "The Army of France has broken your chains: the People of France is the friend of all other Peoples: come to greet it. . . ."

It was during the enactment of these events that Pitt formed his only attachment. During the winter of 1796-7 it was generally noted that he was paying marked attention to Lord and Lady Auckland's daughter, Eleanor Eden. Of course Pitt at Holwood and the Edens at Beckenham were near neighbours, and what could be easier than for the Minister under cover of visiting his friends to woo their daughter? Naturally, there was a flutter of excitement at the news, but Auckland was cautious. ". . . they see much of each other," he wrote, "they converse much together, and I really believe they have sentiments of mutual esteem; but I have no reason to think that it goes further on the part of either, nor do I suppose it is ever likely to go further."[1] Nevertheless it certainly looked for a time as if the affair might prosper. And then of a sudden, after toying for a while with the dream of marriage, Pitt brought the matter to an abrupt termination, in a formal, correct and chilling letter. After some five tedious sentences of apology and regret the letter ran—"Whoever may have the good fortune ever to be united to her is destined to more than his share of human happiness. Whether, at any rate, I could have had any ground to hope that such would have been my lot I am in no degree entitled to guess. I have to reproach myself for ever having indulged the idea on my own part as far as I have done, without asking myself carefully and early enough what were the difficulties in the way of its being realised. I have suffered myself to overlook them too long, but have now at length reflected as fully and as calmly as I am able on every circumstance that ought to have come under my consideration (at least as much for her sake as for my own) I am

[1] Auckland to Beresford, December 22nd, 1796.

compelled to say that I find the obstacles to it decisive and insurmountable."[1] The father's reply to this priggish missive seems to have revealed the feelings of his daughter for it called forth a letter expressing Pitt's deep concern at hearing of "the sentiments of another person, unhappily too nearly interested in the subject in question. . . . Believe me," he added, "I have not lightly or easily sacrificed my best hopes and earnest wishes to my conviction and judgment."[2] Auckland acknowledged this the following day, at the same time expressing the intense sorrow felt both by his wife and his daughter.[3] But Pitt too, it seems, was not unscathed, for some ten days later the Archbishop of Canterbury wrote to Lord Auckland, his brother-in-law, that Pitt was living in complete seclusion, that he had a dreamy, far-away look, and that at a recent meeting of the Council he had appeared with a swollen face and unhealthy appearance.[4]

There is little doubt as to what were the insuperable obstacles to this union. As far back as 1789 Pitt had been in financial difficulties, and early in that year an offer of assistance had come from a friendly quarter. It will be remembered that when the elder Pitts were in trouble through the extravagances of young James Charles, the distressed Hester had appealed to her nephew, Tom, and had not appealed in vain. Now once again that nephew was to offer assistance. "The attention he has given to our finances must have allowed him little time to look into his own," wrote Lord Camelford to Lord Chatham in January 1789, "and I doubt with no eye over them, his *Ministers* have not been so faithful to their trust as he has been to that reposed in him." Moreover, his expenses must have exceeded his official salary. Therefore Tom begs to be allowed to help. "I am well aware," he adds, "that he will find those much better able than I am who upon political speculation would be glad to offer him their services! but God forbid he should be reduced to owe them obligations whilst his own family have it in their power to assist him. He belongs to us, we all partake in his glory —it is not only just, but it is a *right* we *claim* (far better founded than some that are assisted) to share with him the inconvenience which that Glory may have brought upon him."[5] Noble words! But Chatham, it appears, was able to send some reassurances. "You make me very happy in telling me that our friend's affairs are not likely to turn out such as my anxiety for him had made me apprehend," wrote Camelford a few weeks later, "at least that at the worst they are not probably beyond the reach of our united

---

[1] William Pitt to Auckland, January 20th, 1797.
[2] William Pitt to Auckland, January 22nd, 1797.
[3] Auckland to William Pitt, January 23rd, 1797.
[4] Archbishop of Canterbury to Auckland, February 7th, 1797.
[5] Camelford to Chatham, "Carnoles, near Monaco, January 16th, 1789."

efforts. Assure him nothing would be more flattering to me than such a mark of his confidence and affection."[1]

Whether his generous-hearted cousin helped Pitt at this time we do not know; but certain is it that in 1792 he was in difficulties, for he was then compelled to sign two Powers of Attorney to enable Thomas Coutts to receive his salary as First Lord of the Treasury and Chancellor of the Exchequer.[2] Then some four years later we find a solicitor writing to Pitt that Lord Stanhope's agents have been making some pressing enquiries for "an account of the monies due to the children of yr. sister Lady Hester, as their proportion of the money bequeathed to yr. late Brother James Charles." The amount involved he estimates at £244 2s. 8d. and he asks Pitt for instructions.[3] We know from Lord Cranworth's papers that the Minister was compelled at this time to raise a second mortgage on his small Holwood property for £7,000. Moreover, amongst the Pitt manuscripts in the Public Record Office there is a short memorandum in Pitt's hand which, dated 1797, must refer to his expenses at Downing Street or Holwood. This shows wine bills for his steward's room at £300 or more and states that other expenditure of that room might be reduced from £600 to £300 a year, that on his own wardrobe from £600 to £400, and that of the stable from £400 to £300. He also lent money to his mother, as is in fact admitted by Lady Chatham herself in a paper written in April, 1794, for "My dear Sons," after her death. ". . . I have now to say on my own Part," she wrote, "that I beg my *just* Debts *may be* Paid, wh. are exceedings beyond the Income I have had to spend, altho' my dear Sons have done much for me in their kindness and affection for me. I do not condemn myself for having incurred these *exceedings*, because they were not occasioned by *Idle Expences*, but by believing what I did was, from different circumstances, best, *at the Time* it was done. I shall have a very Improved Farm, with, I hope, whenever it may happen, a valuable stock upon it etc. My dear Friend, Mrs. Stapleton, has a demand upon me for all her Attention to me a *Thousand* Ways. I shall trust in yr. generosity to acquit me. . . ."[4] In 1801 the Bishop of Lincoln put her debt to him as high as £5,800. "The

[1] Camelford to Chatham, Monaco, March 9th, 1789.

[2] Coutts to William Pitt, Strand, London, November 17th, 1792.

[3] Ward to William Pitt, Newman Street, October 23rd, 1796.

[4] Lady Chatham "to the Earl of Chatham and the Right Honourable Mr. Pitt." April 2nd, 1794. There is also an addition to the document, dated August 8th, 1794, in which Lady Chatham expresses her "ernest wish that my chaise and little Horses, with my Chestnut Mare may be given to Mrs. Stapleton, also my Silver Tea Urn, and my four Silver Bottle Frames *bought* my myself."

security was transferred to Coutts when he advanced the money. . . . I cannot think that Hollwood would sell for £16,000, except it were by auction. . . ."[1] Chatham, too, borrowed from his brother, and in August 1791 owed him £1,000; and the fact that he lent no aid when William was in serious financial straits after his resignation in 1801 is evidence that the elder brother was then still in low water. Most of these figures are, of course, very rough and ready, especially those in Pitt's own memorandum, but they are typical of his attitude to finance, which was as eccentric and carefree as had been his father's. In 1801 Pitt's debts were thus estimated by the Bishop of Lincoln at just over £45,000:

Estimate of Mr. Pitt's debts in 1801.

To Contra, advanced upon security of
Burton Pynsent	£5,000
Ditto on Bond	6,000
Ditto overdrawn	1,750
Mortgage, Hollwood	11,000
State of Debts 1st February	7,408
Old Debts, Hollwood	2,190
Mr. Soane	2,098
Bills unpaid	9,618
	£45,064[2]

The disaster had not, of course, reached such proportions in 1797, but it is now clear that even then the Prime Minister was heading straight for bankruptcy. No doubt with the thought of marriage, he looked into his affairs. Lord Auckland was not a rich man, and as Eleanor Eden was one of a large family her dowry would be small. Only by giving her father some lucrative post could the obstacle be surmounted, and neither Pitt nor Auckland was the man to descend to such expedients. Indeed, when Mansfield's death made a vacancy in the Lord Presidency of the Council, Pitt did not appoint Auckland to fill it, but at the King's bidding, nominated his own brother, who since his retirement from the Admiralty in December 1794 had retained his seat in the Cabinet as Lord Privy Seal.[3] "You will, I am sure, be pleased to hear that on my arrival at Weymouth it was immediately proposed to me that my brother should succeed in the present

[1] Bishop of Lincoln to Rose, Buckden Palace, July 24th, 1801.
[2] Bishop of Lincoln to Rose, Buckden Palace, August 18th, 1801.
[3] William Pitt to Chatham, Weymouth, Sunday, September 4th, 1796.

vacancy, to the Presidentship of the Council," Pitt wrote to his mother. "I could not wait for his arrival, though he was expected Monday; but left a letter for him to mention the arrangement, which I think he cannot but like as very flattering in the way in which it comes, and it is also materially better in point of income than his present office."[1] So all thoughts of the fair Eleanor were expelled from Pitt's mind, and thus terminated his solitary romance.[2]

Meanwhile, the victorious Bonaparte was sending home treasure from Italy to fill the empty coffers of the State. "Would it not be possible to seize the Casa Santa of Loretto and the immense treasures heaped up there by fifteen centuries of superstition?" asked the avaricious Directors. "They are valued at 10,000,000 livres sterling. This would be a financial operation of the most admirable nature, and would harm nobody except a few monks." No one, of course, cared a fig for a few monks, and money came pouring in. The Directors were hugely delighted. "You are the hero of all France!" they wrote, ". . . the considerable success the Republic owes to your victories proves that your attention is devoted at once to the glory and the interests of your country."

This was the contemptible Government to which Pitt persisted in applying in his vain strivings after peace, and in the summer of 1797 Lord Malmesbury was sent to Lille to negotiate. These conversations led nowhere; but there were soon rumours abroad that the liberal bribery of the French Government would win for Pitt what the more straightforward efforts of Malmesbury could not obtain for him. The French Ministers were receiving huge sums from their General in Italy: how could they be expected to renounce these splendid spoils without assurances of compensation from another quarter? The sum asked, reported Pitt to the King, "is a very large one, amounting to four hundred and fifty thousand pounds," but it would be wisely expended if the conditions be fulfilled before payment "namely that the treaty shall be signed and ratified without delay, leaving this country in possession of the Cape, Ceylon, Cochin and Trinidad, and granting nothing in return. . . ." Moreover the money could be raised from the Indian revenues and the secret service, without any disclosure being made.[3] A few weeks later Pitt wrote George again that ". . . the Directory will still agree to an immediate peace giving to the country both the Cape and Ceylon, on condition of their receiving a large sum of money

[1] William Pitt to Lady Chatham, Downing Street, September 6th, 1796.

[2] Miss Eden subsequently married Lord Hobart, who in 1804 succeeded as Earl of Buckinghamshire.

[3] William Pitt to George III, Holwood, September 6th, 1797.

for their own use. The sum mentioned of £1,200,000 for Ceylon and *two millions* for both."[1] However, Pitt was unduly hopeful, for these dishonourable negotiations came to nothing, and it was to be some years before we were to conclude with France an uneasy peace.

Meanwhile, England's lack of success in the war made peace seem highly desirable. For not only were the victories of Bonaparte in Italy a potential danger, but elsewhere also England and her allies had been sadly unsuccessful. The Duke of York had been driven out of Belgium. All our allies had been forced to make peace with France, and what was worse, two of them, Spain and Holland, had been compelled to desert our cause. But a worse misfortune awaited us, for early in the year the Channel Fleet mutinied and it was only after liberal increases in pay had been granted that the men were persuaded to return to duty. Never again has Britain been in such danger from so awful a cause.

But now the Directors in Paris were looking upon their General's victories with increasing apprehension. True, he was sending home magnificent plunder; but he was at the same time making of himself a great national hero, and for how long would he suffer them to enjoy the spoils of office? At all costs he must be kept from Paris, and they wrote to "advise" him to proceed to Rome, there to extinguish "the torch of fanaticism." "Such," they added, "is the wish of the Directory."[2] But Bonaparte scented mischief and was anxious for peace. Already he had been in negotiation at Tolentine with the Pontiff's envoys, and by a mixture of insinuation and bravado had extracted from them territory and treasure, said to be worth 15,000,000 livres. He must now come to terms with Austria. But desperate as she was, the Viennese Cabinet declined to relinquish conquered territory or to acknowledge the vile Republic that had sent a Hapsburg to the scaffold, unless her greed could be sated and her pride appeased with a compensation sufficiently attractive. Bonaparte had no mind, of course, to offer anything belonging to France; but he had no objection to giving the property of another, if by so doing he could serve his turn. He accordingly suggested to the Austrian emissaries at Leoben that the handing over of Venice might form a suitable basis for peace. The Austrians licked their chops. Whereupon the Venetians obligingly gave the French general the very excuse he needed: on April 17th the inhabitants of Verona suddenly turned on the small French force and massacred the garrison. Bonaparte took a swift revenge.

It was at this critical hour that a grave internal crisis suddenly compromised the government of France. The Directory and the Councils

[1] William Pitt to George III, Downing Street, September 22nd, 1797.
[2] Executive Directory to Bonaparte, February 3rd, 1798.

prepared for battle, and it became clear to Bonaparte that his place was in Paris. At midnight on the 25th Vendemiaire of the year VI[1] in the little village of Campo Formio he signed a treaty under which "The leading Conservative Power in Europe ratified the extraordinary conquests of the Republic."[2] The spoils of ravaged Venice served to sate the thirst of the Court of Vienna and to soften for her the cession of Belgium and Lombardy, whilst it was agreed that matters of special concern to the Germanic Empire should be referred to a future Congress to be held at Rastadt. Bonaparte's triumph was indeed complete. No sooner had the victorious general set his seal to this document than he set out for Paris.

On January 13th, 1798, two ships, a frigate *Perdrix* and a sloop *Favourite*, were moored alongside the dockyard in the English harbour of Antigua. The Commander of the frigate, Captain Fahie, was on leave, and his first lieutenant, Charles Peterson, was left in temporary charge. The Commander of the sloop was none other than Lord Camelford, who, on April 7th of the previous year, had been promoted to the rank of lieutenant, and in August had joined the *Vengeance* with Captain Russell on the Leeward Islands station. Russell, then senior officer at St. Kitts, had appointed Camelford as "acting commander" of the sloop *Favourite* whose Captain was ill; but it appears doubtful whether he had the necessary authority, and under the designation of "lieutenant commanding" the appointment was duly repeated by the Commander-in-Chief at Martinique. It was not long before the important question arose as to whether Camelford or Peterson was the senior officer—the latter being some two years senior on the lieutenant's list, but the former being in command of his sloop, whilst Peterson was only in temporary command of his frigate—and the fiery Pitt determined to put the matter to the test. On January 13th, hostile ships being observed off the island, Camelford sent his rival a formal order to prepare for action, subscribing himself as "Commanding his Majesty's sloop *Favourite* and senior officer"; whereupon Peterson, galled at such effrontery, immediately sent Camelford a counter-order and subscribed himself, "Commander of his Majesty's ship *Perdrix* and senior officer." This was too much for Pitt, who straightway despatched a lieutenant and company of marines to bring the culprit to his senses. But Peterson stood his ground and the lieutenant, fearful of using force against a fellow officer, promptly withdrew. It was clear to Lord Camelford that he must deal with the matter himself. Accordingly, accompanied by marines from the *Favourite*, he went down to the wharf, and Peterson, ordering men from the *Perdrix* to fall in, went ashore at their head to meet him. There stood

---

[1] October 17th, 1797. [2] Fisher, *History of Europe,* Vol. III.

Peterson with drawn sword and backed by a number of his armed crew. Facing him was Camelford, not armed himself, but, like his opponent, supported by his ship's company. High words ensued, and Camelford, advancing to Peterson, enquired if he still refused to obey his orders. "I do," came the firm reply. Camelford then seized a loaded pistol from one of his officers and presenting it at Peterson repeated the question a second and a third time, receiving on each occasion the same answer. At the third refusal he fired with deadly effect, for Peterson fell on his back, neither uttering a word nor moving a muscle. He had been killed instantly. After this decisive termination of the argument, the men retired to their respective ships, and Lord Camelford surrendered himself to Captain Matson of the sloop *Beaver*.

This unhappy affray aroused the most lively indignation throughout Antigua, for the dead man was a native of one of the neighbouring Leeward Islands, and was said to be popular. In consequence, Camelford was only saved from violence by his removal to Martinique, where a court martial was held a week later. According to naval law, it would seem as if Peterson was senior to Camelford, who was certainly junior on the lieutenant's list, but the officers of the court martial appear to have accepted without question the accused's statement of seniority, and on January 25th after five days' hearing they acquitted him. This finding was evidently agreeable to the Admiralty, for in a few months they promoted Camelford, who on his return to England was in October 1798 appointed to the *Charon* to carry to the Mediterranean guns for the arming of the ships being fitted out at Constantinople under the direction of Sir Sidney Smith. It was whilst fitting her out that this eccentric young man came to a remarkable resolution; this was nothing less than to repair secretly to Paris and there to seize and bring back a series of charts which he conceived would be useful in our hostilities against the French.

There was residing in England at this time a distinguished French sailor, Commodore Bompard by name, who had just been captured and was now a prisoner of war. To Bompard, then, Lord Camelford presented himself and by some trickery or other extracted from the exile a letter of introduction to Barras, one of the Directors, in which he was described as a man willing to render important service to France. How Camelford managed to persuade the Frenchman that he would act as a traitor to his country we shall never know; what is certain is that our young adventurer, thus armed with a passport to the French Government, on the evening of Friday, January 18th, 1799, took the night coach to Dover where he arrived early the following morning and went to the City of London Inn. Having breakfasted, he explored the harbour in search of someone with a boat, willing to take him to Deal. At length a boatman of the name of Adams volunteered to take him for a guinea. Having examined his man, Camelford apparently thought him trustworthy, for at length he disclosed that his real destination was Calais, where, he said, he must go in order to dispose in France of some materials and watches which he had for sale. After some bargaining, Adams agreed to take him for a fee of twelve guineas, and to call for him at the inn at six o'clock that evening.

No sooner had these arrangements been made, however, than Adams began to have qualms, and after consulting his brother, who owned a half share in the boat, he repeated his conversation with the stranger to the local customs collector. This man, Newport by name, arranged to hide in the boat with four assistants, and no sooner had Camelford stepped aboard than, exclaiming "You are my prisoner!" he arrested him. The captive surrendered without a struggle and was at once taken to the Customs House to be searched. There they found on him a brace of pistols, a carved doubled-edged dagger about eight inches long, and the tell-tale letter to Barras. It was clear that he must be sent to be interrogated by the Privy Council, and early in the morning of Sunday, January 18th, a post-chaise drew up at the door of the Duke of Portland's house in London. Out of it stepped Lord Camelford accompanied by Newport and the brothers Adams. The Privy Council was immediately summoned, and in view of the fact that the prisoner was Lady Grenville's brother, Pitt sent anxiously to Grenville, then at Dropmore, urgently bidding him to come without delay to town. After a prolonged examination the lords of the Council expressed themselves satisfied that the prisoner had acted from the best of motives in that he had been actuated solely by a desire to do his country service. He was accordingly honourably discharged, and the King's pardon issued under the Great Seal expressly exempted him from the penalties of the Act recently passed which made it a capital offence so much as to embark for the French coast. But if the lords of the Council were satisfied, the lords of the Admiralty apparently were not, for they so disapproved of the offender's conduct as to supersede him in the command of the *Charon*. Whereupon the aggrieved sailor indignantly requested that his name might be struck off the list of Commanders, a course to which their lordships took no exception. Thus abruptly and ingloriously ended the chequered naval career of this adventurous young man.

General Bonaparte reached Paris and went to join his wife at their home in the Rue de la Victoire. All the Capital was agog at the news that the hero was in their midst, but it soon became apparent that he was a very coy hero who refused to show himself. In a few days he went to the Luxembourg there to be formally received by the Directors. He attended a Reception given by Talleyrand in his honour. He attended several meetings of the Institute where he hobnobbed with the intellectuals, and he was himself elected a member of that august body. But he refused to be lionized. He seldom went into society and to the general public he was invisible. "What a modest man he is!" exclaimed all Paris. They could not have been more mistaken! He saw at once that the fruit was not yet ripe for plucking and that he had best quit the Capital: meanwhile, to lie low and avoid exciting jealousies was his wisest course. The Directors had given him command of *l'armée d'Angleterre*, knowing full well that the plan to invade England was doomed to failure. So did Bonaparte, and he determined not to fall into that trap. "Make what efforts we will," he wrote to the Directory, "we shall not for many years acquire control of the seas. To make a descent upon England without being master of the sea is the boldest and most difficult operation ever attempted."[1] For a time, however, he pretended interest in the project, and even went so far as to inspect the active preparations that were afoot in the northern ports; but he was soon begging to be put in command of an expedition against Egypt. The Government, thankful to be rid of him, acquiesced with alacrity. An expedition against England? An expedition against Egypt? To the Directors one plan was as good as another as long as the dangerous firebrand would leave them in peace. So on the 29th Floreal[2] he sailed with thirty-five thousand soldiers, ten thousand sailors and a brilliant staff. He quickly seized Malta and on the 11th Messidor of the year VI[3] he landed in Alexandria. At last the Directors could breathe more freely; their hero had departed!

To counter the threatened danger Pitt brought in a Bill for the better manning of the Navy, explaining to the House his reasons why the measure should pass through all its stages in one day.[4] This suggestion was opposed as unduly precipitate by George Tierney, Member for Southwark. Pitt at once rose. "If the measure be necessary," he asked aggressively, "how can the Hon. gentleman's opposition to it be accounted for but from a desire to obstruct the defence of the country?" The Speaker, appealed to, ruled that it was for Pitt to explain his words. The Minister rose, looked round about him with his haughtiest air, and repeating the offending passage declared in the true Pitt manner, "I will neither retract from nor farther explain my former expressions."

[1] Bonaparte to Directory, February 23rd, 1798.
[2] May 19th.
[3] June 30th, 1798.
[4] William Pitt, House of Commons, May 25th, 1798.

The result was inevitable, and the very next day—Saturday, May 26th—the expected challenge came. At three o'clock on the following afternoon the two parties met on Putney Heath. Two shots each were exchanged without effect, whereupon the seconds interfered and declared that honour was satisfied. Perhaps the most sensible comment was made by the King. "Public characters have no right to weigh alone what they owe themselves," he told his Minister; "they must consider that is due to their country."[1] "I cannot bear the idea of Mr. Pitt *versus* Mr. Tierney," wrote Lord Buckingham to his brother, "Surely he ought to have felt that there were duties that ought to have suggested a very different line of conduct than that of staking his life on such a subject and *versus* such a man."[2] Wilberforce was so shocked that he was anxious to bring the whole question of duelling to the notice of Parliament, and only desisted at his friend's most urgent bidding.[3]

Whilst these events were happening in England, Bonaparte was achieving wonders in Egypt. In three weeks, by the victories of Ramanieh, Chebreiss and the Pyramids, he overwhelmed the fleeing Mamelukes, seized their Capital, and set up his headquarters in Cairo. Nothing so daring, nothing so masterful had been achieved for a generation. But the victorious general remained inactive only a few days. On August 7th leaving Desaix in charge, he set forth to complete the conquest of Egypt. Five days later he was on the borders of the desert, having driven the Mamelukes to the Isthmus of Suez, whence they had retired in confusion to Syria, and there in the hour of his triumph, he received news from Kleber of an appalling disaster. The French fleet, under Brueys, securely anchored in Aboukir Bay some miles east of Alexandria, thus protecting the army of Egypt's communications with the west, had been attacked and routed by Nelson and the British fleet. At this news, the hearts of the troops sank within them. "Here we are," they cried, "abandoned in this barbarous country, without communication with home, without any hope of return." "Well, we have then laid on us the obligation to do great things," rejoined their indomitable commander. "Seas which we do not command separate us from home; but no seas divide us from Africa and Asia. We will found here an Empire." And so saying he immediately set about the subduing and the organizing of the whole of Egypt, which, through the

---

[1] George III to William Pitt, May 30th, 7.43 p.m. The original bears the date of the year 1797, but this must evidently be a slip of the King's hand for 1798 as the reference to the duel is obvious.

[2] Buckingham to Grenville, May 29th, 1798.

[3] William Pitt to Wilberforce "Downing Street, Wednesday, May 30th., 1798," and "Downing Street, Saturday 6 p.m." (June 2nd, 1798.)

disaster in Aboukir Bay, had been rendered even more essential to his future projects.

The autumn and part of the winter of 1798 were passed in the mastering of Upper Egypt. In November Suez was occupied, and late in December the commander-in-chief himself inspected the isthmus by which he must advance to the prosecution of his larger schemes. It was here that he learnt that Djezzar, the Pasha of Syria, had on January 2nd, 1799, occupied the oasis of El Arish in the desert of Suez and was preparing its fortress in a state of defence. Clearly the position was acute, but Bonaparte did not hesitate; he must immediately advance into Syria, in spite of the hostility of the Turks, whom he still hoped to keep neutral. It was only after his troops were already in the desert, marching towards Syria and he himself on the point of joining them, that he learnt that the die was cast and that Turkey had declared war on France.

Bonaparte's first aim was the seizure of El Arish, recently occupied by Djezzar, and early in February General Reynier routed the Turks and laid siege to the citadel. A week later Bonaparte appeared, and within a few days of his arrival the garrison capitulated. Forty-eight hours later the advance from El Arish began. Gaza was soon seized and in little more than a fortnight the port of Jaffa was in French hands. On March 12th commenced the march upon Acre, and on the 17th, at five o'clock in the afternoon, the victorious general looked down upon his goal from the recently captured port town of Haifa. And there lying in the roadstead of Acre he spied two British ships-of-the-line. These, the *Tigre* and the *Theseus*, represented the sea power of Great Britain preparing to foil the evil designs of the great French leader; and the sea power of Great Britain was under the command of a man of genius, Sir Sidney Smith, now destined to bar the way to the most illustrious soldier of modern times.

Bonaparte knew full well the importance of Acre: to advance leaving it unsubdued would be to leave his flank and rear most vulnerable to attack from the sea. If he captured Acre, on the other hand, the whole country might rise in his favour. "If I succeed," he declared during the siege, "I shall find in the city the treasures of the Pasha, and arms for three hundred thousand men. I raise and arm all Syria, so outraged by the ferocity of Djezzar, for whose fall you see the population praying to God at each assault. I march upon Damascus and Aleppo. I swell my army as I advance by all malcontents. I reach Constantinople with armed masses. I over-throw the Turkish Empire. I found in the East a new and great empire which shall fix my place in posterity."[1] Dreams? asks Mahan, and he

[1] *Mémories de Bourrienne*, Vol. II.

reminds us of the exploits of Ibrahim Pasha in 1831 and 1832. If Ibrahim, why not Bonaparte? But, whereas the former succeeded, the latter failed, and after sixty-two days was obliged to raise the siege and to lead his baffled, demoralized army through the sands of the desert back to Egypt.[1] Thus the proud conqueror, his dreams shattered, was forced to retire thwarted and ashamed at the behest of a British naval captain with two ships-of-the-line and a few small craft.

Whilst these stirring events were passing in the east, in Europe a new Coalition was formed which threatened the whole line of French defences from Naples to Amsterdam. Meanwhile in Paris, where the government was rapidly losing its small remaining credit, men began to sigh for the presence of the soldier to rescue them from their dilemmas. But the saviour was at the other end of the world and the French fleet had been destroyed. What hope was there of their deliverance? And then a wonderful thing happened. On the 19th Vendemiare, the strangely garbed messengers of the Directory suddenly made their appearance at the Palais-Bourbon. "Citizens," they declared, "the Directory informs you with great pleasure that it has received news from Egypt. General Berthier, who landed at Frejus on the 17th of this month with General Bonaparte . . ." That was all. Shouting and cheering crowds drowned the rest, for the galleries long rang with the acclamations of the audience. Meanwhile, the general was hastening across France towards the Capital, determined, as he had put it to some friends, "to drive out the lawyers."

At first he thought of becoming a director himself, but he rapidly changed his mind and determined on a partnership with Sieyès. A fictitious Jacobin conspiracy, brandished before the nervous Parisians, formed a sufficient pretext for removing the government temporarily from the Capital, and on the 18th Brumaire[2] the Ancients duly decreed the transference of the Councils to St. Cloud. Of the directors, Sieyès and his friend Ducos resigned as arranged. Gohier, the President, tried to summon a meeting of the Directors, but he could not obtain the necessary three to form a quorum. Moulin alone came. The sole remaining Director, Barras, sent word he was at his toilet and could not come: all he did was to send his secretary, Bottot, to the Tuileries. They soon cajoled him into retiring. Talleyrand came to his house, bearing a dignified letter of resignation and requesting his signature. At this moment Madame Tallien came in, and seeing what was afoot implored Barras to play the man. But, knowing the game was up, he appended his name to the document; thus he signed

---

[1] Mahan, *The Influence of Sea Power on the French Revolution and Empire*, 1793–1812, Vol. I.

[2] November 9th.

himself out of history. The fate of Gobier and Moulin was more unkind; they refused to retire and in consequence found themselves lodged in the Luxembourg. Thus ignominiously and unmourned, the Directory fell.

So far, things had gone well. But when the Councils, gathered at St. Cloud on the following day, showed signs of offering resistance, the sequel was not so satisfactory. Bonaparte addressed the Ancients and made a deplorable figure; his speech was clumsy, confused, incoherent; and to the charge of acting the Caesar, he had no answer at all. Next, he appeared before the Five Hundred, where he was greeted with shouts of "Down with the Traitor!" "Down with the Dictator!" "Outlaw the Tyrant!" In a moment the Mountain was upon him and only with difficulty was he rescued from the throng. A motion to outlaw the general was frustrated by the audacity of the President of the Five Hundred, who chanced to be his own brother, Lucien Bonaparte; whereupon the troops were summoned to eject the Council, and the Ancients promptly passed a decree appointing Bonaparte, Sieyès and Ducos provisional Consuls. At five in the morning the three Consuls took the oath, and departed amidst joyous shouts of "Long live the Republic!" Thus ended the famous *coup d'état* of the 18th Brumaire.

Having gained power by these discreditable means, the First Consul was not slow to make use of it. He immediately took steps to put an end to the civil war in France, to retrieve the ruined finances and to do everything in his power to improve the spirit and the lot of the French armies. At the same time, on Christmas day, 1799, he despatched personal letters both to George III and to Francis II proposing terms of peace. The former was sent under cover of a short note from Talleyrand to Grenville, requesting its transmission to George III. Though the tone was civil enough, Pitt was unimpressed. ". . . as I think we can have nothing to do but to decline all negotiation at the present moment on the ground that the actual situation in France does not as yet hold out any solid security to be derived from negotiation, taking care, at the same time, to express strongly the eagerness with which we should embrace any opening for general peace whenever such solid security shall appear attainable. This may, I think, be so expressed as to convey to the people of France that the shortest road to peace is by effecting the restoration of Royalty. . . ."[1] The Cabinet in London appears to have been unanimous, and Grenville thus wrote to his brother: "I send you for your New Year's gift a curiosity. I need not tell you that we shall say no—I am occupied in studying how to say it in the manner least shocking to the numerous tribe of those who hate the French and the

---

[1] Pitt to Dundas, Downing Street, Tuesday, December 31st, 1799.

Jacobins, and would to-morrow sign a peace that should put us at the mercy of both."[1] "Your New Year's gift is indeed most curious," came the reply, "and perhaps as a diplomatic piece, is unique. The first paragraph is the only real communication, namely, a notification to King George of the accession of King Bonaparte. . . ."[2] On January 4th, 1800, England replied in the form of a letter from Grenville to Talleyrand. The King, it is stated, had only one wish, to maintain the rights and happiness of his subjects against aggression; but he could not feel that there would be any lessening of the necessity for him to contend for these objects by his entering at present into negotiations with those whom a fresh revolution had so recently placed in power. And to Talleyrand's further plea for the opening of negotiations, Lord Grenville replied on January 20th declining to enter further into the matter, at the same time pointing out that the overtures of France did not extend to England's allies.

Thus ended Bonaparte's famous peace offer, and Pitt, who had been anxious enough to conclude hostilities with the discredited Directory in 1795, refused to negotiate with the Dictator in 1799. And can we, who have lived in the age of dictators, blame him for that? He realized the traitorous cunning, the cold-blooded insincerity of the upstart; he realized the true value to be placed on the word of the tyrant, on the honour of the oligarch. He would be party to a general peace, but he would not come to any separate understanding with Bonaparte. But whilst we may applaud his policy, we can hardly approve Grenville's reply to the First Consul's letter, for what was more calculated to unite Frenchmen under their new government than his slighting reference to their ruler's supposed insecurity? The wording of this document was undoubtedly a psychological blunder of which the great Chatham would never have been guilty.

In Parliament men seem to have thought more of the policy than of the method by which it was carried out, and the Opposition was feeble. In the Lords, the Address was carried by a huge majority, and amongst the minority of six appeared the name of Lord Camelford. In the Commons, the debate was somewhat keener and much more protracted, though ending with the same result. With rare skill and eloquence, the Prime Minister defended the whole conduct of the government. "I see no possibility at this moment of concluding such a peace," he said, "as would justify that liberal intercourse which is the essence of real amity; no chance of terminating the expenses or the anxieties of war, or of restoring to us any of the advantages of established tranquillity; and as a sincere lover of peace, I

[1] Grenville to Buckingham, January 1st, 1800.

[2] Buckingham to Grenville, Stowe, January 2nd, 1800.

cannot be content with its nominal attainment; I must be desirous of pursuing that system which promises to attain, in the end, the permanent enjoyment of its solid and substantial blessings for this country, and for Europe. As a sincere lover of peace, I will not sacrifice it by grasping at the shadow, when the reality is not substantially within my reach."[1] Was not this the very thing that Pitt had done when in the days of the Directory he had sent Malmesbury to Paris and to Lille? The House apparently did not think so, for in spite of all the eloquence of Fox, the Address was carried by 265 votes against 64. "I would demand of the Minister," declaimed Tierney a few days later, "I would demand of the Minister to state in one sentence what is the object of the War."[2] "He defies me to state in one sentence what is the object of the war," was Pitt's instant reply. "I know not whether I can do it in one sentence, but in one word I can tell him that it is Security! Security against a danger the greatest that ever threatened the world. It is security against a danger which never existed in any past period of society. It is security against a danger which in degree and extent was never equalled; against a danger which threatened all the nations of the earth; against a danger which has been resisted by all the nations of Europe, and resisted by none with so much success as by this nation, because by none has it been resisted so uniformly, and with such energy. This country *alone*, of all the nations of Europe, presented barriers the best fitted to resist its progress. We *alone* recognized the necessity of open war, as well with the principles, as the practice of the French revolution." England standing alone against aggression in the nineteenth century, as in the twentieth!

But was the home front firm? "We say that it was to be resisted no less by arms abroad than by precaution at home, that we were to look for protection no less to the courage of our forces than to the wisdom of our councils, no less to military effort than to legislative enactment. At the moment when those who now admit the dangers of Jacobinism while they contend that it is extinct, used to palliate its atrocity, and extenuate its mischief, this House wisely saw that it was necessary to erect a double safeguard against a danger that wrought no less by undisguised hostility than by secret machination. But how long is it since the Hon. Gentleman and his friends have discovered that the dangers of Jacobinism have ceased to exist?" he asked. "How long is it since they have found that the cause of the French Revolution is not the cause of liberty? How or where did the Hon. Gentleman discover that the Jacobinism of Robespierre, of Barrere, the Jacobinism of the Triumvirate, the Jacobinism of the Five Directors,

[1] William Pitt, House of Commons, February 3rd, 1800.

[2] Tierney, House of Commons, February 17th, 1800.

which he acknowledges to be real, has all vanished and disappeared because it has all been centred and condensed in one man, who was reared and nursed in its bosom, whose celebrity was gained under its auspices, and who was at once the child and the champion of all its atrocities and horrors. Our security in negotiation is to be this Bonaparte, who is now the sole organ of all that was formerly dangerous and pestiferous in the revolution. Jacobinism is allowed formerly to have existed, because the power was divided. Now it is single, and it no longer lives. This discovery is new, and I know not how it has been made...."[1] Alter a word here and there and this could be the great voice of Mr. Churchill castigating the tyrant of our days; in fact it is the great voice of Mr. Pitt denouncing the tyrant of his! And in his days, as in ours, there were those who could hardly be persuaded of the reality of the danger. But such was the force of the Prime Minister's eloquence that even the wavering Wilberforce was satisfied. "January 24. I wrote to Pitt, and he sent for me to town. I saw him. Till then I was strongly disposed to condemn the rejection of Bonaparte's offer to treat: greatly shocked at it; he shook me. January 27. Slowly came over to approve of Bonaparte's offer though not of Lord Grenville's letter."[2] How wonderful was the eloquence of this remarkable Prime Minister!

And indeed the peril was great, for Bonaparte was even now showing what credit could be given to his pacific overtures by marching at the head of his army across the Alps, seizing Milan, and giving battle to the Austrian troops on the plains of Marengo. At the same time the French forces in Germany were being equally successful. There, General Moreau led his men across the rivers Rhine and Danube, debouched into the plains of Bavaria, and marched to the gates of Munich. It was at this point that our Ambassador at Vienna, Lord Minto, was instructed to announce that England, whilst unwilling to negotiate with France separately, was prepared to take part in a negotiation for a general peace; and before the year was out, Grenville's brother, Thomas, was nominated as our representative at the intended Congress of Luneville.

It was not, however, an affair of foreign policy, but the tangled skein of Irish affairs that brought the Government down. Early in 1795, Pitt sent over as Lord-Lieutenant a wealthy Whig nobleman, Lord Fitzwilliam, a known friend to the Roman Catholic claims. Unfortunately, however, Fitzwilliam, a self-opinionated and loquacious man, commenced at once to blab of what he proposed to do; and no sooner had he arrived in Ireland than he began dismissing high officials, who were not slow in carrying their

[1] William Pitt, House of Commons, February 17th, 1800.

[2] Wilberforce, *Diary*.

complaints to London. The result was that it became necessary at once to recall the precipitate Viceroy. But the damage had been done, and Ireland soon fell a prey to organized Terror. During 1796 there broke out that rebellion which, though sullied by horrible barbarities, yet gave fame to Wolfe Tone and to that strange romantic figure, Lord Edward Fitzgerald, the Bonnie Prince Charlie of Irish history. The outbreak was quickly crushed, but it was becoming abundantly clear that there was only one satisfactory solution of the difficulty; the English and Irish Parliaments must be united as the English and Scottish legislatures had been in 1707. To effect this, which really involved the Irish Parliament voting an end to its existence, Pitt sent over as Chief Secretary a young friend and budding genius, Lord Castlereagh, whose mission was "to arrange the affair," or in plain English, to bribe the borough proprietors with the pensions, sinecures and titles they so much coveted. Castlereagh was remarkably successful, with the result that, without giving any definite promise, but on the implied understanding that union would be followed by concessions to the Catholics, bills were duly passed through both parliaments, enacting that four spiritual and twenty-eight temporal lords and one hundred commoners should represent Ireland at Westminister. A new Great Seal and a new Royal Standard were prepared for the United Kingdom of Great Britain and Ireland, and on the first day of 1801 the King's new title was duly proclaimed. And then, when all difficulties seemed to have been surmounted, of a sudden a formidable obstacle arose and on the rock the bark of the Ministry was destined to founder.

In September, 1800, as soon as the bills had been passed in the Irish and English parliaments, Pitt summoned a meeting of the Cabinet to consider how best the implied understanding could be fulfilled. He said nothing to the King, thinking perhaps by means of his persuasive powers to make him acquiesce when a plan was prepared. Nothing could have been more ill-advised, for George's views were known; and as far back as 1795, on the advice of Lord Loughborough, he had expressed apprehension that to consent to emancipation would be a breach of his coronation oath. Now, on receipt of Pitt's summons to the Cabinet,[1] Loughborough, who chance to be with the King, showed him the letter and excited him to resistance. George III, thus fortified, made no secret of his views. "I shall reckon any man my personal enemy," he declared, "who proposes such a measure"—and he went so far as to beg Addington, the Speaker of the House of Commons and Pitt's friend, to remonstrate with the Prime Minister. On January 31st, Pitt wrote his sovereign a long letter in which he set forth the general grounds of his desire for emancipation

[1] William Pitt to Loughborough, September 25th, 1800.

and added that a refusal must be followed by his resignation.[1] The King, after taking counsel with Addington, replied that he was bound by his coronation oath to refuse consent, and proposed that neither of them should say any more on the subject.[2] But Pitt, adamant, replied that he must retire as soon as a new Ministry could be formed,[3] and two days later the king regretfully accepted his resignation.[4] "My dear Pitt," he wrote, "as you are closing, much to my sorrow, your political career, I cannot help expressing the joy I feel that the Ways and Means for the present year have been this day agreed in the Committee without any debate and apparently to the satisfaction of the House. G.R."[5] Not "Mr. Pitt," but "My dear Pitt." That token of regard was the only recognition for his long services that this proud man would accept from his Sovereign.

The letter just quoted referred to the Budget which Pitt had introduced that day owing to the formation of the new Ministry being delayed because Pitt's successor was Speaker of the House of Commons and it was necessary to find a new Speaker to take his place. Meanwhile, Addington was busy with the formation of his Government. But he had not concluded this work before the King's health once more broke down. In the middle of February he fell ill with a feverish cold; then, towards the end of the month, it became evident that after an interval of twelve years, the calamity of 1788 was upon him again.

On Sunday, February 22nd, Addington had an audience of the Sovereign, and it was only too plain that his mind was deranged. All the old symptoms—the hurried speech, the wandering excitability, the confused and inarticulate chatter—had returned, and soon the Prince of Wales, thinking his hour had come, began to bestir himself. Then just when men thought that the dreaded regency was upon them, the King recovered. That was early in March and George promptly sent Pitt a message through his doctors. "Tell him," he said, "that I am now quite well—quite recovered from my illness; but what has *he* not to answer for who is the cause of my having been ill at all?" Pitt was deeply mortified, and indeed it was difficult to reconcile this cruel message with the King's letter of only a few weeks back. Would an assurance that he would never again trouble the

[1] William Pitt to George III, Downing Street, Saturday, January 31st, 1801.

[2] George III to William Pitt, Queen's House, February 1st, 1801.

[3] William Pitt to George III, Downing Street, Tuesday, February 3rd, 1801.

[4] George III to William Pitt, Queen's House, February 5th, 1801.

[5] George III to William Pitt, February 18th, 1801, 8 p.m.

King on the Catholic question "be material to his health?" he asked. "Certainly," Dr. Willis replied, "and to his life also." The fallen Minister did not hesitate: he bade the doctor give the King the necessary assurance.[1]

Thus ended the great Administration of William Pitt. It had lasted just seventeen years. Before long, in the hour of England's direst need he was to be recalled to the helm.

> "And O! if again the rude whirlwind should rise,
> The dawning of peace should fresh darkness deform,
> The regrets of the good and the fears of the wise,
> Shall turn to the pilot that weathered the storm."[2]

But he was then but a shadow of his former self and the strength of the pilot was no longer sufficient to "weather the storm."

[1] Colchester, *Diaries*, Vol. I. Lord Malmesbury states that Pitt himself wrote the King a contrite letter (Malmesbury, *Diaries*, Vol. IV), but this seems unlikely. Stanhope, *Life of Pitt*, Vol. III.

[2] Canning's well-known song, "The Pilot that weathered the Storm," of which I have quoted the last verse, was first sung at the dinner held in celebration of Pitt's birthday, May 28th, 1802.

BOOK III

Decline of the House of Pitt

CHAPTER I

The Stanhopes of Chevening and the House of Pitt

IN the days when Mr. Pitt was governing England, there lived in a modest house in Chevening Park an old lady of great beauty and charm. This was the dowager Lady Stanhope, widow of the second and mother of the third lord, and she it was who had written so happily to her great friend, Lady Chatham, in those far off days in 1774 when young Mahon was marrying sweet Hester Pitt and both families were rejoicing in the match. As the years passed, the two mothers continued to correspond, and the old dowager in Kent was wont to write all the family news to the old dowager in Somerset. Mahon and Hester had had three daughters, Hester, Griselda and Lucy, before the young mother died some six years after their marriage. "The Three Graces have just left me," wrote the fond grandmother. "They drank tea with me, and we were a very happy *parti carré*."[1] "The three and the governess dined with me yesterday, very happy, very busy, finishing a trimming they have worked to present to Lady Stanhope on her birthday, and I hear were out in the garden by five o'clock in the morning and erected a small theatre of hurdles and boughs, in which they acted a play composed by Griselda for her, Lucy and brothers to act. Hester, too tall to match, was chief engineer."

As the girls grew older there was news of gaiety. "About a week ago my five females were at a great ball and supper and they took the two eldest boys with them. After supper the ladies retired and the two little boys remained, and thought themselves, no doubt, persons of importance. The gentlemen said to M.: 'Come, you shall be our toast-master'; and he accepted with the greatest gravity. The first toast he gave was: 'To the immortal memory of Lord Chatham.'" Oh, tactful Mahon! "I do love him for it, more than I can tell you, 'tis a sweet dear and a sensible, for it came from his heart and head, both good as you see. . . ."[2]

But however gaily Lady Stanhope might write, it may be doubted if life at Chevening was very pleasant in the days of her son. At least the children did not find it so. We have seen Charles Stanhope in his public career, now we are to catch a glimpse of him in his own home. The first

[1] Lady Stanhope to Lady Chatham, November 29th, 1790.
[2] Lady Stanhope to Lady Chatham, April 17th, 1795.

disturbing influence we find is that of his second wife, Louisa Stanhope, who seems to have had all the frigid pride of the Grenvilles without any of the charm of her mother, the gay and merry Peggy Banks of long ago. Her whole life was passed in a whirl of fashionable excitement, so that she had little time to spare for her family; whilst Lord Stanhope, intent on his philosophical pursuits, immersed in the business of his public life, indifferent to the somewhat hard charms of his formal wife, spent his time advocating liberty abroad and acting the stern autocrat at home. "Lord Stanhope called and spent an hour or two with me," wrote his friend, Lord Holland. "He was very entertaining and full of encomiums of you, though you shared them with *Blacksmiths* in general, who in body and mind, he said, were superior to most classes of men. 'Not a stroke on the anvil without intellect—such amazing, such charming intellect, citizen.'"[1] At home he was very different. "His rule was absolute," wrote his grand-daughter, the Duchess of Cleveland, "his word was law—the law of the Medes and Persians, from which there was no appeal—and he forced the most implicit and unquestioning obedience."[2] It was in this uncongenial atmosphere that the children were brought up.

Of the three girls, we know, of course, much the most of the eldest. Lady Lucy, the youngest, was the beauty of the family, Lady Griselda the wisest, but Lady Hester by far the most interesting. Tall, stately, aristocratic, with dazzling complexion and expressive features, her blue, flashing eyes, now lighting up at some pleasing fancy, now darting scorn at some poor trifler, she recalled the *hauteur* of her terrible grandsire, and like Chatham in days long passed, compelled attention in any circle. "I am an aristocrat, and I make a boast of it," she once declared. "We shall see what will come of people's conundrums about equality. I hate a pack of dirty Jacobins, that only want to get people out of a good place to get into it themselves."[3]

But though the ascendency of the eldest girl was absolute, it was the youngest who first openly rebelled, and towards the close of 1796 we have her grandmother writing to Hester Chatham: "Since my last, I received a present of game from those who, for some time, have taken up much of my thoughts. I took the hint and wrote, desiring they would dine here to take a share of it, which they did yesterday, and all seemed pleased with me. I think now the ice has been broken and melted I need not write

[1] Holland to Caroline Fox, London, July 7th, 1799.

[2] Cleveland. *The Life and Letters of Lady Hester Stanhope.*

[3] *Memoirs of Lady Hester Stanhope as related by herself in conversation with her Physician,* Vol. II.

anything more and that you will now be easy on this subject."[1] The allusion in this letter is to a terrible event of that year. Lady Lucy, then only just sixteen, had fallen in love with the family doctor, Thomas Taylor, of Sevenoaks, and without her father's sanction had married him! Lord Stanhope's democratic principles did not cover such a *mésalliance*, and though Taylor was a man of irreproachable character, and was subsequently assisted by the great Mr. Pitt himself, neither he nor his young wife had since been received at Chevening.

Within a few months of this unhappy event, Lord Stanhope was to lose another daughter, for later in the same year Lady Griselda also left home, and took refuge in a cottage near Walmer Castle, lent her by Pitt. Four years later she married John Tekell, an army officer, whose circumstances, to quote Lord Chatham, were very confined though neither Chatham nor William thought that that consideration alone should be an obstacle to the match. Both brothers, however, urged their niece to mention the intended marriage to her father,[2] who nevertheless, remained unmoved. "My grandfather," writes the Duchess of Cleveland, "offered no opposition to his daughters' departures, though when Lady Griselda left he was heard to compare himself to Lear, quoting the line (certainly applicable): 'I never gave thee kingdoms.'"[3] Of his daughters, the children of his first wife, only one now remained; and Lady Hester Stanhope was destined ere long to add to her father's troubles.

Of the Stanhope brothers, young Mahon, unfortunately, had an upbringing at home unsuitable for a boy, and he was soon to deplore the wasted years. At last, in 1801, when he entered his twentieth year, he begged to be allowed to go to college and made proposals, drawn up by Pitt, regarding the entail. To these suggestions he received a blank refusal; and finding to his horror that his father's true object was to gain the power of disposing of the estate, he turned, in the hour of his distress, to his half-sister, the masterful Hester, who promptly packed him off abroad. Lord Stanhope of course was furious, and in face of these events it became impossible for Hester to remain any longer at Chevening; in consequence she went to live with her grandmother, Lady Chatham, at Burton Pynsent. Here she was thankful to learn that the high and mighty Mr. Pitt approved the news of her brother's departure. "Oh! delightful, charming!" she wrote to her friend, Francis Jackson, who had facilitated Mahon's escape, "this evening's post has not only brought me your letter, but a volume from

---

[1] Lady Stanhope to Lady Chatham, October 6th, 1796.

[2] Chatham to William Pitt, Ipswich, January 26th, 1800.

[3] Cleveland, *The Life and Letters of Lady Hester Stanhope.*

Mr. Pitt . . ." who ". . . speaks in the highest terms of approbation of all that has been done, which pleases me mightily and gives me every assurance that both now and hereafter he will do everything in his power for dear Mahon. . . ." Then she makes the sensible resolution of seeing a good deal of her distinguished uncle. "How instinct taught me to love this 'Great Man,' and if I had not kept sight of him at a *distance*, what would have become of us all? He means to come here this summer. . . ."[1]

It was not long before the two younger Stanhopes, left at Chevening, were following the example of their elder brother. "You will, I am sure, be happy to hear that all goes on well," wrote Hester. "Charles has a Commission in the 25th Foot, now at Gibraltar. . . . I heard to-day from James's Captain (a great friend of mine) ; he says he never had a boy before in his ship he was so fond of."[2]

In the summer of that year, we begin to hear distressing news of Lady Chatham. ". . . Dear Grandmamma's health having undergone so great a change since I arrived in the winter," wrote Hester, "has been in times the source not only of uneasiness, but of melancholy reflection, as when I once part with her, I have little chance of ever seeing her again."[3] Yet in the following September Hester left England to join Mahon on the Continent. On the way to Dover she stopped at Walmer to visit her uncle William. "Hester arrived here yesterday on her way to join her travelling friends at Dover," wrote Pitt to his mother's friend, Mrs. Stapleton. "I hope to enjoy the pleasure of her society, at all events till Monday, and perhaps if the winds are contrary, some days longer."[4] Hester was "enchanted with everything here. I have never seen the face of a woman till to-day. Charming!—nothing but pleasant men. But I leave them all on Thursday."[5]

On her return to England in the spring of 1803, Hester was greeted with distressing news. Early in April Lady Chatham had died at Burton Pynsent. They buried her near her husband in Westminster Abbey, and as her grand-daughter gazed down upon her tomb, sad thoughts must have chased each other through the portals of her mind. She had lost a dear friend. She had lost a happy home, for the Burton estate had passed to her elder uncle, Chatham, who had assumed protection of his other niece, the orphaned Harriot Eliot. She had, as it seemed, lost all. Yet this hour

[1] Lady Hester Stanhope to Jackson, April 19th, 1801.
[2] Lady Hester Stanhope to Jackson, Seymour Street, February 13th, 1802.
[3] Lady Hester Stanhope to Jackson, Burton Pynsent, June 13th (1802).
[4] William Pitt to Mrs. Stapleton, Walmer Castle, September 17th, 1802.
[5] Lady Hester Stanhope to Jackson, September 21st, 1802.

of sorrow was for the mourning Hester the precursor of great events, and the next four years were to prove the fullest and the happiest she would ever know.

May 1803. In the great bed in the darkened best bedroom at Camelford House lay Lady Camelford. She was not an old woman for she was only in her sixty-fifth year, nor was she suffering from any bodily infirmity. She was dying of a broken heart.

As she lay in the semi-darkness, her mind travelled back to the days of her youth, and of the tragedy of poor Mary's infatuation for that dreadful Jack Smith. And then her own Tom Pitt had come to woo and claim her as his bride. How wonderful he had been to Mary in her trouble—how generous, gentle, thoughtful and kind. Poor Mary! What a life she had led—surely she had been punished enough for the dreadful folly of her marriage. But she had had her compensations too, for how proud, how intensely and how justly proud she had been of her three fine sons. What splendid men they were and especially, of course, Sidney, a national hero. She too, his aunt, had been proud of him. She remembered so well his return to England in the autumn of 1801. She was at Brighton at the time, and with what pleasure she had written to welcome him home. How she had wished that her rheumatism had not made it impossible for her to go to London to see her nephew. But she had written nevertheless, about his private affairs, lest he might be in want of financial assistance. ". . . I wish you to tell me whether I shall send you an order upon Messrs. Drummond for £200 for your immediate use. The £200 I once named to you are still in my strong closet, certainly never to be applied in the manner your generous nature suggested."[1] How sad it was that dear Mary had not survived to see her son in the hour of his triumph! But she had lived long enough to know of his greatness. Nearly three years ago it was—July 1800—when she had died, and with startling suddenness. Her solicitor was with her, for she was busy settling her affairs. He went to a table for pen, ink and paper, and upon turning round found her dead.[2] Poor Mary —but that was the way to die. Not to linger, oh, never to linger! . . .

And her own life? It had started so fair, and now it was ending so miserably. One blessing she had. Her daughter, dear Annette, ever kind and dutiful, had caused her no concern. She had married, and, thank God! been happy with that grave, stern, cold man, Lord Grenville, who had been so prominent a member of his cousin's ministry. A thousand pities

[1] Lady Camelford to Smith, November 12th, 1801.
[2] Cooke to Smith, London, September 6th, 1800.

they had no children, but it was too late now. . . . Certainly her dear daughter had made him an excellent wife and had greatly helped his career. If only her son had been more like her, or more like his cousin, Sidney. She recalled the words her husband had addressed to him in the paper he had drawn up at Petersham Lodge back in 1781, when he wrote of his marriage "with the most amiable and best of women who has proved as much a blessing to her children, as a comfort to her Husband, that never thinks he can repay the obligation which he owes to her tenderness and affection. The great inheritance she brings is the smallest of the obligations you owe her," he had stated, "may you long enjoy the advantage of her life which every day that opens your reason will render you more sensible of." "The obligations you owe her . . ." thus her dear husband had written; and how had their son repaid her? Oh, how could he harass her so? She recalled the awful affliction from which her dear husband had suffered in his youth. Thank God, it had vanished with the years, and, though he was never robust, had left him unscathed. Could it be that it had passed to their son in this different, but terrible form? Could it be—could it possibly be—that on him too had fallen the scourge that had struck down so many members of the family, the curse of the Pitts?

She recalled her son's lamentable conduct under Captain Vancouver. She recalled the dreadful affray in the harbour of Antigua in 1798. She recalled her son's discreditable attempt to cross to France which had resulted in his examination before the Privy Council. True, he had been discharged from custody, but his career had been ruined. And since then, what had Thomas sought to do? To be forgotten, to sink into blameless seclusion? Far from it. The misguided young man had seen fit to take up his residence in London where he had quickly contrived to acquire an unenviable notoriety for the violence and disorderliness of his conduct. The poor dying woman recalled the lamentable scene in Drury Lane theatre in 1799, when her son had assaulted a perfectly harmless stranger of the name of Humphries, had three times knocked him down. That mischief had cost the assailant £500 in damages. She recalled, too, that disgraceful scene when her son, returning home with his friend, Captain Barrie, at one o'clock in the morning, had seen fit to beat up the watch in Cavendish Square. The guardians, asleep at their posts, had been sharply awakened by a rain of blows on their backs. Two of them, starting up, had been laid prostrate in the gutter; but the others, springing to their rattles, quickly brought a body of colleagues to their aid. After a sharp encounter, the two friends had been escorted to the watch-house, where, we are told, his lordship seemed to find himself perfectly at home. He persisted from folly to folly, no matter what one said . . . useless to try to intervene . . . his affliction . . .

the curse . . . the scourge of the Pitts. . . . But where . . . and when would it end. . . . ? It was to end very soon now in sordid tragedy. But the poor, sorrowing mother was spared the dismal climax . . . she was tired . . . so very tired . . . she would try to sleep awhile . . . she turned her face to the wall. . . .[1]

Soon after Mr. Pitt vacated his official residence in Downing Street, he retired to Walmer Castle. He was at this time much harassed by his financial affairs, which had gradually become more and more involved. As far back as 1797 his friend Rose had estimated Pitt's debts at between £30,000 and £40,000, including two mortgages for £4,000 and £7,000 on Holwood,[2] and some three years later we find him writing to the Bishop of Lincoln with the news that bailiffs threatened the seizure of his furniture in Downing Street for debts of £600 and £400. "Something must be done before Pitt's return to Town. His expenses in the last years were nearly £26,000. I am quite certain Holwood must be parted with."[3]

But in truth the Pitt finances are shrouded in mystery. "There is great perplexity about Pitt's affairs," wrote Rose to the Bishop of Lincoln in the summer of 1801. "If Holwood fetches a good price, the sum of £24,000 will set the matter at rest. Pitt's diamonds have been sold for £680 to pay pressing claims. The unpaid bills now amount to £9,618. Old debts come to £9,600 more. . . . The debt due to Banker (£5,800) cannot surely be a separate one of Pitt's; for I think he could give no security for it. Probably it is a debt contracted jointly with Lord Chatham, the whole of which Pitt may have to pay. Of the last sum, which in his deep distress he borrowed on the security of Holwood, he gave (I know) £1,000 to Lord Chatham."[4] In his reply the bishop throws light on the £25,000 debt which he believed was a sum advanced by Thomas Coutts to Lady Chatham upon Burton Pynsent.[5] We now know, what then was only suspected, that Pitt had had to help his mother, and it seems that the advances on the Somerset estate amounted in all to the huge sum of £11,750. No wonder that these severe drains on his resources rendered him insolvent!

It was evident that something must be done. His friends were anxious to help, but Pitt resolutely declined to accept such assistance.[6] On this failing the great merchants of the City of London renewed their offer made

[1] Lady Camelford died at Camelford House on May 5th, 1803.

[2] Rose, *Diaries and Correspondence*, Vol. I.

[3] Rose to Bishop of Lincoln, October 18th, 1800.

[4] Rose to Bishop of Lincoln, Christchurch, July 21st, 1801.

[5] Bishop of Lincoln, to Rose, July 24th, 1801.

[6] Rose, *Diary*, March 19th, 1801.

in 1787 of the princely sum of £100,000, but this too was refused; and the King's anxiety to relieve the situation by the secret payment to Rose of £30,000 from his Privy Purse was found to be impracticable without the transaction being disclosed to the debtor. Finally the only alternative to bankruptcy was found to be a subscription amongst a few chosen friends and £11,700 was thus raised. With this sum the most pressing claims were met. The sale of Holwood to Sir George Pocock for £15,000[1] further relieved the situation for after the deduction of the two mortgages there was left £4,000 at his disposal. Thus were the worst of Pitt's embarrassments overcome; henceforth, he was able to live in reasonable comfort, though of course with a drastically reduced establishment.

Whilst the retiring Minister's affairs were causing his friends so much anxiety, the new Minister was without difficulty forming his Government. Addington was in a strong position. He was secure in Pitt's support and he was the chosen minister of the Sovereign. Moreover, he was fortunate in public affairs. By the glorious victory of Copenhagen, Denmark was forced to cede from the recently formed Armed Neutrality. In St. Petersburg, a dark deed performed in the still watches of the night removed the new Tsar, the insane Francophil Paul Petrovitch. His successor was eager to come to terms with England and soon amicable relations were restored between Russia and Great Britain. In Egypt, too, the news was favourable. Early in March, a British force of some fourteen thousand men, commanded by Sir Ralph Abercromby, appeared off the coast of Aboukir, routed the opposing French force under General Friant and within a few days had advanced to the heights overlooking Alexandria. At these alarming tidings, the main body of French troops under Menou made haste to march from Cairo, and on March 21st joined battle with the invaders. But the French were repulsed at all quarters and with heavy losses; and within a few weeks General Hutchinson, who had succeeded to the command of the fallen Abercromby, was enabled to besiege one French force under Belliard in Cairo and another under Menou in Alexandria. Belliard capitulated towards the close of June, Menou before the close of August. Thus was Egypt reconquered from the French invaders.

But the country was hungry for peace. So also was the French dictator, who needed a respite to reorganize his forces. Accordingly, on October 1st, 1801, an uneasy truce was signed under which Great Britain agreed to give up to France, Spain and Holland all their possessions recently conquered by her, save only Trinidad and Ceylon, to retire from Elba and to hand back Malta to the Knights of St. John. The French agreed to restore Egypt,

---

[1] He soon afterwards resold the property, and some twenty years later Pitt's house was entirely demolished.

which they had already lost, to the Sultan, and Portugal was preserved entire. The Cape of Good Hope was to be open to the commerce of both contracting parties. Pitt was satisfied with the terms which ". . . though not in every point precisely all that one would wish, are certainly highly creditable, and on the whole very advantageous."[1] And again the next day he wrote to Mulgrave. "I cannot help regretting the Cape of Good Hope, though I know many great authorities do not attach to it the same importance that I do. In other respects I think the treaty very advantageous, and on the whole satisfactory; and the stipulations in favour of your Allies are peculiarly creditable."[2]

But whilst Pitt was approving, Grenville, Windham and Canning were appalled. Grenville was especially indignant at a treaty, "of which we give up everything, everywhere, except Ceylon and Trinidad," as he wrote to Dundas, "even Malta and what is, if possible, more than that—even the Cape of Good Hope;"[3] and he had already made arrangements to retire to Dropmore. "I have been fortunate enough to sell my house in town very advantageously," he reported to his friend, Lord Carysfort, "a circumstance not indifferent to me, as I certainly have not made my fortune in office; and I now look to the expectation of remaining chiefly at Dropmore, with the exception only of an occasional attendance in Parliament on great days.[4] Pitt, regretful at this disagreement with his cousin, proposed a meeting.[5] Grenville consented, but coolly observed that the differences were fundamental and could not be concealed.[6] In November in the House of Commons, Pitt defended the preliminaries of peace. If we could not retain both Malta and Trinidad, he commended Ministers for choosing Trinidad, for the sight of the Union Jack at Malta would have hurt the pride of France. A strange choice and a strange reason for it! He deemed the Cape of Good Hope of first-rate importance, but inferior to Ceylon. Curious reckoning! He deplored our failure to restore the House of Savoy to its capital, Turin, but the chief object of the War, the security of Great Britain, had been achieved. He admitted that the restoration of the French monarchy would have offered a better safeguard for peace; but we had never made a point of restoration, though if the Allies had fulfilled their duties even that might have been achieved. But what of the future? And here Pitt aired some

[1] William Pitt to Long, Park Place, October 1st, 1801.
[2] William Pitt to Mulgrave, Park Place (October 2nd, 1801).
[3] Grenville to Dundas, Dropmore, October 4th, 1801.
[4] Grenville to Carysfort, Camelford House, April 21st, 1801.
[5] William Pitt to Grenville, Holwood, October 5th, 1801.
[6] Grenville to William Pitt, Dropmore, October 6th, 1801.

strange views. "What might be the future object of the chief Consul of France, I know not," he declared. "But if it were to exercise a military deception, I will venture to predict that he will not select this country for the first object of attack. And if we are true to ourselves, we have little to fear from that attack, come when it may."

But though we might appease, we must likewise arm. "But though I do not entertain apprehensions," he continued, "yet I cannot concur with those who think we ought to lay aside all caution; if such policy were adopted, there would indeed be ground for most serious apprehension. . . . Let us try to remove animosity and irritation between the two countries, which . . . will not be done by paying abject court to France. We must depend for security upon ourselves. If, however, the views of France are correspondent with our own, we have every prospect of enjoying a long peace. I see some symptoms that they are, though upon this I have no certain knowledge; but I will never rely upon personal character for the security of my country. I am inclined to hope everything that is good, but I am bound to act as if I found otherwise."[1] Peace in our time! Appeasement and rearmament! Have we not in our own days heard the echo of Pitt's words?

And it was not long before facts belied his hopes. Within six months Bonaparte had perpetrated many breaches of faith against which, unfortunately, the Addington Cabinet made no protest. Some of Pitt's friends tried to elicit from him expressions of disapproval, but having promised Addington his support he deemed himself in honour bound to remain silent. Most of his time was spent at Walmer where he was active in improving the grounds adjoining the Castle and in farming some neighbouring land of which he had recently taken a lease. But at Christmas he visited Cuffnells, Rose's house in the New Forest, where he received a letter from Addington requesting an interview. So it was arranged that early in the new year he should stay a few days with the Prime Minister at White Lodge in Richmond Park. There are several versions of what passed during this visit. All we positively know is that on January 11th Pitt wrote from the Wilderness, Lord Camden's place in Kent, that he was in accord with the Government policy for foreign affairs, but that he had been unable to convince Addington of his financial errors. Nevertheless, he refused to attack the Ministry and he urged moderation on his friends.

Meanwhile, foreign affairs were going from bad to worse, and the report of Sebastiani, Bonaparte's envoy to the Levant, published in the *Moniteur* on January 30th, 1803, was so hostile and threatening as to cause

[1] William Pitt, House of Commons, November 3rd, 1801.

even the supine Addington to apply to Parliament for 10,000 additional seamen and the forming of a militia. On February 10th Lord Whitworth, the British Ambassador to France, had a heated and monologistical interview with the First Consul, for apparently dictators have not changed much in the last hundred and fifty years! In the face of such truculence it is hardly surprising if Grenville should write thus to his cousin, "Unless our present difficulties can be removed by some miracle, for nothing else could do it, I am confident that the public will not any longer bear with the imbecility of the present Government. . . . Whenever this happens, a call will be made upon you such as you cannot decline."[1] During the winter of 1802–3, further correspondence passed between the cousins, but Pitt still refused to take any decisive action.[2] At last in March, 1803, Addington himself determined to sound Pitt again and he despatched to Walmer, Pitt's old friend, Henry Dundas, now Lord Melville, to see what he could do. The jovial Melville moved circumspectly, and it was not until the two friends had enjoyed the mellowing effects of a good dinner and plenty of wine that he ventured to broach the subject about which he had come. The proposal he was commissioned to bring was that Addington and Pitt should both serve under Pitt's brother, Chatham, as Prime Minister. How much of this preposterous proposal Melville was able to voice is uncertain. "Really," exclaimed Pitt to Wilberforce afterwards, "I had not the curiosity to ask what I was to be."[3] But however abruptly Pitt may have stopped Melville that night, he heard him out the next day and to the proposal he returned an uncompromising refusal.[4]

But Addington would not take no for an answer and he promptly despatched Charles Long to the Kentish coast with the message that he was anxious to reinstate Pitt as Prime Minister if it appeared at an interview that their views on certain matters coincided. Pitt readily agreed to meet Addington at Long's house, Bromley Hill, and an appointment was made for April 10th. As Addington's emissary was preparing to leave next day, however, he observed Lord Grenville drive up to Pitt's door, and to this visit the Prime Minister ever afterwards ascribed the ill-success of the negotiations which ensued.[5] At the famous interview, Pitt demanded that

[1] Grenville to William Pitt, Dropmore, November 8th, 1802.

[2] William Pitt to Grenville, Bath, November 16th, 1802; Grenville to William Pitt, Dropmore, November 16th, 1802; William Pitt to Grenville, Bath, December 3rd, 1802; William Pitt to Grenville, Walmer Castle, February 3rd, 1803.

[3] *Life of William Wilberforce by his sons,* Vol. III.

[4] Melville to Addington, Walmer Castle, March 22nd, 1803. This letter was largely dictated by Pitt.

[5] Pellew, *Life of Lord Sidmouth,* Vol. II.

Grenville, Melville, Windham and Spencer should enter the Cabinet with him; and to these terms Addington demurred but promised to consult his colleagues. Ministers at once raised violent objections to Grenville and Windham, expressing the greatest indignation at Pitt's attitude. On these views being reported to him Pitt merely replied that he had said his last word; but he subsequently wrote to Addington to amplify and clarify his point of view, so that his stand should not be misunderstood by the King.[1]

Thus ended these abortive negotiations. On May 18th, war was declared with France, and Pitt hastened to London for the first time for two and a half years to take his seat in parliament. "I have been a long time truant," he declared to the Speaker, as they shook hands. "What does he mean to say of the Ministers?" demanded Malmesbury of Canning. "He means," came the reply, "to fire over the heads of the Government—that is, not to blame or praise them, but to support the war measures and to confine himself to this." The speech he made that day has been generally said to have been one of the greatest of his career.[2] "Never was any speech so cheered, or such incessant and loud applause," records Lord Malmesbury. "It was strong in support of war, but he was silent as to Ministers and his silence, either as to blame or praise, was naturally construed into negative censure."[3] Addington's reply only sufficed to show his mediocrity, but thanks largely to Pitt, the Government triumphed by 398 to 67 votes. Soon after the debate Pitt retired to Walmer once more, where he found a new activity to employ his restless spirit—the raising and drilling of the Cinque Port Volunteers.

Immediately upon the renewal of the war, the First Consul began his energetic measures for the invasion of England, and the vast camp, which sprang up along the heights overlooking Boulogne was frequently encouraged by the presence of the first soldier of France. From Brest to Antwerp, we are told, fifty thousand more troops stood to arms. To effect the hazardous passage of the Channel, a fleet of flat-bottomed boats and other vessels could be seen mustered along the French shore. All was ready or was being

[1] For fuller details of the negotiations see Colchester, *Diary and Correspondence*, Vol. I, and Pellew, *Life of Lord Sidmouth*, Vol. II. Two letters from Lord Redesdale to Pitt (Pitt MSS. Public Record Office) indicate the intense pressure that was being brought to bear on Pitt whilst out of office. Redesdale to Pitt, Albemarle Street, April 16th and 17th, 1803. Redesdale, formerly Sir John Mitford, and now Lord Chancellor of Ireland, had been present at the conference at Bromley.

[2] William Pitt, House of Commons, May 23rd, 1803. Unfortunately, by some error the reporters were excluded from the House with the result that virtually nothing of the great occasion survives.

[3] Malmesbury, *Diaries and Correspondence*, Vol. IV.

feverishly prepared.   Against this peril the whole nation stood firm.   The danger was mortal; all men must jump to arms to meet it.

> "No parleying now.   In Britain is one breath;
> We all are with you now from shore to shore; —
> Ye men of Kent, 'tis victory or death!"

Victory or death, and Kent the forefront of the battle!   And where would the Lord Warden be but preparing for the fray?   On him devolved the main responsibility for organizing resistance along the most easily accessible coast from Ramsgate to Rye, and on July 27th, he sent an official offer to raise 3,000 volunteers in Walmer,[1] a total that was reached in a very short time.   He himself as Colonel-in-Chief could be constantly seen on horseback drilling and reviewing his men.   Further along the coast at near-by Deal, where the commander was Lord Carrington, the same activity could be observed; and the two neighbours worked together in friendly rivalry to obtain recruits.   As Constable of Dover Castle, Pitt summoned a meeting of delegates from the Cinque Ports to discuss matters and he contributed £1,000 which he could ill afford towards expenses.   He also took steps to secure enlistment to the new Army of Reserve.   By the end of 1803, more than 10,000 Kentish men had enrolled as volunteers and more than 1,000 in the Army of Reserve.[2]   Pitt took the whole matter most seriously, and his caustic joke at the expense of a battalion who thought more of privileges than duty is well known.   On reading the conditions of service which stipulated all sorts of limitations to their duties, "except in case of actual invasion," with puck-like glee he penned at the foot of the clause stipulating that volunteers should in no event be sent out of the country the stinging comment "except in case of actual invasion."

We are fortunate in having glimpses of Pitt at this time bequeathed to us by a lively pen.   As we have already seen, Hester Stanhope returned to England this summer to find her grandmother dead and her home gone. What was her future to be?   When all seemed most blank, her fortunes suddenly turned, for her Uncle William offered her a home.   "She was his dead sister's child—his favourite sister's child—and she must want for nothing that it was in his power to give."[3]   Henceforth she presided at his board and did the honours to his guests: and he the greatest man in England. What a triumph for a woman of twenty-seven!

[1] William Pitt to Hobart, July 27th, 1803.

[2] The figures for the whole of Great Britain were 379,000 volunteers and 31,000 recruits for the Army of Reserve.

[3] Cleveland, *Life and Letters of Lady Hester Stanhope.*

Pitt had already shown great kindness to the Stanhope family. Both Griselda and Lucy, on quitting their father's house, had received assistance from him. More recently he had shown a like generosity to the brothers also. In December of the previous year, 1802, Mahon had returned from abroad; since then, he had been a frequent guest at Walmer, and his uncle had provided tangible assistance by bestowing upon him the Lieutenancy of Dover Castle. The younger boys, Charles and James, were also cared for by their uncle and were privileged to come to Walmer whenever they chose. "To express the kindness with which Mr. Pitt welcomed my return and proposed my living with him would be impossible," wrote Hester appreciatively to her friend soon after her installation at Walmer Castle, "one would really suppose that all the obligation was on his side. Here, then, am I, happy to a degree, exactly in the sort of society I most like. There are generally three or four men staying in the house, and we dine eight or ten almost every other day. Military and naval characters are constantly welcome here; women are not, I *suppose*, because they do not form any part of our society. You may guess then, what a pretty fuss they make of me!"[1]

And, indeed, Hester Stanhope suddenly let loose in a bachelor's household must have been somewhat terrifying. She was high-spirited, light-hearted, joyful; she had a gay, caustic wit and a mischievous tongue that was never still. She had fascination and charm, but her talent as a mimic doubtless cost her dear. She could enslave; but she could equally repel the toady or the bore with retorts that were faintly reminiscent of her terrible grandsire of long ago. "Hester, Hester, be careful. What are you saying?" her uncle would cry in alarm as some amusing indiscretion in ringing tones would burst from her at the head of his table. But he would laugh at her wit with the rest of the company, and thoroughly enjoy the flood of warm light that she shed on his household. And under her influence and that of her brothers, Charles and James, he would quite unbend. No longer was he the austere statesman, courted and revered; of a sudden he would become an overgrown schoolboy romping with his family. The story is familiar of the Stanhopes' and young Napier's efforts to blacken the great man's face with burnt cork. In the midst of the play Lords Castlereagh and Liverpool were announced. "Let them wait in the other room," bade Pitt, and he continued the battle, belabouring his assailants with a cushion in glorious fun. And then when numbers had told and his face was already smeared— "Stop, this will do," he cried, "I could easily beat you all . . ." (a chorus of jeers at this, no doubt!) "but we must not keep those Grandees waiting any

[1] Lady Hester Stanhope to Jackson, Walmer Castle, November 19th, 1803.

longer." So a towel and basin were hastily produced and with the aid of Napier and the Stanhopes, Mr. Pitt was set aright. "Now show their lordships in," he ordered as the basin was hurriedly hidden behind the sofa. So the visitors entered—Liverpool melancholy, bending, nervous; Castlereagh a model of grace and strength combined—and there they stood beneath the eyes of the astonished rompers, obsequious before the man whom but a moment since they had been belabouring with all the insolence of fun. And Mr. Pitt? How was he? "His tall, ungainly bony figure seemed to grow to the ceiling, his head was thrown back, his eyes fixed immovably in one position as if reading the heavens, and totally regardless of the bending figures near him. For some time they spoke; he made now and then some short observation, and finally, with an abrupt stiff inclination of the body, but without casting his eyes down, dismissed them. Then turning to us with a laugh, caught up his cushions and renewed the fight."[1]

So let us see Mr. Pitt for a moment through the spectacles of this engaging new inmate of Walmer Castle. He attends a review. "Lord and Lady Chatham have been staying here lately. . . . Lord C. never looked so well in his life as at this moment, nor did anybody ever contrive to appear so much of a prince as he does—his led horses, his carriages, his dress, his star and garter, all of which he shows off in his *quiet* way with wonder effect. I like all this sort of thing, and I admire my uncle most particularly when surrounded with a tribe of military attendants. But what is all this pageantry compared with the unaffected simplicity of real greatness! and how indeed does the former shrink before the latter, even in the estimation of its greatest admirers!"[2] "Mr. Pitt absolutely goes through the fatigue of a drill-sergeant. It is parade after parade, at fifteen or twenty miles distant from each other. I often attend him and it's quite as much (I can assure you) as I am equal to, although I am remarkably well just now. The hard riding I do not mind, but to remain almost *still* so many hours on horseback is an incomprehensible bore, and requires more patience than you can easily imagine. . . ."[3] "We are in almost daily expectation of the coming of the French and Mr. Pitt's regiment is now nearly *perfect* enough to receive them. We have the famous 15th Light Dragoons in our barracks; also the Northampton and Berkshire Militia. The first and last of these I command and have an orderly dragoon whenever I please from the former, and the band of the latter."[4] The Home Guard a century and a half ago!

[1] Napier, *Life of Sir C. J. Napier.*
[2] Lady Hester Stanhope to Haddington, Walmer Castle, November 15th, 1803.
[3] Lady Hester Stanhope to Jackson, Walmer Castle, November 19th, 1803.
[4] Lady Hester Stanhope to Jackson, Walmer Castle, January 14th, 1804.

Pitt himself was pleased with his work. ". . . I wish the arrangements for defence were as forward everywhere else as they are in Hythe Bay under General Moore. We begin now to have no other fear in that quarter than that the enemy will not give us the opportunity of putting our preparations to the proof, and will select some other point which we should not be in reach of in the first instance."[1] Pitt was constantly singing the praises of General John Moore, who was a frequent guest at the Castle. Hester therefore had ample opportunity to become acquainted with him. She observed his tall and graceful person, his handsome, clear-cut features, and his winning address. She observed his soldierly bearing, his efficiency, and his old-world charm. She observed the respect with which her uncle held him, how he always spoke of the General with admiration, and how, on receiving a note from him at Deal, he would show it to the company, pointing out the grace and felicity of its style. She observed, and she soon decided that she liked very much this friend of her family. *Friend* of her family . . . that set her thinking awhile. . . .

Hester had not long been installed at Walmer before young Mahon announced his engagement to a daughter of Pitt's neighbour, Lord Carrington. This gave him a chance to write asking for his father's blessing.[2] Stanhope replied immediately; it was a kind letter, but there was one ominous passage. "Your close connection with Mr. Pitt and certain other persons of his description will certainly prevent our being reconciled."[3] The wedding duly took place on November 19th, being solemnized in the dining-room of Deal Castle, and Pitt, as a friend of one and near connection of the other family, was present at the ceremony.

Meanwhile, public affairs were going from bad to worse, and as the peril of invasion grew, lack of confidence in Addington's ministry increased. Lord Grenville was anxious for a junction of himself with his cousin and Fox to overturn the Government, but Pitt would not hear of it and purposely delayed his return to London.[4] And then, just as matters looked like coming to a head everything was thrown into confusion by the renewed mental instability of the King. For two days he was thought to be dying; for a week he was completely deranged, and there was talk of a regency again. The Prince of Wales observed with his usual taste that his father's illness *must* last for several months, and when this remark was reported by Malmes-

---

[1] William Pitt to Rose, October 18th, 1803.

[2] Mahon to Stanhope, 52 Manchester Street, June 10th, 1803.

[3] Stanhope to Mahon, June 10th, 1803.

[4] Grenville to William Pitt, South Audley Street, January 31st, 1804. The original is docketed in Pitt's hand as "answered" though no copy of the reply is extant. It was, however, most certainly in the negative.

bury to Pitt, he exclaimed from Shakespeare: "Thy wish was father, Harry, to that thought."[1] The usual series of intrigues ensued and in view of these disgraceful plottings at a time of national danger, Pitt suddenly changed his plans and announced to Malmesbury that, whilst he would not unite with the Grenville party to overthrow Addington, yet he would not refuse to take office if the Minister would resign. But the King was slowly recovering, and when towards the end of April he was convalescent, Pitt wrote to him of his intention to declare in Parliament his dissatisfaction with the Ministry.[2] Two days later he attacked the Government in the House of Commons.[3] At this onslaught, Addington, now thoroughly alarmed, formally resigned and advised the King to confer with Pitt. To George III's appeal for a plan for a new Government, Pitt replied in a lengthy letter in which he strove to set forth the arguments in favour of a combined Government and required the royal sanction to confer with Fox and Grenville.[4] This not unnaturally irritated the King, who replied demanding a renewed pledge against Catholic Emancipation.[5] Pitt thereupon declared his adherence to the pledge of 1801 and requested an audience.[6]

On the following day, accordingly, the retired statesman had his first audience for over three years. The dire peril of the country and the total inability of the Ministry to grapple with the emergency had brought him to the fore. Though his health had for some time been uncertain, he must emerge from his retirement to take in her hour of danger the helm of state.

On the evening of March 6th, 1804, there was seated at one of the tables at the Prince of Wales's Coffee House in Oxford Street a man of the name of Best, known to be one of the deadliest pistol shots in England. Up to him there suddenly stalked a young man, obviously in a great passion, who was perfectly well known to him. "I find, sir," he burst forth, "that you have spoken of me in the most unwarrantable terms," and on Best assuring him that he did not know what he was talking about, he was

[1] Malmesbury, *Diaries and Correspondence*, Vol. IV.

[2] William Pitt to George III, York Place, April 21st, 1803. Endorsed thus on the copy: "Transmitted through the Lord Chancellor on Sunday April 22nd, and delivered by him to the King on Friday 27th." For fuller details see *Secret Correspondence connected with Mr. Pitt's return to office in 1804*, compiled from the Melville MSS. at Melville Castle and edited by Lord Mahon.

[3] William Pitt, House of Commons, April 23rd, 1803.

[4] William Pitt to Lord Chancellor (to be laid before the King), York Place, May 2nd, 1804.

[5] George III to William Pitt, Queen's Palace, May 5th, 1804.

[6] William Pitt to George III, York Place, Sunday, May 6th, 1804.

promptly declared to be "a scoundrel, a liar and a ruffian." The attacker was Lord Camelford, and it subsequently transpired that a certain Mrs. Simmons, who at one time had been Best's mistress, had reported that Best had said to her something to Camelford's prejudice. On hearing this, Best sent Lord Camelford the most positive assurances that the information he had been given was entirely untrue, and that as he had acted hastily under a false impression, he would be satisfied by the retraction of the expressions used. This Camelford absolutely refused. It was clear where things were heading, and an information was duly lodged at Marlborough Street. But the police officers were tardy and until almost two o'clock the following morning they took no measures to prevent the meeting. Then they posted some men at Camelford's door; but it was too late. Between one and two o'clock he had quitted his lodgings so as to avoid their attentions; but not before he had added a declaration to his Will which shows his fundamentally noble disposition. He frankly admitted being the aggressor in the quarrel, and continued, ". . . should I, therefore lose my life in a con-test of my own seeking, I most solemnly forbid any of my friends or rela-tions, let them be of whatsoever description they may, from instituting any vexatious proceedings against my antagonist; and should, notwithstanding the above declaration on my part, the laws of the land be put in force against him, I desire that this part of my Will may be made known to the King, in order that his royal heart may be moved to extend his mercy towards him."

Early that morning, Camelford and Best again met at the coffee-house, where the latter once more begged his friend to retract. "Camelford," he said, "we have been friends, and I know the unsuspecting generosity of your nature. Upon my honour, you have been imposed upon by a strumpet. Do not insist on expressions under which one of us must fall." But though he knew himself in the wrong, Camelford was too obstinate to agree. "Best, this is child's play," was his answer, "the thing must go on."

There was nothing more to be said. The antagonists met near Holland House at about eight o'clock the same morning. They put up their horses at the "Horse and Groom" and then walked into the fields behind Holland House, where Melbury Road now runs. When all was ready, Camelford fired and missed. Then after a moment's pause, his opponent fired with telling effect. Best and the seconds at once rushed to the wounded man. "Best, I am a dead man," he exclaimed, "but I freely forgive you." But the sound of shots had been heard and already Lord Holland's gardeners were approaching. It was urgently necessary, therefore, for Best and his seconds to seek safety in flight. Lord Camelford was moved to Little

Boconnoc

ANNE PITT, Lady Grenville, daughter of Thomas Pitt, Lord Camelford
Hoppner

Holland House, and urgent messages were sent for medical assistance and for the relatives. The first relative to arrive was William Cockburne, Camelford's cousin, who subsequently wrote an account of his death;[1] he now sent messages to the Buckinghams at Stowe and the Grenvilles at Dropmore. Lord and Lady Grenville hastened to the bedside, but Lady Grenville, who was in great distress, was not allowed to see her brother. Other members of the Pitt family do not appear to have been much moved by the disaster, though Hester Stanhope had some cryptic comments to make. ". . . Lord Camelford has been shot in a duel and there is no chance of his recovering," she wrote to her friend, Jackson. "You know my opinion of him, I believe, therefore can judge if I am not likely to lament his untimely end. He had vices, but also great virtues, but they were not known to the world at large. . . ."[2] There was, as Lady Hester says, not the slightest hope of his recovery. He lingered on from Thursday to Saturday evening, when, at about half-past eight, he died.

By a codicil to his Will, Camelford desired to be buried in an indicated spot within the Canton of Berne, Switzerland, which he had loved as a child; and in a letter to his cousin, Sir Sidney Smith, he requested him to arrange for his body to be removed as soon as possible and to be buried at a special site where three trees grew overlooking the lake of St. Pierre. As the renewal of war with France made this temporarily impossible, the body was embalmed, packed in a long basket and lodged in the crypt of St. Anne's Church, Soho. When the war was ended, the body could not be found, nor has it ever been recovered. Thus ignominiously perished Thomas Pitt, second Lord Camelford, head of the House of Pitt.[3]

"Never in any conversation I have had with him in my life has he so baffled me." Thus Pitt greeted the Lord Chancellor after his three hours' audience with the King on May 7th, 1804. Yet he had been surprisingly

[1] Cockburne, "An authentic account of the late unfortunate Death of Lord Camelford, with an extract from his lordship's will and some remarks on his character."

[2] Lady Hester Stanhope to Jackson, York Place, March 8th, 1804. In her *Memoirs*, written in old age, she speaks well of him.

[3] Camelford was unmarried; the peerage therefore became extinct. By his Will he left practically the whole of his estate to his sister, Lady Grenville, who subsequently bequeathed the property to her late husband's nephew, a member of the Fortescue family. Accordingly, at her death in 1864, Lord Grenville's property of Dropmore and the Pitt Cornish estate of Boconnoc passed to the Fortescues. The former has recently been sold; the latter is still in Fortescue hands. The pair of pistols used by Lord Camelford in the duel are still preserved at Boconnoc.

successful. George had been most gracious[1] and Pitt managed to prevail on him to admit Lord Grenville and his followers to the new Ministry. Only upon Fox was there an absolute veto. Accordingly, as soon as he had left Buckingham House Pitt sent Canning to Grenville and Lord Granville Leveson Gower to Fox to acquaint them with what had passed. The latter, sated with the joys of retirement at Ann's Hill, took the honourable course of renouncing all claims; the former received his cousin coldly, doubted if he or his followers would join without Fox, but promised to consult his friends. A meeting was accordingly held at Camelford House, since the recent tragedy near Holland House the property of Lady Grenville, when the Grenvillites agreed that in the face of Fox's exclusion they could not join the new Government, and Grenville was requested to write to Pitt to that effect.[2] In face of this, the Cabinet was inevitably a weak one, and Pitt was most indignant at the refusal of his kinsman's aid. "I will teach that proud man," he is supposed to have exclaimed, "that in the service and with the confidence of the King, I can do without him, though my health is such that it may cost me my life."

But a further matter added to his indignation: unfortunately, Lord Grenville's letter of May 8th though commencing "My dear Pitt," and concluding "Most affectionately yours," was published in the Press and became the manifesto of the Opposition. This was a blow which Pitt could not parry without disclosing to the public the personal feelings of the King, and though there is nothing to show that Lord Grenville was himself responsible, Pitt could never forgive him. Indeed, we may be sure that in fact Grenville did not desire any breach with his cousin. At about this time he published a small volume containing the series of letters which the great Lord Chatham had addressed in 1754 and the following years to his nephew Thomas Pitt, afterwards the first Lord Camelford, to guide and direct him in his studies.[3] On Lady Camelford's death these letters had passed to her son-in-law. This volume, which appeared in May 1804, contained a flattering prefix addressed to Pitt. Lord Grenville accompanied the personal copy which he sent to his relative with a touching note. "My dear Pitt," he wrote, "I send you at last the letters which you saw in manuscript last summer. . . . I know there is no fear of your thinking that political differences (be they more or less) will alter in my mind a friendship of more than twenty years' standing; but it is satisfactory to be able to

[1] Rose, *Diaries and Correspondence*, Vol. II.

[2] Grenville to William Pitt, May 8th, 1804. The Whigs met at Carlton House and voted unanimously against taking office without Fox.

[3] Extracts from some of these letters appear earlier in this work.

testify this feeling publicly."[1] To this letter, no answer seems to have been returned, and Grenville was deeply hurt.

Whilst Pitt was Cabinet-making and Grenville and his party were sulking in their tents, the First Consul was showing ever-increasing hostility to England. His invasion armada was still assembled and maintained along the French coast; though the less far-seeing seemed to think the danger passed. "Can anything equal the ridicule of Pitt," wrote Grenville bitterly, "riding about from Downing Street to Wimbledon, and from Wimbledon to Coxheath to inspect military carriages, impregnable batteries and Lord Chatham's reviews? Can he possibly be serious in expecting Bonaparte now? Fifty more questions one might ask, if any part of his conduct admitted of any discussion on the ordinary principles of reason and common sense."[2] Yet, in spite of Grenville's sneer, the danger was real, and no minister could afford to ignore it. Hitherto, in the renewed struggle with France we had stood alone—England once more a solitary barrier against tyranny and oppression, but, as with the great tyrant of our own day, the French dictator overreached himself. On May 18th with the greatest possible solemnity and amid a vast concourse of spectators, the First Consul was proclaimed Sovereign of the French with the title of Emperor. Nothing was more calculated to rouse the hereditary rulers of Europe than this arrogant assumption of regal powers by a presumptuous upstart, and in these circumstances the efforts for peace of Livingston, the anti-British United States Minister to France, were from the first doomed.

Whilst the Emperor of the French was showing his increased hostility to England, whilst Fox and the Grenvillites stood aloof, whilst the Prime Minister strove to instil martial enthusiasm into the volunteers, efforts were seriously hampered by the eccentricities and the mental aberrations of the Sovereign. King George, never completely recovered from the worst effects of his recent illness, was now more fussy, more irritable, more incoherent than ever. He displayed at this time a marked and most inconvenient preference for the company of servants. He made capricious changes in the royal household, dismissing the Queen's favourite coachman, converting grooms to footmen and footmen to grooms to the distraction of the Court. He became convinced that the French would land, not in Kent or Essex as was generally expected, but in Dorset, and he planned the assembly of a large military force in that country to meet the expected blow; from this aberration he was only with difficulty dissuaded by the arguments of the Duke of York. At the same time there were the usual

[1] Grenville to Pitt, Camelford House, May 16th, 1804.

[2] Grenville to Buckingham, August 25th, 1804.

hostilities between the King and the Prince of Wales, and the wayward conduct of the Princess of Wales to contend with. Pitt indeed did his utmost to bring father and son together, but the only result of his efforts was a fruitless interview between them. Indeed, when we think of the distractions that Pitt had to suffer at this time—the dangers from abroad, the confusion at home, and a weak Cabinet to combat all these difficulties—need we wonder at the words of Lady Hester Stanhope thus describing in her Lebanon fastness many years later a day in the life of the Minister? "When I think of the ingratitude of the English nation to Mr. Pitt," she exclaimed, "for all his personal sacrifice and disinterestedness, for his life wasted in the service of his country!"—and here the proud recluse burst into tears. "People little know what he had to do. Up at eight in the morning, with people enough to see for a week; obliged to talk all the time he was at breakfast, and receiving first one, then another, until four o'clock; then eating a mutton-chop, hurrying off to the House, and there badgered and compelled to speak and waste his lungs until two or three in the morning!—who could stand it? After this, treated as he was, and having eaten nothing, in a manner of speaking, all day, he would sup with Dundas, Huskisson, Rose, Mr. Long, and such persons, and then go to bed to get three or four hours' sleep, and to renew the same thing the next day, the next and the next." At Walmer things were easier, and his health improved; but in London during the sitting of parliament, what a life was his: "Roused from his sleep (for he was a good sleeper) with a despatch from Lord Melville;—then down to Windsor; then if he had half-an-hour to spare, trying to swallow something;—Mr. Adams with a paper, Mr. Long with another; then Mr. Rose: then with a little bottle of cordial confection in his pocket, off to the House until three or four in the morning; then home to a hot supper for two or three hours more, to talk over what was to be done next day: and wine and wine! Scarcely up next morning, when tat-tat-tat—twenty or thirty people one after another, and the horses walking before the door from two till sunset, waiting for him. It was enough to kill a man—it was murder!"[1]

Amidst all these difficulties, at home and abroad, in December 1804 Pitt's Cabinet suffered the loss of Lord Harrowby, who met with an accident. Though Harrowby was no genius, it was not easy to fill his place. So Pitt determined if possible on reinforcing the ranks of his government by a reconciliation with Addington. A meeting between the two old friends was soon arranged at Hawkesbury's residence, Coombe Wood, near Richmond Park. "I rejoice to take you by the hand again,"

---

[1] *Memoirs of Lady Hester Stanhope as related to her Physician*, Vol. II.

exclaimed Pitt to Addington on entering; whereupon a talk of three hours' duration ensued. As a result a thorough reconciliation was effected, and Addington agreed to accept a peerage and to take the Presidency of the Council in place of the ailing Portland. Pitt and his brother, Chatham, were thoroughly satisfied, but men like Rose, Camden and Canning were disgusted, and the last-named went so far as to write a long and bitter letter of protest to Lady Hester Stanhope.[1]

Whilst these events were happening at home, Pitt was anxiously pursuing his diplomatic negotiations. For some time now, England had stood alone against all the malice and the might of imperial France. He was determined that, if he could help it she should stand alone no longer. Of recent months, mainly through the bravado of Napoleon, grave differences had broken out between the Courts of Paris and of St. Petersburg, and Pitt was quick to seize the advantage. As a result, a treaty between England and Russia was concluded, under which the two powers agreed to endeavour to form a general league of the Great Powers of Europe and to collect upon the Continent a force of half a million men. The Emperor Francis and Sweden both acceded to the Treaty, and thus under Pitt's guidance the third Coalition was formed against revolutionary France.

But even while the negotiations for this alliance were afoot, the restless Napoleon was making history. On May 26th in solemn state in the great Cathedral of Milan, he was crowned King of Italy. No sooner had he committed that offence than he committed two others. He annexed to France the Republic of Genoa, and he granted to his sister, the Princess Elisa Baciocchi, the fief of Lucca. What more evidence did men require of the restless, the limitless ambition of this terrible man? Yet, with all his ambitions beyond the Alps, Napoleon still cast envious eyes on these island shores. On the evening of July 8th he left Turin; on the morning of the 11th he reached Fontainebleau. A month later, back in his camp at Boulogne, he was as intent as ever on scaling the opposite cliffs. "The English do not know what is coming to them," he wrote grimly to Dacrès, his Minister of Marine. "If we can but be masters of the passage for twelve hours, England will have ceased to be."[2] Twelve hours! They were not destined to be masters for twelve minutes! This is no place for telling how that dreadful danger was faced and overcome. The machinations of Villeneuve were matched by the genius of Nelson. Before he sailed the great Admiral had an interview with Pitt in Downing Street: it was the only time they ever met. "Mr. Pitt paid me a compliment, which I believe he would not have paid to a Prince of the Blood," reported Nelson with

[1] Canning to Lady Hester Stanhope, South Hill, January 1st, 1805.
[2] Emperor Napoleon to Dacrès, August 4th, 1805.

pardonable pride. "When I rose to go, he left the room with me and attended me to the carriage." As these two great men strode through the ante-room they passed a waiting visitor, Sir Arthur Wellesley, just back from India. So for a brief moment were gathered together in one room three of the foremost figures in English history—the greatest statesman, the greatest seaman of the day, and the future hero of Waterloo.

Meanwhile, the Austrian forces under the command of General Mack, thinking that the French Emperor had mind only for the projected invasion of England, had passed the River Inn and advanced into Bavaria. But unbeknown to Mack, Napoleon had suddenly reversed his plans. On September 2nd, the Emperor had left Boulogne. After a short wait in Paris on the 24th, he left the Tuileries and two days later reached Strasburg. Mack had taken up a strong position at Ulm, commanding the course of the Danube, so as to confront the enemy as he advanced from the Rhine. But the French commander, with the skill of the genius, by a series of forced marches, took him in the rear, cutting off the Austrians from their lines of communication. Confusion reigned; ruin ensued. Mack's troops broke into two bodies; one fell back in the direction of the Tyrol, the other in that of Bohemia. It was evident that all was lost, and in a few days he had no alternative to unconditional surrender. This was perhaps the heaviest reverse that ever befell the Imperial House of Germany.

The tidings of the disaster trickled through to London, first as unauthenticated rumour. On November 2nd, Lord Malmesbury, sitting next to Pitt at a dinner party, mentioned the report he had heard. "Don't believe a word of it; it is all fiction," replied Pitt testily and in a voice loud enough to be heard by all the company. But next day, Sunday, about one o'clock the Prime Minister and Lord Mulgrave came to Lord Malmesbury's house in Spring Gardens with a Dutch newspaper giving a full account of the capitulation, and begged him to translate it for them. "I observed but too clearly the effect it had on Pitt, though he did his utmost to conceal it," recorded Malmesbury. "This was the last time I saw him. The visit has left an indelible impression on my mind as his manner and look were not his own, and gave me, in spite of myself, a foreboding of the loss with which we were threatened."[1] Four days later the gloomy tidings of this disaster were swiftly followed by news of a very different order. The maritime might of France had been shattered off Cape Trafalgar and the glorious commander had fallen in the fray. Never throughout the length and breadth of the land was joy so mingled with sorrow, and even Pitt was

[1] Malmesbury, *Diaries and Correspondence*, Vol. II.

so moved by conflicting emotions that, though the soundest of sleepers, he could not rest.

On November 9th the Prime Minister attended the Lord Mayor's Banquet. When he rose to respond to the host who had proposed his health as "the Saviour of Europe," it was observed that he seemed much exhausted. But his reply, though perhaps the shortest speech in history, has become immortal. It opened softly. "I return you many thanks for the honour you have done me"; he said, "but Europe is not saved by any single man." Then in ringing vibrant tones reminiscent of happier days, "England has saved herself by her exertions, and will, as I trust, save Europe by her example." That was all; and as the magic words echoed and re-echoed amid the ancient rafters of Guildhall, they were wafted in ever-gathering *crescendo* around the world.

CHAPTER II

Uncle and Niece

WHILST Napoleon was achieving fresh successes over the Russians and Austrians, culminating in the overwhelming victory of Austerlitz, Mr. Pitt was drinking the waters of Bath and endeavouring to recruit his failing strength. Early in the new year, however, he set out for London, which he was anxious to reach for the meeting of Parliament on January 21st, 1806. Yet he was very ill, and on his arrival at Bowling Green House, the villa on Putney Heath which he had leased some eighteen months previously, Hester Stanhope, who welcomed him at the door, was shocked at the change she saw in him. She helped the weary invalid from the coach, and as he passed through the hall towards the stairs he spied a map of Europe hanging on the wall. He paused to gaze wistfully upon it; then he turned to those at his side. "Roll up that map," he ordered, "it will not be wanted these ten years."[1]

On the morrow—Sunday, January 12th—Pitt wrote to Lord Wellesley to welcome him home from India and to bid him come to Putney. "I am recovering rather slowly from a series of stomach complaints, followed

---

[1] Another version of this familiar story places the scene of it as Shockerwick House, near Bath, where Pitt, on a visit of inspection to the picture gallery, is supposed to be gazing at Gainsborough's portrait of the actor, Quin, and to be recalling Churchill's lines:

> Nature, in spite of all his skill, crept in—
> Horatio, Dorax, Falstaff—still 'twas Quin.

Suddenly a courier, splashed with mud, darts in with despatches. Pitt opens them and reads hurriedly. He turns pale, calls for brandy and a map, then almost in a faint he is helped to his carriage uttering the historic phrase. Peach, *Historic Houses in Bath and their Associations*. In *The Dynasts* Thomas Hardy places the incident in the week after Austerlitz (*The Dynasts*, I, Act vi, Sc. 7), but this is evidently wrong. There can be no certainty as to when Pitt actually uttered the words, but I have preferred to follow Lord Stanhope and to place them at the moment of his return to Bowling Green House. Against the Bath theory is the fact, pointed out by Dr. Holland Rose, that the news of Austerlitz did not come as one sudden overwhelming shock; it filtered through by degrees. Holland Rose, *William Pitt and the Great War*. Professor Barnes doubts if the famous words ever were really uttered by Pitt at all. Barnes, *George III and William Pitt, 1783–1806*. But if that were so, would not the story have died long ago?

by severe attacks of gout," he wrote, "but I believe I am now in the way of real amendment."[1]   On the following morning he was well enough to take an airing in his coach, but later the same day he was much agitated by a visit from two of his principal colleagues, Hawkesbury and Castlereagh, who came to consult him on the question of recalling the British troops sent as reinforcements to the north of Germany.   Nevertheless, the next day Pitt was once more able to go out in his carriage.   But this was his last airing; he never left the house again.   In the afternoon his brother called. Later Wellesley came for what was to prove a last farewell and the patient fainted before his friend had left the room.   The visitor retired with mournful foreboding, knowing full well that the end was near.   ". . . I warned Lord Grenville of Mr. Pitt's approaching death.   He received the fatal intelligence with the utmost feeling in an agony of tears and immediately determined that all hostility in Parliament should be suspended." Poor Grenville, poor, grave, proud, obstinate Grenville—Grenville with the mask off—Grenville in an agony of tears!

In truth Pitt was sinking fast.   He was very weak and faint from want of nourishment, and his pulse was far too high.   Yet his thoughts were for others, and he made signs for paper and ink, to pen his last requests; but his strength was insufficient and he only succeeded in tracing strokes which could not be deciphered.   His thoughts were with his nieces too, and he dictated to Bishop Tomline, "I wish £1,000 or £1,200 a year to be given to my nieces if the public should think my long services deserving of it; but," he added modestly, "I do not presume to think I have earned it." His favourite, Hester, sought to see him at this time, but Farquhar was anxious to spare the invalid the agony of parting.   During his temporary absence, however, she slipped into his bedroom, there to receive her uncle's blessing and a fond farewell.   "Dear Soul, I know she loves me," muttered the dying man to her brother James shortly after she had left him.   "Where is Hester?" he kept murmuring.   "Where is Hester?   Is Hester gone?"

To Bishop Tomline, who besought him to prepare his mind to receive the Sacrament, he excused himself, pleading that he lacked the necessary strength.   Tomline then begged to be allowed to pray with him.   To this he readily agreed, though he had small hopes of its efficacy for one who had neglected prayer so long.   During the night of January 22–23rd the cares of State seemed to press upon him.   To James Stanhope, who seldom left his side, he spoke often of a private letter he was expecting from Lord Harrowby, and enquired from time to time the direction of the wind. "East!   Ah, that will do," he muttered, answering himself.   "That will do,

[1] William Pitt to Wellesley, Putney Hill, Sunday, January 12th, 1806.

that will bring him quick." At times he fell into conversation with the
messenger, at times he attended a debate in the House of Commons. "Hear,
Hear! Hear, Hear!" he gasped. As the new day was born, the twenty-
fifth anniversary of his entry into parliament, there were heard for the first
time the fatal rattles in his throat. Now he was calm and sleep enfolded
him. Now he moaned and cried, "O dear! O Lord!" But he lingered
on, and only towards half-past two was it observed that his extremities were
growing cold. Then at last to James Stanhope there came with strange
clearness in the stillness of the night, the whispered words, "Oh, my country! How I leave my country."[1] From that time forth he never spoke or
moved: and so he lay until, some three hours before the dawn, his spirit
fled in a long-drawn sigh.

A month later, in the presence of a great company, he was borne to
his last resting-place and with great pomp his coffin was lowered into the
vault in full view of the effigy of his illustrious sire. "It seemed," said
Wilberforce, "as though his statue were looking down with consternation
into the grave which was opened for his favourite son, the last perpetuator
of the name."[2] "What grave contains such a father and such a son?" wrote
Wellesley many years later. "What sepulchre embosoms the remains of
so much human excellence and glory?"[3] And to a sorrowing nation the
Border Minstrel sang his mournful lay:

> "Now is the stately column broke
> The Beacon light is quench'd in smoke,
> The trumpet's silver sound is still
> The warder silent on the hill."[4]

"Be my fate what it may," wrote the bereaved Hester, "I am prepared
to meet the worst, conscious that I have already received from Providence
many blessings I do not deserve, therefore I have no right to expect more.
. . . You have no idea of the consolation it is to me that I received the
last blessing of that beloved angel; and that, when forbid to see him (because
it was thought he would not know me) I took my own way, and dis-
obeyed unnatural commands. My voice recalled his scattered senses, and
he was perfectly collected the whole time I was with him; and when I
departed, and though his ideas became confused, he continued to name

---

[1] Disraeli's oft-told story about Bellamy's pork pies and Pitt's last words, seems to
have no authenticity.
[2] *Life of William Wilberforce*, by his sons, Vol. III.
[3] Wellesley to ——?, November 22nd, 1836.
[4] Scott, *Marmion*.

me with affection. This proud pre-eminence over the rest of the world will compensate me for many future sorrows which his loss must entail upon us."[1] And indeed her prospects were gloomy. Hitherto courted and fawned upon by all as the niece and hostess of the greatest man in England, she was now no longer a person of the first importance. Homeless and adrift, she was for a time received into the house of her kinsman, Lord Harrington; but soon afterwards when, in accordance with her uncle's dying wish, Parliament granted her a pension of £1,200 a year,[2] she took a house in Montagu Square, there to make a home for her two younger brothers. But fond as she was of them, these arrangements did not bring happiness. The London of Montagu Square seemed far removed from the London of Downing Street; the friends of the young Stanhopes very different from the friends of William Pitt. She was, in the words of her niece and biographer, "a dethroned princess. She had been accustomed to queen it in society, to be courted, consulted, and applauded, and could not endure to find herself now of little or no account."[3] The result of this state of mind was inevitable. She became irritable, suspicious, quick-tempered, unbearable; she alienated her best friends, those very persons most anxious to help in her hour of need. With Lord Mahon she had definitely quarrelled because of his alleged ingratitude for all she had done for him. With her Uncle Chatham she was soon on bad terms; and to her cousin Grenville she would scarcely speak. With such forthrightness, such autocratic manners, such intolerance, there was no room for compromise, no room for concessions. Poor Hester Stanhope was her own worst enemy, and none could help her in her hour of sorrow.

In more normal circumstances one so situated might turn to her father for help, but no forgiveness could be expected from the dread Lord of Chevening, and never again was she destined to darken his doors. Moreover, Lord Stanhope's troubles were accumulating fast. For some years there had been disagreements between him and his eldest son about the management of the family estates, and early in 1808 these came before the Courts. It is unnecessary to follow the unhappy lawsuit of *Mahon* v. *Stanhope* through all the labyrinths of the Court of Chancery. Suffice it to say that the decision of the Master of the Rolls in favour of the son, was a bitter pill for the father, a humiliation under which he smarted to his dying day.[4]

[1] Lady Hester Stanhope to Adams, South Hill, January 26th, 1806.

[2] Pensions of £600 a year were at the same time voted to Lord Stanhope's other daughters, Lady Griselda Tekell and Lady Lucy Taylor.

[3] Cleveland, *Life and Letters of Lady Hester Stanhope*.

[4] For details of this litigation, see Stanhope & Gooch, *Life of Charles, 3rd Earl Stanhope*.

Furthermore, at some uncertain date about this time, the last legitimate inmate left Chevening for ever. The much tried Louisa Stanhope had contrived to put up with her wayward lord's passions and with the family upheavals, but the installation of a rival in the house proved too much for her forbearance. It seems that about 1805 or 1806 a certain Mrs. Walburgh Lackner, a foreign music teacher of whom little is known, had become practically a resident at Chevening. Her presence could hardly have been congenial to Lady Stanhope, but it is probable that she countenanced it for a time. Eventually, however, she left her husband's roof, never to return. Thenceforth Louisa divided her time between Tunbridge Wells and London, though after Charles Stanhope's death she was a frequent visitor to the family home. Thus the gifted, imperious lord of Chevening had driven the whole of his family from his doors. Now he was left, an ageing, sorrowing man with his thoughts, his mistress and his devoted mother who loved him still.

It can thus be seen that Chevening was no place for Hester Stanhope. Yet amid all the sadness and disappointment of these times, there was still one joy left in her life, and that joy was her uncle's friend, General Moore. It has often been denied that Lady Hester and Sir John Moore[1] were betrothed, but there were strong rumours at the time that there was an understanding, if not an engagement, and Hester's statement in Syria years later that Moore was the man she was to have married is certainly evidence, if of nothing more, of her own willingness for the union. To General Moore, appointed Commander-in-Chief in Portugal, Charles Stanhope went out as aide-de-camp. "Charles's Regiment was in the number of those named to remain in Portugal under Sir Henry Buzzard," wrote Moore to Hester, "this was breaking his heart, and so was it mine—but I have at last, contrived an arrangement, in concert with Sir Henry, who is the most liberal of men, to take the 50th. with me, and now all is well. The regiments are already marching. His will move in a few days, and as soon as I have seen everything in train here, I shall push on, and get to their head. Pray for good weather; if it rains the torrents will swell, and be impassable, and I shall be accounted a bungler . . . I wish you were here with us. The climate now is charming; we should give you riding enough, and in your red habit, à l'Amazone, you would animate and do us all much good."[2] Pleasant memories of joyful days at Walmer! Hester à l'Amazone—a happy thought!"

Before long Hester is asking Moore to take her other brother. "I shall

---

[1] Moore had been made a Knight of the Bath in 1804.

[2] Moore to Lady Hester Stanhope, Lisbon, October 16th, 1808.

be very glad to receive James if he wishes to come to me as an extra aide-de-camp," he replies, "though I have already too many, and am, or shall be obliged to take a young Fitz Clarence. But I have a sincere regard for James, and besides, can refuse you nothing. . . ." Then he strikes an ominous note, "He will, however, come too late; I shall already be beaten. I am within four marches of the French, with only a third of my force, and as the Spaniards have been dispersed in all quarters, my junction with the other two-thirds is very precarious, and when we do join we shall be very inferior to the enemy."[1] "Charles is not yet arrived," he wrote three days later. "His was one of the last regiments that left Lisbon, and was not intended to join us, if I, in compassion to his melancholy countenance, had not found a pretext." Then he sounds a note of warning. "We are in a scrape, but I hope we shall have spirit to get out of it; you must, however, be prepared to hear bad news. . . ." And he concludes his letter with these memorable words: "Farewell, my dear Lady Hester. If I extricate myself and those with me from our present difficulties, and if I can beat the French, I shall return to you with satisfaction, but if not, it will be better I shall never quit Spain."[2]

The immediate effect of the death of Pitt was the dissolution of the Government. The King turned first to Hawkesbury and then to Grenville who promptly made it plain that in his view no Government could survive that did not include the formidable figure of Charles Fox. "I thought so, and meant it so," was the King's only comment. Thus given a free hand, the new Minister encountered little difficulty in forming the Ministry that came to be known as "All the Talents." But though dubbed with this flattering title, the new Government was not destined long to survive; yet even its short life is honourably remembered for one redeeming measure, the abolition of the slave trade. Its weakness, however, was much increased in September 1806 by the death of Fox, whose remains were with great pomp interred near those of that illustrious rival who had preceded him by so short a time across the Styx.

But whilst Grenville and his Cabinet were struggling with affairs at home, events were moving rapidly on the Continent. In June 1806 Napoleon converted the Batavian Republic into the Kingdom of Holland, the crown of which he placed upon the brow of his brother, Louis. In July was formed the Confederation of the Rhine, which parted the Western States from the Holy Roman Empire, and united them under the control

[1] Moore to Lady Hester Stanhope, Salamanca, November 20th, 1808.

[2] Moore to Lady Hester Stanhope, Salamanca, November 23rd, 1808.

of France. A few weeks later, Francis II formally renounced his ancient but now empty title and the Holy Roman Empire ceased to be. In February the King of Prussia concluded a shameful bargain with the French dictator whereby in return for the bribe of Hanover, he was to join in an alliance against England and to close his ports to English ships. Ashamed at his duplicity, he long strove to conceal this ignominious and disgraceful alliance; but in deceit he was no match for Napoleon, and at last he was provoked into staking all on a single-handed contest with his tyrannical ally. On October 1st, he declared war; within a fortnight the army of Prussia—the child of that mighty force of which the great Frederick had been the parent —was all but annihilated at the battles of Jena and Anerstädt.

Too much occupied with affairs at home, the Grenville Cabinet contented themselves with despatching to the Continent a number of small expeditions that had no results save to excite the derision of our foes. And then in March 1807 the Government fell in a manner very similar to the fall of Pitt in 1801. The Duke of Bedford, the Lord-Lieutenant of Ireland, having urged the importance of making some concession to Roman Catholics, Howick moved for leave to bring in a Bill opening all commissions in the Army and Navy to persons of that faith.[1] The King refused his sanction, and the Government agreed to withdraw the measure. But George III was not content, and he required his Ministers to give a written pledge never again to press upon him any request for further concessions to the Roman Catholics. Very naturally Ministers declined, and they accepted the alternative of resignation.

The new Ministry was formed under the nominal and feeble headship of the Duke of Portland, but with a pale, thin, wizened little barrister for its real leader, for Spencer Perceval, second son of the second Earl of Egmont, became Chancellor of the Exchequer and Leader of the House of Commons. The change of Government made little alteration in our insular attitude to affairs abroad, and it was therefore perhaps hardly to be wondered at if the Tsar, whose army had recently suffered a notable defeat at the hands of Napoleon at Friedland, at once resentful at England's failure to aid him in the hour of his need and dazzled by the subtle flattery of his wily conqueror, should welcome overtures for peace at the expense of Great Britain and should indulge his fancy in dreams of a regenerated Europe divided between himself as Emperor of the East and Napoleon as Emperor of the West. Blinded by visions of this order, Alexander I held a three-hour conference with Napoleon on a raft moored in the Niemen; the off-spring of this

---

[1] By an Irish Act of 1743, Commissions in the Army up to the rank of Colonel only were open to Roman Catholics, and the King had reluctantly consented to extend this concession to Catholics throughout his dominions.

meeting was the Treaty of Tilsit. The general effect of this agreement was the abject humiliation of Prussia who was required to surrender almost half her territory; to recognize Napoleon's new creations, including the Kingdom of Westphalia, formed for his brother Jerome, in the valleys of the Ems, Oder and Weser, and the Grand Duchy of Warsaw, formed for the King of Saxony out of Prussian gains in the second and third partitions of Poland; to surrender Berlin and other fortresses until the payment of an exorbitant indemnity had been completed, and to make common cause with France and Russia against England. Faced with this menace, Britain replied by Orders in Council forbidding neutral ships, on penalty of seizure, to trade with French ports; and as the world was soon to learn, the Mistress of the Seas was in a favourable position to fulfil this threat. Thus once again through the supremacy of the British fleet were we enabled to cry defiance at our foes.

We left Sir John Moore in command of the British forces in Spain. "We are in a scrape," he had written, "but I hope we shall have spirit to get out of it; you must, however, be prepared for bad news."[1] This was no exaggeration; for he had just received the most alarming intelligence. The Spanish force with which he had been sent to co-operate, had suffered at the hands of the French a series of terrible disasters and was retiring in rout and confusion before the enemy. Faced with this position, Moore ordered his subordinate, General Baird, to retreat immediately on Coruña, he himself preparing to retire to Lisbon. In a few days, however, fresh intelligence caused him to change his plans. He recalled Baird, who had commenced his retreat; and on December 11th, in spite of having heard two days previously the news that Napoleon had captured the Spanish capital, the advance was continued. At about this time Moore learnt from a captured despatch that the Emperor was unaware of his presence and that Marshal Soult, lying in an isolated position at Soldaña on the river Carrion with less than 20,000 men, might possibly be cut off. The temptation to surprise Soult was too great; and turning north with that object in view, on December 19th, he joined Baird. Two days later the united forces of 27,000 men entered Sahagun.

At this apparently favourable juncture, Sir John Moore learnt for the first time that Napoleon at last knew of his whereabouts and had already quitted Madrid with the main body of his army, amounting to 42,000 men, in order to cut off his retreat and to crush him where he stood. Moore did not hesitate. Without a moment's delay he commenced his retreat

[1] Moore to Lady Hester Stanhope, Salamanca, November 20th, 1808.

335

westward on the Benavente-Astorga road on his way to Vigo and Coruña. And now it was a race for time. Napoleon drove his luckless troops in the midst of a blizzard at breakneck speed across the snow of the Guadarrama pass and over the fertile plains of old Castile. The race was too hot for many a man and many a steed and long was the line of miserable, exhausted beings left in the wake of the pursuing force. But in spite of all Napoleon's efforts Moore was too quick for him. When on December 28th the cavalry of the Emperor's vanguard reached the Esla, the British troops were safely across and out of the clutches of their would-be destroyers. Three days later, on January 1st, 1809, at Astorga, Napoleon gave up the pursuit; thereafter the chase was entrusted to the corps of Ney and Soult, a body of about 45,000 men.

But if the pace was hot for the French army, so it was for the British, and our troops, dispirited, demoralized and worn out by continuous marching, were soon out of hand; and when on January 12th the British army at last reached Coruña, two days before the arrival of the transport fleet delayed by storms, it was in a sorry plight. On January 14th the ships came up and embarkation began. But Soult was hard on their heels and to secure a quiet departure on the 16th, Moore was compelled to turn at bay. But that interval, four days' rest and the prospect of coming to grips with the enemy at last, brought the men to their senses; as if by magic they changed from an undisciplined, rebellious rabble to an army worthy of the highest traditions—worthy of the great commander who for the last time led them into battle.

During the afternoon of January 16th the French attacked. For a moment they looked like outflanking the British, but Moore was not so easily trapped and a dreadful volley into the midst of the oncoming French killed a vast number and threw the rest into confusion. Then it was the turn of the 50th, commanded by Charles Napier and Charles Stanhope. "Well done the fiftieth! Well done my Majors!" shouted the Commander as they charged and drove back the enemy with great slaughter. But alas! young Stanhope was killed in the fray and Napier was wounded and made prisoner. The general was everywhere shouting encouragement to his men. "Highlanders, remember Egypt!" he cried. "My brave 42nd, join your comrades, ammunition is coming: and you still have your bayonets." They heard his voice, the brave, familiar, frendly voice, rising amid the din of battle, and they rallied at his word. With him they felt unbeatable. They knew that where the fray was hottest, there would be found their brave commander.

Whilst Moore stood, watching the course of the battle, a shot wrenched off the leg of a man of the 42nd Regiment. He screamed horribly and, rolling on the ground in his agony, was fain to break the line. "This is nothing, my lads; keep your ranks," shouted the general. "Take that man away," he ordered. He spoke severely, but his words had a calming effect on the soldiers. Then turning to the sufferer, "My good fellow, don't make such a noise," he bade, "we must bear these things better." A moment later the general himself was struck and hurled from his horse to the ground. The ball had carried away his left shoulder, and had shattered the collar-bone and part of the chest; his arm was hanging by the flesh. Not a muscle of his face moved; not a sigh escaped him; not by so much as a wince did he show himself conscious of pain. He half raised himself, clutched the arm of a fellow officer and gazed anxiously at the Highlanders in the heat of the battle. "They are advancing," whispered his companion, and at that his face lighted. "You can be of no service to me," he said to the surgeons, anxiously summoned, "go to the wounded soldiers to whom you may be useful." As they bore him, wrapped in a blanket, from the field, his sword became entangled against his wound, but he would not suffer it to be unbuckled. "It is as well as it is," he muttered, "I had rather it should go out of the field with me." And so they bore him towards Coruña.

By the time they reached the port, it was almost dark; and to his great friend, Colonel Anderson, he for the first time showed momentary weakness: "Anderson, don't leave me," he whispered pathetically. But instantly he recovered, and he kept asking if the French were beaten, and showed the greatest satisfaction on receiving an affirmative reply. But the agony was terrible and a deathly pallor overspread his fine, clear-cut features. "Anderson, you know that I have always wished to die this way," he muttered. Gradually his thoughts turned to home. "I hope the people of England will be satisfied! I hope my country will do me justice!" After a short interval, he spoke again, "Anderson, you will see my friends as soon as you can. Tell them . . . everything. . . . Say to my mother. . . ." His voice faltered and whether from emotion or weakness he could not continue. Then he changed the subject. "Hope! . . . Hope! . . . I have much to say to him . . . but cannot get it out. . . ." He asked continuously if all his aides-de-camp were safe, and they forbore to tell him that Sir Harry Burrard's son was mortally wounded. He spoke of his Will and of his wishes for the members of his staff. He enquired again if the French were beaten, and expressed the utmost satisfaction at their rout. "I feel myself so strong . . ." he continued, "I fear I shall be long dying. . . ." But he was visibly sinking. "It's great uneasiness . . ." he murmured, "it's great pain. . . ." At this moment, two of his aides-de-camp, Percy and Stanhope, entered, and he spoke kindly to both. After a pause he caught the latter's eye. "Stanhope," he muttered softly, "Stanhope, remember me to your sister." He never spoke again. He remained quiet and unmoved awhile, until at last Death, approaching, gently touched him with her beckoning hand.

At midnight, under cover of darkness, they buried him in the Citadel of Coruña. No shroud enveloped, no coffin encased the corpse of the hero. Wrapped in his military cloak he was interred by the officers of his staff with few prayers and no salute. The guns of the foe paid his funeral honours and the Spanish commander, the Marquis de la Romana, subsequently raised a monument to his memory on the field of battle.[1]

In England a sorrowing Hester, anxious that her hero's reputation should be duly honoured, wrote eagerly to her cousin, the Prime Minister, that the great Mr. Pitt, who had always thought so highly of the general, had promised him the command of 30,000 men for a great invasion of France, but that Moore, after having reconnoitred the coast had "judged it prudent to give up the plan." She wrote, too, "of the unlimited confidence Mr. Pitt placed in Sir John Moore's judgment and exertions," and she expressed apprehensions lest the Ministers should "persecute him beyond the grave by blackening his memory and diminishing the honours he is so well entitled to from his country. . . ."[2] An aggressive letter: nor did she address her Uncle Chatham in milder terms, "I feel your kind attentions at this unhappy moment as much as I felt your neglect of me under similar affecting circumstances," she wrote. "I thank God James is spared me, and try to console myself with the idea that if beloved Charles could have chosen his death, it would have been to have shared the glorious one of our dear friend, the ever lamented general."[3]

Whilst in this unhappy state of mind, she bethought herself of the solitude of Wales where the previous year she had passed a pleasant holiday, and she wrote to a friend there asking him to make arrangements for her reception in the cottage at Glen Irfon, where she had before been made comfortable. Her wants were modest indeed. "I want the parlour," she wrote, "the little room above it for my bedroom, and the little room next for a dressing-room, a door to be made near the window to communicate

[1] It was Romana who raised the monument and not Soult as stated by Sir William Napier. Napier, *History of the War in the Peninsula and the South of France*. Vol. I. The memorial, which was of a temporary nature, was in 1811 converted into a permanent one by order of the Prince Regent. It was further restored and improved in 1834.

[2] Lady Hester Stanhope to Grenville, Montagu Square, January 25th (1809).

[3] Lady Hester Stanhope to Chatham, undated.

with the bedroom. The room over the kitchen for my maids, and a bed in the loft or elsewhere for a boy. The parlour must have two rush chairs or wooden ones, and be carpeted all over with green baize, or coarse grey cloth, like soldiers' great coats, a table to dine on, a fly-table, and shelves for books. The bedroom must have two chairs, a bath—no bed, as I shall bring down a camp bed and furniture complete. Beside carpets I shall expect to find a chest of drawers. The dressing-room must have two chairs, and a table with a looking-glass, two wash-hand basins, two water jugs, one large stone pitcher for water, two large tumbler glasses, and two large cups for soap, a tin kettle for warm water, and a little strip of carpet before the table. . . ." She required no attendance and she offered "£25 for part of the months of May, June, July, August, September and part of October. . . ."[1] The terms were accepted and in a few weeks Lady Hester moved in. She spent most of the summer in this rural retreat, and by the autumn had regained her health amid the peace and quiet of the Welsh mountains.

By the time Hester Stanhope returned to London she had matured her plans. The fashionable world disgusted her. All the zest and interest in life had gone. Her friends had failed: some had deserted; with others she was in open antagonism. But worse than that, an ungrateful country had not paid her lost hero the honour that she thought his due. A change of air and scene would be welcome and might do her good. She therefore determined to quit England forthwith and, as she hoped, find solace in a foreign clime. Someone tried to stop her, but she would have none of it, "Go out of England I am determined," she wrote to her kinsman, General Grenville, "& I will go in some vessel I am sure will be taken for I have not the least dread of being ill treated by the french, & at all events I w^d rather be at their mercy than at that of any creature called a friend of Mr. Pitt's. . . . If after Mr. P. has added during his Administration 600 Ships (line of B & frigates) to the naval force of this country, a relation or even a friend of his cannot be accommodated with a passage in one of them is rather hard, & if they do not intend to do the thing handsomely they may let it alone. I am much too ill to be so worried. I will give you no further trouble on this subject for I will ask for nothing *more & refuse* every offer. . . . James has the sweetest temper in the world, but I have not; that is to say I speak my sentiments, they are not dictated by passion but by reflection. . . . James *shall not go* if I go in any other vessel than a frigate."[2] Grenville apparently tried to help, but it was in vain. "I have desired James not to come up," she wrote,

[1] Lady Hester Stanhope to Price, Montagu Square, April 24th, 1908.

[2] Lady Hester Stanhope to Grenville, undated.

"for I shall take a lodging near Portsmouth & wait events. When I am better I shall set off. A thousand thanks for yr. kind offers, but to *argue* with facts is useless."[1] In a few weeks she sailed: and as she stood on deck and watched the shores of her native land slowly recede from view, how astonished she would have been could she have foreseen the truth— that she was sailing never to return.

[1] Lady Hester Stanhope to Grenville, undated.

CHAPTER III

The Passing of the Pitts

THE first light on July 28th, 1809, revealed a vast armada setting sail from the Downs. As the sun rose high in the heavens, it whitened the ocean with its sails as it made its leisurely way towards the mouth of the Scheldt and the great naval base at Antwerp. The object of the vast enterprise was the destruction of the fleet which Napoleon had assembled to launch his long-projected assault upon the shores of England. The Admiral in charge of the naval operations was Sir Richard Strachan; the commander of the land forces was Lieutenant-General Lord Chatham.

Why a man so destitute of ability and experience, so indolent and pleasure-loving, so vain and self-satisfied as John Chatham, should have been entrusted with so momentous an undertaking it is difficult to say,[1] and soon the appointment was being severely criticized even by his own connections. "The miserable certainty however of 35,000 of our best and last troops being put under Lord Chatham," wrote Thomas Grenville a few weeks ere the armament set sail, "destroys all other interest beyond that of the extreme apprehensions which must be entertained for all who go under such orders to such an expedition."[2] "There are all sorts of stories afoot about our new commander," he wrote a month later. "I saw a letter from Dover from an acquaintance of yours and mine which says that the wind was fair two days ago, and six expresses were sent one after another to *Ramsgate, where Lord Chatham slept*, to conjure him to embark with all haste and not to lose the tide; he would not get up or bestir himself, and he lost the tide, and the wind was no longer favourable in the ensuing tide. Nor is this all. They ordered from the Admiralty that three of the lightest men of war of the expedition should, at all events, go on to join the squadron which was cruising off the Scheldt; one of these was the *Venerable*, but Lord Chatham's trunks and servants being aboard, he refused to let the *Venerable* stir, and only two ships went instead of three. These are two happy specimens of

---

[1] But in the subsequent parliamentary enquiry, the Commander-in-Chief, Sir David Dundas, expressed himself as satisfied as to the propriety of Chatham's appointment.

[2] Thomas Grenville to Lord Grenville, Cleveland Square, June 12th, 1809.

the new command."[1] "I suppose you know," wrote a friend to Lord Buckingham, "that Popham wrote from on board the *Venerable* at Deal, after Lord Chatham had embarked 'that nothing could be expected from a man, so perfectly ignorant of his profession, and so incapable of acting.'"[2]

For a time, however, fortune seemed to favour our arms. On July 30th some 20,000 were disembarked on the Island of Walcheren, and by the 31st the principal towns, including Middleburg and Veere,[3] were firmly in our hands. Thus the Veergat, the narrow channel leading to South Beveland, was laid open and that island exposed to the full force of our attack. On the morning of August 2nd, Goes, its capital, opened its gates; in the evening Bahtz capitulated. So the entire island had been reduced. At about the same time Strachan ordered ships to be sent to the Western Scheldt above Flushing to try to prevent supplies being despatched by the Ghent Canal or ferried down the river. Thus Flushing, which was not thought to be heavily defended, was not only besieged from the land side but was also threatened from the sea; and the enemy's position there was evidently insecure. In some three days both channels of the Scheldt were alive with English ships and more than two-thirds of the distance to Antwerp had been covered; what could not resolution have achieved?

The instructions that had been sent to Lord Chatham were clear and concise. But the secret orders which he had received from Lord Castlereagh emphasized the secondary importance of capturing South Beveland and Walcheren: the essential purpose of the whole expedition was the rapid seizure of the naval base of Antwerp, the loss of which would have been a formidable blow at Napoleon's invasion plans.[4] But this required resolution, and how could the Government have expected such conduct from a man of the temperament of John Chatham? All men knew his nature, and even his officers despised him. "The dissensions amongst the Generals are very great . . ." wrote Temple to his father, "an officer upon the staff said he should not have known of the existence of a commander-in-chief had he not seen in his garden at Batz two turtles sprawling upon their backs; he was never visible until two o'clock, and in the luxury of a London kitchen was he living within twelve miles of the enemy, whilst his army were living upon salt meat and biscuit, without tents or covering

[1] Thomas Grenville to Lord Grenville, Cleveland Square, July 20th, 1809.

[2] Freemantle to Buckingham, Englefield Green, August 16th, 1809.

[3] Sometimes called Ter Veere or Campveer.

[4] Castlereagh to Chatham, Secret Instructions, June 1809.

of any sort, and in water. The sick list of the army, when these people came away, amounted to 5,000."[1]

Nothing was more certain, nothing more evident, than Chatham's total inadequacy for the task. His orders and common sense alike bade him thrust on with all speed to Antwerp, there to overwhelm the enemy before he could recover from the shock of our landing. Instead, Chatham devoted the whole of his energies to the subordinate object of reducing Flushing. On August 4th he announced the surrender of the Fort of Ramakins, the Scheldt to attack Flushing from the sea and to cut off all communication effect of which was to enable the fleet, by coming round into the West between Cadsand and Walcheren. Later a conference was held between Chatham and Strachan, the only account of which comes from the pen of Lord Chatham[2] and must therefore be taken with reserve. "I urged strongly the necessity of proceeding up the west Scheldt without delay," notes Chatham, "and stated to him that I had taken measures to move as large a part of the force as South Beveland would provide for through that island in order to embarrass the navigation of the Scheldt with as few transports as possible." He outlined his plans for achieving these objects. "This plan the Admiral thought would lessen the difficulties of the navigation," but he made trouble about bringing in the men-of-war to these confined waters. "I told him that I should move the troops by land without delay," noted Chatham, "but the transported could not go up the Scheldt but under his protection."[3]

Meanwhile, the investiture of Flushing proceeded apace; and between two and three o'clock in the morning of August 16th, when the town was a shambles, the French Commander was at last compelled to capitulate.

To the Government this seemed a mighty victory, and Castlereagh hastened to express to the Commander "the great satisfaction with which the King has received the intelligence of the surrender of the fortress of Flushing. . . ."[4] But the official view was over-optimistic, for in fact the resolution of Flushing had saved Antwerp, to the succour of which enemy troops had been rushed from all directions. For a time the British made some attempt to press on up the river, but they achieved little; and it was not long before the naval commander was reporting to the General the impossibility of the Navy moving higher up the Scheldt with the enemy

[1] Temple to Buckingham, Dover, September 3rd, 1809.

[2] In the Pitt MSS. Public Record Office.

[3] Chatham's Notes of Conference, August 6th, 1809.

[4] Castlereagh to Chatham, August 21st, 1809.

in possession of Lillo and Luffenshoek: he accordingly urged an immediate decision as to future operations "in consequence of the advanced state of the season, and the shortness of our provisions and water." So seriously did he view the situation that Strachan accompanied his official despatch with a private letter urging that "the transports with Horses on should go . . . to get a supply of Water with as little delay as possible."[1] Next day he followed this up with yet another despatch, in which he reminded Chatham that "you have not a week's provision for the Army, and we have not above four for the Navy, which when we come to divide with you, will reduce us to about 10 days." He asks the General for an immediate decision, warns him of the serious consequences that may arise from delay, and he begs with the utmost insistence for permission to report matters home.[2] Crossing this appeal came one from the military commander agreeing with all the contentions in Strachan's letter "not only on account of the important considerations you represent of the advanced season of the year, and the shortage of provisions and water, but I am sorry to add, on account of the alarming progress of sickness in this army."[3]

The terrible malady was due to the well-known malarial climate of Walcheren and South Beveland, against which no remedies had been provided, and the men were sinking fast. In view of this serious situation, Chatham called a council of war of his generals, all of whom were decidedly of the opinion that no operations against Antwerp could be successfully taken; and two days later he announced to Strachan his determination, "in consequence particularly of the increasing sickness of the Troops to a very alarming extent," to withdraw and embark immediately, "such of the Troops as shall not be wanted for the defence of Walcheren. . . ."[4] This sudden decision put the Admiral in a quandary, and he was not slow to point out "the necessity I am under in compliance with my orders of endeavouring to destroy the navigation of the Scheldt before I fall back with the ships of the Fleet . . ." which would take at least ten days or a fortnight.[5] Ten days or a fortnight! But Chatham was in a hurry to be off, and would not listen. If a few days would have sufficed, well and good; but ". . . I cannot feel myself justified under these circumstances in risquing the total ruin of the Army which must I fear be the inevitable consequence of keeping them in their present situation through the most unhealthy period of the

[1] Strachan to Chatham, August 26th, 1809.
[2] Strachan to Chatham, August 27th, 1809.
[3] Chatham to Strachan, August 27th, 1809.
[4] Chatham to Strachan, August 28th, 1809.
[5] Strachan to Chatham, August 29th, 1809.

year which is just now commencing."[1] The island of Walcheren, it was hoped, might still be retained so as to bottle up the mouth of the Scheldt; and some fifteen thousand men were left as a garrison. Having made these arrangements, on September 14th the inglorious commander sailed for home.

The fate of the troops amid the pestilential swamps of Walcheren was awful indeed. By the end of September close upon half the whole force was in hospital and deaths numbered from two to three hundred in a week. It was clear this could not long continue, and before Christmas we had quitted the whole island after losing some seven thousand men in the enterprise and inflicting on the remainder the seeds of a disease that they were destined to carry in their systems till their dying day.

It was inevitable that the utter and complete failure of the expedition should lead to a storm of abuse throughout England, and the Government sought to cast the whole of the blame on the lazy and incompetent commander. "I see accordingly in the *Courier* of the last night, and in the papers of this morning," wrote Lord Auckland, "that the ministerial war is begun against Lord Chatham . . . if there be any sense remaining among our countrymen they will naturally and reasonably discover that Ministers are and ought to be responsible for employing incompetent instruments."[2] Not unnaturally, Chatham was indignant at this treatment. "I understand the quarrel has risen to the highest pitch between Lord Chatham and Castlereagh, and that the former vows vengeance for the cruelty of throwing the whole blame of the failure of the expedition on him. It is quite impossible he can sit quietly by and see all the government papers full of abuse of him, and the defence of the Ministers built on his misconduct."[3]

Were it not for the fact that during the progress of the parliamentary enquiry into the failure of the expedition, Chatham took advantage of his position as a Privy Councillor and a peer to claim a private audience of the King, and to present a partisan report, our sympathy would go out to the victim of this ministerial displeasure. Moreover, in connection with this memorial, Lord Buckingham brings a grave charge against both George III and Chatham. "Lord Chatham must, I think, be ruined by his *double*-dealing, for I have no doubt but that the paper in question was delivered in October and re-dated to February 14th for the purpose of avoiding to the King the dilemma of having withheld such a paper after promising to Parliament to lay before them the necessary papers

---

[1] Chatham to Strachan, August 30th, 1809.

[2] Auckland to Grenville, Eden Farm, September 5th, 1809.

[3] Freemantle to Buckingham, Englefield Green, September 12th, 1809.

respecting Walcheren. Nothing but a direct falsehood can now keep back that fact, and I agree with you that this part of the story will pinch at Windsor more severely than any other part of the transaction."[1] Within a few days Chatham was to give his explanation of this to the Committee—an explanation that has done nothing to raise his name with posterity. Sir Richard Strachan, not unnaturally incensed at Chatham's partisan report, made haste to compose a counter-statement which he presented to the Government: in this he charged the general with gross laziness and unpunctuality and applied to him the sobriquet "the late" Earl of Chatham.[2] Thus the General blamed the Admiral, and the Admiral blamed the General; meanwhile, the wits chanted their well-known lines and all England laughed or sighed at the absurd quarrel between the commanders.

Whilst the General and the Admiral were thus employed, the Committee's investigations continued. "Lord Chatham is frightened out of his senses at the thought of appearing to answer at the bar," wrote Freemantle to Buckingham, "and I know there are some of those who acted under him, who are most eager to give their opinions."[3] Nor did his relations and friends regard his chances as rosy. "Lord Chatham's situation seems quite desperate," wrote Grenville to his brother. "He has got into a scrape, from which I don't see how it is possible for him to extricate himself."[4] ". . . I shall be curious to know how Lord Chatham gets out of his entanglements," wrote Lord Auckland. "His evidence is that of a man who has lost today the entire recollection of what he said yesterday, and wanders consequently into inconsistencies and incorrectness in points of fact. His worthy colleagues clearly wish to put all their sins on his back, and to send him into the wilderness with their maledictions. If there be any sense or spirit left in the country, they will fail in that speculation."[5] On that unworthy note the enquiry opened.

When the Committee sat, some strange things quickly came to light. Neither the Physician-General nor the Surgeon-General of the Forces was ever consulted before the expedition sailed, nor was the Inspector-General of the Army Hospitals ever consulted at all, though it was common knowledge that the prevalence of fever in and around Walcheren made special safeguards essential. The first requisition for additional medicines was received on September 18th; yet it was not passed to the Storekeeper until

[1] Buckingham to Grenville, Stowe, February 25th (1810).
[2] Strachan to Government, London, March 5th, 1810.
[3] Freemantle to Buckingham, Stanhope Street, January 29th, 1810.
[4] Grenville to Buckingham, Camelford House, February 24th, 1810.
[5] Auckland to Grenville, Eden Farm, March 5th, 1809. *Private.*

Chevening

JOHN PITT, Earl of Chatham, son of William Pitt, Earl of Chatham
Romney

the 27th and not shipped until the 30th. The medicines were, in fact, received at Walcheren on October 15th, over a month from the day on which the requisition had been despatched. Not until September 10th, when fever was already raging among the troops and four days before Chatham returned home, was Sir Lucas Pepys, Physician-General to the Forces, ever consulted, and then he was merely bidden to visit Harwich to investigate the state of those sufferers who had returned from the Continent. Then again, the Chairman of the Transport Board gave the startling testimony that only two hospital ships, the *Asia* and the *Aurora* were sent out with the expedition and that these were capable of accommodating in all no more than some one hundred and twenty patients. It was under such disgraceful conditions of neglect that our men were allowed to suffer and die amongst the unhealthy swamps of Western Holland.

Sir Richard Strachan, in his evidence attributed much of the failure of the operation to the very unfavourable weather encountered, and it is only fair that due weight should be given to this factor; but he had to make the damaging admission that he suffered from almost entire lack of knowledge of the navigation of the Scheldt; that he knew little of the best landing places on Walcheren, Cadsand and in the neighbourhood of Santrliet, and that he was totally ignorant of the nature of the fortifications at Antwerp, Lillo and Liefkenshoeik.

But if Strachan's evidence was disturbing, Chatham's was positively damning. In the course of his examination he was forced to admit that, when he left England, he had been given to understand that the works at Antwerp were in a very bad state of repair, and that no guns were mounted on the ramparts, whereas the exact opposite proved the truth; that, though he had entertained grave doubts of the accuracy of these reports, he had made no efforts to verify or falsify them; that he did not know that the approaches to Antwerp could be flooded, that the citadel commanded the arsenal and the dockyard, that the enemies' ships, fully laden with guns and stores, could retire to within one mile of Ruplemonde, some five miles from Antwerp, and that without guns and stores, they could go to the fortified town of Dendermonde, some fifteen miles higher still. It further transpired that, owing to interminable delays, the expedition did not sail from England until the unhealthy season of the year had actually started—though in his letter of August 30th he had foolishly written on risking the lives of his men if kept in their present situation "through the most unhealthy period of the year which is just now commencing."[1]—and that great damage had been thereby caused by the loss of secrecy. "This is one of our secret

[1] Chatham to Strachan, August 30th, 1809.

347

Expeditions, the precise object of which is known to all the world," wrote an acute contemporary observer. "No one, however, can justly be blamed for this," he comments. "If anything be impossible, it is for England to have a secret Expedition. The nature of the preparations, the multitude of persons necessarily in the secret, very intelligibly point out the purpose of the armament; and accordingly a fleet is no sooner collected in any of our outports, than every inhabitant of the town will whisper to you its destination."[1] We who have witnessed the marvel of a twentieth century invasion may well smile at this comment upon one nigh on a century and a half ago!

Lord Chatham was further questioned on his memorial, which, as we have seen, though dated October 15th, was not presented to the King until February 14th during the actual progress of the enquiry. By way of explanation he stated that it was dated the day it was drawn up, but he did not deliver it earlier because he did not think it would be right for him to state in advance what in fact would constitute his defence in case of an enquiry. To the question why he chose February 14th he replied that there was no particular significance in the exact date except that it was a levee day; but that he wished to deliver it about that time because he knew that the Admiral "would be called upon to make some narrative of his proceedings and I was very anxious that they should both come up precisely at the same time, that I should not state my narrative first before any statement was given in by him."

On this specious explanation worse was to follow. Had he delivered any other paper, narrative, memorial or memorandum of any sort to the King? "The paper which is now before the House is my official Report of my proceedings," Chatham replied. "When I am asked with respect to any other paper, or to any other circumstances not coming under that description, I do not feel myself at liberty to enter at all into any examination of that sort, and I must beg to decline giving any answer to the question put to me." On being pressed, Chatham persisted in his refusal; on being asked on what grounds he refused, he merely replied that he declined answering the questions: "I have stated all I did in my military capacity, which is, that I delivered my official report to the King on the 14th February; on the contents of that report I am ready to give any information." And there the matter rested.

But though the evidence before the Committee with regard to his conduct gravely besmirched Chatham's reputation and was fully enough to ruin most men, yet it was not many months before he was promoted to

[1] *Letters from Flushing*, by an Officer of the Eighty-First Regiment.

the rank of full general.[1] Moreover, on the death of the Duke of York in 1820, he was appointed Governor of Gibraltar, a post he held until his death fifteen years later. Never perhaps in all our history have gross incompetence and culpable inefficiency been so generously requited!

We left Hester Stanhope sailing from England on February 10th, 1810. With her were her brother James, in spite of all her protests, James's friend, Nassau Sutton, Dr. Meryon, the physician who many years later was to give the world the entertaining but unreliable memoirs that have been already quoted, Elizabeth Williams a personal maid, and a man-servant. At Gibraltar they separated; James joined the Guards at Cadiz, Sutton went on to Minorca, and Lady Hester, with her doctor and attendants, sailed for Malta. Their stay there was short, however, for by August 2nd the party were bound for Zante, whence they went to Patres. Here they were joined by Lord Sligo and a certain Michael Bruce, and they all embarked together in a felucca for Corinth. A few weeks later they were in Athens. From Athens, Lady Hester went to Constantinople, and thence, after a short stay, she set out for Egypt. On the way she was shipwrecked in the Sea of Marmora and nearly lost her life. But she quite lost all her wardrobe, and as no English-style clothes were to be had, she had no alternative to dressing as a Turk—not a Turkish woman, for then she could not speak to a man—"but as an Asiatic Turk in a travelling dress—just a sort of silk and cotton shirt; next a striped silk and cotton waistcoat; over that another with sleeves, and over that a cotton short jacket without sleeves or half-sleeves, beautifully worked in coloured twist, a large pair of breeches, and Turkish boots, a sash into which goes a brace of pistols, a knife, and a sort of short sword, a belt for powder and shot made of variegated leather, which goes over the shoulder, the pouches the same, and a turban of several colours, put on in a particular way with a large bunch of natural flowers on one side. This is the dress of the common Asiatic; the great men are covered with gold and embroidery, and nothing can be more splendid and becoming than their dress. At this moment I am a wretched figure—half a Greek, half a Turk, but most of all like a blackguard (gallongi), a Turkish sailor."[2] The oriental dress that Lady Hester had now adopted she was destined never to discard.

[1] January 1st, 1812.

[2] Lady Hester Stanhope to Murray, "The Island of Rhodes, January 2nd, 1812."

From Rhodes, the wanderer embarked for Alexandria,[1] and a few weeks later we find her in Cairo, where the Pasha did her much honour. But in no place did she stay long, and we shortly hear of her at Jerusalem, Damascus, Latakia, Palmyra, Acre, Jaffa and Sayda. At Latakia, where Lady Hester rented a house on the shore, alarming reports reached the party. "The plague is all over Syria (Aleppo excepted)," she wrote to General Sir Hildebrand Oakes, the Governor of Malta, who had shown her much attention when her party had stopped at the island on their way out from England. "Here, thank God, it has been slight, and is upon the wane as is the case everywhere where it has been for some time. . . ." But she made up her mind that summer to leave Syria in October, which "is the best month to leave the coast, after the equinoctial gales are over . . ." she told Oakes.[2] Yet, when October came, it was not she who left, but her friend and companion, Michael Bruce, summoned home, if we are to believe the Duchess of Cleveland, by an insistent father. Moreover, she tells us, "He had probably had enough of the East, and felt he could not remain much longer away without expatriating himself altogether. But he and Lady Hester parted with mutual regret."[3] Mutual regret! It was, it seems, something quite different from that.

It was the early spring of 1810 when Michael Bruce first met Lady Hester Stanhope and he had remained the constant companion of her wanderings until summoned home in October 1813. Bruce was, as we know, an experienced traveller in the Orient, clever and ambitious; and in a few years he was to prove himself a man of daring and resource, for he was one of the three who, in April 1816, contrived the escape of Count Lavallette, condemned to death for high treason, on the very eve of his intended execution. He was probably younger than Hester Stanhope, and of not so strong a character as she; and during their three years together he had conceived

---

[1] Extract from Muster Book of H.M.S. *Salsette*, 9th Feby. 1812.
Rhodes. Passengers to Egypt.

Rt. Hon. Lady Hester Stanhope

Bruce	Gentleman
Pearce	"
Merryean	"
Fry	Servant

Left on 16th Feby.

Extract from Log Book of H.M.S. *Salsette* (en route for Alexandria).
"16th Feby. 1812.
. . . saluted Lady Hester Stanhope with 13 guns on her leaving the ship."
Public Record Office, Admiralty, 37.3660.

[2] Lady Hester Stanhope to Oakes, "Latakia, July 15th. 1813."

[3] Cleveland, *The Life and Letters of Lady Hester Stanhope*.

the most profound admiration for his brilliant companion—a sentiment that had not gone unrequited. Moreover, they had common aspirations for the promotion of knowledge of the East that might be of value and importance. This, of course, would cost money: but Bruce had a wealthy father, and not without difficulty he prevailed upon Hester to share his allowance, partly for her comfort and partly to promote the causes they both had at heart.[1] "I was a little hurt at observing from the tone of your letter that you did not feel disposed to keep the promise which you made me before I left Latachia—of drawing on me for whatever was necessary for your comfort," he wrote some three months after his departure. "The sum first, I believe, was £1,000 per annum. Now my dear love, I can enter into all your feelings, and I am sure that nobody can entertain a higher admiration for your lofty and dis-interested spirit than I do. Indeed, the more I reflect upon your character, your talents, and your history, the more I am lost in wonder; and look upon you not only as the most extraordinary, but the first of created beings. But in this case, my dear love, it is not a work of merit, but of duty, which I am performing. Are you not labouring in my vocation? Is it not for my benefit that you are collecting all this information? And would it be just that the whole bulk of the expense should fall upon you? By consenting to keep your promise, so far from accepting, you confer a favour. . . ." There then follows much of his father and his circumstances. "The wonderful changes which have taken place in Europe since the date of *his* last letter will, I am sure, have relieved him from his commercial embarrassments. But whether this is the case, or not, is nothing to the purpose. He confesses that he is a man of very large fortune, and he might at least make me an allowance of Two Thousand pounds a year, and can I do less than make one one-half to you? Do not, at least, deprive me of the gratification of making so proper a use of my money. £1,000 will be more than sufficient for me; for I shall live very retired, and principally in my father's house. I shall come to a very clear understanding with him upon this, as well as upon every point, immediately

[1] The truth of these facts is established by a number of letters and extracts from letters that were formerly at Stowe and are now in the British Museum. Add MSS. 42,057. I am indebted to the Rev. G.W. T. Tyndale Biscoe for the following information with regard to these letters. At the sale of the effects from Stowe many years ago, a Buckingham tradesman bought a number of sacks filled with books, letters and other documents, and promptly sold them to a lady of the parish who was anxious that they should not fall into improper hands. Some of these sacks she gave to Mr. Tyndale Biscoe for the benefit of the finances of the church. Among the contents, there were found a small number of letters to and from Lady Hester Stanhope.

upon my return to England."[1] No more of this extract exists, but some nine months later he writes from London that he has seen his father and explained ". . . that, as long as we were separated, I wished that your income should be equal to mine, and that the portion I gave you must depend upon the allowance which he could afford to make me. He answered—that the present state of his fortune would permit him to give me £2,500 per annum, so that I make over to you £600 a year, which will make our incomes equal. . . . He authorises you to draw on him privately so that this transaction will be known to only us three. I then made another request of my father, which was that in case of any accident happening to me, he would pay to you, for the remainder of your life, £800 a year. To this he assented with the greatest pleasure; and said that he would have paid that or any other sum I might have named, and should execute it as a sacred duty."[2]

But the romance was shortlived, it seems, for before long Hester is writing "Dearest B." that "As I find, by the French papers, that you are going to be married, it will be proper that all correspondence should cease between us." So she wishes to clear up some points "before all sort of intercourse is broken off between us." "When I allowed myself to accept an increase of income from you," she wrote, "I had two motives for so doing; first, that the world might not say that you had deserted me in a foreign country, and left me in bad circumstances; next, I wished to carry into execution some plans I had in contemplation, and to pick up information which might hereafter be useful to you, if you became a public character; and if not, that which would be interesting to you as a literary man, and add to your fame in that character." There follows many pages of detail as to how the money has been expended. "I have never kept a horse for myself for three years. . . . I have always been drest like a common person, except when absolute necessity required I should be otherwise. I have observed, in every thing, the strictest economy in my house, and in every thing respecting myself. Every farthing I have spent has been for what I considered either public objects or your future advantage. . . . Such then are the objects your money has accomplished: I hope, when you reflect, you will not regret it; and that you will think (as it w^d equally have been spent) that it was better bestowed than in frivolity at Paris." But Bruce's father had lost his money, and had she known, she would have accepted nothing.

[1] Headed "Extract from a letter of Mr. B's dated Constple. Jan 20th. 1814." The whole is in Meryon's hand.

[2] Headed "Nothing more said about money matters until in a letter dated September 29th. 1814 from London." The whole is in Meryon's hand.

"But how could I suspect anything, after the allowance he had made you, and the promise you had made me? . . . From your silence I could learn nothing, except that I feared you had no longer any friendship for me: and, if it was sheer neglect, it raised a feeling of anger, if not contempt, in my heart, that any man, who professed to have feeling, could thus tamper with that of another. This is the truth; and, added to many disadvantageous histories I had heard of you (true or false), I had reason to fear you avoided writing to me. . . ." And when she thought of his neglect, "I do not know whether a feeling of indignation at your negligence, or that of regret at your want of confidence, or anxiety about you, were the uppermost." Her mind had been "upon the rack"; so he must forgive whatever she may have written under these impressions. "Had I loved you less, I might have been more cool; but coolness is a quality I never yet had, or shall, I fear, possess until I am interred in the grave." But enough of the past: now for the future. "Do not be uneasy about me in any way, or fancy your marriage pains me. On the contrary, you know I often told you, when I took pains to correct your faults, it would not be myself who would profit by your improvement, but some other woman more worthy of you: that for your mutual happiness, you must correct your temper: and I am too happy to have learnt from some of our common friends of late, that it's much altered for the better. May you be happy, my once dearest friend! If you are so, I shall consider that that share of happiness, which fate has chosen through life to deprive me of, is better thrown into your scale. . . ." As for herself, she is worn out and cannot live long. She had wished to see her brother and some of her friends once more, but they have deserted her. "If those, who have had experience of my character," she writes pathetically, "cannot give me credit for honour, disinterestedness, and integrity, without statements that I am neither mad nor unprincipled, I must content myself with y^r flattering hope that strangers will be more just to my present conduct as well as to my memory."

> "By foreign hands her humble grave adorn'd;
> By strangers honour'd, and by strangers mourn'd!"

She concludes a thirteen-sheet letter by asking Bruce's directions as to the disposal of his papers in her hands, and by asking his and his father's forgiveness for any harshness on her part. "Adieu, fare well, my once dearest B! I must call you so no more—but I never shall cease to pray for your prosperity and your happiness."[1]

---

[1] Lady Hester Stanhope to Bruce, undated. The letter is in Meryon's hand, but it is signed by Lady Hester, and there is a postscript in her hand.

Brave words! But the desertion of Bruce had left her in a sorry plight. "It is the first time in my life I was ever in debt, although I have been often very poor." She wrote to her kinsman, General Grenville, at about this time. "The unforeseen circumstances had embarrassed me on the one hand, and B's giddiness on the other involved me in difficulties. I must now just clearly state to you that, when he took his leave of me, he insisted upon my accepting £1,000 a year; which I did not exactly accept, but did not absolutely refuse for fear of hurting his feelings, and thinking it was not right to take advantage of what any man might say when agitated and affected as he was. But when, at the end of six months, he still repeated the same thing, and conjured me to accept it upon his account to pursue certain plans and gain information which might be useful to him; and gave also a favourable account of his father's circumstances; all my scruples were at an end . . . I thought it might be carrying false pride and independence too far for you to run the risk of the world's saying that he had left me ill-provided for in a strange country, surrounded by difficulties. . . . The events which have taken place since the period I spoke, you are fully aware of. Therefore I will not refer to them."[1]

First Moore; now Bruce. Thus, in misery and disappointment ended the second romance of Lady Hester Stanhope. She was alone once more; and after further wanderings she was destined to settle among the half-savage tribes on the slopes of Mount Lebanon. Her first retreat was an old ruined monastery about two miles from Sidon, but this was far too small for her requirements, and shortly afterwards she leased a house near Jôon, or Djoun as the French spell it, from a Damascus merchant named Joseph Seweyah. This was Dar Jôon; and was destined to be her home till her dying day.

Knowing her isolated position, her family and friends sought to bring her home, but she would have none of it. "I think so ill of affairs in general, that I feel no great wish to leave this quiet country, for no where can a popular stranger be more at liberty, and more comfortable. I suit the people and they suit me," she wrote to General Grenville in March 1815. ". . . for I enjoy not only the privilege of a Turk, but also their confidence, and they will talk to me upon subjects, which few Christians dare to question them upon."[2] "I began this the beginning of March now it is the 23rd. of April and I am returning from Ascalon where my business took me," she wrote in the postscript. "I am now writing from a forest of orange trees

[1] Lady Hester Stanhope to Grenville, undated. Another portion of this very long letter is very inaccurately transcribed by the Duchess of Cleveland, who gives it as to General Anderson: but that seems to be incorrect.

[2] Lady Hester Stanhope to Grenville, "begun in March 1815 upon the road to Acre."

in full bloom near Jaffa, you can have no idea of the perfume they give or of their beauty for these are not trimmed into sort of wigs, as at Gibraltar, Malta and the Greek islands or placed in straight lines, but wild like forest trees and the shade is so thick that you hardly want a tent." Of the Greeks she thinks them poorly, and dubs them ". . . all a nasty *cunning, cowardly, discontented* people. The Arabs tho' rascals are ten thousand times better . . ."

"You have no idea how all the strange people like me, or how they interest and amuse me, and what admirable talents they have compared with Europeans in general," she wrote to the same correspondent later that year. "It is a very happy thing for me that I can continue to pass my time tolerably pleasant here, for when Europe will be settled God only knows! Our army has done every thing, crowned heads and big-wigs nothing, for what in God's name can they mean by sending Bonaparti to England? Here it is reported that he is to be tried, but surely that is too mad? They better take care how they make a *precedent* of trying a *bad King*, a man at least who was once acknowledged *one* by all Europe."[1] But as time passed, and still her family tried to persuade her to return, her temper became more uncertain. "Cease, therefore, to torment me," she wrote passionately to her cousin, Lord Buckingham in the Spring of 1816. "I will not live in Europe, even were I, in flying from it, compelled to beg my bread. . . . I will not be a martyr for nothing. The grand-daughter of Lord Chatham, the niece of the illustrious Pitt, feels herself blush, as she writes, that she was born in England. . . ."[2] There then followed much abuse of her country. "I am sick and tired of being worried out of my life upon every subject great or small and fifty lies being told of me, which the *silence* if not the approbation of my family, sanction in the world." She wrote to General Grenville some three years later. "To England, to my country, disgraced in the annals of history will I never return. It is true since that in my travels I have seen (or rather suffered) what w^d turn a child grey in its cradle, but I w^d sooner die upon the burning sands of Africa than add one link to that chain which is now binding justice, honor, Humanity and independence in eternal bondage. . . . I will have nothing more to do with those who treat with contempt the judgment of one whose foresight has often proved useful to them, and in future I shall refer to strangers whom [sic] may judge me by the rules of Justice only . . . let James follow the head of the family if he pleases, I wish not either to the head or the tail; but the adopted child of

---

[1] Lady Hester Stanhope to Grenville, "From a Hamlet on the Top of Mount Lebanon, Sept. 15th. 1815."

[2] Lady Hester Stanhope to Buckingham, Mount Lebanon, April 22nd. 1816. This was the second Marquis, who succeeded his father in 1813, and was created in 1822 Duke of Buckingham and Chandos.

reason in a remote part of the world, whence I may leave my bones in peace, and my reputation to the mercy of savages. General, dear General, my blood boils when I hear . . ."[1] The remainder of this impassioned outburst is lost, but her words have a wild ring as they come to us down the years.

The village of Djoun, peopled by that strange, half-savage Mohammedan tribe, the Druses, was perched high on a curiously shaped conical barrow surmounted by a tableland, and this plateau gave ample space for the enlargement of her new property. So Lady Hester Stanhope soon set about erecting a number of additional buildings around Dar Jôon in order to increase the accommodation available for guests and to supply herself with stabling, cottages, offices and other outhouses. She also formed a richly diversified garden, ornamented with all manner of pavilions, arbours and fountains, which Meryon favourably compared to any that could be found at home. To ensure herself absolute privacy round the whole, she built a high wall. Amidst these picturesque surroundings the English wanderer lived in considerable state, being waited upon by upwards of thirty personal attendants, and dispensed open-handed charity so that she came to be looked upon with a mixture of awe and reverence by the half-wild tribes of the mountain. In the summer of 1821, there were rumours of revolution and of a Russian war in the East, but Hester could write to General Grenville with sublime self-confidence, "things have been bad, likely to be very very bad, yet do not be uneasy about me. I have ever done my duty to God, and my fellow creatures to the extent of my power, and therefore *fear nothing*. . . . Never believe what is said of Orientals," she added, "they are not known by Europeans, whose brutal ignorance of the sublime and of what ought to be the most interesting to man, every day becomes more and more disgusting to me. . . ." She writes wildly of strange horrors to come such as "you have never yet seen, or perhaps can form an idea of." Then ". . . the tyrant, the interested wretch, and the illiteral one will tremble upon the dunghill, and upon the throne. . . ."[2] In a few months, she is writing of revolution: the Pacha of Acre and the Emir Beshyr are rebels, and the latter has fled to Europe. "If he comes to England," she writes, "take care of him, he is as false as Hell, and whatever he may *propose* himself, he will say was proposed to him, and he refused it, for it is very clear he means to return." Acre is being besieged, but "Scarcity is what I most dread, by the number of troops and Paches which are

---

[1] Lady Hester Stanhope to Grenville, "The wilds of Libanon, July 29th. 1819."

[2] Lady Hester Stanhope to Grenville, "3rd. of May 1821," endorsed "This private for you and Ld G."

arrived and arriving. In some places you can find not a single thing either of provision, or furniture, all is hid or buried under ground. . . ." Derwish Pasha is in command of the troops before Acre, but he has proved himself her friend. Unfortunately, however, "He is a very good man, but *no soldier*, so slow in his motions! If he be beat, his troops will all Desert and lay waste the country like a hord of banditti, and the Pacha of Acre will become more wicked than ever. One of his last acts before the arrival of Derwish Pacha was to condemn to death 21 innocent persons. A great Judge was one, he escaped here for protection. I did not *hide him* and his *relation* but *openly* said I w^d *never give them up* to the Pacha, and that the first person he sent here after then I s^d cut off his head with my sabre, for these were men condemned by *caprice*, not by either the *Sultan* or the *law*. In about ten days Derwish Pacha arrived, and relieved me of my charge. . . ."[1]

The power and influence which she thus achieved over the rude native population of Lebanon became the very breath of life to the strange, lonely, proud, imperious woman, the voluntary exile from her native land; so that as this half-superstitious veneration increased—for the Druses came to look upon her as a kind of prophetess—Hester was careful to encourage it further by insensibly introducing Eastern manners and customs into her daily life. For some time now she had assumed the garb of the Orient, but hitherto she had still retained many of the European modes to which she had been born. But gradually these, too, were laid aside so that Dr. Meryon, who had returned to England on Hester's settling on Mount Lebanon, but revisited her in Syria in 1819, was quick to notice that she had in the meantime completely familiarized herself with the ways of the East, conducting her establishment entirely in the Turkish manner, and adopting even much of their medical empiricism. This was too much for the prim doctor, who promptly returned to England—not much to his employer's regret, it would seem. "The Doctor who is the bearer of this is a good sort of dull slow man," she wrote to General Grenville early in 1817, "He was a great fop and fool, when he first came into the East, but I have cured him of these failings: having a sort of impediment in his speech, he is an unpleasant man to converse with, but he is *honest*, tho' nothing will ever make him bright. I am not fond of confidences, and therefore never placed any in him, until this last year, when his being obliged to write some letters for me which the state of my health at that moment prevented me from being able to undertake myself made it necessary I sd. speak a little openly to him upon my own situation, which I do

---

[1] Lady Hester Stanhope to Grenville. Undated.

not regret, as he has behaved I think even better since, and he has made himself very useful in many ways, which I had had no right to expect of a doctor, or indeed hardly of a very fine gentleman servant I feel myself greatly obliged to him for this, as I have no one about me whom I can place confidence in as to honesty, who can speak the language. . . ."[1]

But all this splendour, of course, cost money, and it is not surprising, therefore, that before long, Lady Hester Stanhope was in sorry straits. For a time she managed to prevail upon various Levantine usurers to advance her considerable sums on note of hand, but though no climax in her affairs was to arise for some years, already in 1825 her financial position was becoming difficult. Towards the end of 1824 a true friend appeared in the person of Captain Yorke, the Commander of the *Alacrity* cruising in the Levant, whose family was intimately known to the Stanhopes. This young man was one of the few of her countrymen received by Lady Hester at this time, and, grieved at his hostess's lack of funds, wrote anxiously to her Uncle Chatham. "As she was open and frank with me, she made me understand that absolute want of money was a great source of uneasiness to her; the house she now lives in belonging to a Turk in Constantinople, who threatens to turn her out when her lease was out, which was three months when I saw her, if she does not pay £500 for the entire purchase of the place. She has not the money, she tells me. Another source of misery was the want of some good people about her, a steady man-servant and a maid; she begins much to feel the want of these comforts, and I assure you they are absolutely necessary for her. She is very forlorn, and her mind has taken a very serious turn, much impaired, and full of magic and divination. Nothing will ever induce her to return to her native land; in fact, it is a dangerous experiment to try and persuade her; but what would make her comfortable, and as happy as she can be made in this world, would be the purchase of Djoun for her, and send such people as I have described out to her. She never will herself make known to her family her distress; her mind is too high, and knowing what *I* do, I felt it my duty to her, and to my fellow-creature, to make it known to one of her family. You, my Lord, I know, and you can make it known to her brother, James, of whom she never ceases to talk, and for whom she retains the warmest affection." And he begged that she should never know he had written this letter. "Her mind is so high, that, did she know I wrote this, she would never bear to hear my name again."[2]

It is unlikely that this letter brought assistance. In the first place, the

[1] Lady Hester Stanhope to Grenville, "Mount Lebanon, Jany. 1st. 1817."

[2] Yorke to Chatham, H.M.S. *Alacrity*, February 25th, 1825.

much-loved brother, James, died by his own hand within a few weeks of the writing of this letter. But two years back he had lost his wife,[1] who died in childbirth, and Hester had only heard of this six months later. "To write—not to write—no proper conveyance—what to say—after a year, perhaps to open the wounds of his heart without being able to pour in one drop of the balm of Consolation?" So she had written to Dr. Meryon. "What I say would be vain. He considers me as a sort of poor mad woman, who has once loved him, therefore he is kind to me; but as to my opinion having weight—no! To be considered as a sort of object is not flattering; but so let it be. There is no remedy for it, or other wiles except in the hand of God, which, if He will stretch forth to save me, all may vanish; if not, I shall vanish, for I am quite worn out. . . ."[2] Depressed by this loss, poor James, in March, 1825, went out and hanged himself. We do not know when the proud, haughty exile heard of his suicide, or how she mourned him; but even in those days of sorrow her thoughts did not turn to home, and words of sympathy from England were neither welcomed nor acknowledged. Her only surviving sister, Lady Griselda Tekell,[3] by breaking the long silence, hoped to cheer her sister and wrote her several times after their brother's death. "I thought it would be consolatory to her to hear something of his child and the rest of the family," she recorded. "My letters were written in a kind and conciliatory spirit, and did not enter into any family disagreements, but she took no notice whatever of them." We cannot judge of this for the letters have not been found. But they were the only communications that had passed between the sisters since the elder left England in 1810, and there was to be no further intercourse between them for the fourteen years remaining of their joint lives.[4]

And from John Chatham what could be expected? All his life he had been impecunious, and it is unlikely that he had at the time money to spare for a niece who had often treated him in cavalier fashion, and for whom he could not have cared. As far back as the summer of 1785, we find him borrowing the sum of £3,150 from three money-lenders, and nine years later two separate sums of £3,000 and £4,000 from his banker, Thomas Coutts. Yet in spite of these loans, he was unable to maintain Burton

[1] Stanhope had married in 1820 Lady Frederica Murray, daughter of the 3rd Earl of Mansfield.

[2] Lady Hester Stanhope to Meryon, July 30th, 1823.

[3] Lady Lucy Taylor had died on March 1st, 1814, leaving three sons and four daughters.

[4] Lady Hester died on June 23rd, 1839. Her sister, however, lived on for a great many years, and died at Bagshot on October 13th, 1851, at the age of seventy-three.

Pynsent, and a cry of sorrow comes to us from the faithful Mrs. Stapleton, at the neglect into which her beloved Burton was being allowed to fall. "Oh! Mr. Pitt, words cannot figure to you the Torture I suffer from the humiliated state of the adored, distinguish'd Burton, does not there yet remain Powers of redemption from the threaten'd final disgraceful distruction of it? I never name the too painful subject, and avoid as much as possible seeing or hearing any thing leading to it, but that is insufficient to Banish It from my sleeping or waking thoughts; and void of sensibility must I be could it be otherwise. The loss of Her dear to me as myself was in the course of *Nature*, and Time would have soften'd the Change; and assisting in, or seeing what was so dear to Her, and for more than Its own supreme Merits, cherish'd and preserved, I should still have been happy. Her *Confidence* was in your self. For loving it as your Father did, fearing the turn of your Brother's mind was bent on other (illegible) but thank Goods left the World free from the apprehsion of what has already taken place. It's possible the Proud Pillar may Bow as its Lord passes to the Government. Oh, Mr. Pitt, it's a misfortune to have a feeling Heart. God Bless you and preserve your Health, and bring you successfully through your arduous situation. How often have *we* stood at the Windows, watching you Walking or sitting 'upon your own Troy Hill seeming to overlook the World, which for it's Benefit you appear'd Born to Rule.'"[1] What could poor, impecunious William do to stifle this cry of anguish? His brother, as always, was in want of money, and Burton Pynsent must be sacrificed. In fact it was shortly afterwards sold to a family of the name of Pinney. Yet, in spite of that, John Chatham was still in want of cash, and later he assigned five policies of insurance on his life as security for a loan of £7,000. These transactions seem to have assisted the improvident Chatham for a time, for we find no evidence of any further borrowings for some years. But early in 1821 he appears to be in difficulties again, for he then borrowed £6,900 from Joseph Ward and Francis Robertson and £4,100 from John Burke; and he followed that up five years later by mortgaging his London house in Chester Street, Berkeley Square, to the dowager Lady Suffield for a loan of £3,000.

Yet in spite of all his faults, we must not withhold entirely our sympathy from Lord Chatham. A haughty, proud man, the son of one genius and the elder brother of another, life must have brought him many disappointments; the heir to honours won by another and to an estate impaired and altogether inadequate to support the high rank his father had bequeathed him, his life must have been one long burden. But over and above the

---

[1] Mrs. Stapleton to William Pitt, Andlem, April 20th, 1805.

ordinary commitments this unfortunate man was subject to expenses that he could not avoid—expenses attendant upon a sickly wife. As far back as 1806 we hear of Lady Chatham's ill-health, and her husband was even forced to express a doubt as to whether he would be able to leave her to act as chief mourner at his brother's funeral.[1] Then towards the end of the following year some ugly rumours were rife as to the invalid's condition. "When I was in town yesterday morning on the business of the Westminster improvements, I was told by a person likely to be correct, that Lady Chatham is at Frognall (in this neighbourhood) under some symptoms of a mental derangement," wrote Lord Auckland to Lord Grenville. "I most sincerely hope that this report may be without foundation."[2] But, alas! the report was not ill-founded, for two months later we hear, "Lady Chatham is much disordered in her senses, and that circumstance is said to have confirmed Lord Chatham in his determination not to succeed the Duke of Portland. . . ."[3] Must we not pity a man, however unattractive, vain, pompous, stupid, who has the great misfortune to be thus circumstanced? But be that as it may, as a helper of his niece in her trouble, John Chatham could have been but a broken reed. It is clear enough that no assistance could be looked for from that quarter.

And so the years dragged slowly by until, in 1828 poor Hester Stanhope was to suffer the irreparable loss of Elizabeth Williams, the personal maid who had sailed from England with her in the *Jason* in 1810, and had remained for many years, first as servant and later as secretary,[4] companion and friend. So now Hester was alone indeed, far from her family and home, without a fellow-countryman to help or cherish her. What news had she from England? She certainly heard of her father's death—he died of dropsy at Chevening on December 15th, 1816—but did she hear other news of family and connections? Did she hear of the sale by the bachelor Lord Rivers[5] of the family estate of Strathfieldsaye, and of its purchase by the nation for the country's greatest hero, the Duke of Wellington? Did she hear, and if so, what did she think, of the Grenville triumph in 1822, when the head of that well-rewarded family was raised to ducal rank? But just as they reached the summit, the sun of fortune was destined to shine no more upon the proud lords of Stowe—such is the frailty of

[1] Chatham to Dartmouth, St. James's Square, February 6th, 1806.

[2] Auckland to Grenville, Eden Farm, November 6th, 1807. (Private and Confidential.)

[3] Thomas Grenville to Lord Grenville, Cleveland Square, January 9th, 1808.

[4] Many of Lady Hester's letters were written by Miss Williams.

[5] The second Lord. See family tree.

human ambitions. Within a few years of the creation, through his reckless expenditure on the luxuries of art and literature, and the munifi-
cence with which he had entertained the royal family of France, the new
Duke of Buckingham and Chandos found himself in such embarrassed
circumstances that he was forced to retire to the Continent for awhile.
The final crash, however, was to come in the days of his son, but this
calamity Hester was not destined to see.[1] With the death of the third
Duke all these new great honours became extinct, minor honours were
dissipated, and little was left of Grenville grandeur.[2] In 1823, by far the
ablest member of this family was struck down, for in that year Lord Grenville suffered a paralytic attack from which he was never destined completely to recover, and though he lived for above ten years more,[3] he took
little further part in public affairs. In the autumn of the following year,
the candle of the most stupid and useless of the Pitts was snuffed out, for
on September 24th, 1835, John Chatham breathed his last in London in his
eightieth year. Did Hester hear of the ruin of William Morton Pitt,
son of her grandfather's cousin and friend, the Great Commoner of the
West? How this talented, well-meaning man managed to dissipate the
vast fortune left him by his father, John Pitt of Encombe, must remain a
mystery. All that is certain is that he was the ruin of his house; and after
having sat in the House of Commons as member for Dorsetshire for close
on half a century, he was compelled to part with Encombe, which Chatham
had so loved to visit in his hours of leisure. Kingston, too, had later to be
given up; and thus the wealthiest branch of the House of Pitt, once powerful
and distinguished, sank into the obscurity of a landless middle-class. How
much of these events came to the ear of the solitary exile in a distant land?

As the years passed poor Hester's debts mounted; and with increasing
trouble it appears that her imagination so mastered her reason that she
became the frequent dupe of impostors. Thus on one occasion a man,
pretending to bear a message from the Dukes of Sussex and Bedford with
offers of pecuniary assistance, obtained complete possession of her confidence

[1] On August 31st, 1847, the effects at Stowe and elsewhere were seized by the
bailiffs, and on September 12th, Buckingham left England with liabilities said to be
about a million.

[2] On the death of the third duke on March 26th, 1889, the dukedom became
extinct: but the earldom of Temple passed to his nephew, William Stephen Gore
Langton, the Scottish barony of Kinloss to his eldest daughter, Lady Mary Morgan,
and the Viscountcy of Cobham to Lord Lyttelton. The great mansion of Stowe,
for so long the scene of so much splendour, was subsequently sold, and is now the
seat of a celebrated Public School.

[3] He died at Dropmore on January 12th, 1834.

which it may be readily supposed he soon turned to his own profit and to her loss. On another occasion, news having reached her that a certain Colonel Needham—perhaps some relation of the Robert Needham or Nedham who had married her great-aunt, Catherine Pitt, many years ago —had bequeathed his Irish property to William Pitt, who predeceased him by a few days, she gradually became convinced that his heir-at-law, Lord Kilmorey, was bound to make over the whole estates to her, if not in his lifetime, at least after his death; and for many years she was in anxious expectation of a favourable answer on this head from Sir Francis Burdett, to whom she had written as her agent, but who doubtless regarded the whole affair as some sorry Irish jest or poor Syrian fantasy.

And so things moved from bad to worse, until on January 27th, 1838, the climax came. On that day, the Consular Agent at Sayda, one Abela, desired to see Lady Hester in order to deliver into her hands a letter from the Consul at Beyrout. She refused to receive him, and after some altercation, he was forced to hand the letter to Dr. Meryon. Hester Stanhope was in a state of wild excitement, for here surely was the long-awaited reply from Sir Francis Burdett. Here after all the long weary months of waiting was good news at last—the end of all her worries, all her sorrows. But alas, it was very different. It was headed "Cairo, January 10th, 1838," and was signed "Patrick Campbell, H.M.'s Agent for Egypt and Syria." In eighteen months the lonely exile was dead—this letter may not unjustly be termed the death-blow of Lady Hester Stanhope.

Some years previously, a money-lender of the name of Homsy, to whom Lady Hester was alleged to owe 5,250 dollars, petitioned the Viceroy of Egypt to assist him on the plea that the loss of this sum—then worth slightly over £1,000—reduced him to abject beggary; and Mehemet Ali applied to Colonel Campbell, the Consul-General in Syria, to obtain payment of the debt. This put Campbell in a quandary, for though it had become customary for the Consuls to adjudicate in cases where English subjects were involved, yet in the event of their refusing to accept the decision, the Consul had no power to enforce it; and, as Campbell knew full well, there was no hope of Lady Hester accepting any decision that he might give. He accordingly applied for instructions to the Foreign Secretary, the Duke of Wellington,[1] who declined to allow him to interfere. This settled the matter for the moment; but towards the end of the following year, Colonel Campbell again communicated with the Foreign Office to point out the great inconvenience entailed by conforming to his instructions.[2] This time the Attorney-General was consulted, and that pundit reported

---

[1] Campbell to Wellington, October 22nd, 1834.
[2] Campbell to Wellington, December 19th, 1835.

that, inconvenience or no inconvenience, the Secretary of State's decision must be upheld; the British Consuls had no powers to adjudicate between British and Turkish subjects except by agreement between the parties. This seemed final, and so the matter was allowed to rest for nearly two years; and then—Homsy having become yet more importunate—Campbell wrote a vigorous letter to the new Secretary of State, Lord Palmerston. Palmerston, it appears, was sympathetic towards the money-lender. He issued orders that, in the event of Lady Hester refusing to pay the amount due, she should be coerced by means of the confiscation of her pension and it was the Consul's letter announcing this decision that Hester received on January 27th, 1838.

On the proud exile the staggering blow had fallen; but even now she could not forget that she was a Pitt and she would not truckle. "My grandfather and Mr. Pitt did something, I think, to Keep the Brunswick family on the throne," was her acid comment, "and yet the grand-daughter of the old king, without hearing the circumstances of my getting into debt, or whether the story is true (for it might be false) sends to deprive me of my pension in a foreign country, when I may remain and starve. . . . But now, since they have chosen to make a bankrupt of me, I shall come out with a few things that will make them ashamed. The old king wrote down on the paper, 'Let her have the greatest pension that can be granted to a woman.' If he were to rise up and see me now!"

But this was no time for moaning, there was work to be done. First, she must reply to Campbell, whom she bade send her the official order from the Foreign Office and the creditor's statement of claim.[1] To Meryon, acting as her secretary, who asked how she would subscribe herself, "Say nothing," she replied. "How many times I have said I could never call myself the humble servant of anybody. I hate and detest all these compliments, so unmeaning and so false. . . ." And then after some hesitation she decided on a desperate course—she would write direct to the Queen. Having arrived at this determination, she did not long delay, and within a few days a turbulent letter was composed and despatched under cover of one to Lord Palmerston. She also wrote the same day to the Duke of Wellington, telling him how her embarrassments had come about, by helping the oppressed "the host of orphans, and widows, and little children, whom to feed and clothe for nearly two years took away all the ready money with which I ought in part to have paid my debts, and caused new ones." And now she had been dubbed "a swindler": what right, she demanded, had the Queen to meddle with her affairs? "In due time, please God, I should

[1] Lady Hester Stanhope to Campbell, Djoun, February 4th, 1838.

have known how to arrange to satisfy everybody, even if I left myself a beggar. If she pretended to have a right to stop my pension, I resign it altogether, as well as the name of an English subject, for there is no family has served their country and the Crown more faithfully than mine has done; and I am not inclined to be treated with *moins d'egards* than was formerly shown to a gentlemanlike highwayman." Then, after more in this strain, and also an unjustifiable attack on her brother for having dined with Lord Holland to meet Fox when Pitt was on his death-bed, an aspersion which Lord Stanhope was later forced publicly to deny,[1] she wrote to the Duke these memorable words: "There is no-one more capable of making the Queen understand that a Pitt is a unique race than your grace. There is no trifling with them."[2] There is indeed no suppressing so proud, so dominant a spirit!

But though no earthly power could overcome this indomitable woman, there is one power against which it is vain for mortals to contend. During the summer of 1838 she received from Lord Palmerston the reply to her letter to the Queen.[3] It was not unfriendly, but to it she returned a lengthy and turbulent rejoinder. "If your diplomatic despatches are as obscure as the one which lies before me, it is no wonder that England should cease to have that proud preponderance in her foreign relations, which she could once boast of. . . ." And then after much fiery language of that sort, "Your Lordship talks to me of the capitulations with the Sublime Porte," she wrote arrogantly. "What has that to do with a private individual having exceeded his finances, in trying to do good? If there is any punishment for that, you had better begin with your ambassadors, who have often indebted themselves at the different Courts of Europe, as well as at Constantinople. I myself am so attached to the Sultan that, were the reward of such conduct that of losing my head, I should kiss the sabre wielded by so mighty a hand, yet, at the same time, treat with the utmost contempt your trumpery agents, as I shall never admit of their having the smallest power over me; if I did, I should belie my origin."[4] That was her last word. Having despatched that proud reply to her tormentor, she walled herself up in her mountain home, and declined to admit guests. Thus isolated and alone the self-appointed prisoner prepared to receive the only visitor whom nothing could exclude.

[1] When the absurd statement was put in print in the second volume of Meryon's book, Lord Stanhope publicly denied the story in a letter to *The Times*.

[2] Lady Hester Stanhope to Wellington, Djoun, Mount Lebanon, February 12th, 1838.

[3] Palmerston to Lady Hester Stanhope, Foreign Office, April 25th, 1838.

[4] Lady Hester Stanhope to Palmerston, Djoun, Mount Lebanon, July 1st, 1838.

As the year advanced, her health sensibly declined. In October, we learn that many of those around her were ill. "Everybody is laid up here," she wrote to Dr. Meryon, who had recently left for England and was destined never to see her again. "The early rain has caused illness everywhere. . . . The mountain is in a very disturbed state; but my habitation is well walled in. . . ."[1] Not unnaturally she was not at all well amidst such unhealthy surroundings; but though weaker, there was fight in her still. "As to the Government, Lord P. has acted like a blackguard to allow of a dirty agent to threaten me"; she wrote to Lord Hardwicke the same month, "but I have not done with him, and he will hereafter see, those who have Pitt blood in their veins are no *swindlers*, nor are they cowards, or will they bear a *threat* even from a crowned head. You know I am no longer an English subject; I would rather live under a Hottentot King, than be subjected to the caprice of a childish queen, governed by such ministers."[2]

During the second half of 1838 and the early months of 1839, further letters were exchanged with Lord Hardwicke, who was anxious that Hester should return to England and see to her affairs. But this she would never do, and by now her strength was quite inadequate for such an effort. "May it please the all-powerful Commander of events," she wrote on June 6th, and the quantity of words omitted shows her failing powers, "to give me a fair hour in which I may be able to give evidence to the world of my gratitude for your (having) thus kindly interested yourself (in) my affairs, where others have forsaken (me). What you say about my coming to England I understand, and (it) appears very reasonable, but I cannot (and) will never go there but *in chains*, therefore that subject must never more be mentioned. I have reflected, and *feel* that God will not forsake (me). . . . For God's sake, do not let my impudent relations interfere in my concerns, or look over my account at Coutts'. Did ever anyone hear of conduct like what theirs has been? Do not be unhappy about my future fate. I have done what I believe my duty, the duty of every one of *every religion*: I have no reproaches to make myself, but that I went rather too far; but such is my nature, and a happy nature too, who can make up its mind to everything but insult. I have been treated like a vile criminal, but God is great!!!"[3] A fortnight after penning these awful words, she was at peace.

And now great weakness overcame her, so that she could not rise from bed. It was clear that she was dying. Yet who tended her, who nursed her? There was no kindred hand to clasp in hers, no comforting voice to

[1] Lady Hester Stanhope to Meryon, October 1838.

[2] Lady Hester Stanhope to Hardwicke, Djoun, October 21st, 1838.

[3] Lady Hester Stanhope to Hardwicke, Djoun, June 6th, 1839.

murmur a prayer for her departing soul. Her retainers, some twenty-eight in number, heedless, uncaring, stood whispering by, watching the blinking of those dark, familiar, flashing eyes; then they fled, seizing as they went all the plunder upon which they could lay their thieving hands. Meanwhile, as she lay there awaiting the inevitable end, the British Consul at Beyrout, Niven Moore, having heard of Hester's illness, was riding over the mountain to her aid, bringing with him William McClure Thomson, an American missionary. They left about ten o'clock and reached their destination some nine hours later. At Djoun, there was a deathly silence. No one greeted the visitors, and for a time they wandered from room to room. Then at last they came upon her they sought—her great body stretched out, her fine aristocratic, commanding features rendered gaunt by wasting and by the pose of death, looking like some distorted image of the mighty Chatham.

It was a night of tropical heat, and the Consul decided that the funeral rites must be performed immediately. Lady Hester had left instructions that she wished to be buried on a certain site in her grounds. Here in the midst of a grove of myrtle and bay trees was a garden-house screened by a trellis-work arbour, up which rose-trees, jasmine and woodbine had been cunningly trained. This had been a favourite resort during her lifetime. It was the spot she had chosen for her last resting-place. So having encased her in a plain deal coffin, they summoned the absconding servants and bade them bear their mistress to her selected grave. About midnight this strange, mixed company set forth, their way lighted by the flares of torches and lanterns, and with difficulty they made their way amid the winding alleys of the garden towards the tomb. The American missionary, who was to perform the ceremony, took a wrong path and for some time wandered amongst the labyrinthine mazes of the grounds. When at length he reached the arbour a strange, bizarre and horrible sight presented itself to his astonished eyes. The body of a Frenchman had been buried in the vault many years before, and in the haste of opening the grave, these bones had been taken out and hurriedly placed at the head. There now they were in ghastly disarray, the disorderly heap surmounted by the skull, into each of the eye-sockets of which a lighted taper had been thrust. It was under the flickering light from this hideous, grinning spectacle that the bewildered priest must play his part; and as the dread familiar words echoed amid the tomb— "I am the resurrection and the life . . . I know that my Redeemer liveth. . . . We brought nothing into the world, and it is certain we can carry nothing out. The Lord gave, and the Lord hath taken away; blessed be the name of the Lord"—the flesh of the living may well have chilled at the presence of Death, in spite of the heat of the tropical night. Never, perhaps since the world began, have the solemn, dread last rites been performed amid sadder or more grotesque surroundings.

The melancholy coincidence that likened the burial of the half-forgotten outcast to that just thirty years before of the noble man she had loved was too evident to pass unnoticed. At the dead of night, far from home, in silence and by the fitful light of flickering lanterns, these two were laid to their rest, and the only one of her own nation who attended the proud daughter of the Stanhopes bore the honoured name of Moore. But whereas a concourse of his own sorrowing countrymen, without perchance a single eye unwatered, followed the great commander to his grave, not one of those who bore the proud exile to her tomb had any affection or feeling for her whose body they were committing to the earth. The Hero of Coruña they left alone in his glory; the Exile of Lebanon they left alone—to neglect, desolation, decay, oblivion.

> "Here didst thou dwell, here schemes of pleasure plan,
> Beneath yon mountain's ever beauteous brow:
> But now, as if a thing unblest by Man,
> Thy fairy dwelling is as lone as Thou!
> Here giant weeds a passage scarce allow
> To Halls deserted, portals gaping wide:
> Fresh lessons to the thinking bosom, how
> Vain are the pleasaunces on earth supplied,
> Swept into wrecks anon by Time's ungentle tide!"[1]

[1] Byron, *Childe Harold's Pilgrimage*, Canto I, Stanza XXIII.

L'ENVOI

My task is done. The story of the Pitts is told. And to the reader who likes a moral to adorn a tale, what says this book? That genius and eccentricity are not so far apart, that he who climbs up to the summit is not so far removed from him who goes down into the depth? Perhaps; but I am content to leave such questions to wiser heads than mine. I seek to point no moral to adorn my tale. The House of Pitt, made illustrious by its greatest sons, needs no such decking. Four-square it stands to all the winds that blow. And to its sons and daughters—queer compounds of human frailties—we must bid a last farewell. Sinking to sleep once more amid the eternal shades, they are at peace—and all their world is still.

SIR WILLIAM PITT =
1559–1636,
of Hartley Westpall
and Strathfieldsaye, a
Commissioner of the Navy.

EDWARD PITT, = RACHEL, dau. of
1592–1643, of   Sir George Morton
Strathfieldsaye.   Milborne St. And
                    Co. Dorset.

= JANE, dau. of   Other   JOHN PITT = CATHERIN
ye.   John Savage, 1st Earl   Children.   dau. of
      Rivers, and widow 1st   Nichola
      of George Brydges, 6th   Venabl
      Lord Chandos and   of And
      2nd of Sir William   Co. Ha
      Sidley of Aylesford,
      Co. Kent, Bt.

EORGE PITT, = (2) LORA, dau. of   Other   JOHN PITT, = SARAH,
1663–1735,   Audley Grey of   Children.   Consul at   widow
of Strathfieldsaye. Kingston   Masulipatam. —. Wa
                  Maureward,
                  Co. Dorset.
                  Died 1750.

PITT   = MARCIA, dau. of   Other   GEORGE MORTON PITT =
Encombe,   Marcus Anthony   Children.   of Twickenham,
Dorset, and   Morgan.   Co. Middlesex.
ıninghill,   Governor of Fort
Berks.   St. George.
d 1787.   Died Feb. 1756.

                            Other Children.

·T,   = MARY, dau. of   Other   (1) MARGARET, = WILLIAM MORTON
              Emanuel Scrope   Children.   dau. of   PITT, 1754–1836
rtsmouth.   Howe, 2nd.   John Gambier,   of Kingston Ho
1809.   Viscount Howe.   Governor of   Co. Dorset.
                                             Bahamas.
                                             Died Nov. 1818.
                                                          *

VARD LIGONIER, = PENELOPE. = (2) SMITH.   MARCIA LUCY, = JAMES LAN
-1782, Visct. later Born   ? A Private   1756–1822.   of Bramh
Ligonier,   1749.   in the Horse   Co. York.
.-Gen.   Guards.   Died Apri

:s,
of Francis
Rigby, of   *
·y Hall,
ssex.

GEORGE
of Str
Died

(1) LUCY, dau of Tho
Pile of Baverstock,
Wilts., and widow
Laurence Lowe of
Shaftesbury, Co.
Dorset. Died 169

GEORGE PITT   = MARY LOUISA,
of Strathfieldsaye.   dau. of
Died Oct. 1745.   John Bernier
                          of Strasbourg,
                          Germany.

GEORGE PITT,   = PENELOPE,   SIR V
1721–1803, 1st   dau. of   AU
Lord Rivers, Envoy   Sir Henry   Gen
to Court of Turin,   Atkins of   Gov
Amb. to Spain.   Clapham, Co.   Die
                        Surrey, Bt.

GEORGE PITT,   LOUISA.   = PETER BECKFOR
1751–1828,   Died   of Stapleton,
2nd Lord   1791.   Co. Dorset.
Rivers.   Died 1810.

WILLIAM HORACE BECKFORD,   =
1777–1831, Afterwards
Pitt-Rivers, 3rd Lord
Rivers under special
remainder.

PITT-RIVER

ITH, dau. of
ːicholas Cadbury
f Wareham,
o. Dorset.

Other
Children.

ROBERT PITT
of Blandford.

THOMAS PITT.
A Master in
Chancery.

ROBERT PITT
of Blandford
F.R.S.
Died Jan.
1711–12.

CHRISTOPHER PITT
of Blandford.
Died 1723.

r,

ɔPHIA, dau. of
—. Bugden and
sometime wife of
George Drake, Governor
of Fort St. George.

CHRISTOPHER PITT,
1699–1748.
Rector of Pimperne.
Poet and Translator.

ROBERT PITT,
1714–1750. Rector
of Ower Moigne,
Co. Dorset.

(2) MARIA, = THOMAS Pɪ
dau. of   of Bocon
General   Swallowfɪ
Murray.   Lord Waɪ
              Stannarie
              Steward ɾ
              of Cornwː
              Died Julɣ

= (2) GRACE AMELIA,
dau. of
Henry Seymer.
Died July 1836.

HARRIOT, = BROWNLOW BERTIE,
1745–1763.   1729–1809,
              5th Duke of
              Ancaster and
              Kestevan.

THOMAS
1736–1ˀ
Lord Cː

*

ox

THOMAS
1775–
2nd L

321.

INDEX

Abercromby, Sir Ralph, 310.
Aboukir Bay, Battle of, 291–2.
Acre, 292, 356–7.
Addington, Dr. Anthony, 170–1, 191, 194.
Addington, Henry (1st Viscount Sidmouth), 298–9, 310, 312–14, 318–19, 324–5.
"Advice in Writing," 145.
Albany, Countess of, 186–8, 273.
Alexander I, Tsar of Russia, 334.
Alfieri, Count Vittorio, 178–9, 182–8, 273.
Allen, Ralph, 101–2.
Almanara, Battle of, 30.
Alvinzi, Baron of, 280–1.
Amelia, Princess, 126.
America, 157, 160–4, 173, 199–201, 214, 216, 218–19.
Amherst, Baron, 123, 144.
Anne, Queen, 29–30, 32, 37–40.
Anson, George Lord, 146.
Antigua, 287–8, 308.
Antwerp, 341–4, 347.
Appleby, 212–13, 227, 231.
Arcot, 125.
Arden, Richard Pepper (Lord Alvanley), 227.
Argyll, 2nd Duke of, 39.
Armistead, Mrs., 231, 241, 252.
Assid Khan, 8, 11n.
Auckland, William Eden, 1st Baron, 240, 253, 269, 281–2, 284, 345–6, 361.
Augusta, Princess of Wales, 71, 91, 121, 143, 150, 151.
Aurangzib, Mogul, 3, 5n., 8, 10–11, 124.
Austria, 256–7, 262, 264, 274–5, 280, 286–7, 297, 325–6, 328.
Ayscough, Anne (née Lyttelton), 80n.
Ayscough, Dr. Francis, 68, 80–2, 88, 90, 97, 113.

Baker, Sir George, 242, 245.
Banks, Peggy (Peggy Grenville), 104, 212, 304.
Barras, Comte de, 276, 278, 288–9, 293.
Barré, Isaac, 214.
Bastille, Fall of, 253, 259–60.
Bath, 21–3, 67, 86, 100–1, 106–7, 127–8, 130, 174–5, 197, 206–8, 328.
Bath, Earl of, 128.
Bavaria, 256, 326.
Beauchamp, Lord, 229.
Beaufoy, Henry, 246.
Beaulieu, Marshal, 280.
Beckford, Peter, 186n., 244n., 273n.

Beckford, William, 149, 153, 190.
Bedford, Duchess of, 131.
Bedford, 4th Duke of, 75, 85, 145n., 146, 150.
Beggar's Opera, The, 154.
Belasyse, Mary, see Pitt, Mary.
Belgium, 275, 278, 286–7.
Bellenden, Mary, 61, 66.
Bengal, 125–6.
Berenger, Richard, 110–11.
Bertie, Lord Brownlow, 77–8.
Best, Mr., 319–20.
Black Hole of Calcutta, 125–6.
Blandford St. Mary, 4, 14, 21, 35, 57.
Boconnoc, Cornwall, 47–8, 65, 81–2, 85, 87–9, 140–1, 174n., 196, 204n., 321n.
Bolingbroke, Henry St. John, Viscount, 38–9, 70–1, 73, 91.
Bolingbroke, Viscountess, 72, 91.
Bompard, Commodore, 288.
Bonaparte, Lucien, 294.
Bonaparte, Napoleon, see Napoleon, Emperor.
Boscawen, Mrs, 205, 238.
Boulogne, 314, 325.
Bouchain, Siege of, 36.
"Boy Patriots," 70–2.
Bridport, Admiral Viscount, 103.
Brighton, 191–2.
Bristol, 2nd Earl of, 137, 145.
Brown, "Capability," 156.
Bruce, Michael, 349–54.
Brunswick, Duke of, 264–5.
Buckingham, George Grenville, Marquis of (2nd Earl Temple), 211, 218–19, 223, 226, 229–30, 241, 248, 268–70, 272, 291, 294–5, 342, 345–6.
Buckingham, Marchioness of, 252–3.
Buckingham and Chandos, 1st Duke of, 355n., 361–2.
Buckingham and Chandos, 2nd Duke of, 362n.
Bulkeley, Lord, 250, 252.
Bunbury, Lady Sarah, 101.
Burchett, William, 60.
Burdett, Sir Francis, 363.
Burgoyne, General, 199.
Burke, Edmund, 159, 165, 172, 214–16, 228, 235, 248–9, 260.
Burney, Fanny, 142.
Burton Pynsent, Somerset, 155–6, 159, 169, 170n., 191, 193, 197–8, 238, 241, 284, 305–6, 309, 359–60.

INDEX

Bute, Countess of, 131, 204.
Bute, 3rd Earl of, 139, 141–4, 147, 149–50, 151–3, 190, 203.
Buzot, M., 277.
Byng, Admiral, 115, 119–20.

Camden, 1st Earl, 164*n*., 173, 214, 229, 247, 312, 325.
Camelford, Lady (Anne Wilkinson), 175, 177–8, 196, 268, 307–9.
Camelford, Thomas Pitt, 1st Lord, 48, 53, 64, 66, 85, 172, 205, 271–3; relations with Chatham, 85, 89–90, 99–100, 127, 132–3, 151, 174, 204*n*., 322; and Boconnoc, 88, 141; leaves father, 89–90; travels abroad, 135–7, 140, 204–5, 268, 272; fits of, 136; in Parliament, 144, 216–17, 220, 223; given office, 151; marriage, 174, 178, 307–8; and Smith, 177–8, 206–9; children, 196, 222, 267; lends to Lady Chatham, 198, 282; refuses office, 222; raised to peerage, 231; and daughter's marriage, 267–70; death, 273; offers help to William, 282–3.
Camelford, Thomas Pitt, 2nd Lord, 267, 270–3, 287–9, 295, 308, 319–21.
Campbell, Colonel Patrick, 363–4.
Campo Formio, Treaty of, 287.
Canada, 123–4, 144–5, 194.
Canning, George, 311, 314, 322, 325.
Cape of Good Hope, 278, 285, 311.
Carleton, General, 194, 199–200.
Carmarthen, Lord, *see* Leeds, Duke of.
Caroline, Queen, 61–3, 66, 71.
Carrington, Lord, 315, 318.
Carteret, Lord (Earl of Granville), 70, 73–6, 145.
Castlereagh, Viscount, 298, 316–17, 329, 342–3, 345.
Cathcart, Lady (*née* Hamilton), 111–12.
Catherine the Great, 149–50, 256–7, 262.
Catholic Emancipation, 298–300, 319, 334.
Cavendish, Lord John, 230.
Ceylon, 285–6, 310–11.
Charlotte, Queen, 242–5, 247, 252, 264.
Chatelet, Duc du, 259.
Chatham, Hester Pitt, Countess of (*née* Grenville), 104, 109–11, 155*n*., 166, 168, 172–3, 196, 200, 210, 213, 219, 267, 282, 360; marriage, 111–13; letters, 122–3, 129, 193, 237; children, 126–7, 191–3; given peerage, 147–9; sees to husband's affairs, 169, 171, 197–8; brings up grand-daughter, 238–40; William's loans to, 283, 309; last letter of, 283; and Hester Stanhope, 305–6; death, 306.
Chatham, John Pitt, 2nd Earl of, 122, 156*n*., 166–7, 192–3, 201, 203, 210, 231, 271, 282, 305–6, 309, 313, 317, 325, 329; birth, 126–7; in Canada, 194, 199–200; marriage, 224; at Admiralty, 241; Garter for, 258; President of Council, 284–5; and Hester Stanhope, 331, 338, 358–9;

leads expedition to Scheldt, 341–9; pecuniary difficulties, 359–60; death, 362.
Chatham, Mary Pitt, Countess of (*née* Townshend), 224, 317, 361.
Chatham, William Pitt, 1st Earl of, 27, 46, 54, 56, 63–5, 143*n*., 181–2; at Oxford, 57–8; at Eton, 59–60; maiden speech, 63, 71; and sister Ann, 65, 68, 72, 91–3, 127–31, 147–8; returned to Parliament, 70, 90, 133; speeches, 73–4, 114–15, 146, 150, 155, 160–3, 190, 200–2, 215; disliked by George II, 73, 76, 91, 107–8, 120; legacies to, 74–5, 155–6; gout of, 74, 86, 100–1, 106–7, 157, 168; in office, 76, 115, 121, 158, 165; relations with brother, 81, 87–8, 133–5; and nephew, 85, 89–90, 99–100, 126–7, 132–3, 151, 174, 204*n*., 322; and sister Elizabeth, 93–8; hosts and friends of, 100–4; marriage, 109, 111–13; helps Prussia, 121–2; and George III, 142, 147, 153–4, 157–8, 160, 163–5, 168–9, 171–2; and war with France, 144–6, 150; arrogance, 145*n*., 167, 190; resigns Seals, 146–7, 171, 197; accepts peerage, 147, 166–7; and America, 157, 160–3, 173, 199–201; illness, 165, 167–71, 196; reconciled to Grenvilles, 172; in Lords, 173, 190, 200–2; family life, 191–9; financial difficulties, 197–9; death, 203; funeral, 210; and parliamentary reform, 217.
Chauvelin, 264, 273.
Chesterfield, 4th Earl of, 70–2, 73, 75–6, 96.
Chevening, Kent, 49–50, 52, 172, 211, 303–5, 332.
Cholmondeley, Charles, 41, 46, 48, 58.
Cholmondeley, Essex (*née* Pitt), 21–4, 26, 33, 41–2, 45, 106.
Cholmondeley, Thomas, 97, 195–6.
Clarkson, Thomas, 240.
Cleveland, Duchess of, 304–5, 350, 354*n*.
Clive, Robert, Baron, 125, 197.
Closterseven, Convention of, 121–2.
Cobham, Hester Grenville, Countess, 104–6.
Cobham, Richard Temple, Viscount, 70, 73, 76, 104–5.
Cockburne, William, 321.
Compton, Sir Spencer, 61–3.
Consulate, the, 294–5.
Conway, General, 159–60, 162, 181*n*.
Cope, Mr., 18–20.
Copenhagen, Battle of, 310.
Corbett, Sir William, 65.
Cornbury, Viscount, 67, 70.
Coruña, 335–8.
Coutts, Thomas, 197–9, 283–4, 309, 359.
Coventry, Countess of, 179.
Cumberland, Duke of, 121, 157, 159*n*.
Curgenven, Thomas, 14, 16, 26.

Danton, G. J., 266, 275, 278–9.
Daud Khan, 3, 11.
Daun, General, 121–2.

INDEX

Declaratory Act, 164.
Delany, Mrs., 132, 196, 205–6, 238.
Devonshire, 4th Duke of, 115, 145*n.*, 146.
Devonshire, Georgiana, Duchess of, 232.
Digby, Colonel, 245.
Dingley, Charles, 167–8.
Directory, the, 280, 285–6, 290, 293–4, 296.
Djoun, 354, 356–8, 367.
Dropmore, Burnham, 269–70, 311, 321*n.*
Drummond, John, 27.
Ducos, Consul, 293–4.
Duffell, Dr., 206.
Dumouriez, General, 264–6, 274–5.
Duncannon, Viscountess, 232.
Dundas, Henry, *see* Melville, 1st Viscount.
Dunning, John, 173, 214.
Dupleix, J. F., 125.
Dutens, Louis, 95–6.

East India Company, 3, 5–7, 27–8, 124, 235.
Eden, Hon. Eleanor, 281–2, 284–5.
Eden, William, *see* Auckland, Baron.
Effingham, Countess of, 244.
Egremont, Earl of, 151, 153.
Egypt, 290–2, 310.
Eldon, Earl of (Sir John Scott), 227–8, 263.
Eliot, Edward, 215, 224–5, 237, 239–40.
Eliot, Harriot, 238–40, 306.
Eliot, Lady Harriot (*née* Pitt), 167, 172–3, 191–2, 211, 237–8.
Elizabeth, Tsaritsa, 149.
Encombe, Dorset, 100, 362.
Estrées, General d', 121.
Evance, Sir Stephen, 12, 15, 18*n.*, 19–20, 28.

Ferdinand of Brunswick, Prince, 122, 179.
Fielding, Henry, 101–2.
Fitzgerald, Lord Edward, 298.
Fitzwilliam, Earl, 297.
Flushing, 343.
Foncesca, Alvarez de, 18*n.*, 19–20.
Fort St. George, 3, 10–11, 14–15, 76–7.
Fort William, 125.
Fouquier-Tinville, A. Q., 276.
Fox, Charles James, 214, 216, 218–22, 225–32, 234–6, 241, 247–9, 251, 260, 274, 296, 318–19, 322–3, 333, 365.
Fox, Henry, *see* Holland, 1st Baron.
France, 72, 88, 93–6, 121, 124, 127, 144–5, 199, 201–2, 219, 240, 257–62, 264–7, 273–9, 285–7, 293–7, 310–12, 314, 323, 325, 334–5.
Francis II, Emperor, 294, 325, 334.
Francis, Sir Philip, 136, 171, 235.
Franklin, Dr., 218.
Frederick II, King of Prussia, 119, 121–3, 149, 256–7.
Frederick, Prince of Wales, 69–71, 80–2, 143.
Frederick William II, King of Prussia, 257, 262.
French Revolution, 253–5, 259–62, 264–7, 273–9.

Gainsborough, Thomas, 102.
Garrick, David, 102.
Geary, Admiral Francis, 109–10, 119*n.*
George I, King of England (Elector), 37, 41–2, 50, 55, 74.
George II, King of England (Duke of Cambridge, Prince of Wales), 37, 50–1, 55, 61–3, 71, 76, 81, 91, 114, 119–21, 126.
George III, King of England (Prince of Wales), 71, 80, 144, 145*n.*, 149–50, 152, 173–4, 214, 217, 222–3, 263, 271, 285, 324; succeeds to throne, 141–2; favourite of, 142–3, 151; and Chatham, 147, 153–4, 157–8, 160, 164–5, 168–71, 197, 203; and Pitt, 222, 229, 231–3, 234–6, 291, 298–9, 310, 321–2; objects to India Bill, 226; insanity of, 242–7, 251–3, 299, 318–19, 323; and French Revolution, 262, 264, 273; Napoleon's letter to, 294–5; and Catholic Emancipation, 298–300, 319, 334; and 2nd Earl of Chatham, 345, 348.
George IV, King of England (Prince of Wales), 232, 244–5, 247–52, 299, 318, 324.
Gibbon, Edward, 215, 234.
"Gironde, the," 275–6.
Godolphin, Countess of, 75.
Godolphin, 1st Earl of, 29–30, 36–7.
Gower, 2nd Earl, 222, 231.
Grafton, 3rd Duke of, 159–60, 163–5, 168–9, 171, 173, 174*n.*, 190, 222.
Grandison, Lady, 16, 33–5, 44–5, 48, 63, 64*n.*
Grandison, Lord, 195.
Grantham, Lord, 219.
Granville, Countess, 74.
Granville, Earl, *see* Carteret, Lord.
Grattan, Henry, 237.
Grenville, Elizabeth (*née* Wyndham), 109–11, 127*n.*
Grenville, General, 250, 339, 354–7.
Grenville, George, 70, 72–3, 76, 103–4, 106, 108, 110, 111, 115, 127, 132, 151–4, 157–160, 162, 172–3, 211.
Grenville, Henry, 104, 106, 113, 212.
Grenville, Hester, *see* Cobham, Countess.
Grenville, James, 104, 106, 109, 113, 146*n.*, 159, 229.
Grenville, Lady (Anne Pitt), 222, 267–70, 307–8, 321–2.
Grenville, Lady Hester, *see* Chatham, Countess of.
Grenville, Richard, *see* Temple, Earl.
Grenville, Thomas (d. 1749), 104, 109.
Grenville, Thomas, M.P., 211, 218–19, 297, 341.
Grenville, William Wyndham, Baron, 211, 218–20, 222, 230, 241, 249, 253, 264, 274, 289, 313–14, 321, 346; on Prince of Wales, 250; raised to peerage, 258; marriage, 267–70, 307–8; and Napoleon's letter, 294–5, 297; on truce with France, 311; and Fox, 318–19, 322, 333; estranged

373

from Pitt, 322–3; and death of Pitt, 329; and Hester Stanhope, 331, 338; forms Ministry, 333–4; stroke of, 362.
Grimaldi, Marquis, 145, 150.
Gustavus II, King of Sweden, 257, 262, 264, 277.

Hagley, Worcestershire, 66, 102–3.
Halifax, 2nd Earl of, 146, 151, 154.
Hamilton, Jane, see Cathcart, Lady.
Hannam, John, 98.
Hanover, 121, 334.
Harcourt, 1st Viscount, 37.
Harcourt, 2nd Viscount, 206–7.
Hardwicke, 1st Earl of, 108, 114, 146, 153, 173.
Hardwicke, 4th Earl of, 366.
Harley, Robert (Earl of Oxford and Mortimer), 28, 30, 36, 38–9, 73.
Harrington, 1st Earl of, 69.
Harrington, 2nd Earl of, 267.
Harrington, 3rd Earl of, 331.
Harrowby, Baron, 324, 329.
Harvey, Edward, 42n.
Hastings, Warren, 240.
Hawkesbury, Baron (afterwards 2nd Earl of Liverpool), 324, 329, 333.
Hayes Place, Kent, 102, 122–3, 156, 169–70, 172, 191, 197–8, 203, 213, 224.
Henley, Lord Chancellor, 146.
Hervey, Baron, 66, 69–71, 132, 145n., 273.
Hoare, William, 102.
Holland, 257, 267, 274, 278, 286, 310, 333.
Holland, Henry Fox, 1st Baron, 81, 97, 107, 113–15, 120, 150, 151, 167.
Holland, Stephen Fox, 2nd Baron, 253, 304, 365.
Holwood, Kent, 237, 241, 269, 283–4, 309–10.
Holy Roman Empire, 333–4.
Hood, Alexander, 103, 165, 167, 191, 194–5, 198–9, 212, 224, 240.
Hood, Molly (née West), 103, 165, 167, 198.
Hood, Samuel, 1st Viscount, 194–5, 277–8.
Howard, Mrs., 52–3.
Howe, Earl, 231, 241, 278.
Huntingdon, Earl of, 204.
Hurd, Bishop, 242–3.

Independence, Declaration of, 199.
India, 3–15, 27–8, 76–7, 124–6, 144, 219, 234–5.
India Bill, 225–6, 228–30.
Innes, Jane, see Pitt, Jane.
Ireland, 235, 297–8.
Italy, 96–7, 137, 204–5, 272–3, 280–1, 285–6, 297.

Jacobins, 260, 275, 296–7.
Johnson, Sir Henry, 10.
Joseph II, Emperor, 256–7.
Joubert, Marshal, 281.
"Junius," 171.

Kellerman, General, 265.
Kildare, Marchioness of, 179.
Kingston, Duchess of, 204n.
Kinnoul, Earl of, 137.

Lafayette, General, 264.
Lebanon, 354, 356–7.
Lee, Sir George, 120.
Leeds, 5th Duke of (Lord Carmarthen), 231.
Legge, Chancellor, 108, 112, 115.
Lennox, Lady Sarah, 151.
Leopold II, Emperor, 257, 262–4.
Lepell, Mary, 66, 145n.
Leveson Gower, Lord Granville, 322.
Lignitz, Battle of, 122–3.
Ligonier, Field-Marshal Earl, 146, 179, 182.
Ligonier, Viscount, 179, 182–4, 186.
Ligonier, Viscountess (Penelope Pitt), 179, 182–8.
Littleton, Sir Thomas, 22.
Liverpool, 1st Earl of, 316–17.
Londonderry, Countess of (Lady Frances Pitt), 41, 48–9, 53.
Londonderry, Thomas Pitt, 1st Earl of, 36, 41, 43, 46–7, 49n., 51, 53–4, 58–9.
Londonderry, 2nd Earl of, 53n.
Londonderry, 3rd Earl of, 53n.
Long, Charles, 313, 324.
Lonsdale, Lord, 250.
Loughborough, Lord, 298.
Louis XVI, King of France, 256, 260, 262, 264–6, 273.
Louisburg, 123–4.
Luneville, Congress of, 297.
Lyttelton, Dr. Charles, Dean of Exeter, 83–5, 136, 138.
Lyttelton, Lord (George), 64–6, 68, 70, 73, 76, 83, 86, 102–4, 107–8, 112–13, 133, 138.
Lyttelton, Molly, 64.
Lyttelton, Sir Richard, 66, 89–90, 132, 137, 140, 174.
Lyttelton, Sir Thomas, 64, 80n., 83.

Mack, General, 275, 277, 326.
Madrid, 137, 335.
Madras, 4, 7, 27, 125.
Maestricht, 256–7, 274.
Mahon, Lady Hester (née Pitt), 127n., 166–7, 172–3, 193–4, 211, 283.
Mahon, Lord, see Stanhope, 3rd Earl of; Stanhope, 4th Earl of.
Malmesbury, 1st Earl of, 285, 296, 300n., 314, 318–19, 326.
Malta, 290, 310–11, 349–50.
Mann, Sir Horace, 96–7, 140, 182, 203.
Mansfield, Earl of, 70, 107, 146, 177–8, 209, 284.
Maria Theresa, Empress, 256.
Marie Antoinette, Queen of France, 225, 256, 260, 262, 264–5, 276.
Marlborough, Duke of, 29–30, 35–6, 39.
Marlborough, Sarah, Duchess of, 30, 37, 74–5.

INDEX

Masham, Mrs., 30, 38.
Masulipatam, 5, 7–9.
Mawarden Court, 4, 14, 35.
Melville, Henry Dundas, 1st Viscount, 229, 259, 311, 313–14, 324.
Meryon, Dr., 349, 352n., 353n., 356–7, 359, 363, 365n., 366.
Miller, Sanderson, 102–4.
Minorca, 115, 119–20, 219.
Mirabeau, Comte de, 260–2.
Miranda, General, 274.
Montagu, Fred, 205.
Montagu, Elizabeth, 66.
Montagu, Lady Mary and Edward Wortley, 143.
Montagu, Mrs., 102–3, 138.
Moore, Niven, 367–8.
Moore, Sir John, 318, 332–3, 335–8, 368.
Mornington, Lord, 270.
"Mountain, the," 275, 294.
Murray, William, see Mansfield, Earl of.

Napier, Charles, 316–17, 336.
Napoleon, Emperor, 277, 280–1, 285–7, 289–95, 297, 312–13, 314, 323, 325, 328, 333–6, 355.
Necker, M. and Mme, 225.
Nedham, Catherine (née Pitt), 46, 65, 106, 195.
Nedham, George, 195.
Nedham, Robert, 65n., 70n.
Nedham, William, 195.
Needham, Colonel, 363.
Nelson, Horatio, Lord, 278, 291, 325–6.
Netherlands, 256, 264, 266, 274–5, 278.
Newcastle, 1st Duke of, 52, 69, 75–6, 86–8, 105–8, 113–15, 120, 133, 138–9, 143n., 144, 145n., 146, 150, 160, 163.
Noailles, Vicomte de, 259.
Norris, Sir William, 8–11.
North, Lord (2nd Earl of Guilford), 174, 189, 197, 199, 214–17, 220, 222–3, 229.
North Briton, 152, 155.
North End, Hampstead, 167–9.
Northington, Lord Chancellor, 186.
Northumberland, 1st Duke of, 154.

Oakes, General Sir Hildebrand, 350.
Okehampton, 70n., 138, 144.
Old Sarum, 4, 25, 32, 70n., 82, 134–5, 138, 144, 217, 223.
Oliver, Dr. William, 128.
Ongley, Samuel, 14.
Orford, Earl of, see Walpole, Sir Robert.
Ormonde, 2nd Duke of, 36, 42–3.
Oswald, Richard, 218.
Oxford and Mortimer, Earl of, see Harley, Robert.

Palmerston, Viscount, 364–6.
Paris, Treaty of, 150, 155.
Pelham, 2nd Baron, 227.
Pelham, Henry, 69, 75–6, 91, 106.

Pembroke, Countess of, 267.
Pembroke, 9th Earl of, 111.
Perceval, Spencer, 334.
Peter III, Tsar of Russia, 149–50.
Peterborough, Earl of, 29, 31.
Peterson, Charles, 287–8.
Phelps, Mr., 180–1.
Philippe Égalité, 266, 276.
Pitt, Amelia (Mrs. Spry), 66, 83–5, 90, 135, 137–8, 140.
Pitt, Ann, 46, 65–8, 71–2, 91–2, 106, 112, 123, 127–32, 147–9, 203–7.
Pitt, Anne, see Grenville, Lady.
Pitt, Catherine, see Nedham, Catherine.
Pitt, Christian (née Lyttelton), 64–6, 80n., 83, 85.
Pitt, Christian (Mrs. Saunders), 66, 83–5, 90, 135, 137–8, 140.
Pitt, Dr. Christopher, 78.
Pitt, Dr. Robert, 21, 78.
Pitt, Elizabeth Villiers, 35, 46, 87, 93–9.
Pitt, Essex, see Cholmondeley, Essex.
Pitt, George (1st, of Strathfieldsaye), 20, 26, 33, 44, 50.
Pitt, George (2nd, of Strathfieldsaye), 78, 100.
Pitt, George (3rd, of Strathfieldsaye), 100.
Pitt, George, see Rivers, 1st Lord.
Pitt, George Morton, 76–7.
Pitt, Harriet (b. 1704), 22, 46, 56, 64–5.
Pitt, Harriet (Lady Brownlow Bertie), 77.
Pitt, Harriet (née Villiers), 16–17, 22, 24, 27, 34–5, 43, 45, 52–3, 54.
Pitt, James Charles, 191–5, 198, 201, 210, 212–13, 282–3.
Pitt, Jane, 4, 14–17, 21–7, 54, 64.
Pitt, John, see Chatham, 2nd Earl of.
Pitt, John (Colonel), 5, 16, 41, 46, 48, 53–5, 59.
Pitt, John (Consul), 5–10, 16, 76.
Pitt, John (Cornet), 21.
Pitt, John (of Encombe), 92, 100–1, 112, 227–8, 362.
Pitt, Lady Frances, see Londonderry, Countess of.
Pitt, Lady Harriot, see Eliot, Lady Harriot.
Pitt, Lady Hester (née Grenville), see Chatham, Countess of.
Pitt, Lady Hester, see Mahon, Lady Hester.
Pitt, Laura (née Grey), 100.
Pitt, Louisa (Mrs. Beckford), 186n., 244n.
Pitt, Lucy, see Stanhope, Countess of.
Pitt, Mary, 41, 87–8, 134–5, 196.
Pitt, Penelope, see Ligonier, Viscountess.
Pitt, Penelope (Mrs. George), 179–82.
Pitt, Priscilla, 58.
Pitt, Rev. Christopher, 78–9, 159n.
Pitt, Robert, 4–5, 13–26, 32, 34–6, 41–5, 52, 55, 57–9.
Pitt, Thomas (Governor), 50, 52, 124; in India, 3–8, 10–15, 27; diamond, 11–20, 33, 41, 46–7; family dissensions, 22–7, 43–5, 55; returns to England, 27–8; in

Parliament, 32, 36, 41–2; Whig principles, 32, 39, 42–3; in London, 33–5; received by King, 41; Governor of Jamaica, 45–6; grandchildren, 46, 52, 56; buys land, 47–8; death, 57; on duties of M.P., 139.

Pitt, Thomas (Master in Chancery), 21.

Pitt, Thomas (brother of Chatham), 33, 46, 56, 63, 84; allowance, 57; seizes property, 64; marriages, 64–6, 140; harshness, 65; enters Parliament, 70n., 138–9, 144; mismanages electoral business, 80–1; pecuniary difficulties, 81–2, 86–90, 133–5, 137–9; flies abroad, 88–90, 133; returns, 132–5; left by daughters, 137–8; death, 140.

Pitt, Thomas, see Camelford, 1st Lord.

Pitt, Thomas, see Camelford, 2nd Lord.

Pitt, William, see Chatham, 1st Earl of.

Pitt William, 123, 132, 165, 166–7, 200–1, 203, 289, 305, 360; illness, 172, 193; childhood, 191–3, 195; at Cambridge, 193–4, 210; and death of Chatham, 203, 210; called to Bar, 211; returned to Parliament, 212–13; speeches, 215–16, 220–1, 232–3, 260, 266, 295–7, 311–12, 314, 327; and parliamentary reform, 217, 223, 235–6; Chancellor of Exchequer, 219; refuses office, 222; visits Continent, 224–5; first Administration, 227–33, 234–7, 240–1, 300; financial policy, 234–5, 263; pecuniary difficulties, 237, 251, 282–4, 309–10; and regency question, 247–8, 251; foreign policy, 257–8, 262, 274, 285, 294–7, 325; and French Revolution, 260, 264, 266–7, 274, 296; romance, 281–2, 284–5; fights duel, 290–1; and Napoleon's peace offer, 294–7; and Catholic Emancipation, 298, 300; resigns, 299; and Hester Stanhope, 305–6, 315–18; in retirement, 309, 312–18; defends treaty with France, 311–12; asked to serve under Chatham, 313; prepares for invasion, 314–15, 317–18, 323; second Administration, 319, 321–7; death, 328–30.

Pitt, William (d. 1708), 23–4.

Pitt, William Morton, 112, 227–8, 362.

Pitt Diamond, 11–20, 33, 41, 46–7.

"Plain, the," 275.

Pocock, Sir George, 310.

Pope, Alexander, 102.

Portland, 3rd Duke of, 222, 226, 230, 325, 334, 361.

Portugal, 274, 311, 332.

Pretyman, Rev. George, 193.

Pringle, Sir William, 240.

Prussia, 121–2, 256–7, 262, 264–5, 274, 334–5.

Pulteney, William (Earl of Bath), 38, 63, 70–1, 73, 134.

Pynsent, Sir William, 155–6.

Quebec, 123–4.

Queensberry, Kitty, Duchess of, 66–7.

Quiberon Bay, Battle of, 124.

Quin, James, 102, 328n.

Ramchund, 3, 11–13, 47.

Revolution Society in London, 246, 253–5.

Rhine, Confederation of, 333.

Richardson, Samuel, 101.

Richmond, 3rd Duke of, 202, 226.

Ridgeway, Lady Frances, see Londonderry, Countess of.

Rigby, Richard, 85.

Rivers, George Pitt, 1st Baron, 170, 179–182, 186.

Rivers, George Pitt, 2nd Baron, 186n., 361.

Rivers, Lady (Penelope Pitt), 179–82.

Robespierre, M., 261, 275–6, 278–9.

Robinson, John, 228–9.

Robinson, Sir Thomas (Lord Grantham), 86, 107, 113–14, 120.

Rochefoucauld, Duc de la, 254.

Rockingham, 2nd Marquis of, 159, 163–4, 172–3, 181n., 214, 217, 219.

Rodney, Admiral, 133.

Romana, Marquis de la, 338.

Rondet, Laurent, 46–7.

Rose, Mr., 309–10, 312, 324–5.

Russia, 149–50, 256–7, 274, 310, 325, 328, 334–5.

Sacheverell, Dr., 29–30.

Sackville, Lord George, 122, 175, 179.

Sandwich, 4th Earl of, 154–5.

Saragossa, Battle of, 31.

Saunders, Thomas, 137–8, 140.

Saxe-Coburg, Prince of, 275, 277.

Scheldt, expedition to, 341–5, 347.

Scott, Sir John, see Eldon, Baron.

Sharp, Granville, 240.

Shelburne, Earl of, 133, 164n., 214, 218–22.

Shenstone, William, 102–3.

Sheridan, Richard Brinsley, 220, 235, 247–9, 254.

Shrewsbury, Duke of, 30, 39–40.

Siddons, Mrs., 243.

Sieyès, Abbé, 293–4.

Slave Trade, abolition of, 240–1, 333.

Sligo, Marquess of, 349.

Smith, Admiral, 103, 119n.

Smith, Captain John, 175–8, 206–9.

Smith, Charles Douglas, 206–9.

Smith, John Spencer, 206–7, 277.

Smith, Mary (née Wilkinson), 175–8, 206–9, 307.

Smith, Sir Sidney, 206–7, 209–10, 251, 253, 277–8, 288, 292–3, 307, 321.

Somerset, Duchess of, 38.

Somerset, 6th Duke of, 39.

Sophia, Electress of Hanover, 37.

Soubise, Prince de, 121–2.

Soult, Marshal, 335–6, 338n.

South Sea Bubble, 51.
Spain, 136–7, 145–7, 149, 219, 258, 274, 286, 310, 335–8.
Spanish Succession, War of, 29–32.
Sparry, Mrs. (Pam), 166, 192–3.
Spencer, Earl, 230, 314.
Spencer, John, 75.
Spry, Dr. William, 141.
Staël, Mme de, 225.
Stamp Act, 157, 160, 163–4.
Stanhope, Charles (d. 1809), 306, 316–17, 331–3, 336, 338.
Stanhope, Charles, 3rd Earl (Lord Mahon), 201, 210, 215, 231, 274, 318; marriages, 194, 211–12, Chairman of Revolution Society, 246, 253–5; unhappy home, 303–5, 331–2; death, 361.
Stanhope, Countess (née Louisa Grenville), 212, 304, 332.
Stanhope, Countess (née Lucy Pitt), 26–7, 34, 42–4, 48–50, 52–3, 55.
Stanhope, Countess (wife of 2nd Earl), 159, 194, 303–4, 332.
Stanhope, James, 306, 316–17, 329–31, 332–3, 337–9, 349, 355, 358–9.
Stanhope, James, 1st Earl, 29–32, 34, 38–9, 41–3, 48–52, 55, 78.
Stanhope, Lady Griselda, see Tekell, Lady Griselda.
Stanhope, Lady Hester, 211n., 212, 303–7, 315–18, 321, 324–5, 328–33, 338–40, 349–59, 361–8.
Stanhope, Lady Lucy, see Taylor, Lady Lucy.
Stanhope, Philip, 2nd Earl, 56, 59, 172.
Stanhope, Philip Henry, 4th Earl (Lord Mahon), 303, 305–6, 316, 318, 331, 365.
Stapleton, Mrs., 238, 283, 306, 360.
Starhemberg, Marshal, 30–2.
Stewart, General, 35, 44, 46, 63–4.
Stowe, 70, 103–4, 111, 172–3, 224, 226, 252–3, 269–70, 351n., 362n.
Strachan, Sir Richard, 341–4, 346–7.
Strange, John, 205.
Stratford under the Castle, 4, 14, 21, 34.
Strathfieldsaye, 20, 180, 361.
Strathmore, Earl of, 136–7.
Suffolk, Henrietta, Countess of, 66–7, 72, 127, 167.
Sunderland, 3rd Earl of, 30, 50, 52, 75.
Surajah Dowlah, 125–6.
Swallowfield, Berkshire, 47–8, 56, 81.
Sweden, 257, 262, 264, 277, 325.
Sydney, Lord (Tommy Townshend), 214, 219, 224, 231, 236.
Syria, 292, 350, 354–7.

Talbot, Lord, 93, 95.
Talleyrand, Prince, 224, 261, 264, 273–4, 290, 293–4.
Taylor, Dr. Thomas, 305.
Taylor, Lady Lucy (née Stanhope), 211n., 303–5, 316, 359n.

Tekell, John, 305.
Tekell, Lady Griselda (née Stanhope), 211n., 303–5, 316, 359.
Temple, Countess, 168.
Temple, George Grenville, 2nd Earl, see Buckingham, Marquis of.
Temple, Lord, 342.
Temple, Richard Grenville-Temple, 1st Earl, 70, 73, 104–6, 108, 115, 119, 145–7, 149, 156–9, 164, 167, 172, 198, 202, 211, 218.
Terror, the, 275–9.
Thomson, William McClure, 367–8.
Thurlow, 1st Baron, 218, 226, 229, 231, 247, 249, 263.
Tierney, George, 290–1, 296.
Tilsit, Treaty of, 335.
Tomline, Bishop, 230, 329.
Tooke, Horne, 254.
Towshend, Charles, 143, 159.
Townshend, 2nd Marquis of, 223, 248.
Townshend, Mary Elizabeth, see Chatham, Countess of.
Townshend, Viscount, 50, 61.
Townshend, Viscountess, 55, 91.
Trafalgar, Battle of, 326.
Tunbridge Wells, 103, 127–8, 175–6, 206.
Turkey, 256–7, 292.

Upper Ossory, Lady, 174.
Utrecht, Treaty of, 36.

Valmy, 265–6.
Vancouver, Captain George, 271–2, 308.
Vane, Anne, 69–70.
Vendôme, Duke of, 31.
Vergennes, Comte de, 218, 240, 257.
Victoria, Queen, 364–5.
Villiers, Harriet, see Pitt, Harriet.
Villiers, Lord, 64, 203.

Walcheren, expedition to, 342, 344–7.
Walmer Castle, 305–6, 309, 312, 314–17, 324.
Walpole, Horace, 73, 93, 96–8, 115, 120, 131–2, 136, 140, 150, 153n., 160, 167, 170, 174, 179, 182, 203–6, 216, 220.
Walpole, Mrs., 55.
Walpole, Sir Robert (Earl of Orford), 38, 50, 61–3, 69–74, 133, 157.
Walpole, Thomas, 156, 170.
Washington, George, 200.
Wedderburn, Alexander, 247.
Wellington, Arthur Wellesley 1st Duke of, 182n., 326, 328–30, 361, 363–4.
Wentworth, Lady, 33.
West, Admiral William and Gilbert, 103.
West, Dr., Prebendary of Winchester, 103.
West, Molly, see Hood, Molly.
West, Mrs. Frances, 199.
West, Temple, 199.
Wharton, Duke of, 51.
Whitworth, Lord, 313.

Wilberforce, William, 215, 224-5, 236, 240-1, 291, 297, 313, 330.
Wilkes, John, 152-5, 167*n*., 171, 173, 249.
Wilkinson, Ann, *see* Camelford, Lady.
Wilkinson, Mary, *see* Smith, Mary.
Wilkinson, Pinckney, 174-8, 206-9, 217.
Williams, Elizabeth, 349, 361.
Willis, Dr. Francis, 247, 249, 300.
Wilmington, Lord, 69.
Wilson, Edward, 166, 192-3.
Windham, William, 311, 314.
Wolfe, James, 124.
Wotton, 108-9, 111.

Wyndham, Colonel John, 24, 33.
Wyndham, Elizabeth, *see* Grenville, Elizabeth.

Yarmouth, Countess of, 126, 128.
York, Duke of, 244, 249-52, 277-8, 286, 323, 349.
Yorke, Captain, 358.
Yorke, Charles, 173.
Young, Sir William, 248.

Zulficar Khan, 8-10.